Powers

This volume has emerged from a collaboration among:

The NWO Research Council for the Humanities (GW),
The NWO Research Council for Social Sciences (MaGW), and
The Netherlands Foundation for the Advancement of Tropical Research (WOTRO).

Netherlands Organisation for Scientific Research

THE FUTURE OF THE RELIGIOUS PAST

Hent de Vries, General Editor

In what sense are the legacies of religion—its powers, words, things, and gestures—disarticulating and reconstellating themselves as the elementary forms of life in the twenty-first century? This sequence of five volumes publishes work drawn from an international research project that seeks to answer this question.

REGISTERED
STATE OF NEW YORK
REDEMPTION
CENTER

OPEN

Powers

RELIGION AS A SOCIAL AND SPIRITUAL FORCE

Edited by MEERTEN B. TER BORG

and JAN WILLEM VAN HENTEN

FORDHAM UNIVERSITY PRESS   NEW YORK   2010

Printed in the United States of America
12 11 10   5 4 3 2 1
First edition

Contents

Illustrations

Preface

This volume radically undermines the idea that the political relevance of religion is something of the past. It deals with the nexus of religion and power. Power is now seen as a central aspect of religion, not only because of the ingrained conviction of many—in the West as well as the East—that we are currently witnessing a strong revival of religion, but also because of a reassessment of religion in relevant scholarly disciplines, especially the sociology and anthropology of religion. Power and religion are omnipresent and pervade all human (inter)actions. There is no human act that does not include some kind of faith in a positive outcome and no deed in which power does not play some role. This book elaborates the manifold and fascinating interconnections between power and religion.

The interrelations of religion and power make religion an important means of exercising power. People use religion as an instrument to enhance their power or improve their status, whether personally or at the level of the nation-state. Religion defines power relations as being self-evident, with a superhuman determination. Those who have power will do everything to boost this function, but will also confront opposition and will discover that religion has an independent dynamic. Thus, religion is in principle ambiguous in its relation to power: it can empower as well as disempower people and can function as a critique of existing power relations. Besides, there is the consolatory function of religion, by which religion helps in expressing feelings, offers ways of compensating and healing, and helps make feelings of powerlessness bearable. In addition to exploring these aspects of religion, the volume also deals in detail with various tools religion can use in order to achieve its goals, including visual imagery, art, film, and music.

This book is the first themed volume to emerge from the Future of the Religious Past project of the Netherlands Organisation for Scientific Research (NWO), in which scholars from various fields and countries research new forms of religion. Apart from *Powers*, there will be subsequent volumes entitled *Things*, *Gestures*, and *Words*. Most of the contributions to this book were presented during the Future of the Religious Past conference Religion and Power in Amsterdam, on June 26 and 27, 2006, where a number of fascinating and productive ideas about this theme were presented. We make no attempt to deal with the theme of religion and power exhaustively. That would not be possible with so rich a theme.

We would like to thank the other members of the Dutch program committee and the distinguished members of the Future's international advisory board for their suggestions and support during the preparation of both conference and volume. We warmly thank Dr. Marc Linssen and Danielle Vermeer of NWO for their ongoing assistance during the entire project, as well as Charlotte Faber for her generous and highly efficient support with all sorts of practicalities before and during the conference. We also thank the staff of the Amsterdam University Theatre for hosting the conference in a most welcoming way. Special thanks go to Hent de Vries, the chairperson of the program committee and chief editor of the series, who made several important suggestions. We most warmly thank Helen Tartar, Editorial Director of Fordham University Press, who guided the production of this book from the beginning to the very end. She read the entire manuscript in a meticulous way and made many invaluable comments to us as editors as well as to the individual authors. Her unremitting editorial care greatly improved the coherence and readability of this book. Finally, we thank Neil Hertz, who provided the wonderful photographs for the book's cover and display pages.

Meerten B. ter Borg and Jan Willem van Henten
Leiden and Amsterdam, Summer 2009

Powers

Introduction

Meerten B. ter Borg and Jan Willem van Henten

Religion and Power: Why?

Several scenes in the Hollywood comedy *Bruce Almighty*, about a human person who temporarily takes over God's job, illustrate how religion is inextricably bound up with power.[1] The movie's main theme concerns the unsuccessful performance of a local TV reporter, Bruce Nolan (Jim Carrey), as God. Taking over God's role becomes a spiritual journey for Bruce, during which he learns—with God's help—to become a responsible human being. However, Bruce starts off in this film as a loser and a cynic. In one of the first scenes, Bruce drops off his girlfriend Grace at a blood drive and ridicules the idea of giving blood for the benefit of others. Nevertheless, Grace gives Bruce a present, a set of prayer beads made by the children at her nursery. The next scenes show one disaster after the other for Bruce, who keeps provoking God and ignoring the messages God is sending him. He ruins a report at Niagara Falls and gets into a car accident exactly at the moment he is looking at the prayer beads below the dashboard. Standing beside his damaged car, Bruce throws the prayer beads into the water with an unmistakable gesture. The conclusion is obvious: there is no religion for Bruce when there is no power. The flip side of this negative conclusion is elaborated in the subsequent scenes, during which Bruce acts as a substitute for God. Performing as God, Bruce constantly exerts his powers, mainly in his own interests. He interferes in nature and history, and manipulates humans as well as animals in order to save his relationship with Grace. At a certain moment he enjoys his divine powers so much that God calls him to account, asking Bruce, "Having fun?"[2]

This book also deals with the nexus of religion and power. Many now see power as being a central aspect of religion. There are at least two reasons for

1

this reassessment of religion and power. One has to do with the ingrained conviction of many—in the West as well as the East—that we are currently witnessing a revival of religion. This suggests, of course, that religion is a powerful phenomenon. The other reason is tied up with the critical assessments of the history of the disciplines involved in the study of religion, especially sociology and anthropology. Let us start with the second reason.

In retrospect, previous scholarly paradigms in the scholarship on religion turn out to have been influenced by prevailing power constellations and mainstream religious conventions in earlier times. Sociology of religion can serve as an example. The history of this subdiscipline has been strongly influenced by the social emancipation of the middle classes and by the "cult of progress" that dominated the nineteenth century in the West. Sociology of religion is a child of the French Revolution. On the progressive side of the political spectrum, the idea prevailed, inspired by Auguste Comte and others, that religion was an outdated predecessor of true, scientific knowledge.[3] On the conservative end, the sociology of religion was influenced by the notion that the disappearance of religion would reduce social cohesion, corrupt the social order, and vitiate moral awareness. The fact that religion became subordinated to the idea of progress also meant that the churches gradually lost their dominant position in society; this, in turn, resulted in religion being banished from its central place in general sociological theory. Religion became the subject of a subdiscipline with a low status within the profession as a whole.

A similar development occurred in the field of anthropology of religion. This development was shaped not by the enhanced importance of a social group but by another power constellation, colonialism. One could argue that, in the first instance, anthropology was more or less intended to be a tool of the colonizers.[4] The conscious or subconscious aim of anthropologists of religion was, therefore, basically to strengthen the power of the colonizers. They did this by conceiving of non-Western religions, in terms of both content and social function, as more rudimentary versions of Christianity. This view offered a perspective for understanding subjugated nations and made it all the more easy to dominate, convert, and—where the comparison with Christianity was involved—patronize them.

Characteristic of both the anthropology and the sociology of religion in these early periods was that the study of religion was anything but unbiased. Both disciplines did not take the individual merits of religions other than Christianity into account. Instead, these religions were studied from a perspective that presupposed a position of superiority and domination. Religion was perceived as something irrational, a concomitant of a more or less bizarre view of the world. Attention was paid mainly to factors that are highly characteristic of the established Christian religion: particular items of belief and specific rituals. Faith in these items of belief was seen as a private matter, and ritual regarded as something that could only derive from faith. Moreover, many middle-class people saw both faith and ritual as factors that delayed the process of modernization. Being obstacles to progress, they had to be eliminated. As a result, religion was marginalized in nineteenth- and twentieth-century power constellations. The ongoing process of unchurching, particularly in Western Europe, was seen as an undeniable indicator of this process. And the intellectual impact of these trends in Europe meant that the marginalization of religion was, for a long time, even postulated for the United States.[5] This changed only during the Reagan era, when the Christian right gained immense influence in the U.S. political landscape. At that point, the first cracks in the belief in an inescapable secularization of the United States started to appear.

Thus, arguably the traditional view of religion, as it took shape in the West in the nineteenth and twentieth centuries, arose from the hegemony of Western civilization. The social function of this approach to religion is rather clear: it confirmed that Western civilization was more sophisticated than any other and thereby legitimated Western supremacy. Ironically, if religion was perceived as a power factor at all in this period, it was considered to be a passive one. It was supposed to be an obstacle to the development of peoples and societies. Even the American administration under the pious Baptist president Jimmy Carter did not think religion could be a positive source of power. In consequence, the West was simply flabbergasted by Ayatollah Khomeini's Iranian revolution in the late 1970s. And this brings us to the first reason mentioned above, the revival of religion starting in the last quarter of the twentieth century.

Many writers in various contexts have observed signs of people's (re)turn to religion, and scholars of religion have discussed this revival of religion at length. Indeed, the book series to which this volume belongs is part of this scholarship.[6] The revival of religion is visible in contemporary culture, including the performing arts as well as film, but scholars have also pointed to important shifts in the public sphere. Religion has definitely played an important role in public debates about violence in the West since 9/11, despite the fact that Muslim leaders explain in public speeches as well as on the Internet that their religion forbids violence against innocent people and civilians. The former Pope John Paul II frequently called for ending senseless violence during mass meetings covered by the media. Many people feel that religion is a very important factor in the rise of violence, even at the level of the local community. Nevertheless, religious revivals that have a major political impact, sometimes even on a global scale, receive the most attention. This results from their success for insiders as well as from the highly ambiguous feelings—if not downright fear—about religious revivals that are perceived as fundamentalism and fanaticism.[7] Many people in the West would assign Ayatollah Khomeini's revolution in Iran to this league and quickly add Muslim organizations like Hezbollah and Hamas, or the Egyptian Muslim Brotherhood. The political power that is released by these movements has been an important spur to our discussion here. The success of such so-called fundamentalist Islamic organizations in mobilizing political protest was already impressive long before 9/11.

Even for those who tend to perceive this freshly generated power mainly as folly, it does, in any case, radically undermine the idea that the political relevance of religion is a thing of the past.

An additional significant factor in this reconfiguration of power on the global front is the West's Pyrrhic victory in the Cold War. In consequence, a transparently bipolar world, inspired by two competing modernist ideologies, has been replaced by a chaotic, multi-focal world, based on multiple foundations. Religion is often considered to be one of those foundations. Because of this perceived lack of order and stability in the current world, the dominance of the Western world, led by the United States, is no longer self-evident. Other foundational ideas, ideologies other than modernist views, also need to be taken seriously. Conflicting powers and foundational ideas in the modern world, both in the media and in academia—notions such as tradition and religion, as well as their significance in the world—are slowly but steadily being reevaluated. One of the most significant manifestations of this development, of which this book is part, concerns the study of religion as a power factor. Postcolonial studies have brought to light that the colonial situation, which was the focus of the early studies in the new field of the anthropology of religion, was thoroughly interwoven with the complex power relations between the colonial authorities and the colonized. Several contributions to this book show, for instance, that in Africa outside urban centers indigenous religious leaders were used as a means of governing the rural population. This is a second indication of the close connection between religion and power. In fact, religion and power are omnipresent in the modern world, and there are countless ways to investigate the interplay of the two.

Power and Religion: Omnipresent but Hard to Define

Power and religion share a number of characteristics, the most important being omnipresence. Power and religion pervade all human actions and interactions. There is no human act that does not involve some kind of faith in a positive outcome and no deed in which power does not play some role. That is why power and religion are such common and familiar phenomena that it is almost impossible truly to have an idea of all the things they entail. No agreement has therefore been reached on the definition of either one of them. But this should not bother us too much. In the field of religious studies, all definitions turn out to be unsatisfying in the end, as there are always aspects that defy definition. Therefore, in this introduction we forego giving a definition of either of these terms. Power and religion are what is described as such in a given context, in ways that are plausible and appear unconstrained. It may be quite substantial and obvious, as is apparent from Mark Juergensmeyer's contribution "Symbolic Violence: Religion and Empowerment." It can also be rather implicit, as the contribution by Mieke Bal, "Religion and Powerlessness: Elena in *Nothing is Missing*," shows.[8] And regardless of the method of investigation, it remains impossible to get a handle on more than one or a couple of aspects at the same time. Obviously, the study of power and the study of religion are both characterized by a multiplicity of approaches, schools, and paradigms. Further on in this introduction we will briefly indicate the approaches to religion and power that are being elaborated in this volume.

The familiar intangibility and omnipresence of religion and power are reflected in the fact that they are not dependent upon institutions. They exist both in institutionalized and noninstitutionalized forms. They can also both evolve from noninstitutionalized to institutionalized forms and vice versa. This explains how religious practices, institutionalized in churches, dogmas, or prescribed rituals, can be replaced by more spontaneous and intuitive forms of devotion in certain parts of the world. These can, in turn, evolve into more official forms of religion. The same is true for power. Power relations that emerge gradually in societies can eventually become formalized. From being almost imperceptible but generally accepted power constellations, they can grow into official political formations. That is how states originate.

The independence of religion and power from formal institutions means that they can be present at various levels simultaneously. In fact, every official religion, however well circumscribed and how strictly upheld it may be, shows parallel manifestations of faith: notions and customs that believers practice more or less covertly and that the religion's official institutions often describe as superstition. Scholars of religion should be conscious of this fact. This also holds true for power. That is the reason why sociologists and political scientists have been trained to look at formal as well as informal power structures. A representative picture of reality can result only from looking at both. Likewise, a distinction between the visible and invisible aspects of religion would be helpful, as Peter van der Veer argues in this book. Van der Veer points to the dialectic of the seen and the unseen in practices connected with religion and the nation-state. A focus on the visual register—flags, headscarves, pilgrimages etc.—requires a strong awareness of both what is made visible in state practices and what is made invisible—for example, the political and economic power of the state and the secret service.

As several of the contributions in this book show, another consequence of the omnipresence of power and religion is that they appear on every imaginable level. Power occurs on the level of individual lives—as Mieke Bal's contribution about the Romanian Orthodox Christian mother Elena and José van Santen's case study of the young Muslim woman Maimouna demonstrate—as well as on the macro-level of society. The same is true for religion. People create their personal form of religion, but at the same time people feel that they are part of a global religious community. In between the individual articulations of religion and global religious organizations, many forms of religious practice are possible, or at least imaginable. The connection between the two is often different from what one would assume when looking at it from the perspective of a strict professional theologian. Social research in the Netherlands shows, for instance, that many Christians believe in reincarnation, although this does not fit into the Christian dogma.

The intangibility of both religion and power also implies that people are often only partially conscious of their presence. This can lead to misunderstandings, for instance, in surveys of persons' involvement in religion. Most religious people only become aware of their religiosity once they are asked about it, and often not even then. Often, the reactions pollsters get to questions of faith in the Western world are along the lines of: "Sorry, I'll ask my wife. Honey, what do we believe in?" Apparently, very few people are religious at the level of discursive awareness. The parallel with power is once again obvious. A husband is often unaware of the amount of power his wife has over him. A sociological analysis and a critical attitude toward ideology are necessary to bring power relations to light. The discursivity of religion and power is a matter of degrees, and this book seeks to demonstrate as much. Several of the actors appearing in the articles in this book consciously use religious notions to increase their power. Others appear to be barely aware of the fact that they are involved in a power struggle in which religion plays a role.

A side effect of the importance of religion and power, as well as the interrelations of both in people's lives, makes research into them rather difficult. People are often not pleased with research outcomes concerning these two topics. They get under their skin or threaten their vested interests and positions.

Have the new power relationships in the world made it necessary to reassess the current conception of power? No. Given the shifting power relationships within the Western world, fed by a striving for emancipation inherent to Western culture, conceptual chaos broke out long ago. The authoritarian, top-down notion of power, which goes back to Hobbes, came under pressure as early as the 1800s.[9] Marx undermined this notion by inverting it. Not those who were considered the "powers that be" have the actual power, but rather those who have to obey their orders.[10] In the second half of the twentieth century, this idea finally led to the notion, at least in the humanities, that the exercise of power is a structural characteristic of society. The persons who are supposed to be in power are not the ones who actually exercise that power; rather, the structures, networks, or vocabularies in which these persons are involved exercise power over them. This idea leads to a variety of theoretical problems. If the notion of structure is opposed to the notion of action, how, then, is it possible for a structure to act, that is, to exercise power? This question resulted in the insight that everybody within one's networks exercises power over everybody else, using the power capital they have. Once more, power was described in terms of *actors*, and this inspired the notion of *empowerment*. It is a notion that is very useful for understanding religion as a means of power, as we will see in the next sections.

The emergence of a multi-focal world in the twentieth century did not, therefore, lead to conceptual confusion regarding the notion of power. The confusion was already there, but the new world powers did contribute to a clarification of the way in which power works. As a result, we can see that power, however one might conceive of it, is in itself plural in nature.

The same is true for religion. That is why the title of this volume is in the plural: *Powers*. Pluralism is the distinguishing characteristic of the methodology of the new study of religion. It not only reflects the plurality of religion, as is also apparent from this volume, but also points to unstable and dynamic power relations. Now that the old Western idea of eroding religions, which were nothing more than minor added dimensions in the bare struggle for power, has to be revised, we are likely to encounter many dilemmas. How, for instance, does religion relate to folklore, to tradition, to theology, to belief, and to faith? Where do we find religion, and how do we study it? The consequence is a great sense of conceptual confusion. One of the functions of the NWO program The Future of the Religious Past is, at the very least, to make this confusion more visible.

Religion as a Means of Exercising Power

Because of their omnipresence, religion and power are strongly interwoven. These interconnections make religion a preeminent means of exercising power: using religion as an instrument to enhance one's power in a power struggle or to improve one's status or position in power is discussed in several contributions to this volume. Religious convictions are the mold in which people shape their ideas about their social positions. The measure to which one gets what one deserves or not is often measured in religious terms. Religious arguments are proffered about the need and nature of the actions that are about to be taken. Because of its religious nature, the argumentation often assumes a supernatural aura of inevitability. In addition, religion has an ideological function: certain aspects of reality are emphasized at the expense of others. This ideological function can be a product of the worldly interests of the powers that be, but can also be an unintended consequence of the dynamics of religion. Religion defines power relations as self-evident, with a superhuman determination. Those who have power will do everything to boost this function, but will also be confronted with opposition and the independent dynamics of religion.

Several essays in this volume deal with religion as a means of exercising power. André Droogers elaborates the functions of power at the level of a cult in a fascinating way in his contribution, "The Recovery of Perverted Religion: Internal Power Processes and the Vicissitudes of Religious Experience." The fictitious story of St. Esteban shows how religion comes about and how religious experiences empower people. Any cult has three features in his view: a transcendental dimension of the experience with the sacred; an internal dimension of the organization of the cult and the religious group; and an external dimension of the relationship with the rest of society. Power constellations and power processes are connected with all three features, in different ways. Power within the religious group of the cult, for example, results from the fact that religious virtuosos are scarce. This implies that they have power over others, especially when communicating their experience as a message, directly or through spokespersons. Their tool of power is language, particularly metaphor, which may become a key trope of religion (e.g., bread as Christ's body). Playfulness and the creative interaction with religious experience are reduced as religious leaders control what challenges their power structures.

Another contribution deals with religion and power at the level of the nation-state. Cheikh Guèye and Olivia Gervasoni's "The Mourid Brotherhood at the Center of Senegalese Political Life: A Dialectic of State and Religious Power" concerns the complex relationship between Senegalese state authorities and the Muslim Mourid Brotherhood, which consists of *marabouts*, who are Sufi spiritual leaders, and their disciples. Originally, the Mourid Brotherhood focused on personal devotion, and the Mourid principles were not to be applied directly to politics. Nevertheless, in the 1990s *marabouts* joined electoral tickets and Mourid lobby groups were formed. In 2000 a member of the Mourid Brotherhood, Abdoulaye Wade, became president and liberated the state from "the sin of secularism." The president's affiliation threatens to personalize the relationship between the state and Mouridism, with political power taking on a religious quality given Wade's potential role as "President of the Mourids." Wade quite successfully draws on Mourid religious symbolism to achieve his goals. The growing involvement of the Mourid Brotherhood in state affairs is a success story, but it also constitutes a danger: the Mourids may come to feel that the state belongs to them and that they can do what they please with it. This indicates the risks involved when religion is used as a means to exercise power. This leads us to the critical function of religion in connection with power: religion not only defines power but also evaluates it.

Religion as Critique of Power

A capability to support and strengthen power relations implies a capability to question them. The capability to legitimize power relations implies a capability to perceive them as illegitimate. People in power can hold each other to religious values and keep each other in check that way. However, believers can also reject claims to power on the basis of religion. Competing believers can attempt to improve their positions on the basis of shared religious convictions. Religion is used to perpetuate power relations but also to change them. It can inspire uprisings against what are perceived to be unfair power relations and thus lead to power struggles in which any means are permitted in an attempt to achieve justice, since the struggle is divinely sanctioned. The battle becomes a sacred war, and anyone who falls has not simply died but passed on as a martyr, for a cause that is unreservedly good. In this way, religion can give people courage to rise above what they experience as injustice.

Anna-Karina Hermkens's case study of the religious dimension of a complex power struggle at Bougainville, a small island group in the South Pacific, in "The Power of Mary in Secessionist Warfare: Catholicism and Political Crisis in Bougainville, Papua New Guinea," elaborates the double role of religion as empowerment and inspiration of resistance. From 1988 until the late 1990s, people on Bougainville Island were immersed in a vicious war that destroyed nearly all infrastructure and social services. Religion, particularly Catholicism, played a major role during and after the crisis. The Bougainville struggle for independence was conceptualized as a holy war, which helped to create clear boundaries between "us" and "them" in the struggle to re-trieve social control and power from the forces of evil, including the foreign mining company that exploited Bougainville's rich copper reserves. In order to empower resistance and legitimate the crisis, God was called upon in "an ideology of resistance." Francis Ona, a landowner who became a popular leader in the struggle, devoted his life to "Mama Maria," thereby appropriat-ing the whole of Bougainville with divine sanction. The religious devotions of others were deeply intertwined with indigenous concepts and beliefs as well as with the politics of the crisis. People believed that peace could be achieved through prayers, especially pleas directed to Mary, the mother of Jesus Christ. Thus, Mary's power became intertwined with national identity con-structions and attempts to realize a more just and responsible society at Bougainville.

Religion's Tools

Religion can use various tools in order to achieve its goals, and these tools often overlap with other means of power. David Morgan's contribution, "Seeing Nationhood: Images of American Identity," surveys one of these tools—the use of images, art as well as popular imagery—in constructing American national identity. He argues that national identity, civil piety, and reli-gion are intertwined in these identity constructions. An image in an early schoolbook, for exam-ple, shows George Washington at prayer on the eve of battle, thereby pointing to the combination of religious and national identities. Marsh's painting of Brooklyn's skyline demon-strates how the land was transformed into a modern metropolis. Cityscapes show the strength of American power: humanity replacing God. Morgan argues for the existence of two civil religions: patriotism, which emphasizes individual rights and dissent, totemized by the Statue of Liberty; and nationalism, which totemizes the American flag as a symbol of national unity.

Another tool of religion in politics concerns, of course, law. Again, this tool can be used in very different ways and have contradictory consequences. In countries with a strict separation between religion and state, the law is frequently used to ban religion from the public sphere, as José van Santen's case study of North Cameroon shows. North Cameroon shows at the same time how trends in society undermine such a policy or even go against it. Interestingly, the opposite case—namely, states in which religious law has been incorporated into the state's judicial system—show a complex outcome with contradictory trends. Shamil Jeppie's contribution, "Sharia and State in the Sudan: From Late Colonialism to Late Islamism," exemplifies this. Jeppie traces the interconnections between *sharia* as a body of law and the political context of the Sudan. The British colonial authorities introduced *sharia* to help control the Muslim population. After Sudan's independence in 1956, sharia became bound up with questions of the constitution, replacing the English Common Law. In 1983, Ja'afar Numayri, Sudan's president from 1969 to 1985, put all the penal aspects of sharia into practice, with the support of Sudan's Islamists. Nevertheless, although sharia is currently Sudan's dominant legal system, the constitution of 1998 is not explicit about its significance. Controversial aspects of sharia that go against international conventions or standards of human rights are relaxed or not implemented at all.

Peter van der Veer analyzes yet another tool with which religion exerts power in political contexts in his essay: "The Visible and the Invisible in South Asia": constructions of sacred space. He discusses the role of visual imagery involved in "producing the nation-as-space" at a specific border location, the Kargil area in the northwest of India, which borders Pakistan and is a site of dispute and armed conflict. The sheer fact that India tries to control this uninhabitable area shows the importance of the nation-as-space. The Indian language of patriotism used during this conflict includes phrases like "unrelenting courage" and "brave soldiers," and also demonstrates how the landscape functions as a background for heroism as a representation of the honor and sovereignty of the nation. The Kargil example links up with other constructions of the Indian nation-as-space. For Savarkar, the ideologue of *Hindutva*, the basis of the Hindu nation is the sacred geography of India. Savarkar's ideology of a sacred fatherland for Hindus was made visible in the 1980s with rituals that are derived from pilgrimage. The United Hindu Party (VHP) experimented on a large scale with the ritual in what is called "a sacrifice for unity" (*ekatmatayajna*) in 1983. Hindu pilgrimage increased the national integration of Hindus and pointed to the geographical unity of India as a sacred space (*kshetra*) of Hindus. Three major pilgrimage routes crossed in Nagpur, where the headquarters of the Rashtriya Swayamsevak Sangh (a Hindu nationalist organization of volunteers) are. This ritual of unity, through its mappings, makes other possible mappings by non-Hindus invisible.

Religion as a Way of Release, Consolation, and Personal Empowerment

There are many situations in which a fight for power is not the issue and religion does not play a role as a means of enhancing one's power. Here, the role of religion merely concerns the expression of feelings, ways of compensating for, healing, and making sense of experiences of injustice and suffering. Thus, in addition to the function of religion as a means of expressing, interpreting, and enhancing power in social and political contexts ("king by the grace of God . . ."), religion can also help to find a place and a meaning for feelings of powerlessness. Religion can make impotence bearable. This is its consolatory function. However, even if religion as an expression of feelings of impotence may seem to be "power neutral," it often still possesses a covert power function. With his famous phrase "religion is the opiate of the people," Marx argues that the consoling function of religion can also be a cause of religious power relationships. Yet when the reality of a situation is accepted for religious reasons, a stoic attitude may remain as a silent protest against what should not have been.

Several chapters in this book address this role of religion as a way of release, consolation, and antidote to feelings of loss, pain, and powerlessness. Catrien Notermans presents a case study of a pilgrimage to Lourdes in her contribution, "The Power of the Less Powerful: Making Memory on a Pilgrimage to Lourdes." Combining anthropology of religion with narrative theory of memory, Notermans analyzes how pilgrims to Lourdes narrate and reenact painful and nostalgic memories related to their illnesses as well as their family histories. Pilgrimage empowers the less powerful. Many pilgrims have feelings of loss. They relate stories about family members who have suffered and died, and they have often sacrificed their own pain for the benefit of others. Lourdes allows them to put themselves in first place at least once. The religious symbolism of human suffering and distress at Lourdes becomes a vocabulary for the pilgrims to narrate and experience their pain, make it public, and reclaim the power denied to them. Telling the stories of their medical problems allows these pilgrims to experience some control over their illness when medicine seems to overlook and disempower them. At home again, the pilgrims feel satisfied, because their previously painful memories have been transformed. Through their narratives during the pilgrimage, the pilgrims feel empowered to continue the healing process through the emotional change and relief they experienced.

Mieke Bal's contribution, "Religion and Powerlessness: Elena in *Nothing Is Missing*," also touches upon the function of religion as a way of offering release and consolation. Bal transcribes a half-hour conversation between Elena and her son Simion, who left Romania for Canada. She also provides a running commentary in an attempt to understand what is going on in this interaction. Elena invokes God and considers Holy Mary to be the force behind her son's talents. Over and over she expresses her powerlessness, and the role of religion in the empowerment of Elena is ambiguous, as we will see.

Mark Juergensmeyer deals with the topical subject of the interconnections between religion and violence, which, in his opinion, is closely connected with the striving for empowerment.[11] In his essay "Symbolic Violence: Religion and Empowerment," he explores why symbolic violence, inspired at least to a certain extent by religion, conveys experiences of empowerment. He argues that violent acts themselves, including suicide missions, provide empowerment as an antidote to humiliation. At times these acts also result in political change. The performance of violence as an act of empowerment results in real power, but it is symbolic as well, and its outcome is usually very different from traditional conquests. The term *symbolic* illustrates, in this connection, that the target is outside the field of immediate action and that the act can be understood as a symbol, a ritual, or a sacred drama. The death of Jesus as symbolized in the Eucharist/Communion, for example, becomes a metaphor for salvation and ultimately leads to the transformation of death into life.

Crucial to Juergensmeyer's argument is that religious violence should be explained by the impact of war as a leading idea in religious discourse. The outcome of war is a new social order. When war and religion are fused there is a "cosmic war": a war undertaken on behalf of God or carried out by God, which legitimates and empowers the group that entered the battle in question. Obviously, personal empowerment goes hand in hand with group empowerment in Juergensmeyer's approach. This is apparent from the fact that many perpetrators of religious violence not only have communities of support but also empower these communities. They highlight the religious and political goals that are important for the groups that support the divinely sanctioned battle, but also inspire them because they function as models for these groups. They also legitimate the authority of the insider community, and disqualify the sovereignty and laws of its opponents.[12]

In his contribution, "Political Theology: The Authority of God," Avishai Margalit focuses on another aspect of power: legitimization by appealing to God. Margalit develops a genealogy of authority in three stages: the authority of God, the authority of the messengers of the word of God, and the authority of the word of God in terms of the authority of Holy Scripture. However, these authorities do not result in clear-cut legitimizations of power, because the way they are understood is highly dependent on the way humans understand God.

Juergensmeyer presupposes in his contribution that there are complex tensions between religious goals and established practices or regulations within society. This also becomes apparent from José van Santen's story about Maimouna, a young Muslim woman. In her contribution, "'Without my headscarf I feel naked': Veiling, *Laïcité*, Politics, and Islamist Discourse in North Cameroon," van Santen asks what the impact of Islamic discourse about the "veil" is on the personal life of women in contemporary North Cameroon. Currently, there is a symbiotic relationship between Islam and politics in North Cameroon, and the political elite is Muslim, by contrast to the Christian south of the country. However, the concept of *laïcité*, inherited from the French colonizers, determines state regulations. The Cameroonian state thus imposes the recent French ban on displaying overt symbols of religion in public schools. Many Muslim women, therefore, did not go to school, because their fathers did not want them to remove their headscarves. Since the 1990s, the relationship between state and religion has been changing. Veiling has become a motive for the establishment of Islamic private schools, and girls have an increasing place within them. Paradoxically, many girls who consider themselves good Muslims do not see the need to wear the veil. They consider the emphasis on veiling (particularly the *hijab*) an undesirable influence from the "white Pakistani" (in fact Saudi-Arabian) imams and religious leaders who began to preach in 1992 in North Cameroon. Yet wearing or rejecting the veil cannot be an autonomous individual act. The decision is guided by institutions, politics, and the discourse of what it means to be a good Muslim in the officially laical society of current Cameroon.

The case study of Maimouna in North Cameroon is just one example among many others of the clash between the aspirations of religion and the independent dynamics of a society. As a matter of fact, in most cases only a small part of society consists of what Max Weber calls "religious virtuosos."[13] The great majority of people just aspire to a life that is bearable and satisfying. They aim for not too much power, but also not too little, not much glory, but also no humiliation. Most religious people tend to strive for an Aristotelian middle ground: religion without fanaticism. Because of its function as a means of power, religion tends to oscillate between the two extremes of zero power and full control. In more secularized societies, the religious dimension of power struggles is frequently more limited, and often merely implicit. The values that play a role here are not necessarily divine, but are no less absolute for all that. Religion, therefore, tends to be an element in a whole repertoire of power, and as such it is interwoven with other means of power.

Religion as Artistic Expression and Empowerment

David Morgan's contribution about the importance of images for the construction of American identity indicates that art can be a significant medium for the expression and reinterpretation of religious motifs, traditions, and conventions in a national context. Two other contributions focus on the multi-faceted role of music as a medium of religion and power. This music can also be transformed and reinterpreted when performances are transferred from an original sacred place to audiences in other contexts.

Rokus de Groot's essay "Music, Religion, and Power: *Qawwali* as Empowering Disempowerment" deals with the practices and transformations of *qawwali*, a musical genre that originated in Pakistan and India. *Qawwali* is an Indian-Pakistan ritual of poetry, which was originally performed to music in Sufi shrines but was developed by a single practitioner, Nusrat Fateh Ali Khan, into performances on a global scale. *Qawwali* performances highlight the mystical state that should lead to surrender and the experience of Allah's love by the members of the audience. De Groot analyzes musical events, poetical texts, audience responses, and the spirituality of the music in its original as well as its (com)modified Western settings. He explains how *qawwali* is traditionally performed in *dargahs*, tombs of the saints, epiphanic places where time and eternity intersect. Concert *qawwali* became popular because of Nusrat's commercial performances. Although Nusrat stresses that his performances are a bridge to other nations for the Sufi mystical tradition, they also draw upon Western notions of the deification of the artist. The transfer of *qawwali* practices from shrines to the concert stage has, therefore, important consequences for the spiritual role of the music as well as for the performers and their audiences.

In "John Cage and the Mystification of Musical Silence," Jael Kraut analyzes the compositions of John Cage, a composer who uses silence as a means of religious empowerment to unify humankind with the cosmos and nature. Cage sought to silence music step by step, culminating in his silent piece *4′33″*. He reversed the status of the instrument, using nonmusical instruments and the "prepared piano," a piano transformed by adding bolts and other objects. Cage was fascinated with Indian aesthetics and with Zen Buddhism: the Buddhist ideal of the "negation of the will" prompted him to develop an aesthetic and spiritual silence in both his life and his work. Kraut claims that Cage became immersed in concern for a spiritualized silence and thus was blinded to how his historical situation affected his possibilities as a composer. Kraut also offers a critique of Cage's ideas: Cage seeks a musical identification with nature, but the nature he has in mind is exceedingly manipulated.

Another contribution combines the recycling of religious tropes in the medium of film with the theme of the power of martyrs. In "Maternal Martyrdom: *Alien3* and the Power of the Female Martyr," Laura Copier interprets Lieutenant Ripley, the female character in *Alien3* who jumps into molten lead to save humanity from the alien queen she is hosting, as a martyr. She compares Ripley to Perpetua, the famous ancient female martyr. Building on Mieke Bal's work on quotation, she asks to what extent the contemporary and popular representation of Ripley reconfigures her historical predecessors such as Perpetua as female martyrs. Copier further utilizes Elizabeth Castelli's analysis of gender as malleable to analyze female martyrs: Castelli argues that women martyrs typically adopted masculine features and abandoned their femininity, thereby transgressing and reaffirming gender difference. Significantly, Perpetua is a mother, but her baby does not stay with her in prison. And in Perpetua's fourth vision she is stripped naked and becomes a man, indicating that she is ready to face martyrdom. Perpetua's story has thus been taken to imply that mothers cannot be martyrs and vice versa, but *Aliens3* offers an alternative scenario. Although Ripley is strong and masculine, she embraces her motherhood at the moment of her self-sacrifice. The four different endings to *Alien3* in the DVD version lead to various interpretations of Ripley's role as martyr and mother. The special edition ending reaffirms the classical discourse of martyrs. In the theatrical version Ripley's maternity does not take away from her martyr's act of self-sacrifice for humanity.

In an imaginative and highly original way, Mieke Bal's contribution is also highly relevant as an artistic expression of religion and power. Bal uses the medium of a video installation as an innovative way of contributing to scholarly debates. "Elena" is an episode from her multiple-screen video installation *Nothing Is Missing* (2006–7). This installation shows videos of women being interviewed by people who are very close to them, but whose relationship with these women has been interrupted due to migration.[14] The videos are filmed in close-up to provide a monument to the women's profound losses. They force the viewer to look the women in the eyes, to listen to their foreign languages, which leaves the audience no other option than to engage and relate to the women's body language. In her contribution, Bal takes this role as viewer and interpreter upon herself in her comments.

Religion: Empowerment, Disempowerment, or Both?

Scott Appleby argues, building on Rudolph Otto, that responses to manifestations of the sacred are neither good nor bad in themselves. Positive or destructive actions following upon an encounter with the sacred depend on specific interpretations by the religious actors. Appleby notes: "Within its realm [i.e., the realm of the sacred] power is undifferentiated, neither creative nor destructive in itself, but capable both of generating and extinguishing life."[15] Thus, whether religion empowers or disempowers its adherents is dependent on the specific case discussed, and it is a matter that is in principle subjective. It depends on the interpretations of the religious persons themselves, as well as on the scholars who observe and interpret their actions. Moreover, the appraisal of the outcome of religious experiences and acts is in principle a normative assessment, because there is no agreement about what is considered good or bad in the global world.

Many contributions in this volume focus foremost upon empowerment, the supposedly positive consequence of religion, but several highlight the ambiguity of the sacred in connection with power. Peter van der Veer emphasizes that the very same symbols can be considered to be tokens either of loyalty or of disloyalty to the state, depending on the interpreters as well as on the context in which the symbols are used. Mieke Bal's chapter on Elena calls into question whether Elena's Christian faith empowers her. In her running commentary, Bal's underlying question is whether religion empowers or disempowers Elena. She leaves the question deliberately unanswered. Several of Elena's statements seem ambiguous. Bal, interpreting these words, suggests much more explicitly than Elena that God has been stingy and cruel. Elena had only two sons: one died, and the other went to Canada. Elena could not say this herself, because it would challenge the comfort of her belief. Instead, she blames herself: "What did I do wrong?" Some of Elena's phrases express feelings of powerlessness. Most explicit is her statement "God has beaten me." Nevertheless, Elena does give God credit for her son's success. God remains a ploy in spite of his lack of justice. Resignation is a "back-up" option in negative situations, apparently: "God, rather than happiness, has the last word."

David Morgan points to the disempowerment of "the other" in his contribution. He argues that imagining nationhood requires casting a "liminal gaze" outside of the borders as a means of demarcating the boundaries of kin and kind from the "other." This gaze can be turned to "the other," for example, to the Native American, who must either vanish or be assimilated. One of Morgan's images is a photograph of Hiawatha paddling off into the sunset. One immediately assumes that it represents the idea that America has been given to white Americans for the progress of their civilization. Yet Native Americans themselves turn out to be the source of the photograph. Hiawatha has become a Christ figure, and through him Native Americans experience redemptive suffering. This shows that the tools used by the dominant culture can also be implemented by the oppressed.

In their contribution, "'Bolivarian' Anti-Semitism," Claudio Lomnitz and Rafael Sánchez also focus on the use of religious symbolism to disempower others. They offer a survey of recent cases of anti-Semitism in Venezuela, which are, in their opinion, directly related to Hugo Chávez's attempts to stabilize his position as the nation's leader. Lomnitz and Sánchez argue that the attack on the Tiferet Israel Synagogue in Caracas on January 30, 2009, is part of a continuous stream of anti-Semitic statements and acts in Venezuela, which associate the Jews with Hitler and the devil through the symbolism of swastikas and the number 666, the Mark of the Beast in Revelation 13:18. Such anti-Semitism helps to construct the regime's opponents as enemies of the state, which is personified in Chávez, by associating them with shit, Zionist imperialism, and the Jews. It thus legitimates either expelling these outsiders from the body of the nation or subjecting them to the will of the people. Lomnitz and Sánchez also argue that this ideology has a firm basis in the work of the Argentine Holocaust denier Norberto Ceresole, who acted as Chávez's adviser, rather than in the writings of the great liberator Simón Bolívar.

Two contributors, finally, ask themselves what can be done to defend against the destructive consequences of religion. Mark Juergensmeyer wonders whether it is possible to contain or redirect war as the central factor in manifestations of religious violence. He refers in this connection to helpful discussions by Thomas Aquinas, Reinhold Niebuhr, René Girard, and Mahatma Gandhi. Paradoxically, he concludes that the cure for war, especially religious war, can be religion, so long as it focuses on the sanctity of life. André Droogers also reflects upon a policy to counter the danger that religion leads to disempowerment. In the epilogue to his chapter, he mentions four implications of his analysis of power in the context of a cult: (1) an awareness of how power operates and how it affects the religious experience may prevent perversions of power; (2) religious leaders should promote and facilitate religious experiences instead of frustrating them; (3) focusing upon the initial religious experience may foreground weakness and vulnerability instead of power and also counter the criticism of religion; (4) a new conception of power, focusing upon the promotion of life, should ensure that power does not pervert religious experience.

This Volume: Four Sections

The foregoing discussion of the multiple and diverse interconnections of religion and power underlies the setup of this volume in four sections. It also explains the plural *Powers* of the title: religion empowers people in manifold ways and at various levels, from the individual life of a religious person to the scenario of the entire world. Besides empowerment, religion also helps to express feelings of powerlessness and can lead to the disempowerment of insiders as well as outsiders in a religious community.

All contributions concentrate on the dynamics of "lived religion" in recent or even contemporary contexts. Some chapters focus on religion in the West, but we deliberately chose a multiple perspective on a global scale, extending from the Western World (the United States and Europe) to the East (India and Pakistan), the Pacific, and Africa (Senegal, Sudan, Cameroon, and Egypt). Some chapters also deal with processes of migration between these areas (Romania to Canada, India to the West).

The volume's first section, "Macropolitics" still needs some explanation because it has not been explicitly discussed in this Introduction so far. It deals with the role of religion on the world stage. The return of the religious on a geopolitical scale, observed by many commentators, often conflicts with the self-interpretation of modern states and their citizens. The emergence of a supposedly enlightened public sphere went hand in hand with the formulation of ideals of identity and self-determination, individual autonomy and universalist cosmopolitanism. These trends seem at odds with the heteronomy and particularism commonly ascribed to religious doctrine and its practices. Current tendencies toward globalization and the almost unchallenged appeal of free-market capitalism have reinforced the self-congratulatory narrative of Western "secularist" modernity. The predominance of this narrative obscures the fact that the concept of the political has always been contingent, if not upon the authority or the explicit sanction of a dominant religion, then at least upon a plausible translation and renegotiation of the central categories of this religion's historical beliefs. This was true both in premodern times and during the first establishment of nation-states; the same holds true for the new geopolitics in the wake of globalization and its medium, "informationalism."[16]

The contributions to this section (André Droogers, Mark Juergensmeyer, Avishai Margalit, and Talal Asad) all address issues that have been associated with trends on a global scale: religion as empowerment as well as disempowerment, the interconnections between religion and violence, notions of authority, and, finally, the revival of religion itself. Some of these contributions problematize these supposed globally trends and point to tensions between these trends and local particularities. Importantly, in this section the contribution by Talal Asad radically criticizes the assumption that religious changes can be explained by the assumption of global trends.

In "Explaining the Global Religious Revival: the Egyptian Case," Asad wonders which religion is meant when scholars point to the so-called world-wide religious revival. He discusses several explanations of this revival: (1) religion as a response to acute economic and sociological problems, (2) the need to find a new cultural identity, and (3) the need for reassurance in a time of rapid change and instability. He surveys these hypotheses by connecting them to the world of Islam in current Egypt, arguing that political Islam in Egypt is inconceivable without the formation of the nation-state and its ambitions, and that reinterpretations of Islam are a major factor. For example, the old Islamic notion of *da'wa*—of calling one's fellows to become better Muslims—is being reformulated from its previous primary preoccupation with ritual practice and religious doctrine to include material welfare: the provision of cheap medicines, loans, youth clubs, emergency shelters, etc., because the state is increasingly unable or unwilling to provide these things. Asad concludes that there is no unitary phenomenon to be explained. "Religion"—even "fundamentalist religion"—is not a homogeneous phenomenon. The disparate phenomena that we group together as "a world-wide religious revival" deal with questions about morality, politics, faith, and spirituality that lead in very different directions. They do not express a single movement, a single sensibility, a single existential orientation. Perhaps they share only this: a rejection of the self-assured promises of secularism linked up with the ideal of rationalist progress.

The volume's second part, "The Nation," deals with religion and politics on a national scale, since religion is constitutive of the modern nation-state, as Peter van der Veer argues. Religion can also play a major role in the state's legitimization, as is apparent from several contributions in this section (see above, under "Religion as a Means of Exercising Power"). The "religious" and the "secular" are, therefore, mutually dependent. The contributions to the third section, "The Individual: Between Powerlessness and Empowerment," deal with individuals and how religion helps to empower them but also can lead to their disempowerment. The fourth part, "Power: Artistic Representations," offers three case studies of ways in which art—music and film—can be a means of imagining the intangible and a medium of power.

PART I

Macropolitics

The Recovery of Perverted Religion

Internal Power Processes and the Vicissitudes of Religious Experience

André Droogers

A Story

In Gabriel García Márquez's story "The Handsomest Drowned Man in the World,"[1] the children of a fishermen's village on a desertlike cape find the body of a drowned man, a man of abnormal size, washed up on the beach. The children don't know what to do with the giant dead man. All afternoon they play with the corpse, until somebody happens to see what they are doing. The men then carry the body to the nearest house. They wonder why the corpse is so huge. Has the seawater gotten into his bones? Did he continue to grow after death?

The men go to surrounding villages to see whether someone is missing. As is the custom, the women take care of the dead man. Once they finish cleaning the corpse, they are left breathless by this man's beauty and virility. They see that he has borne his death with pride. They keep staring at him, but he simply is too huge for their imagination. While sewing pants from a piece of sail and a shirt from bridal linen, they imagine how his life has been, how happy his wife must have been with him, how he attracted fish by calling them by their name, and how springs began to flow when he worked on the land. Did he know the secret word that makes a woman pick a flower and put it in her hair? They compare the drowned man with their husbands—who in no way can bear the comparison. This man could do more in one night than their husbands in their whole lives. They thus wander through the maze of their fantasy until the eldest woman, more out of compassion than passion, sighs: "He has the face of someone called Esteban." At dawn they cover his face with a handkerchief, so that the light will not bother him.

Gradually the women grow aware of the tragic irrevocability of Esteban's death. Their eyes fill with tears; they go from sighing to wailing and then sing the traditional dirge, improvising new lyrics for Esteban. When the men return from the other villages with the news that nobody is missing, the women smile in the midst of their tears: "He is ours!" The men don't see the point and wonder what, in their absence, has happened to the women.

Thus the women bring Esteban to life. The men wish to get rid of the dead man. As is the burial custom, the corpse will be thrown off the cliffs. In this village, committing to the earth is committing to the sea. The men tie an old anchor to the body so that it will be gone once and for all. Whereas the men want to return to their normal tasks, the women invent reasons to tarry. They add relics to the litter that the men have made from the remains of a foremast and gaff. The men ask why the stranger deserves decorations worthy of a main altar. But when the women remove the handkerchief from Esteban's face, the men are left breathless, too.

Esteban is then given a splendid funeral. Some of the women, who have gone to other villages to get flowers for the burial, return with other women, who feel that something extraordinary is happening. In order not to return Esteban to the sea as an orphan, he is given a father and a mother, uncles and aunts, from among the best people. He is promoted to being kin. Being much more alive than he is, the dead man's splendor is experienced by the villagers as contrasting with their own dullness. In the end they remove the anchor so that Esteban will be able to return—if he wishes to do so.

When they throw Esteban's body off the cliffs, they hold their breath for the fraction of centuries—as García Márquez puts it—that the corpse needs to reach the sea. All know that their lives will be different from now on. Henceforth their village is known as Esteban's village.

A Sequel

If García Márquez were an anthropologist—which in a way he is—he might have continued the story in the following way. The Esteban stories that people tell make a saint out of the drowned giant. One fisherman starts carving small statues out of driftwood. From homes where such an image adorns the house altar, the first miracles are reported. When children play in a dry field just outside the village, a spring bursts forth. The water is said to have healing power. After some months a small chapel is erected on the spot where Esteban's body was thrown off the cliffs. Esteban's statue is given a central position on the altar. The anchor that the men had tied to Esteban's litter is placed as a cross on the chapel wall. People come regularly to the chapel to pray.

When more miracles are reported, people from other villages come to the chapel as well. Soon the chapel becomes a pilgrimage point. Especially during weekends, buses bring pilgrims to Esteban's village. Pilgrims sing the dirge that the women improvised during their wake. Each pilgrim brings a small litter bearing a statue of St. Esteban. Between the litter and the statue are hidden small notes, on which are written requests for help. These mini-litters are thrown off the cliff. Exactly a year after his funeral, Esteban's saint's day is held for the first time, and a procession with Esteban's statue is performed, partly with fishing ships on the sea.

The changes in the village draw the attention of the priest who twice a year comes to the fishermen's village to say mass, marry couples, and baptize newborn babies. He reports the events to his bishop, who sends a priest and a nun to offer pastoral care to the pilgrims. The church pays for the erection of a huge statue of St. Esteban at the entrance to the village. During St. Esteban's Day the bishop himself comes to the chapel to say an open-air mass and to lead the procession. In his sermon, he refers to the sea as the symbol of chaos, to the ship as a symbol of the church, to St. Peter as a fisher of men, and to St. Esteban, the New Testament martyr St. Stephen. The people hardly listen. They came to seek a miracle.

Once the pilgrimage influences daily life, politicians become interested. At election time they are conspicuously present. During the annual procession, they are the bishop's guests on the boat with St. Esteban's statue. They emphasize that, thanks to them, the road to the village has been asphalted. They also have invested government money in upgrading the fishing port into a marina.

Some of the fishermen in the village understand the chances brought to their corner of the world by the new era that began with Esteban. They start souvenir shops with Esteban statues and holy spring water. Restaurants open, where Esteban's fish is the best-selling dish on the menu. Entrepreneurs using machines have taken the place of the first sculptor. In turn, they are put out of business when plastic statues are sold with labels that say in small print "Made in China." After some time, the first hotel is opened, soon followed by an apartment complex. Two years later, a casino is built. Travel agencies organize brief excursions on the sea in fishing boats, which by now no longer serve to catch fish. A holiday in Esteban's village is advertised in the national newspapers and weeklies as an attractive combination of beauty, folklore, and leisure.

Only the women who were present during the wake still remember the extraordinary experience that the body of the handsomest drowned man in the world brought into their lives.

Religion's Seedbed

Though this account is fictional, the case is plausible. A religious cult emerges from a mixture of events and experiences, coincidences and strategies, well-being and suffering, joy and sadness, Eros and Thanatos, a moment of insight and a hundred years of solitude. Even a dead body is able to inspire a message of life and hope. To the women, the drowned man belongs to the gray area between death and life. He is a border man, found on the beach, at the margin between sea and land. His huge, dead presence interrupts the dull routine of their daily lives. His beauty and virility suggest a possibility of life beyond death. In an odor of sanctity a cult comes to life. Persons, feelings, events, interpretations, and local customs come together in a constellation that generates creativity and has its own dynamic. The unexpected power of a drowned man is explored in a cult that empowers his followers. In short: this is how religion can come about.

Within this context, power—understood here as the capacity to influence other people's behavior, even against their will—is present from the very start. In García Márquez's story, power distribution is primarily organized around gender differences. Men and women differ in their behavior and interpretations. They play the traditional roles that belong to their genders, reflecting a distribution of labor and thereby of power. The men carry the body to the village; the women take care of the corpse. Whereas the giant inspires the men to ask almost scientific questions about the causes of his extraordinary size, the women discover that their deepest desires are addressed. They are the first to sense the dead man's power over their fantasy. The eldest woman among them, the most experienced in life, gives him a name, by which he becomes a person, just as believers tend to personalize their experience with the sacred. This giant Esteban influences the women's behavior, and that is the power he holds over them. The women invest him with qualities that correspond to their ultimate questions and interests. They turn the no-man's-land between death and life into woman's-land, in which they nimbly move between reality and wish, routine and fantasy, the profane and the sacred, strength and weakness. They rehabilitate life as a value. These women understand the promise of different gender relations that the giant's corpse represents. Though initially the men behave as the owners of the funeral, following their traditional power position, they soon have to accept the women's leadership. Once the handkerchief is removed, they too become enchanted by the drowned man's charisma. From then on the women dominate the men's behavior.

Only in the sequel, once the church, the politicians, and the entrepreneurs enter the scene, is male dominance restored. Other forms of power distribution, based on other resources, though still with a gender dimension, then become prominent. Through their activities, including those of a profane nature, stakeholders influence the cult and the form it takes. From the moment it proves to be a success, the Esteban cult is subjected to changes. The women who were the first to recognize Esteban's importance could not have imagined the form the cult would take. Their original version coexists with new versions that match the interests of all the categories of people involved, each in their own ways: men, locals, pilgrims, clergy, politicians, and entrepreneurs. In this constellation, probably the women's version has changed as well.

Three Dimensions

Together, all these actors represent the three dimensions that are present in any religion or cult: (1) a transcendental dimension, consisting in the experience with the sacred, (2) an internal dimension, consisting in the organization of the cult and of the religious group, and (3) an external dimension, consisting in the relationship with the rest of society. Each of these dimensions has its own power constellation and mechanisms. The power dynamics in each dimension influence the form the cult takes. Together, the three dimensions represent a unique but ever-changing religious repertoire, and they all influence each other.[2]

The first dimension, that of the experience of the sacred, is basic to any religious group. Cults around a charismatic person, alive or dead, are quite common, and some have been the start of world religions. In various religious contexts, the repertoires that direct transcendental experience are remarkably similar, often personalizing the sacred. In being given form, the God, gods, spirits, saints, etc. of the transcendental dimension are defined by their power features. Power is the primary feature of their identity. In their behavior, believers are influenced by these sacred powers and in turn seek to influence them, that is, exercise power over them. A link is made between the experience of the sacred and daily problem solving, including the experiences of hunger, infertility, and illness. The contact with the sacred may produce security and empowerment, though it may also lead to existential insecurity and feelings of inferiority. Both views legitimize sacred power. The sacred often takes a bodily form, as in Esteban's case, just as it is often experienced in a corporeal way. Though people usually view the source of the experience as located outside the believer, they feel it as a presence in their bodies. Life and death, as corporeal experiences, are common themes, as are affliction and well-being, good and evil. Effective moral principles may produce a system of divine and human control over the body, sustained by positive and negative sanctions. Power is an important ingredient in such a system. Besides, often a perspective on time and history develops, including both an interpretation of the body's limited life span and a perspective on the history of humanity.

Interestingly, in the experience of the sacred not just its force but also its weakness may be prominent. Thus, Esteban's dead body seems to represent the absolute loss of power of somebody who used to be a giant. Yet the women imagine this body back to life and thereby recuperate its vitality. Despite—or thanks to—its weakness, this intriguing, huge, and once-powerful corpse then suggests various things: the good life, abundance, the perfect husband, beauty, and virility. Religious creativity transforms death into life and vulnerability into power, and it plays with these possibilities. Religious heroes may seek vulnerability, suffer humiliation, or sacrifice themselves for the good of believers. Power thus represents a way of moving along a spectrum

27

rather than taking a fixed position of strength. Superiority and authority may be based on a position of inferiority and powerlessness.

Turning now to the second dimension, that of internal organization, power is present from the start when a person shares his or her religious experience with other people. As we have seen, this process has its own dynamics. In the Esteban cult, the gender-based distribution of power changes in the course of time. Once the experience of sacred power is shared with others, internal power mechanisms are activated. The cult must be organized, as when, in Esteban's cult, clergy and entrepreneurs take the initiative to establish some infrastructure. The success of any cult demands some form of control, to guarantee that both the cult and normal life may continue. Religious and secular authorities have a common interest in this regard. Control by the clergy has the advantage of creating a predictable, repeatable framework on the basis of the original experience or event. In St. Esteban's cult, the diocese's pastoral care and the annual feast provide such a framework. Continuity is guaranteed. The message is made accessible to all. After the inchoate start of a cult, sensible, level-headed organizers play their role in a down-to-earth and matter-of-fact strategic way.

The third dimension, the external relationships of the religious group, concerns the mutual power relationship between a religious group and the larger society of which it is a part. When the message that comes with a religious experience includes the instruction that it must be spread, the wider society is involved from the start. Moreover, the message itself may include some element that seeks to transform society. Cults often contain a blueprint for society, just as the women saw in Esteban the perspective for a better life.

In sum, a personal experience with the power of the sacred, when shared with others, is the start of a process characterized by a variety of power mechanisms. This process involves all three dimensions. What is fed from the transcendental dimension into the internal and external dimensions is modified and returned. The idiosyncratic triangle of the three dimensions in their mutual influence is ruled in large part by power processes. It gives a religion or cult its unique and exclusive identity.

The Effect of Internal Power Processes on Religious Experience

In the beginnings of many religions, a religious virtuoso, male or female, has an extraordinary and often dramatic experience of the sacred—a dream, a vision, bodily ecstasy. This kind of peak experience is not equally or democratically distributed, which is one of the reasons why power is there from the start. Religious experience is a scarce resource and thereby plays the same role in power processes as do other scarce resources, whose control is the basis for power.

This holds even more when the original religious experience includes the explicit task of communicating the message to others and thus seeking to influence their behavior. Besides, the extraordinary nature of the experience draws the attention of those who are not as virtuosic but feel attracted by the experience and hope to share it. The possibility of empowerment draws especially the less powerful into the new cult. When miracles occur, the virtuoso may gain even more power over followers, using paranormal gifts.

The exceptionality of the experience also means that it is difficult to transmit. The founding experience usually is too individual to be shared. Almost by definition the relationship of the virtuoso with the sacred excludes any other person. It may be a lonely mission, an unwelcome vocation that therefore initially is often refused, as is clear from stories about religious founders.[3]

This favors the rise of power mechanisms. The religious virtuoso is not necessarily also a rhetorical virtuoso. A spokesperson with a gift for communication may succeed in making the virtuoso's experience understandable. This communicator will then easily occupy a position of power next to her or him. Though driven by the best intentions, such spokespersons usually have an interest in controlling access to their virtuoso. Correspondingly, their knowledge and their gift for translation remain scarce resources. When sacred texts are being produced or when rituals emerge, words, images, and gestures are strictly controlled. Generations of codifiers and clergy contribute to the elaboration of the codex and its interpretations.

The longer ago it was that the basic first experience happened, the more difficult it is to relive that experience. The impossible task of staying as close to the original experience as possible inevitably activates power mechanisms. Codification serves to safeguard the original. Since clear communication is important in the exercise of leadership, the original experience is stripped of its unruly, contradictory, and unmanageable elements. It is simplified to a transmittable and controllable message. The translation from the dimension of the experience with the sacred into the internal and external dimensions demands a workable version of what happened. In order to establish itself, power defines its own conditions. An effective system of thought and action is built, with its own presuppositions and logic. Conflicts will then arise about the right interpretation. Moreover, new virtuosos add their experiences and versions. The power game is played. Schisms and reforms result.

The codification process leads to a paradox. The more religious leaders strive to be faithful to—their version of—the precious original message, the greater the risk that the basic experience will become bleak, domesticated, sterile, and petrified. People become estranged from that experience. Once Esteban's cult is fully established, the essence of the fisherwomen's experience has almost been forgotten.

If we subsequently take a closer look at the spokespersons' tools, we discover new reasons why power is constantly present in religious contexts. Language is an important instrument. Roland Barthes has suggested that language, beyond facilitating what can be said, obliges us to say things in a particular way, which for him is a reason to call language "fascist."[4] In other words, language serves the powers that be. Moreover, language is not a perfect instrument. Linda Sexton suggests that texts tell lies to create truth.[5] In a more playful way, Brazilian poet Mário Quintana wrote this aphorism, entitled "The Thing": "You think something, finally write something else, and the reader understands something different again . . . and in the meantime the proper thing begins to suspect that it was not properly said at all."[6]

Symbols are almost by definition multilayered and polyinterpretable. Metaphors abound in religions, but they have the disadvantage that they always are translations of meanings from one domain, understandable to the user, to another domain that needs to be clarified. An example is the phrase "I was touched by God's hand." The tactile experience, known to all, is used to describe a puzzling religious experience. Translating from one domain to another, metaphors open the door to more than one interpretation and thus to conflict. Often the problem is which meaning from the clear domain has been selected. Examples are the metaphor of the cross in Christian and that of jihad in Islamic theology. Moreover, metaphors are comparisons that in the end do not hold. As Sally McFague has put it, metaphors "always contain the whisper, 'it is *and it is not.*'"[7]

Under the impact of power, metaphors have often been transformed into clearer tropes. The multilayered nature of metaphors is reduced. Thereby the trope may lose much of its depth. This occurs when a metaphor is taken more literally, reducing the two domains to one, turning it into a metonymy. By the *pars pro toto* rule, a partial experience then represents a larger domain, for example, God's hand is God as directly and bodily experienced.[8] If one particular meaning is selected, to be used only in specific contexts that serve as sacred spaces and times, the metaphor is transformed into a sign, for example, when bread is transubstantiated into Christ's body. Such a sign may become the key trope of a religion.

Codification is most visible in ritual, therefore, having given such actions the connotation of being controlled, prescribed, standardized, traditional behavior, even to the point of having lost their meaning.[9] Religious leadership uses the ritual sphere as a domain for exercising power by regulating access to it, making ritual knowledge scarce. In consequence, ritual experts may come to be considered the proprietors of a religion. In dogma, the same mechanisms occur, making a particular belief, its tropes, and its control the shibboleth for inclusion into or exclusion from a religious group.

Beyond the scarcity of the religious experience and the effects of efforts to share it, the social makes itself felt in two ways in relation to individual experience, This happens first of all in the religious experience itself, despite its being presented as individual. And eventually the followers organize themselves.

Ever since William James,[10] the view that individual experience of the sacred is essential to religious practice has been a common one. Many religions start from a very individual experience. When believers locate the initiative for the experience of the sacred in the supra-human, divine sphere, making it an exclusive revelation to an elected person, the human and social side of the experience tends to be forgotten or denied. However, it is important to be aware of the social nature of the individual experience and of its exact relationship with the social framework. The form given to this lone experience is social. It will, in large part, reflect the imagery that is part of the prevailing culture. Thus, even where individuals seek the experience of the sacred in isolation and silence, this usually takes a more or less prescribed form, as happens in the vision quest of the Plains Indians or in various forms of mysticism. Social and power mechanisms are already present in the virtuoso's experience. Power is there from the start, not only as sacred power but also in the social context of the founder's experience.

Whether the virtuoso embraces the experience or tries to ignore it, sooner or later other people will hear about it. This is certainly the case when the need to share the experience of the sacred with others is part of the virtuoso's revealed mission. But the experience may also be so overwhelming and bring so much joy and well-being that the virtuoso, even without being commanded to by the sacred, feels urged to share its richness with others. Once the news is spread, the social side becomes stronger. A cult grows into a movement, which in turn becomes a full-fledged institution. A stimulating experience in the dimension of the contact with the sacred demands translation into both the internal and the external dimensions, especially when the core message addresses society in general, whether it accepts the new message or not.

In the social sciences' study of religion, social and sacred powers have been considered together. In its most explicitly Durkheimian account of the sacred, the group is considered not only the primary context of the cult but also its object. In fact, there are striking similarities between the power of the group and that of the sacred. Both will survive the believers, both have ultimate authority over the individual, both represent norms and values, and both are able to control, reward, and punish people. Consequently, sacred and social forms mirror each other. Although scholarly discourse has emphasized how the religious mirrors the social, the reverse is possible as well, as we will see.

The story of the drowned man can be read in this light. The women around Esteban's body celebrate togetherness. Similarly, Esteban is posthumously adopted as a family member, making the village one big family, called Esteban's village. The women's imagination, as provoked by the dead man, reflects the local customs and worries. The struggle to survive is the setting for the drama that evolves. Interestingly, the children who find the corpse do not know what to do with it, obviously because they have not yet been fully socialized. Once the adults take over, the distribution of roles reflects their socialization, including the internal division of labor and thereby power relations. When the eldest woman pronounces the name of the drowned man, she does so from her position of authority.

And yet individuality is not absent. Every individual woman has her own story of the drowned man. The same can be said of the men, even though they keep their distance. Each pilgrim who later visits Esteban's village has his or her own experience of the saint. Even each priest, politician, or entrepreneur guards his individual image of what Esteban stands for.

One more aspect of power is that it regards society as a whole. Thus leadership in the religious field must articulate itself in relation to leaders of other sectors in society, those who direct economics, politics, and even art. Being stakeholders on the same stage, they must come to some understanding with each other. Usually this results in a form of mutual support, reinforcing each other's power, though conflicts are part of the repertoire as well.

Finally, power relations internal to the group reduce the playfulness and creativity that is often present in the first experience with the sacred. Play can be characterized, in the spirit of Victor Turner, as "the capacity to deal simultaneously and subjunctively with two or more ways of classifying reality."[11] The term *subjunctively* distinguishes play from the "indicative mood," the domain of the "as is." The subjunctive mood is "used to express supposition, desire, hypothesis, or possibility."[12] These elements are often present in an experience with the sacred, as we can see in the women's experience as they gather around Esteban's corpse. Imagining Esteban's life, they play with possibilities and express their desires. What they hypothesize becomes real to them.

Basically, religion presupposes that people are able to deal with two realities at the same time, one their own and the other of a sacred nature—even though in their experience there may be only one reality, in which human beings and sacred entities interact, so that the distinction stems from a secularized perspective. Religion can be understood as an application of the human capacity for play, art being another field that, in all its diverse manifestations, depends on this ability. Religion, like art, depends upon human creativity. The same gift of being able to deal with two realities is present in metaphor, as a way of playing with the meanings of two domains. As I have suggested, despite their shortcomings, metaphors are important tools for the religious imagination, just as they are widely used in art.

However, as we have seen, those in power usually prefer clear positions, since these can easily be controlled. The unlimited creativity that is an effect of playful behavior challenges established power structures. An effort is made to put religion and art at the service of those in power. Play supports this because a serious side is built into it. Though performed with a wink, it is done within the rules of a presupposed reality, whether that of a sports game or of a religious ritual. This serious side of play is the connecting point for those in power—who seldom wink. A situation that is playful may be domesticated into a serious activity with clear and thereby controllable meanings. Given that the nature of religious activities as being scarce, inexpressible, and social creates opportunities for those in power to alter the nature of the religious experience, their strained relationship with the playfulness that is so characteristic of that experience deprives it of its most basic cause: the way in which another reality is imagined into being. In consequence, the scarcity, the inexpressibility, and the social nature of religious experiences become even more prominent. Accordingly, in many religions seriousness has overcome playfulness. What was tentatively suggested becomes a proclaimed reality that must be defended, instead of being a phase in an ongoing, permanently experimental discovery.

Recuperating the Original

The impact of power on religious experience seems inevitable. Yet each of the circumstances that were mentioned as favoring a corrosion by power mechanisms of that first experience could also lead to a return to the origins, starting a new cycle and reducing established power's impact. Other connotations and meanings of the same circumstances may then weaken that impact.

The scarcity of the experience may be remembered, despite broad acceptance and divulgation of a particular established tradition. Persons may then abandon routine and open themselves again to exceptional and extraordinary sensations, beyond the prescribed. This can take the form of a return to the origins. The notion of purity, whether of a moral, a ritual, or a doctrinal nature, is already familiar to many religions. It may also lead people to start a reform movement that does away with the extras that have been added to the relatively simple experience of the founders—as if the women in Márquez's story were to abandon the whole subsequent cultic infrastructure and return to their experience during the wake around his corpse. The dimension of the sacred experience is rehabilitated against dominance by the internal and sometimes also the external dimensions.

In returning to the primal situation, the exclusivity of the first experience is reemphasized. A new cult group may be formed, one that the established religious authorities will probably label a sect, thus making outsiders of what initially were insiders. Where religious and secular authorities are allied, the members of a reform group may be persecuted because of their deviation from the established norms and forms, disturbing normal life in society. In its turn, the new group will condemn the leadership's deviation from the original message and practice, including its behavior regarding the external dimension. Its leader may behave as a prophet or as a mystic, creating a new original starting point. Sometimes such a movement profiles itself as popular, against the official version of the religion, becoming official religion once it becomes successful and is subsequently institutionalized. Whatever the concrete form of a reform movement, a return to the origins creates a problem for those in power, both internally and externally.

Similarly, the difficulty of expressing the message fully may stimulate people to explore new ways to render the original experience, despite accepted forms and perhaps as a protest against their insufficiency. Depending on the degree of freedom left for individual agency, change may occur. This can take several forms. As soon as people, by their own account, discover what the founding experience was about and have the opportunity to go through a similar spiritual but especially corporeal event, they will share that existential sensation with others. Language does not only limit expression, it also allows for the evocation of the inexpressible, especially in poetry.

Another way in which the limited nature of a religion's expressions is discovered stems from the globalization process. Though religions, in their splendid isolation, may be remarkably successful in ignoring the existence of other religions, the perforation of former boundaries opens up other religious repertoires to believers. One reaction may be to stress the uniqueness and exclusivity of a religion's proper convictions, but recognition of familiar elements in other religions is possible as well. Forms of syncretism will emerge.[13] Thus, meditation practices may be adopted from another context, as when Roman Catholic monks use Zen techniques. If the overwhelming basic experience is difficult to express, any other means of expression that become available are welcomed.

Besides, in the encounter with other religions, believers, especially those socialized in their own religion's claims to exclusivity, will raise the question of how these other religions must be regarded. If adepts base themselves on an overpowering religious experience that represents the unique heritage and conviction of their own religion, they may undertake to convert "pagans," despite the fact that they are almost always believers in another religion. Yet the existence of other religions may also inspire at least some believers to question the validity of their own exclusive truth. Between the poles of exclusion and tolerance, a whole spectrum of positions is available. Challenged by the existence of other religions, religious discourses nowadays usually incorporate some view concerning the truth of other religions. Religious diversity may then, for example, be understood as a result of the difficulty of expressing and interpreting an overwhelming religious experience. Religious relativism may occur, in which the value of any religious view is acknowledged. This has been the case with liberal Christian theology since the emerging field of religious studies introduced academia to the knowledge of other world religions.

In all these cases, the way power is exercised may change. Any reform movement puts those in power in a delicate position: to tolerate or exclude? Power may be reinforced by claims to exclusivity, but there may also be an adaptation. In her long history, the Roman Catholic Church has assimilated reform movements as new monastic orders. The encounter with other forms of religion may also reduce power's effects. When walls are broken down, cohesion and control become more difficult. Syncretism usually challenges the leadership, who therefore tend to condemn it. In several ways syncretism can be understood as the opposite of fundamentalism.[14] Globalization changes power positions. The leadership may choose to adapt itself to the new situation and, for example, seek a dialogue with other religious leaders, stressing the world religions' role in solving the world's problems. Recent scholarly criticism of the notions of "religion" and "world religion" may encourage taking a less exclusivist position.[15] Whatever the merits or shortcomings of Samuel Huntington's thesis of a "clash of civilizations," it may have opened religious leaders' eyes to the consequences of exclusivist positions, which are usually maintained through the use of power. The time for a kind of United Religions has not yet come. Such an organization would have even less power than the United Nations, but it could be more than a utopian idea.

A group's social control may limit its members' possibilities, yet a group's social mechanisms may also lead to a reformation of standard practice. In fact, power mechanisms include competition for influence. Any effort to influence other people's behavior may generate protest. Power's impact is therefore not constant but has its own dynamics. If the pressure of power and control grows too strong, fission and a new group may result. Factions may develop, each choosing elements from beliefs or practice as an emblem for its cause. Personal conflicts can be the catalyst of a reform movement. A new version draws new believers. Every three generations or so, religious groups may show a tidal movement between conformity and protest, between institutionalization and a fresh patterning of relationships, between routinization and prophecy.

In the Durkheimian approach, as summarized above, the mirroring relation between a group's processes and its religious ideas and practices leaves room for changes in the constellation of power, especially since power is not a stable phenomenon. When a group's characteristics change, including its distribution of power, this will sooner or later be mirrored in its beliefs and rituals. A first-generation Pentecostal church therefore differs from a third- or fourth-generation community.[16] A splinter group may want to return to the origins, but it will inevitably move through the same cycle as its predecessor. But a change in religious beliefs and practices may have consequences for the social structure, including the distribution of power. Though resilient to change, power mechanisms will sooner or later have to reflect the values expressed in religious discourse.

Finally, if playfulness is not completely eclipsed by seriousness, it may reveal the relativity of even the most serious religious praxis, especially when the capacity to see two realities at once suggests new experiences of newly evoked realities. Though believers usually do not think in terms of play, just as they do not often use terms like *power* and *syncretism*, the universal capacity for play may impel them. This is especially possible when orthodoxy is weak. Believers then are able to experiment with experiences and interpretations without control by clergy. When other repertoires than that of one's own group are readily available, play with alternatives also becomes possible. Equally, when the distance between believers, on the one hand, and God, gods, spirits, etc., on the other hand, is not overemphasized, experiments are allowed in the relationships between the two. Through such experiments, believers may seek means of empowerment, especially when they are operating from a position of weakness and affliction. The latent capacity to play with more then one reality is a threat to any religious power, as I have suggested.

Epilogue

Our example has demonstrated the ambiguous nature of the relationship between power and religion. The typical characteristics of the religious field—in particular, the scarcity of religious experience, the difficulty in communicating it, the subjection to social forms attendant on it, and the role of the capacity for play—can simultaneously reinforce and weaken the position of those in power. In practice, however, power more often alters the original religious experience than the reverse.

This tentative and more or less objective analysis has some subjective consequences that normally are not mentioned in academic discourse. In terms of the applied study of religion, four implications of the approach developed above can be mentioned, as a subjective epilogue to the picture given so far. These concern (1) religiously inspired conflicts, (2) the optimal chances for a religion that thrives and survives, (3) the critique of religion, and (4) a new definition of power.

First, the daily news presents us with many examples of how religious conviction can result in conflict, motivating parties to wage war on each other. (See the chapter by Mark Juergensmeyer in this volume.) Some consciousness of how power operates and how it affects religious experience could help actors involved in these disputes to reach a peaceful solution. If differences between religions are primarily understood as a consequence of basically profane power processes rather than as based on incommensurable religious experiences, it will be easier for religions to coexist, even while believers continue to adhere fully to their own religion. The conflicts themselves can then be understood as part of the essentialist perversion that power processes have generated, constructing difference out of rather similar religious experiences. If that perversion were understood, all parties involved would be more hesitant to identify with a religious system and practice that has imperceptibly but strongly deviated from the core message that everyone claims to be defending. The Huntington scenario of a clash of civilizations could then be avoided. Religions can do away with their essentializing tendencies. Similarly, reference to the role of play in the emergence of religious experience could make conflicting parties more conscious of the relative and limited value of the positions that are being defended. This need not imply a total undermining of that position, since—I have explained—play must be done in a serious manner. But a modest degree of consciousness of the relevance of alternatives is already helpful. This is possible without selling out one's own convictions, especially when commonalities in religious experience are rediscovered. Degenerate religion can then be regenerated, as we have seen.

Second, in seeking success for their group, religious leadership would be well advised to develop forms in which the execution of power favors religious experiences instead of frustrating them. This inevitably means relinquishing some of their competencies. Yet leadership will gain in authority—as distinguished from power—by doing so. Given how power processes frustrate believers' religious experience, such a move would be in the interest of the religion concerned. In strongly secularized Western European countries, the de-institutionalization of religion has enabled the rise of noninstitutionalized expressions of religiosity, that is, those in which power resides primarily in the experience of the sacred, not in an internal dimension headed by a religious institution's leadership. In other countries, especially in the Southern Hemisphere, Pentecostal churches have flourished.[17] Although some of these churches have developed a very strong leadership, one of the main reasons for their success is the central place they give to religious experience, especially through the charismata of the Holy Ghost. But even in more traditional religious institutions and in the North, experience—in any form—can be rehabilitated as soon as leaders become aware of its power for believers. Power will then be minimal and just functional. Rituals will serve to create conditions for the revival of experience. Then the leaders' power will merely facilitate religious experience, instead of domesticating it. Room can thus again be opened for the immediacy of religious experience, reducing the role of mediating persons and instances to an unavoidable minimum.

Third, in much secularizing critique of religion, special attention has been given to the role of power, whether that of sacred entities or of religious leadership. Since secularization primarily refers to Christianity, the doctrine and practice of that religion have been subjected to critique. Believers have asked why, given God's supposedly absolute power, He allows evil and disaster to happen. The abuse of power by church officials has equally been a reason for abandoning religion. Interestingly, power and empowerment have been important elements in several scholarly explanations of religion from different disciplines, sometimes linked to a secularizing point of view or at least inspired by amazement at the persistence of religion. It would be interesting, by contrast, to begin with the initial religious experience as the basis for an explanation of religion, taking into account that there is a difference between the founders' inspiration and the subsequent institutional, doctrinal, and ritual forms their message has been given, including the dimension of power. Instead of focusing on power, scholars might then give due attention to the role of weakness and vulnerability. This could change both the critique and the explanation of religion.

A final consequence of the approach developed here is that, as a lesson—admittedly subjective—from studying the religious field, it is possible to suggest new definitions of power. In her study of women's role in church base communities in Brazil, Els Jacobs reports that poor women view their own power, as distinguished from that of men, particularly in the church, as their capacity "to survive and live."[18] Notwithstanding religious wars and the use of violence in the name of religion, the promotion of life is a value respected in all religions. When this value is violated, power mechanisms are usually the main cause. Male leaders are dominant in this process. Their view of power matches the causal, mechanistic, almost technical emphasis in Weber's definition, which presents power as the capacity to influence other people's behavior, even against their will, using all resources available. The notion of power that emerges from the Brazilian women's perspective focuses on influencing other people's behavior by creating conditions that improve their lives and increase their well-being. As an engaged counterpoint to the usual distanced definition, this way of looking at power can have interesting consequences. My earlier plea for the avoidance of conflict and for a minimal form of power in religious institutions can easily be combined with the female definition of power, having the promotion of life as its core value. The available resources would serve the same goal, but now not as mechanistic pressure on other people's behavior. Power may still be the capacity to influence other people's behavior, but it can use all available resources to serve the promotion of life. Power in this sense would never pervert religious experience, since the promotion of life is central to that experience. The women around Esteban understood this core value.

Symbolic Violence

Religion and Empowerment

Mark Juergensmeyer

From Bali to New York City and from Mumbai to Madrid, images of religion have become fused with scenes of violent protests against the political order. Islamic activists in the Middle East, Christian militia in the United States, Jewish zealots in Israel, and Buddhist militants in Sri Lanka exemplify the many rebellious challenges to the secular state that have erupted around the world. They have employed religion as a way of legitimizing the power of antiauthoritarian movements. In none of these cases is religion the sole cause of violence—these are movements for political empowerment, not theological contests. Yet religion has become a problematic partner in some of the most virulent political movements of our generation.

In this essay I want to explore why this is so: why religious symbols convey an experience of empowerment and why this experience is intimately related to violence. I find that the idea of cosmic war is at the center of many of these outbursts of religious violence, and I probe the significance of ultimate warfare as a way of conveying power and meaning. I also try to imagine a way that images of ultimate conflict can be defused, so that lives can be spared the savagery of warfare even when the symbolic potency of the bellicose images remains intact.

Understanding the role of religion in providing a sense of empowerment might help to explain what may appear to be some of the more puzzling features of modern acts of terrorism and religious violence: assaults by extremist groups on opponents who are infinitely better armed. These attacks—including suicide missions undertaken by ardent followers of a desperate cause—seem destined to fail. It is hard to take seriously the notion that these are rational efforts to achieve power, at least by ordinary calculations. Yet to those undertaking them, there may be something exhilarating, perhaps even rewarding, about the struggle itself. This sense of empowerment may make the effort seem worthwhile. It can also, at times, lead to real political change.

"To die in this way"—through suicide bombings—the political head of the Hamas movement told me, "is better than to die daily in frustration and humiliation."[1] He went on to say that, in his view, the very nature of Islam is to defend "dignity, land, and honor." He then related a story that the prophet had told about a woman who fasted daily, yet was doomed to hell because she humiliated her neighbors. The point of the story, he said, is that dishonoring someone is the worst act that one can do, and the only thing that can counter it is dignity—the honor provided by religion and the courage of being a defender of the faith. In a curious way, then, both religion and violence are seen as antidotes to humiliation.

Countering dishonor with piety and struggle is a theme that runs through many incidents of religious violence in recent years. A Jewish extremist in Israel, Dr. Baruch Goldstein, felt compelled to kill innocent Muslims in the shrine of the Tomb of the Patriarchs in Hebron because he felt Jews had been dishonored. A similar sense of pride was exhibited in the nervous bravado of the Palestinian Hamas suicide bombers in the videotapes made the night before their actions and in the assured self-confidence of Mohammad Attah and other hijackers of the airplanes that attacked the World Trade Center and the Pentagon on September 11, 2001, as seen on the videotapes of security cameras as they entered the airports on their tragic mission. Sikh militants were so angered that the government ignored them that they turned to violence in order to force the government to take them seriously.[2] Shoko Asahara, the leader of the Buddhist new religious movement who ordered the nerve-gas attack on the Tokyo subways, wanted to be not only "like a king," as one of his former followers told me, but also "like Christ."[3] These are all examples of symbolic empowerment related both to religion and to violence.

By describing this feeling of strength as "symbolic empowerment," I do not mean to imply that the empowerment is not real. After all, a sense of power is largely a matter of perception, and in many cases the power that the activists obtained had a very real impact on their community, their relationships, and themselves, as well as on the political authorities who feared them and granted them the respect of notoriety. But symbolic expressions of violence—performance violence, as I have described it elsewhere—are empowering in a special way, for they do not lead to conquests of territory or personnel in the traditional definition of military success.[4] For most of these quixotic fighters, success consisted simply in waging the struggle—the heady confidence they received by being soldiers for a great cause, even if the battles were not won, or even winnable, in ordinary military terms.

By calling these violent acts "symbolic," I mean that they are intended to illustrate or refer to something beyond their immediate target: a grander conquest, for instance, or a struggle more awesome than meets the eye. As Mahmud Abouhalima, a Muslim activist who was involved in the 1993 attack on the World Trade Center, told me in an interview in prison, the bombing of a public building may dramatically indicate to the populace that the government or the economic forces behind the building are seen as enemies, to show the world that they have been targeted as satanic foes.[5] The point of the attack, then, was to produce a graphic and easily understandable object lesson. Such explosive scenarios are not tactics directed toward an immediate, earthly, or strategic goal but dramatic events intended to impress through their symbolic significance. As such, they can be analyzed as one would any other symbol, ritual, or sacred drama.

Hence, acts of religious violence are about religion as much as they are about violence. They are about religion because religion provides a way of thinking about the world that provides a sense of ultimate order. It takes the messy uncertainties of life, the dangers and the nagging sense of chaos, and gives them meaning. It locates disorder within a triumphant pattern of order. It does this especially effectively in thinking about the most difficult moment of chaos in one's personal life—in thinking about death.

Symbolic Violence

Let us take a familiar ritual as an example of the ability of religion to provide a sense of order in the face of violence and death. This example is the central moment of Christian worship, the Eucharist, which many Protestant Christians call Communion. It is perhaps the most domestic and reassuring of Christian rituals in that its performance is meant to provide a sense of security, calm, and repose. And yet the Eucharist is also a ritual that is about violence and death.

The high point of this most sacred of Christian rituals is literally beyond words and involves an act. Specifically, it is an act of ingestion, in which each worshipper eats a tiny portion of blessed bread and drinks a few sips of consecrated wine. The worshippers are told that they are eating the body and drinking the blood of Christ himself.

As Sigmund Freud and a host of other scholarly analysts have reminded us, the Eucharist is indeed the commemoration of a sacrificial death. It recalls the last meal of Jesus Christ, a Jewish *Seder* service held during the holy day of Passover, but it also enacts the killing of Jesus himself. The bread and wine of the Eucharist is literally, according to some traditional Roman Catholic teachings, transformed into the broken body and shed blood of Jesus in a process called transubstantiation. Not all Christians accept this literal interpretation, but they do believe

41

that the elements of the Eucharist are the representation of the sacrifice of Jesus on the cross. The crucifixion is the central Christian moment, and the cross its primary symbol. What gives this death meaning, of course, is the resurrection, the Easter occasion in which Christ rises from the tomb three days after his body is interred and death is defeated by an eternally present Christ. But this triumphant moment would not be possible without the death that preceded it, a death that is fundamentally a sacrificial act.

This central idea of sacrifice unites Christianity with virtually every other religious tradition on the planet. Sacrifice—and particularly blood sacrifice, the offering of an animal or perhaps even a human—is one of the earliest forms of religious activity and is a common feature of ancient religious cultures from biblical Israel to Vedic India.. In contemporary forms of religious expression, sacrifice is usually represented in a symbolic or metaphorical way, but these representations are often regarded as vestiges of what was originally a common practice.

A long lineage of scholars from Freud and Emile Durkheim to contemporary theorists such as Maurice Bloch, Walter Burkert, and René Girard have pondered the origins of religion and speculated on the centrality of violence—especially sacrifice—to religion and why this is so.[6] Freud, for instance, thought that sacrifice was significant because it provided a symbolic displacement for real acts of violence.[7] Other theorists saw in sacrifice forms of communication between sacred and mundane levels of existence, and the rite was important because it became a metaphor for meaning itself.[8]

These are thoughtful and often contradictory theories, but some common themes run through all of them. Most of these theories focus on sacrifice not only because it is ubiquitous to religion and in most cases can be traced to antiquity, but also for two other reasons. One is that scholars sense that something about this rite is fundamental to the religious imagination. If one can make sense of it, one can understand religion itself. The other observation is the obvious one: sacrifice is about death.

Thus there is near unanimity among these scholars that ritual expressions of killing and dying, and ways of thinking about death, are central to religion. What strikes me as interesting about this discussion is that it often misses the point, that these symbolic rites of sacrifice are always found within a larger context of religious behavior. That is to say, sacrifice is part of a larger structure of religious activity and meaning that illumines the significance of the rite: for instance, the distribution of the sacrificial elements of the Eucharist takes place within a ritual designed to magnify the differences between the sacred and mundane levels of existence and to highlight the tension between them.

Hence the dramatic moment of ritualized sacrifice in Christianity occurs in the context of opposition. It is a comforting religious act in that it symbolically overcomes struggle and despair and turns death into timeless life. The inadequacies of the human condition—its weakness and confusion—are overcome in the recognition of a divine intervention that tips the balance in favor of humanity and rescues the fallen. Thus the sacrifice becomes a metaphor for salvation, and salvation the resolution of an eternal conflict—the apotheosis of a sort of grand and timeless war.

Indeed, religious rites do in a symbolic way what war does; they enact victory over discord. Religious acts begin with acknowledging the confusion and turbulence of life. For most worshippers who recite liturgical prayers, these opening petitions conjure up an existential state of disorder—they are invocations of the faithful's own limitations, their sinfulness, and, most of all, their mortality. To be reminded of the human condition is to be apprised of its capricious and mortal end. The religious images of sacrifice revel in this reality and expose it in what might appear, from an outsider's point of view, a brutal way. In the cathedrals of Central American cities, for instance, one may frequently find representations of life-sized figures of Jesus in what appear to be glass coffins, as if he had come straight off the cross. The bloody wounds of his crucifixion still glow vividly red. Yet to the faithful these are positive images, since the end of the sacrificial ritual—and the end of the Passion narrative about the death and resurrection of Christ—is the transformation of death into life.

Why Does Religion Need Violence?

At the heart of the ideas of both war and religion is the notion of alternative reality. Both war and religion present an alternate order of existential tension and moral contest that locates within them any apparent anomalies in life, such as bombing attacks or the persistence of sin. The main difference between the two is that war offers a mundane form of alternative reality—a different way of understanding the configuration of social order—and religion provides a vision of an order of reality that is ultimately transcendent.

As the gritty images of the bloodied Christ and the dramatic act of ritual cannibalism in the Christian Eucharist indicate, it is important for religion to portray the anomaly of mortality in the human condition in a vivid way. This is part of the reason why images of war are so vital to religious art, legends, and iconography. But another reason is that the image of war is a convenient metaphor for the way religion works. Like war, religion fastens on irreconcilable oddities in the experience of life and tries to make sense of them by putting them into a different template of consciousness, a grand narrative of conflict. In religion's way of seeing the world, disorder is ultimately reconciled—transformed, really—into order. This is why images of war help the believer understand more clearly how religion goes about its business.

Let us look at an example of how religion uses war to explicate its meaning: the biblical idea of Armageddon as portrayed in the *Left Behind* novels.[9] The *Left Behind* novels are a spectacularly successful fictional series based on the drama of the end times as portrayed in the New Testament book of Revelation. With a combined sales of over sixty million, the *Left Behind* novels have become one of the most-read and most profitable publication ventures of all time. Tim LaHaye, an American Christian Evangelical, conceived the series as a way of telling the story of the New Testament account of Armageddon in a modern milieu. LaHaye and his co-author, novelist Jerry Jenkins, had by 2006 completed twelve novels in the series, almost all of which topped the *New York Times* bestseller lists as soon as they were published.

The novels are the fictional account of a group of Christians who are left behind when the prophecy of the end of the world in the biblical book of Revelation comes true. Together these abandoned Christians face the rise of the Antichrist, hideous plagues, and other acts of judgment from God known as the Tribulations, most spectacularly, the cataclysmic battle of Armageddon and the triumphant second coming of Christ. Most readers take the books as the fiction that they are. But some see parallels between the biblical prophecies as vividly described in the novels and real-world events in the present day. In particular, some see similarities between the biblical account of Armageddon, which allegedly will take place in the Middle East, and contemporary confrontations in that region, including the military encounters in Israel and Iraq. After the Israeli incursion into Lebanon in July 2006, the on-line bulletin board of "The Prophecy Club," a membership website related to the book series, was crowded with concerns that the fighting was the fulfillment of the end-times prophecies in the book of Revelation.

The main setting of all the novels is a suburban and modern contemporary life, which most American readers recognize as familiar and comforting. Yet in the midst of the niceties of ordinary affairs, there are rumblings of something profoundly out of synch. As the novels progress, increasingly the spiritual sterility of what passes as normal society is portrayed with a hard edge. It is as if a heartless dictatorial ideology is gradually imposing itself on the social order. Sensitive people—faithful Christian believers—find themselves marginalized, humiliated, and persecuted in a sea of secularism.

But the novels portray Christians as having, as it were, the last laugh. Christians who are true believers are rescued from this earthly travail in an event known as the Rapture. With a whoosh, their bodies are whisked away from worldly reality and transposed to the glorious reality of eternal life. Nothing remains of their earthly existence but piles of old clothing dropped in heaps at the moment when their bodies were transported to the higher regions. They will not be naked in heaven, of course; their modesty will be covered by luminous robes provided in the wondrous world of the Lord.

Meanwhile, on sinful and contentious earth, according to the *Left Behind* novels, a band of half-hearted Christians and secularists who were literally left behind at the glorious moment of the Rapture realize the foolishness of their ways. They convert to true Christianity but must await the time for their own moment of Rapture to come. This produces the dramatic tension for the remainder of the novels—the band of newly converted true Christians struggle to keep their faith through waves of plagues and natural disasters and other forms of persecutions—the Tribulations—sent to earth by God to punish it for its foolish ways. The band of Christians also have to endure the hardships of the reign of the Antichrist—a heartless secularist who just happens to be portrayed in the novels as the Secretary-General of the United Nations. He uses his position of influence to concentrate all political and economic power under his control in the new world order.

The great conflict portrayed in the *Left Behind* novels presents in an interesting way the worldview of religion itself. It pictures a world of normal reality that is somehow deeply insufficient. Those who are sensitive to the fundamental aspects of reality perceive this insufficiency, especially in times of financial crisis, which expose the vulnerability of the mundane aspects of modern life. Hence they are attracted to a different way of thinking about the way the world is, a material world in conflict with a more true and transcendent order provided through a religious view of reality. In the *Left Behind* novels, this alternative reality of religion does not just hint at its existence through mild forms of religious awakening, such as scriptural texts and Sunday sermons. It crashes into our mundane world with a vengeance, in the dramatic moment of the Rapture.

The tension between the two realities—the mundane world and the religious world—is what most of the novel is about. Like all views of war, this conflict comes with moral weight attached to each side. The mundane reality is not just insufficient in its ability to provide meaning and comfort, it is downright evil. The battle between good and evil is presented as a challenge to us, the onlookers, who are forced to make a choice, to join either one side or the other. Like Prince Arjuna hesitating at the fringes of the battle in the Hindu epic *The Mahabharata*, the newly converted Christians in the *Lost Behind* novels realize that avoiding a position in the battle is not an option. The only questions for them are which side they will be on and how they will wage the fight.

Cosmic War

Though they are not the same, war and religion play roles in the human imagination that are so similar that they easily reinforce one another. Both war and religion provide visions of alternative perceptions of order, ways of seeing the world that absorb anomalies and explain why chaos and disorder exist. They explain and ultimately contain and control these untidy and dangerous aspects of life. Both offer hope, prospects for victory that will transmute a messy life into a gloriously successful and triumphant order. Though war's alternative reality is a this-worldly version of reality and religion holds a transcendent vision, they function so similarly that war frequently utilizes religion, and religion often incorporates images of war.

Sometimes the two, religion and war, are fused. This creates a powerful construct of the human imagination that I have called "cosmic war."[10] I have not used the term *holy war* to describe this union of religion and war for several reasons. One is that the term *holy war* is often limited to Islamic ideas, and the notion of cosmic war is a common feature of most religious traditions; it is not solely Muslim. Moreover, scholars and activists sometimes distinguish between holy war and divine war—one is war undertaken on behalf of God, the other is war imagined to be carried out by God. As I have explained in other writings, I use the term *cosmic war* in a way that could refer to either of these ways of thinking about the divine orchestration of warfare. It is a remarkable fusion of the concept of religion and the idea of war that is often expressed in real war and not just in its literary and legendary representations.

As we saw in looking at the *Left Behind* novels, some Christians have taken the idea of apocalyptic war described in the book of Revelation and connected it with current events. This provides them with evidence that the end times are coming to pass in the present day. The cataclysm described in Revelation 16 is in part a "battle," but it also involves a series of acts of nature presumably triggered by God: "flashes of lightening, loud noises, peals of thunder, and a great earthquake such as had never since men were on the earth" (Revelation 16:18). Islands will vanish and mountains will be leveled (Revelation 16:20). At the culmination of the conflict, the old world will be swept away and "a new heaven and a new earth" will be established (Revelation 21:1). A new holy city, a new Jerusalem, will be established, and God will dwell with the citizens. "Behold," the book says, "I make all things new" (Revelation 21:5). Some Christian activists have seen the battles in Iraq and Lebanon and the global *jihadi* struggle as part of the apocalyptic moment described in the book of Revelation. It is viewed as sacred war, God's war, one described in the Bible.

Curiously, this idea of Armageddon has also emerged in a quite different part of the world, in Japan. Seizing on the name given to the battlefield in the final confrontation described in Revelation 16, the Aum Shinrikyo master Shoko Asahara has described his own version of Armageddon. The Aum master prophesied that this new apocalypse will rival World War II in its destructiveness.[11] Most Japanese would take this to mean something even more horrific than the incidents of nuclear annihilation that destroyed the cities of Hiroshima and Nagasaki. Asahara prophesied that nuclear tactics such as these will be multiplied and compounded with biological and chemical nerve-gas attacks. The movement's imagined enemies were a paranoid cornucopia of political powers and social groups, from the Japanese government and the U.S. military to the Freemasons. The Aum Shinrikyo imagined itself to be the lone defender of all that was good in civilization.[12] The terrorist attack in 1995 was meant to illustrate this imagined view of religion and war, and in illustrating it to bring it into reality. If the sarin gas that it unleashed in the Tokyo subways had been produced in a more pure strain, rather than an adulterated form, tens or even hundreds of thousands of innocent Japanese commuters would have been killed. As it turned out, twelve innocent subway riders perished in an agonizing way, and six thousand were injured.

Like some Christians, there are Islamic activists who have seen their struggle as dictated by scripture, in their case by the Qur'an. The ninth section of the Qur'an urges the faithful to stand up in righteous defense against "people who have violated their oaths and intended to expel the Messenger" and those who "attack you first" (*Surah* 9:13). Though the historical context is one in which a fledgling Muslim community is attempting to survive in a hostile environment in the seventh century of the Common Era, some Muslims take this passage from the Qur'an as license to struggle against those in the present day who would try to destroy them and their religion. Like the battles in the Christians' New Testament and the Hebrew Bible, which is respected by Christians, Muslims, and Jews, the skirmishes in the Qur'an are ultimately not human encounters but part of God's war: "fight against them so that Allah will punish them by your hands and disgrace them and give you victory over them and heal the breasts of a believing people" (*Surah* 9:14).

These ideas of spiritual battle, which are found in scripture and employed by activists in such disparate movements as the Aum Shinrikyo, the Christian right, and militant Islam, are shadows of an image that resonates within the worldviews of all religious traditions, the tension between appearance and deeper reality—transcendent versus permanent order. This tension is often portrayed in images of cosmic war. The idea of cosmic war is that of a grand encounter between the forces of order and chaos, played out on an epic scale. Real-world social and political confrontations are swept up into this grand scenario. Conflicts over territory and political control are lifted onto the high proscenium of sacred drama. Such extraordinary images of cosmic war are meta-justifications for religious violence. They not only explain why religious violence happens—why religious persons feel victimized by violence and why they need to take revenge for this violence—but also provide a large worldview, a template of meaning in which religious violence makes sense. In the context of cosmic war, righteous people are impressed into service as soldiers, and great confrontations occur in which noncombatants are killed. But ultimately the righteous will prevail, for cosmic war is, after all, God's war. And God cannot lose.

47

In a sense, there is a bit of cosmic war in all wars. Since war involves the moral absolutism of social conflict, all wars are to some extent forms of meta-conflict, confrontations for which no easy negotiation is possible or expected. All wars involve the idea that opponents are enemies, that enemies are evil, and that great good must prevail. So religious ideas are often in the background of any militant, nonnegotiable dispute. As we have seen, it is easy for sacred language and images to be enlisted in a military cause. Most wars are thought to be conducted for a high moral purpose, and often this means seeing them as blessed by God. For this reason, there is something of a sliding scale between worldly war and cosmic war, between military activities that are rational calculations for the sake of civil order and those that are thought to be manifestations of an ultimate sacred struggle. This means that those who think about how we might live in a world without war must deal with the religious dimensions of the construct—the cosmic war images that may lurk behind military maneuvers and their public supporters—as well as the worldly issues for which a war might be waged.

War Without Blood

Even without being blessed by God, war is such a deep and enduring aspect of the human imagination that it is hard to think of the world without it. Whenever a society is under stress—as frequently societies are—the temptation exists to imagine a different way of understanding the dilemma and its causes, and to pose the idea of an evil enemy engaged in war. Often, of course, the enemies are easy to imagine because they are indeed threatening. They are opponents who want to change, punish, or destroy the policies of a society's public order. It takes only a short stretch of the imagination to think of these foes in absolute terms, not only as political rivals but as demonic creatures set on annihilating a people and their culture. Individuals will find in participating in warfare either vicariously or directly a resolution of these social tensions and also of areas of indecisiveness in their own personal lives. Hence the idea of war will always have a strong appeal on both social and personal levels.

Is it possible, then, to contain or redirect war? The idea of containing war has been a rational goal of most religious traditions. The ethical foundations of most religions have some version of what in Christianity is known as the "just war theory" of conflict. After the conversion of the Roman Emperor Constantine to Christianity in 312 CE, when Christianity became the state religion of an empire, Christian thinkers tried to make sense of the pacifist mandate in the New Testament in light of the need to morally justify the military actions of the state. They tried to reconcile the idea of defensive war with the nonviolent idealism of the Gospels in a way that would not glorify bloodshed.

A fourth-century Christian bishop, Augustine, hit upon a solution. Borrowing the concept of "just war" developed by Cicero in Roman jurisprudence, Augustine expanded upon the notion and set it into context. The perfect ethics of peace that Jesus talked about, Augustine reasoned, was appropriate to the "city of God," to which we should all aspire.[13] We live, however, in a more mundane realm—the "city of man"—where life is less pleasant and force is sometimes necessary to keep evil at bay. Augustine specified the conditions under which a Christian could morally sanction war. He specifically condemns "the lust for power," which he regards as an inappropriate reason for warfare.

These conditions were later refined by the medieval Catholic theologian Thomas Aquinas and have become the bedrock of the Christian Church's teaching on the morality of war ever since.[14] Just-war theory allows for military action only as a last resort, when it will lead to less violence rather than more, when it is conducted for a just cause, and when it is authorized by a proper public authority. As several scholars have noted, Islam and other religious traditions have developed similar equivalents in thinking about the moral criteria within which just warfare is permissible.

Contemporary Christian thinking continues to be guided by just-war criteria. One of the twentieth century's most influential Protestant thinkers, Reinhold Niebuhr, began his career as a pacifist. The evil powers of Hitler and Stalin persuaded Niebuhr that there are moments when the force of evil must be countered by military force for justice to prevail. In an influential essay, "Why the Christian Church Is Not Pacifist," Niebuhr cited the Christian tradition's defense of justice as more important than pacifism when it comes to great encounters in history between evil powers and social order.[15]

Another way of limiting warfare is to redirect the idea of religious violence away from bloodshed. A contemporary theorist, René Girard, has provided an updated version of Freud's insight that ritualized violence can play a role in symbolically defusing a potentially tragic encounter.[16] According to Girard, societies have devised cultural dams to prevent the violence that the rivalry between competitors might produce. One of these cultural institutions is religion, which shelters expressions of cathartic violence in the guise of ritualized sacrifice. Through religion, Girard claims, the death of a sacrificial victim becomes a saving death, and the scapegoat who is the butt of the violence is often celebrated as a culture hero. In Girard's reckoning, religion's increasing role in providing releases for violence's passion reduces the possibility of real violence occurring.

Mohandas Gandhi offers yet another way to domesticate images of violence and war and thereby limit the loss of life that might otherwise occur. Though he has the reputation of being an apostle of nonviolence, Gandhi was fascinated with the idea of conflict and saw it as a way of broadening one's view of the truth. He insisted on looking beyond personal differences in a clash to the larger issues on each side. Every conflict, Gandhi reasons, is a contestation on two levels—between persons and between principles. Behind every fighter is the issue for which the fighter is fighting. Every fight, for Gandhi, is on some level an encounter between differing "angles of vision" illuminating the same truth.[17] This difference in positions—sometimes a difference in worldviews—is what needs to be resolved in order for a fight to finish and the fighters be reconciled. In that sense, Gandhi's methods were more than a way of confronting an enemy; they were a way of dealing with conflict itself.

One could imagine, then, the idea of war being the metaphor for facing conflicts, dealing with the differences behind them, and resolving them, though metaphorical war would forge a resolution through nonviolent ways. Of course, this sober way of dealing with contradictions in social life will never gain the imaginative power of violent warfare and total destruction. But perhaps these martial images can be reserved for the realm of cultural imagination. In an interesting way, then, perhaps the cure for the horrors of war—especially warfare propelled by religious impulses—is religion itself. When religion stays religion—when the transcendent conflict of ultimate values is imagined as residing on a transcendent plane—this imagined warfare can excite human creativity without destroying it. Humans will always imagine war; perhaps it is one of the most creative acts of human consciousness to think in such extraordinary reaches of cosmic confrontation and to pose such dramatic alternatives to reality as war and religion provide. But it is also within the creative power of the species to think reasonably about differences and profoundly respect the sanctity of life. This latter impulse may eventually be war's captain, and humanity's saving grace.

Political Theology

The Authority of God

Avishai Margalit

Two theses that are intimately related to the idea of authority are political theology, associated with the name of Carl Schmitt, and moral theology, associated with Elizabeth Anscombe (though she never used the expression). Political theology is the claim that key notions in modern secular political doctrines are unwittingly moored in theological and teleological world views. These notions in their secularized versions make no sense and can be validated only within the theological frame for which they were designed. "Sovereignty" and "authority" are paradigmatic cases of such key notions. Moral theology is a parallel claim. Key moral notions concerning modern moral doctrines are moored in a theological and teleological frame and gain currency only there. Unmoored, as these notions are in a current secular frame, they have lost their sense. "Obligations" and "duty" are paradigmatic examples of such notions anchored in the old idea of God the law-giver. Without God the law-giver, these notions make very little sense. Secular morality is like the famous explanation of what wireless is. Well, you know what wire is. It is like a dog: you pull its tail in Jerusalem and it barks in Rome. Now, wireless works like wire, but without the dog. Morality without God is like wireless without the dog.

I hold a moderate version of political and moral theology. In my account, authority and sovereignty have contents that are independent of a religious theological frame, yet these notions are in the grip of a theological picture of the world. To be in the grip of a picture is to confuse a model of reality with reality without being aware of it. There are, in fact, two tiers in the picture of God. On the ground level, the idea of the theistic God, as well as the authority of God, is in the grip of a picture of God as the father or God as the king.

51

But, on the second tier, the idea of God the almighty creates a model that greatly intensifies the ideas of authority and sovereignty as models for earthly rulers and states.

Here I will explore an idea of authority as depicted by a religious picture (note the indefinite article). It is a picture, not the picture. It is the picture of God as the supreme decision maker without being a deliberator. I shall call it the decisionist picture of God. His authority is based on his absolute will, unhindered by any laws and rules, in particular, by any laws of morality. To call the decisionist picture of God a fascist picture of god would be abusive, perhaps, but not inaccurate. "That there must be," in the language of the eighteenth-century Blackstone, "a supreme, irresistible, absolute, and uncontrolled authority, in which the . . . right of sovereignty resides" is the idea and ideal that interests me.

Who Needs a Justification of Authority?

Anarchism in political theory has a comparable function to the null hypothesis in science. For political theory to justify authority—any authority—it should first provide cogent arguments why one should not accept the anarchist claim that there is no justification for any political authority.

Let me state briefly an anarchist argument against authority. A familiar idea, expressed in many different ways, is that you can do whatever you like with bayonets but you cannot sit on them. To rule by the use of brute force ("bayonets") is unstable. Rousseau made the point that even the strongest of men has to sleep, and then he is vulnerable: hence the need for legitimacy. A legitimate power gains acceptance in the eyes of its subjects and thus is freed from constant surveillance over them. Legitimacy is a manipulative move by the rulers to reduce the costs of using force; it is based on indoctrination, not on persuasion. Legitimacy is the use of force by other means. Legitimacy by indoctrination is what causes the belief that the state has authority. But this is no justification in the sense of showing that this belief is true.

The anarchist is willing to accept expert authority. Expert advice, however, is different from power, which is authority based on command, not on advice. The anarchist makes the point that authority is a matter of justification and that there is no justification for political authority above and beyond the justification that the reasons for what you are told to do are the reasons you would have adopted (on reflection) by yourself. But such justification has the status of expert advice and not a command by a political authority.

Listening to the anarchist argument, one may be tempted to adopt Ramsey's philosophical strategy to the effect that, if you see a philosophical dispute that goes on for too long without being resolved, see what the two sides to the dispute share in common and deny. The decisionist seems to adopt Ramsey's strategy. He detects that the anarchist and the believer in authority both believe that the issue between them is an issue of justification—justification of power. But whereas the anarchist denies that there is such justification, the believer in authority believes that there is.

The decisionist denies the need for and the importance of justification by giving reasons for the use of power. If one needs a justification for power, it is to be found in the style of using power, not in the reasons for its use. By style he means, for example, being resolved and decisive. Justification by style rather than by content can be as absurd as the deep philosophical joke made by the person who summarized Heidegger's lecture by saying, "I am resolved, I just don't know upon what." There is a whole style of square-jawed politicians who try to assert their authority by being decisive about nothing in particular. But what I have in mind is something far more sinister. Something casts its shadow on the decisionist picture. It is the decisive leader that Schmitt and Heidegger had in mind.

I shall advance my little genealogy of the idea of authority in three stages: first, the authority of God; second, the authority of the messengers of the word of God; and third, the authority of the word of God in terms of the authority of the scriptures.

The Authority of God

When it comes to God, it seems that there is no need to justify his authority. One reason is that it is correlated with God's three attributes. He is omniscient, omnipotent, and supremely benevolent. What better justification is there to obey the commandments of such a perfect being?

It takes Lucifer, the fiery fallen angel, to find these attributes, and especially the benevolence of God, irritating and to try to assert his freedom by rebelling against God's perfection. The point about Lucifer's gesture is found in the Augustinian notion of the will, which includes the possibility of knowing the good and yet doing evil. Augustine's idea was a novel idea in philosophy and theology: it meant that recognizing the maximal attributes of God does not secure actual acceptance of the reign of God.

But this, of course, does not mean that the three attributes do not provide justification. Indeed, the three attributes seem almost self-explanatory. The God of the three attributes is the God of the philosophers. But the God of the philosophers is not the only picture of God that emerges from the scriptures

The Gnostic reading found something very different in the Bible, at least in the Old Testament and in many parts of the New (except the parts ascribed to Paul). The God of the Bible, according to the Gnostics, is a mischievous God who plays nasty tricks on us. This wretched God, the jailor of the world, blocks us from contacting the true God. But then, the Gnostics did not challenge the authority of God; they only quarreled about which God should have that authority.

The Gnostic heretical account is interesting in and of itself. Yet for our concern here the important thing to remember is that the scriptures that are traditionally meant to provide reasons for accepting the authority of God can be read very differently. The trick is that of switching the light, switching from reading the text in the best light to reading it in the worst light. The traditional reading of the Bible tries to present the God of scripture in the best light; the Gnostics present God in the worst light and thus provide powerful reasons for subverting his authority. So the issue of justifying the authority of God depends on the question: Under which description of God should we accept his authority?

As for the God of the philosophers, a tension between God's omnipotence and his benevolence should concern us in justifying His authority. By that I do not mean the banal tension between omnipotence and benevolence, on the one hand, and the evil found in the world, on the other. The tension I have in mind is of a different sort: it is how to reconcile the omnipotence of God and his benevolence so as to avoid the omnipotent God from being constrained by the good. The decisionist holds that a God who is constrained by the good is not omnipotent, and hence being constrained by the good diminishes God's absolute sovereignty. On the decisionist account, God's absolute authority rests on his absolute will, namely, on his capacity to decide, unhindered by anyone or anything. Any of God's decisions may, of course, be dubbed good by definition. This is uninteresting, since had he decided to do the opposite, that too would have been regarded as good by definition. The goodness of his decision is independent of its content. God's will is beyond good and evil. This chain of thoughts concerning God's omnipotence and sovereignty is what invites the decisionist picture of God as the One who is supremely capable of making decisions that are absolutely unconstrained and, especially, not constrained by moral laws.

The tension in the decisionist picture derives from the view that the mind no less than the body is a living phenomenon, and the mind has a psychic force that is exerted on and by its owner to bring about things in the world. This force is the will. The will is what is distinctive to individual personality. God, in the theistic view, has personality without having a body. His will, not his reason, is the most characteristic trait of his personality. God presides over the world the way the mind presides over the body. The will in both cases is what makes for the presiding. The will is manifested in the faculty to decide, but it should be regarded as an internal primary force. In the case of God, it is the force to determine the world. The will, in this view, is the ability to start a causal chain that can be ascribed to the owner of the will. He is the creator of this chain.

God's force is so overpowering that there is no way of recognizing it without admiring and thereby surrendering to this overpowering will. Humans have the will to power; God has the power of the will. This is, in the decisionist picture of God, the true answer of God to Job. Admiration should replace justification.

In the decisionist picture, God's will is, paradoxically, a normative brute force. It is brute force in the sense that it is a will that can bring things about without being constrained by any antecedent reasons, since acting for reasons would mean that independent reasons have power over God and thus undermine God's absolute authority. But a God who acts arbitrarily as a brute force may have mere coercive power over us, without the legitimacy needed for authority. It may be prudent to obey his will, but there is no duty to do so. So the decisionist fantasy wants to ascribe normative existence to and have a sense of duty in bowing down to God's overwhelming will. The decisionist wants to depict God the father and not the Godfather. God as the Godfather is a brute force with no normative force; God the father is a brute force that has normative existence. The will of God, though ultimately arbitrary, is not necessarily a despotic, mischievous will. It can be a benign will, the one we face in meeting the forgiving God; the act of forgiving or amnesty is a benevolent act of sovereignty, which is not justified by reasons of law. It is, rather, a gratuitous act of grace that the sovereign is free to enact. God the father is a forgiving god and not a ferocious, Oriental despotic god, at least not by temperament. He is the benevolent side of the decisionistic picture of God. But the authority of God does not hinge on his being benevolent. God's benevolence is a bonus, not a blinker in harnessing his authority.

Schmitt made an interesting analogy: "the exception in jurisprudence is analogous to the miracle in theology."[1] The point of the analogy is that, when the laws fail to constrain the sovereign, it is precisely then that he manifests his full power to decide and hence his authority. Miracles manifest the sovereignty of God. He can bend the laws of nature to his will and thereby create exceptions to the law. For a political ruler, it is in those instances of exceptions to the law, as in times of war and states of emergency, that nothing constrains his will and his power and authority are exerted fully. This picture explains why fascists thrive on crisis or emergency situations and why war plays such key role in fascist thinking. It is not mere fascination with the excitement of war that is at the center of the fascist picture of politics. It is also fascination with authority. It is in war and emergencies that unrestrained and unconstrained decisionism blooms and the authority of the sovereign is there for anyone to see. But this benighted picture of the sovereign acting outside the law can also be a benign picture of giving amnesty, which the sovereign also exercises outside the law.

We might argue that the human capacity to decide on action is a capacity to act for reasons. Thus the idea of God as a person with a will should also have been based on his capacity to act for reasons—higher reasons, to be sure, but reasons all the same. Acting for reasons as a manifestation of the will is very much played down in the fascist picture of God, as it is in the secular fascist picture of man. The God of hosts, as the supreme commander in the cosmic struggle, is the best exemplar of the will that in the fascist picture commands respect. Respect here means the submission of human will to this overpowering force. Submission of human will does not mean annihilation of human wants; on the contrary, the more one is inclined to do A, the more value is attached to one's refraining from doing A. A famous dictum in rabbinic Judaism says, "One should not say I do not want pork. I do, but what can I do and my father in heaven commands me not to do?" (Sifra, Kedusihm). It is God's will, inexplicable as it is, against your will, and so what can you do? He overpowers you.

Authority lies not with reason but with the power to take big decisions. The authority of God is based on his matchless power to decide. The secular counterpart to the principle of the authority of the big decider is terribly grim. It is the *Führerprinzip*, which establishes the absolute authority of the leader due to his charismatic power as a resolute decider. The fascist picture of God is far from being the most common picture of God, let alone the only picture. But it would be excessively apologetic to deny that there is such a picture. This picture takes the ideas of the absolute authority and sovereignty of God to be the key concepts in depicting God as the king of kings—the only true king, who is also the lord of hosts.

There is another picture of God, which I shall call the feudal picture. In the feudal picture, the authority of the lord and the loyalty owed to him are due to favors that he or his ancestors bestowed on his vassals or on their ancestors. Authority and loyalty are based on gratefulness. In Judaism, it is the gift of creation that was bestowed on humanity, for which each and every human being should be grateful and should obey the will of God. Jews have a special obligation of gratefulness for being delivered from Egypt, "the house of slavery." The justification of feudal authority is based not on what is to be gained in the present or in the future but on what was gained in the past. In the feudal picture of God, God is both a father and a king, and his authority is akin to the authority of both. The authority of the father is due to his giving us life. He is our progenitor. In the case of a king, this usually due to his or his ancestors providing protection when it was most needed. The feudal picture of God does find a need to justify the authority of God. His authority is not self-explanatory. But giving life is a good justification for recognizing authority, whereas acting against the will of one who gave us life is being ungrateful in the extreme.

Two trends in political philosophy are an interest in political power as the main feature of political life and an interest in the justification of political power. The first tries to shy away from the project of justification, though it does deal with justification, nonetheless. One such justification in the decisionist picture is that stable political power produces stability and order. Stability and order, the negation of anarchy, is a good justification of power. The decisionist picture, though belittling the whole idea of the need to justify power, tacitly assumes justification through stability and order. This justification takes the form of justification by protection, which it partly shares with feudal justification.

The decisionist and the feudal pictures together can be termed the protectionist model of authority. Authority is justified if it can provide effective protection for its subjects. God as the best protector of his servants is in line with this picture. The political theology of "security philosophers" such as Hobbes is very much in the grip of this picture. They put a premium on securing life rather than on securing good life and find security to be the only goal worth pursuing in polities. Any power that can secure life is therefore authoritative.

Protection resides in order and stability. Any order and stability justifies the power that is capable of effectively imposing a stable order. The content of the order or the stability is immaterial to the justification of authority. The Sicilian mafia's use of power should be judged in the way that the Spanish government's use of power is to be judged—by the protection it provides. When Schmitt addresses Hobbes's Leviathan as an expression of a kindred decisionist soul, and a protectionist to boot, he endlessly quotes Hobbes's saying: *auctoritas, non veritas*. This is the essence of the political order. The essence of *auctoritas* is order, not moral order but any order, be it in heaven or on earth.

So far we have encountered three justifications for the authority of God. All were dubbed with unflattering titles: the fascist picture based on sheer decisionism, the feudal picture based on gratefulness, and the protectionist ("mafia") picture based on protection. The three pictures and with them the three justifications of the authority of God are by no means the common pictures, but it would be a mistake to view them as merely eccentric.

The Authority of the Messenger

The word of God is conveyed by a messenger, a prophet. How to sort out a true messenger from a false one is a major concern in the Bible. The messenger is not a mere postman, nothing but a vehicle for transmitting the word of God. The most interesting case for current concern with the authority of the messenger in religion and politics is the prophetic authority of Muhammad. In one sense, he is as close as one can be to being God's postman, since Islam makes the strong claim that Muhammad received a book, the Qu'ran, with both words and meanings. But Muhammad's authority cuts much deeper than that of a passive though divine messenger.

In one important sense, Muhammad is more like Jesus than like Moses. This sense is that Muhammad is not only a messenger but the message as well.

Unlike Jesus, the prophet does not have two natures: human and divine. To impute, in Islam, God's nature to anyone or anything is idolatry. The prophet is no exception. But the prophet has two personae: human and prophetic. He is fallible as a human, but in his prophetic mode he is infallible, not just in words but in deeds as well.

So, apart from the Qu'ran, a book conveying the word of God, Muhammad's deeds and words as told by an authentic tradition (*sunnat al-nabi*) is another source of authority in Islam. Even the word of God in the Qu'ran can only be understood in the light of the Sunna. In the case of the Qu'ran, there is both phonetic fanaticism and meaning fanaticism. The words and the meanings are given from heaven. In the case of the holy stories about Muhammad (*hadith*), the meaning or the content of the stories is constant, but there is no phonetic fanaticism with regard to the wording. Different wording does not detract from the normative force of an authentic story about the life of Muhammad in Sunni Islam. In Shiite Islam, this status of authority is transferred in part to the messianic imams. Imitation of Muhammad is not just the pedagogical ideal of imitating the life of a perfect human being. Muhammad led a normative existence, with normative commanding force as to how Muslims ought to lead their lives. His life is a source of authoritative commandments and not just a fountain of good advice. There is a strong doctrine of the infallibility of the prophet and his Godlike authority.

What does it all have to do with the picture of religious decisionism? A great deal, I believe. In Islam, two authentic sources of authority, the Qu'ran and the *Sunnat al-nabi*, give the impression that decisionism does not hold with respect to Islam, for decisionism assumes the unity of the will of God as the only legitimate authority. The impression is wrong. The prophet as prophet has no independent will of his own. Muhammad is a Muslim, namely, one who totally surrenders his will to the will of God.

This point calls for further elucidation. The ultimate sin in Islam, as in Judaism, is the sin of idolatry: in Islam idolatry means not the sin of replacing God (Allah) with another god (a wrong god) but instead adding a partner to God. To view the prophet as a partner to God is a terrible blasphemy. This does not mean that God in his heavenly court has no servants—the angels are such servants. What distinguishes a servant of God from a partner is that he has no will of his own. Al-Gazzali, a great Islamic teacher (d. 1111), expressed it forcefully: "Though men, genii, angels, and devils should conspire together either to put one simple atom in motion or to cause it to cease its motion without His will and approbation, they would not be able to do it." The prophet is no exception. Muhammad's life, I claim, is part of the message of God as much as the word of God revealed to Muhammad. Hence the authentic stories about his life are authoritative stories that express, through the medium of Muhammad's life, the will of God.

The authority of Muhammad in this account does not undermine the decisionist picture of Allah but underscores it. The dialectic here, however, is more complicated. Radical political Islam that plays up Muhammad's authority, especially in political matters, seems to move rapidly from admiration of the prophet to deification of the prophet. It has become clear that modern movements in Islam, be they radically conservative or radically reformist, made their moves by pitting themselves against the authority of the four schools that dominated Islam for hundreds of years, divided by allegiance to the two main original sources of authority—the authority of the Qu'ran and the authority of the Sunna. They were even called the people of the Qu'ran and the people of the *hadith*. There was much tension between these two movements, but they had a common target to attack: the classical law (*taqlid*) and its carriers, the Ulma—the learned establishment. Thus political Islam, in the name of authenticity over corrupt tradition, is veering toward Muhammad's direct rule over the pristine community of the early days. The motive of Islamists is in no way an effort to undermine the authority of God. But turning the *Sunna a-nabi* into the primary source of authority creates a duality of authority, a duality that the Islamists would find shocking.

Let me address a question that hovers over my whole discussion and is very much at the center of Islamic thinking. If justification is not the ground for accepting authority, according to the decisionist picture, what are the proper motives for accepting authority there? The motives for human acceptance of God's authority are of great religious moment, in particular, the relative merit and demerit of accepting God's authority out of love or out of fear. Joseph Raz has insightful things to say about the meaning of accepting God's authority out of love. The lover who wants to have the taste in music that the beloved has may want not just instrumentality to ingratiate herself but, in order to be one with the beloved, to be of one mind. The decisionist picture of religion wants something else: a fusion of fear and love for the veneration of God and the acceptance of his authority. The fusion of love and fear is what creates ambivalence, according to Freud's account: first toward the primal despotic father, and then toward God the Father. The decisionist is interested not in deep psychology but in effective submission; the combination of the two is best for submission. Stalin made his admirers shiver, but many also sobbed bitterly at his funeral. For the decisionist, the combination of a tremor of fear and tears of love is just about right. The decisionist picture of God has a strong hold on political Islam. It is directed against another source of authority in Islam, the legalistic authority of the four schools of Islamic law. As a matter of fact, this source of authority was most influential in shaping religious life in the Islamic world. Of course, this legalistic source of authority presents itself as a derived source of authority relative to the Qu'ran and the Sunna, but in fact it is a source of authority of its own.

The Authority of the Scriptures

For most religious thinkers, God's authority was so obvious that it did not call for any justification. God was posited as the self-justified authority; other authorities were justified by their relation to the authority of God. How does the authority of the word of God fit with the decisionist picture of God? Let me redraw the outlines of the decisionist picture. God is a personality with no body. The main trait of his personality is his will. It is his will, not his reason, that counts, because reason does not individuate a personality. Reason in principle is shared by all. The will of God is the individuative principle of God's personality. The will individuates personality the way matter rather than form individuates in Aristotelian metaphysical substances. Matter is corrupt, so it cannot be imputed to God. Thus the immaterial will is supposed to do the trick of marking God's uniqueness. The will of God is a unifying principle of his complicated personality. It is a simple will. This is at the basis of the decisionist picture of God.

The will of God is expressed by his commands more than by anything else he says and does. To be a believer is to accept his authority and obey his commands. To be a true servant of God is the highest religious status. Moses and Muhammad were such servants—indeed, slaves. To do the will of God is to obey his commands, and to obey his commands calls for an interpretation of his words. There are about six thousand verses in the Qu'ran, but only two hundred of them are conveyed by imperative sentences.

By "command" I understand roughly what Hobbes says: "Does this or does not this, without expecting any other reason than the Will of him that says it." God is a super-commander. But commands call for understanding, an understanding not of the reasons for the command but of what to do. Commands may be baffling; they are not always linguistically marked by imperative moods. The epitome of the biblical law is the Ten Commandments. For the most part, they are marked by the imperative mood of "you shall not" (kill, steal, covet, etc.). But then it is generally accepted that "I am the Lord" is the first commandment. This is given in an indicative statement and does not look like a command. For it to be a command, it should already presuppose the authority of God to command. But to believe in God and to accept his authority is what the first commandment commands. Roughly speaking, Judaism and Islam are action-centered religions better fitting the decisionist picture expressed in commands, whereas Christianity is more a belief-centered religion (man is justified by faith).

The prophet Muhammad was the first to coin the very useful expression "people of the book." He meant Jews and Christians. Muslims, through the messenger Muhammad, join this book club, too. The idea is that all these religions, unlike the religions of the heathens, are scripturally based religions. Jews and Christians are entitled to protection under Islamic rule due to the very fact that they are people of the book. Being people of the book does not mean that there is a primacy of the written word of God over the word that is heard. Indeed, for religious purposes hearing is more important than seeing. Faith, after all, is, in the language of the famous eleventh chapter of Hebrews, "the conviction of things not seen." But whether the scriptures were handed over as a book or were revealed by a spoken word (and were committed to writing by prophets), written canonical texts are at the center of each of these three religions. The authority to determine the canon is important for the understanding of religious and political authority. Indeed, an excellent account of canonization in Judaism can be found in Moshe Halbertal's *People of the Book*.

Who the people of the book are is, on occasion, a highly contestable matter. Heretics swear by the name of the holy books that they and only they are the "true" people of the book. One may argue that, in some peculiar way, "the book" is more important to heretics and fundamentalists than to orthodoxy. Appeal to the book is a way to offset the authority of orthodoxy, which counts, in fact, more on "living traditions" than on the book. Paradoxically put, "the people of the book" are the fundamentalists and the heretics, who try to undermine traditional religious and political authorities by direct appeal to the authority of the book.

What, in the decisionist picture of God, is the right interpretation of scripture? Right interpretation is the interpretation that gets the intentions of God right. But this is easier said than explained. Under the title "the intentional fallacy," William Wimsatt, an influential literary critic, maintained that interpreting a literary text should not be concerned with the author's intention but should be based on the shared linguistic meanings of its words. Various arguments are advanced to promote the idea of "the fallacy," among them a denial of first person authority over one's own words.

For the decisionist picture, God's authority over his own words is of great moment. It ties in with another religious picture of God—the creator picture, or the creator fallacy. On this account, only the creator knows in full the things he created. The potter knows everything there is to know about his products, and the carpenter knows everything about the tables and the cupboards that she produces. God, as the creator of the world, is the sole entity that knows the world, for he created the world. It was stories coming from Prague that exposed the creator picture as a creator fallacy: first, the old story about the Golem and then the new story of the Robots. In both stories the creator lost control over his products. This loss of control over one's artifacts shaped the modern sensibility of not understanding the world created around us. In any case, God is the author of his world. He created the world and handed over a book based on his creation (not quite; in Islam there is a doctrine of the eternity of the Qu'ran), so he is in the best position to know everything about the meanings of its words. Moreover, he is not constrained by the plain meanings of words. He is the sovereign. This last claim is untenable, since the only theory of meaning that goes with such an account is Humpty Dumpty's: "When I use a word it means just what I choose it to mean." Remember how "glory" is famously turned by Humpty Dumpty into "a nice knock down argument"?

The decisionist picture of interpretation is pushed into a Humpty Dumpty position. There is no glory in this account, and it is nothing but a knock-down argument against God's commanding his creatures to obey his will in a language he uses as he pleases. The point is that a decisive and deciding God who exerts his authority by commanding his creatures should make sure that they understand him. And this can be done if, and only if, God speaks in the language of his creatures, which puts many strictures on what he can and cannot say. The decisionist can ignore morality but not linguistics. Human understanding is a constraint on the way God understands himself, even when God is trying to be a decisionist God, who is not constrained by morality.

The decisionist picture of God may not be a coherent picture—a great deal hinges on how we understand God's omnipotence—but this does not stop it from being an influential picture in politics, in theology, and especially in political theology.

Explaining the Global Religious Revival
The Egyptian Case

Talal Asad

It is a truism that global forces have greatly heightened social instability, economic distress, and cultural uncertainty in the contemporary world. The widespread phenomenon of religious revival is said to be part of the picture. How should one explain the resurgence of religion across the world—as a cry of misery, an assertion of identity, a revolt against the uncertainties produced by modernization? It is evident that how we try to explain it will determine our expectation of its promise and its threat. But there is also the question of exactly *what* we are required to explain, of how we are to identify a worldwide phenomenon called the religious revival. Is there an essence here that connects it to what our historians and anthropologists have called the past of religion? In what sense was the Bharatiya Janata Party (BJP) government in India rooted in historical Hinduism? What connects the Christian right alliance with the American presidential administration, or with Islamist opposition groups in Egypt? Should we see al-Qaeda as an integral part of the Islamic revival? Is the growth in everyday piety in numerous countries integral to "fundamentalism"? Should we regard the increasing interest by philosophers, anthropologists, and historians in theological languages as part of the same "religious revival"—even though very many of them are nonbelievers—or simply see them as scholars for whom the language of theology is suggestive of new ways of thinking about some problems in the modern world?

In statistical terms Christianity is, of course, globally pre-eminent. Scattered across the world, Christians now constitute one-third of its population—and a third of them live in what were once Euro-American colonies. It has been pointed out that, although Christianity was brought to these countries by European missionaries, it is now an integral part of the ethnic identity of the populations who profess it. Christian movements in one excolonial country even prosely-tize energetically in another. All of this is part of the global religious revival. By contrast, the spread of Islam over the last two centuries has been globally much less dramatic. A mere fifth of the world's population, Muslims are present in Europe and North America because they have migrated from Africa and Asia, not because of conversion; African-American converts to Islam are the only significant exception to this generalization. In purely statistical terms the relative strength of Muslims in the world is unremarkable. And yes, there are acts of violence carried out by small groups of Muslim militants around the world, but these can scarcely be compared in scale with the recent destruction wrought by Christian American and (to a lesser extent) Jewish Israeli armies. So what are we trying to explain?

I want to begin by focusing on some explanations of the so-called world-wide revival with special reference to the world of Islam, and within it to the part I happen to know best. I shall concentrate on the Arab countries, and particularly on Egypt. I hope, nevertheless, that testing explanations of the religious revival in one country will throw some light on how we might view such explanations in general. Because an important aspect of this "revival" is that, however transnational such movements may be, they are all placed within the context of particular nation-states, and part of their strength comes from their ability to address that context.

The common assumption that the Islamic revival in all its forms needs to be explained by reference to the acute economic and sociological problems of those countries is reflected in media reactions to the 2002 United Nations Development Programme (UNDP) report on Arab countries. Thus, a *New York Times* article on the report by Barbara Crossette quoted extensively from it, focusing on the many negative features in the socioeconomic picture of "Arab culture," and concluded: "Then came the attacks on the United States, giving the report unexpected new relevance as explanations for Arab anger against the West are being sought." The clear implication of this remark, as well as of others in which supposedly authoritative commentators on the Middle East are cited in support, is that the violence connected to political Islam—and perhaps the Islamic revival itself—is generated by the economic uncertainties, political failures, and social instability of something called Arab culture. Thomas Friedman is even more explicit. "If you want to understand the milieu that produced bin Ladenism, and will reproduce it if nothing changes, then read this report."[1] For Friedman and others, the frustrations of uncontrolled change in the Middle East are being directed, through the religious revival, at the innocent West.[2]

So I begin by looking at the "economic distress" explanation. The social composition of each Arab country, and its unique history during and after colonialism, have contributed to considerable variation in the overall picture. But several of these countries have a political-economic feature in common: after the collapse of the attempt to establish welfare states based on attempts at autonomous industrialization (IS), financial bankruptcy following rapid economic liberalization compelled postcolonial governments to resort to foreign loans, a move that led to the structural adjustment (SA) programs being imposed by the International Monetary Fund (IMF) and the World Bank[3]—a phase that coincided with some loosening of state control over public life, including the ending of two decades of fierce state repression of Islamic movements. The economic disruption of life in these countries is not the result of "Arab culture" or of "Islam" but of other factors.[4] The main point I want to endorse here has been made by several acute analysts of the Middle East: that economic and social distress does not explain the existence of Islamic political movements, if only because the main cadres of these movements are generally among the more privileged sectors of society.

These comments apply particularly to the most important Arab country, Egypt, on which I will now concentrate. It is from Egypt, with its history of modern disappointments, that the lead authors of the UNDP report come.[5] And it was in Egypt that the most influential Islamist movement—the Muslim Brotherhood—began. The movement was proscribed by Nasser in the early nineteen-fifties, its cadres imprisoned, tortured, and exiled because of the threat they posed to his one-party government.[6] The lifting of the ban against the Brotherhood by Nasser's successor Sadat was part of a strategy of loosening the hold of Nasserites and Marxists on state power. This is why the left often claims that the Islamic revival in Egypt owes its prominence today to the political manipulations of Sadat's right-wing regime. Sadat's "opening-up" (*infitāh*) of Egypt's political economy certainly provided a public space that allowed Islamist discourses (and others as well) to be expressed. But in my view the increasing political *influence* of Islamists—including, most importantly, of the Muslim Brothers—was a consequence of their appeal to the Egyptian masses and not of Sadat's efforts.[7] There is an old tradition of reform as renewal (*tajdīd*) in Islam, and this has been drawn on again and again in the modern period. There is also a tradition of authoritarianism, inherited, it is said, from the past— although I think it is more useful to focus on *the emergence of the modern nation-state and the transnational market* so that one can distinguish precolonial, colonial, and postcolonial forms of authoritarianism.

In Egypt (as in other Muslim countries), Islamic tradition has always been central to the life of most inhabitants—albeit in different ways in different classes. In that sense the term *revival* may not be appropriate here. The state has sought to use Islamic piety for its own purposes, and different oppositional groups have reinterpreted it for theirs. The discursive tradition has enabled various responses to changing perceptions of threat and reassurance, both within the nation-state and beyond. As circumstances that are the objects of these perceptions have changed, so too has the tradition, and with it the aspirations and sensibilities of its followers. Thus there is now a strong sense of world-wide connection among Muslims, built on circuits of communication and sympathy. The *umma* so conceived is indeed "an imagined community," as Olivier Roy has recently proposed.[8] But unlike him I would emphasize that the world Muslims share with non-Muslims is the scene of complicated interactions between political, economic, and ideological forces, internal *and external*. This imagined community is not isolated, as Roy appears to suggest, and so it cannot be understood on its own. The *umma* is locked into a larger world of powerful interventions and seepages. The economic consequences of these processes have been well analyzed, but there is less understanding of their religious consequences. The Muslim communities in Western countries are an interesting example of this condition—at once residents of numerous liberal democracies that are dominated by non-Muslims and part of the transnational *umma*.[9] But non-Muslim powers are also intimately present in the life of Muslim-majority countries. So the *umma* is not simply an imagined community, it is a moral space within which there is a struggle for right doctrine (orthodoxy). But even this struggle is not simply confined to Muslims as members of the *umma*. They are constantly subject to pressures to incorporate Western liberal traditions (economic as well as cultural) as signs of the modern.

All of this is certainly an important part of the context in which the Islamic revival is located. But when it is suggested that the revival is best understood as a religious mask for political-economic discontent led by ideologues—whether opportunistic or simple-minded—I remain unconvinced.[10] Of course, there are opportunists and fanatics in contemporary Egypt as there are everywhere else. Certainly there is corruption in public life, increasing economic inequality in the country, continuous political repression by the Mubarak regime. But the suggestion of people like Thomas Friedman that Egypt's difficulties (in which the U.S. is, of course, never seen as having any part) create a general state of pathological despair that then leads to "Islamism" is surely disingenuous. The violence of Islamic "fundamentalists" is not the only violence there is—as the indiscriminate brutality of state security forces (including the widespread use of torture) testifies.[11] And although the U.S. is not directly responsible for the political-economic problems encountered in Egypt, its intervention does have something to do with them—and therefore with the ways Egyptians construct their religious politics.

However, my main argument so far is that the personal experience of social and economic difficulties is neither a sufficient nor a necessary cause of political Islam in Egypt—or, for that matter, elsewhere in the region. My suggestion therefore is that, instead of seeing deteriorating social conditions in society as the cause of discontent that is then exploited by Islamists, we should first consider these conditions as the objects of a diverse and evolving religious discourse that engages these conditions and gives them political force.

. . .

It is because explanations of the so-called Islamic revival in terms of economic distress are seen as wanting that an alternative account (which still focuses on the search for security) is gaining popularity. The revival, it is said, is really all about cultural *identity*: In a rapidly changing modern world, individuals (both rich and poor) are seeking a sense of certainty. But I find this explanation equally unpersuasive.[12] True, people who are part of the "Islamic revival" are moved by various interests—and their commitments vary in intensity and seriousness over time. And of course there *are* people for whom "the rhetoric of Islam" is merely a tactic, merely a means for achieving a variety of objectives. But that is also true of people who employ the rhetoric of "freedom and democracy," and yet generally we distinguish (in my view rightly) the moral potentialities of *that* rhetoric from the designs of politicians who use it. Islamic discourse, even the militant forms that advocate a new concept and a radical practice of *jihād*, is about justice in this world—not, of course, for its own sake, but for the sake of a divine dispensation.

A case can be made for saying that some aspects of thinking that arose in the state socialist era have been incorporated into political Islam, including the mainstream, nonviolent form. Perhaps the most important of these is the notion that society has a moral obligation to the underprivileged, so that the idea of justice (*'adl*) is considered to be more important than the notion of freedom (*hurriya*)—although in practice even Islamists know that the two are not easily separated. The idea of justice finds expression not only among small groups of Islamic militants but also in the emergence of new social spaces for the exercise of commitments to the deprived. The old Islamic notion of *da'wa*—of calling one's fellows to become better Muslims—is being reformulated away from its previous primary preoccupation with ritual practice and religious doctrine to include material welfare: the provision of cheap medicines, loans, youth clubs, emergency shelters, and so on, in a state that is increasingly unable or unwilling to provide any of these things. Rules pertaining to religious devotion remain important, but there is now a new opportunity for a discourse of responsibility toward others in society. Charity to the poor has always been a major religious value in Islam (it is one of the five pillars), but many Islamists now say that one cannot be a good Muslim unless one has the material means to ensure health and security in life, that it is therefore a *religious* requirement, a duty of the Muslim community as a whole, to provide these things to all Muslims. Hence it is not the same as individual charity (*sadaqa*), nor the same as the work performed by secular welfare institutions (*mu'asasāt khayria*). The difference consists in the fact that *da'wa* requires an appropriate moral attitude in the giver and seeks a developing moral response in the taker. (This is not only an intellectual viewpoint; the poor are adopting it, too.) The point I want to stress is that the concern here is not with poverty in the abstract, nor simply with it as an occasion for virtuous giving, but with the material deprivation that disables people from living "a virtuous Islamic life." This is usually accompanied by the assumption that a single conception of the virtuous life can and should be imposed on all Muslims, and that a major purpose of the state is to ensure the conditions for its attainment, including the elimination of poverty.

Basic to the discourse and practice of *da'wa* (so I am reminded by many Egyptian friends) is the notion of "thanking the benefactor" (*shukr al-mun'im*)—that is, of thanking the divine giver for his bounty to humankind, which the Qur'an repeatedly speaks of as his wondrous signs (*ayāt*).[13] One may detect an invitation to enchantment in this idea, although the word *sihr*, which is the usual rendering of "enchantment," is never used by Muslims in this context. I refer to it here partly to problematize its use in the standard Weberian account by suggesting that it relates to something rarely noted by social theorists:[14] an encounter with wondrous things and events in the world, a world that, for the Muslim believer, has been made by the Creator.[15] Regarded in this way, "enchantment" is not simply an obstacle to reason, something that has to be shed when modernity is achieved. *It becomes the ground for engaging with the world in a particular way.* Enchantment "charms" one out of a habitual state of indifference into a state of wonder made possible by alerted senses. Of course, enchantment may deceive (the sources of deception are many), but the loss of enchantment is more than simply the removal of a source of delusion. It constitutes a particular *loss*.

I am proposing, in effect, that to deepen our understanding of the so-called religious revival we need to inquire not only into how Muslim intellectuals see "the West" and the political solutions they offer but into what ordinary Muslims themselves say and do in their daily lives, what demands they typically make of their sensations, how they try to discipline themselves to live *as Muslims*—what, in short, becomes "natural" to them, taken for granted. I am not, incidentally, making a plea here for "listening to the Other," about which one hears so much nowadays.[16] My proposal has to do with recognizing the complexity of the notion of "religious agency" and with the need for analyzing the subtle and dynamic ways that intention, action, and ownership of action are brought together in "religious life." (It is a common prejudice to think that for every *action* there corresponds a determinate human actor; the agent may be either less or more than the individual.) Such inquiries have rarely been done adequately, partly because most sociologists dealing with the Muslim world tend to have too impoverished a conception of agency and subjectivity.

At any rate, my own view is that the public Islamic discourse is not simply a response to the anxious question "How can I be true to what I *really* am?" There *are* such concerns, but their proponents are usually Westernized secularists.[17] (When Islamists express that concern, it takes a more complicated form.) What is assumed in such identity discourse is that one has an authentic essence reflected in one's *feeling*, something one has the right to express publicly and have publicly recognized, and that one's primary responsibility is to oneself, to the body, emotion, and mind one owns absolutely. *Yet this assumption is by no means part of the language and mode of life of most ordinary Muslims.*[18]

So I argue that, for most ordinary Muslims, the "Islamic revival" is not a search for cultural identity or authenticity in a time of social instability, that for them other questions are more meaningful: "Since I am a Muslim, how should I behave in accordance with God's commands? Since I live among Muslims, how should we behave toward one another? To which Islamic authority should I turn to find an answer to these and other similar questions?" While most people don't normally ask themselves such abstract questions, *the Islamic discursive tradition*—to which people turn with varying commitment—*does* assume them. (By the Islamic discursive tradition, incidentally, I do not refer to the manipulative intentions of leaders or to the closed world-view of believers but to the space in which verbal, emotional, and bodily resources are made available to Muslims *as Muslims*, to be taught, criticized, defended, and reformulated, in relation to founding texts.) Thus even the material services that the poor are offered, and that the professional syndicates provide,[19] are talked about in a particular religious-moral language—both by activists and by recipients. I want to stress: it is not that the language of cultural identity is never to be found in the "revival." Indeed, it is present, especially in the discourse of intellectuals. But even where the language of cultural identity *is* used by them, the fact that it is accompanied by a sense of spiritual obligation complicates the subjective and discursive object to be explained. It is therefore different from a straightforward "search for identity" in a general period of uncertainty. What one seeks is an agency that is at once one's own (one has chosen it) and not one's own (one submits to divine power).

Apart from such complications, it seems to me that explanations in terms of "identity" generally miss something very important: the fact that the primary form of public discourse about "identity" is attached to the modern state. Here the question that matters is not "Who am I?" but "Who are *you*?" In this context one should not think of the individual's right to express *uniqueness* but of the state's power to identify *similarity*. This concern is with *identification*. Identity in this sense is essential to modern state control and security, which continually records and classifies bodily and verbal signs of identification. The question "Who are you?" is always put by an officer of the state and typically accompanied by a demand for identity papers (*awrāq al-huwīyya*)—especially when crossing national borders. Here the uncertainty is not existential but administrative and political, and the response is not in terms of religion but of techniques of surveillance, as well as coercion, that are at once Western and indigenous. I want to make two points here: first, political Islam is inconceivable without the formation of the nation-state and its ambitions; second, questions about existential identity are related to the modern state's interest in identifying suspicious foreigners and nationals (criminals, traitors, terrorists). Thus loyalty to the state's normative constitution overrides all others and sets limits to the subject's legitimate identity. At the same time, state and market (national and global) are intimately connected, and in an increasingly consumerist economy, consumption—for those able to afford it—has become a duty and a need, indispensable for the individual to express his/her modern identity. The opportunities and constraints of the market for individual consumers, on the one hand, and, on the other hand, the powers of the nation-state, at once solicitous and disciplinary toward a national population, are together more important for the question of identity than the ill-defined notion of "a legacy of authoritarianism" in the Middle East. In fact, I would say that it is only when the ambition of the postcolonial state and the destructiveness of the postcolonial market are taken into account that postcolonial authoritarianism can be fully explained.

. . .

It is a widely reported fact that during the last century movements of Islamic reform have encouraged the deprofessionalization of religious interpretation, and that—together with increasing literacy, the widespread use of audio and video tapes, and now also of the Internet—this has led, in effect, to a significant shift in religious authority. This process of deprofessionalization has often been compared to the Protestant Reformation, and some liberals have pinned their hopes on an outcome similar to that which Europe eventually experienced and defined as "modern." There are certainly some important comparisons to be made here. Among these is the increasing salience given in the reform literature to tenets (*'aqā'id*, sing:*'aqīda*), primarily as an internal state. But the analogy cannot be pressed too far, because obviously the *Christendom* of early Protestant sects was profoundly different from the contemporary world inhabited by Islamist movements. The historian Herbert Butterfield once pointed out that sixteenth-century Protestants were *not* struggling to create the world we call modern, and that the sixteenth-century Catholic Church was *not* determined to prevent that world from emerging. They had their own very special preoccupations, which were expressed through their notions of salvation.[20]

More attention needs to be paid to the idea that the Reformation was a rebellion against a centralized religious authority that sought to control the definition of legitimate knowledge, and that even in the Protestant parts of Christendom official concern to locate, assess, and regulate belief as an internal psychological condition remained strong. Islam, as is well known, never had a centralized religious authority. Nevertheless, for two centuries Muslim societies have had to confront the Euro-American claim to a monopoly of knowledge and the criteria that ensure its legitimacy. For many modern Muslims, claims to knowledge are valid simply because they issue from Euro-America—and only because this is the center of capitalist power. For others, knowledge is "inauthentic" if it comes from "outside." Opponents of "Islamic fundamentalism" find in this latter position evidence of an "antimodern"—because "antiscientific"—mind-set, an expression of the desire to cling to religious certainty in place of scientific skepticism. Yet this judgment is questionable, and not simply because many so-called Islamists are themselves professionally active in the sciences or because they use modern gadgets. Philosophers of science have increasingly come to recognize that there is no single "scientific mindset." Practices that are effective for one set of scientific problems are inappropriate for others. This is true for both the natural and the moral sciences. The notion that there are two blocs of knowledge, one dealing with "nature," the other with "culture," each internally homogeneous, has long been problematized. There is great diversity in the conditions in which knowledge is accumulated, in the techniques on which it draws, and in the ends to which it is applied. Disagreement (technical and ethical) occurs at numerous levels in the world of scientific endeavor. And contrary to popular understanding, skepticism is by no means a continuous or pervasive attitude of modern scientists toward their work.[21] So when people argue against particular political-economic constructions on what they claim are "religious" grounds, they aren't *necessarily* being "antiscientific." The question that needs to be addressed more systematically than it has been is whether, and if so, in precisely what sense, Islamist criticisms of the way the contemporary world is arranged amount to a rejection of scientific knowledge—bearing in mind that science itself is intertwined with the ways we live, and therefore with the ethics of everyday life.

I return now to the phenomenon of world-wide religious resurgence to which I referred at the beginning of my talk. This has been the object of innumerable explanations by scholars and journalists. Common to very many of them is the notion that people need reassurance in a time of rapid change and instability. This is echoed in much that has been written trying to explain the so-called revival in Egypt and fits quite nicely with the "search for identity" idea.

"Modernity," writes Peter Berger in a recent article, "tends to undermine the taken-for-granted certainties by which people lived through most of history. This is an uncomfortable state of affairs, for many an intolerable one, and religious movements that claim to give certainty have great appeal."[22] Karen Armstrong has taken this state of affairs to be an explanation of the growth of fundamentalism: "Fundamentalism," she writes, "speaks to a popular 'desire for impregnable certainty' and simplification in the face of the social dislocations and ambiguities of late modernity."[23] But are the religious movements of which Berger speaks Armstrong's *fundamentalist* movements understood in some narrow sense? Or does the term *fundamentalism* apply to *all* religious commitments because religion by definition offers certainty?

However plausible Berger and Armstrong may seem, they do not attend sufficiently to the conditions that witnessed the rise of secularism, which (so I have argued elsewhere) is more than a political doctrine. Perhaps this is because for most of us moderns secularism isn't in need of explanation—it is simply the self-evident truth of the world in which we now live. The fact remains that explaining the recent "rise of religion" as the resort to certainty in a time of social upheaval tends to ignore the story of the emergence of secularism in modern life.

71

From its beginning modernity has apparently undermined taken-for-granted certainties. All the emblematic writers of the nineteenth century recognized the changing character of modern life. Baudelaire, who introduced the word *modernity,* represented modern life as fleeting, transitory, and arbitrary. His ideas have been central to later discussions about the character of aesthetic sensibilities in modernism. Marx, famously, saw capitalism as a dynamo of change, a kind of permanent revolution in which the relations and forces of production were constantly in the process of being transformed—and with them the entire range of social relations. If social and economic historians are agreed on one thing, it is the accelerating speed and widening scope of social disruptions in people's lives during the last few centuries. Instability and anxiety have accompanied the humanist promise of universal progress. And yet it is in *this* period that secularism—not "religious fundamentalism"—emerged and triumphed in what we now know as the liberal democratic societies of the West. Do we not need to account for this?

A familiar old story about the emergence of modernity is often narrated in this context. Starting in the sixteenth century, the spiritual and political authority of religion began to be progressively undermined by science and materialism. In the eighteenth century, the hegemony of faith gave way to the hegemony of reason. Calculation and practical control of the world by enlightened reason replaced magic and mystery. Progress in knowledge and life was clearly being made. This was what Weber famously called *the disenchantment of the world,* a notion that stands in epistemological contrast to the one I discussed earlier. By the twentieth century, it became increasingly evident that, although scientific discoveries and technological innovations had resulted in clear improvements in the material conditions of life, these were accompanied by another, less happy development, which Weber referred to as "the iron cage." Ultimate values were now elusive, and to make matters worse, even science failed to provide certainty in place of religion. This disappointment with science was linked to an ambivalence about the practical accomplishments of capitalism. The result was what has been called "a crisis of Enlightenment thought," and a resurgence of religion was one of its results.

The second half of the twentieth century—so this narrative goes—witnessed a further erosion of modernity's belief in progress: science could now be linked to the horrors of Nazi death camps, to the instant destruction of Hiroshima and Nagasaki. Increasingly, technology seemed unable to deal with the costs of the progress it had enabled. Enlightenment reason was itself in crisis. "The moral crisis of our time is a crisis of Enlightenment thought," writes the Marxist geographer David Harvey, summing up postmodernist thought. "The affirmations of 'self without God' in the end negated itself because reason, a means, was left, in the absence of God's truth, without any spiritual or moral goal."[24] I am not myself persuaded that there *is* "a crisis of Enlightenment thought" that has now left the modern world morally aimless and spiritually anxious. In Euro-America, neither the political and intellectual elite nor most ordinary people believe they are living through a crisis of Enlightenment thought, although they are aware of the disruptions of advanced capitalism. There are fears about terrorism and job insecurity, there is a widespread lack of confidence in the political process, and—especially in Europe—a dislike of non-European immigrants. But I do not think that all that amounts to a deep civilizational uncertainty about "reason, [which is] a means, [being left] without any spiritual or moral goal."

But even those who believe that there is "a crisis of Enlightenment thought" know that religion in Western Europe is a weak presence, while remaining strong in the Third World. Those countries are of course thought of as premodern in the narrative of modern progress. Yet America, the most modern country of all, appears to be an anomaly. Some scholars have proposed a complicated account to explain this. Thus in *The Romantic Ethic and the Spirit of Modern Consumerism*, Colin Campbell has argued that from the outset there were two ideological tendencies within Protestantism. One—of which Weber wrote—emerged as instrumental rationalism, central to capitalist production. But late capitalism needed something else in addition—an ideological force that would drive mass consumption forward. That force, says Campbell, grew out of the Romantic sensibility, also bequeathed to modernity by Puritanism. As Campbell puts it, "The cultural logic of modernity is not merely that of rationality as expressed in the activities of calculation and experiment; it is also that of passion and the creative dreaming born of longing." The result is the distinctive tension in modern capitalism between dream and reality, between pleasure and utility. "In struggling to cope with the necessity of making trade-offs between need and pleasure, whilst seeking to reconcile their bohemian and bourgeois selves, modern individuals inhabit not just an 'iron cage' of economic necessity, but a castle of romantic dreams, striving through their conduct to turn the one into the other."[25] Campbell's story allows one to make some sense of the persistence, in the world's most dynamic capitalist society, of ideological sources that sustain its religiosity.

However, Campbell is still preoccupied with the question of the re-emergence of religion as a consequence of instability and the longing for lost certainty. If myth and magic have not been entirely eliminated by modernity, so the story goes, this is because the old belief in illusions (paradigmatically, "religion" itself) has simply been replaced by others generated by consumer capitalism. In a more elaborate way Campbell's explanation responds to the same old question about illusions: it is the gap between popular fantasies created and encouraged by consumer capitalism, on the one hand, and, on the other hand, the crises of production that religion seeks to bridge with its own kind of illusory certainty. This is quite an attractive account but not, I think, in the end fully usable for my purpose. Its main value lies in reminding readers that the *materiality* of capitalist consumption goods is inextricably tied up with their *imaginary character*. But it does not explain the strength of "religion" in countries where consumer capitalism is least developed, nor the absence of a revitalized religion in countries where it is relatively well developed—especially Western Europe and Japan. More important, the question that interests me here has to do not with the so-called revival of religion but with the emergence of secularism. And the reason for this interest is that the sociological conditions that are often said to explain the rise of fundamentalist religion in our time are very similar to those that gave rise to secular sensibilities in the modern West. I ask: Does this indicate an overlap between the two? Perhaps an overlap, but not—so I say—an identity.

Let me elaborate by taking up a suggestion of Walter Benjamin's in *The Origins of German Tragic Drama*. In this study Benjamin argues that the continuous tension displayed in baroque drama between the ideal of restoration and the fear of catastrophe should be interpreted in light of the social instability and political violence of early modern times. The emphasis one finds on *this-worldliness* in these plays, so he tells us, is to be understood as a consequence of that tension. Skeptical detachment from all contestable beliefs—*ataraxia*—was conducive to self-preservation, as, in its own way, was the lack of trust in people's motives and actions. The materiality of objects (i.e., the fact that persons and things were to be apprehended and confirmed through the senses) offered a kind of guarantee that people's words no longer afforded. The human body could be enjoyed and attacked and defended against as pure physicality. Social life was full of unpredictable change, alternating delight with menace. In a striking sentence Benjamin writes that *even* "The religious man of the baroque era clings so tightly to the world because of the feeling that he is being driven along a cataract with it." The suggestion here seems to be that the anxieties generated by the subversion of social and moral certainties in early modernity *did* direct people to seek reassurance, but that this did not lead them toward the transcendent—it led them to turn to the material world more insistently than ever before. So it may not be the steady accumulation of facts about the "real" world that underlies secularism but accidental ruptures, shifts in our collective experience, new fears and satisfactions that push us in a particular direction.

In this connection it is worth pondering something else, too. Recent historians of eighteenth-century science have suggested that the Enlightenment fear of the distortion of hard-won "facts" based on sensations led them to disdain the imagination—which they feared had a tendency to create fanciful notions, other worlds, "enchanted worlds." This scientific distrust of the unruly imagination easily fed into a distrust of *the sources* of religion.[26] So the material basis of "facts" generated its own instability because *fear* of the imagination required continual disciplining. As Lorraine Daston has recently reminded us, the so-called skeptical attitude of the scientist toward belief was a *moral* stance but also one that was not (that cannot be) practiced strictly and systematically.[27] This *particular* emphasis on physicality was also at the root of the early modern state and of its neo-stoic theorists—who were among the first to argue for secularism as a means of strengthening the state.[28] Such considerations complicate our story.

Whether Benjamin is completely right or not, we may legitimately wonder whether the process of looking for certainty after doubt has set in is as clear a matter as some of our globalization theorists and intellectual journalists would have us suppose.

The so-called Islamic revival has many different forms, and it includes a revival in interest in Sufism (*tasawwuf*), which is not always regarded as an alternative to "orthodox Islam," with its emphasis on prescribed duties, but is a complement to it. The *political* movements that are included in this general resurgence harness diverse interests and means. Yet it is not uncommon to find all of them treated by both scholars and journalists as "Islamic fundamentalists." Taking this view elides important differences to be found in movements not only as regards political power and democratic potential but also in the theological traditions that inform them. The repeated claim that "fundamentalists" of all kinds can be defined by their "certainty" obscures critical distinctions within that very notion: for example, between those who claim to possess an overpowering intuition that they are subjects of divine illumination and those for whom a (sacred) text with unquestionable authority is a taken-for-granted object in the social world. These two forms of certainty are not the same, nor do they have the same social, political, and theological implications. And they are not subject to the same kind of doubt, nor are they equally available as a solution to existential uncertainty deriving from changes in human experience in the world.

I am, in fact, at a loss as to how I should confirm the proposition that the subversion of "taken-for-granted beliefs" has led the Egyptians I know to seek reassurance in religion. When taken-for-granted beliefs are undermined, one does not restore *them* by turning in a self-conscious way to a particular ideology; what happens is a reorientation of one's commitments. But the new commitment has its own problems. As any serious believer will tell you, far from being a simple guarantee of comfort and security, "religious conviction" opens up its own kinds of anxieties and uncertainties.

In any case, for a millennium Islamic theological and legal discourse has distinguished certainty (*yaqīn*) from doubt (*shakk*) as epistemological states. Jurists have insisted that only revealed texts provide knowledge of which there can be no doubt[29]—that for the rest one must be content with probability, as indicated by prevailing opinion (*ghālib al-zann*). Islamic jurisprudence has always made a distinction between ethical norms that bind the conscience of the individual believer and the norms that the judge is required to apply in legal cases. The individual's conscience (*damīr*) deals with his relation to his God, and in doing so he must refer to absolute criteria. But the individual's conscience is not accessible to others and so will always remain a matter of uncertainty for them. The judge, therefore, must confine himself to his understanding of probable facts (behavior that is visible) and his knowledge of legal norms. The tension between legal and ethical norms, between the judgment of God and that of the human judge, between the individual's conscience and his memory, on the one hand, and the court's final decision, on the other, may result in unavoidable conflicts.[30] But it does not—cannot—lead to a demand for certainty in all things. According to the central tradition of Islam, the domain of uncertainty is always present because it is conceptually necessary for defining, by contrast, the status of revealed knowledge. Hence the ubiquitous phrase expressed by Muslims, *wa allāhu a'lam* (but God knows best—i.e., one cannot be sure). The absence of absolute certainty, whether in the religious law (*fiqh*) or in everyday life, has never been a serious problem in Muslim history. And it is also something with which the Islamists with whom I have interacted are quite familiar.

. . .

Finally, I return to the question with which I began: How should one explain the world-wide revival of religion? I have been trying to suggest that, given the variety of motives, conditions, and feelings, there is no unitary phenomenon to be explained. "Religion"—even "fundamentalist religion"—is not a homogeneous phenomenon. If my argument is acceptable for Egypt, it should be even more acceptable for the world at large. I have proposed elsewhere that the question to ask is not "What is religion?" (to which one response might be: Look at religion "*as* a cultural system") but "How does the concept of religion as a universal arise? And why? How is it defined and with what is it contrasted? And by whom? In what social/historical context? What kinds of sensibilities encourage/discourage its articulation? What is doable in its name?"[31] Since the answers to these questions will differ, so too will the explanation.

But one thing seems clear. The profound problems of globalization in the domain of national and transnational economies have led to skepticism about the zealous pursuit of progress. The Three Horsemen of the Apocalypse—War, Famine, and Pestilence—are still riding high, and they have been joined by a new and more terrible cavalier: the irretrievable degradation of our planet. None of this constitutes a *gap* into which religion "re-enters." All the things that have been called "religious" relate to a variety of responses to outcomes supported or at least condoned by a self-declared "secular discourse" committed to the continuous development of national populations.

One common thought seems to be this: If being modern requires that every country become secular, and if secular culture discourages us from intruding our ethical judgments on others, how can one respond adequately to the horrors perpetrated in the political domain? The disparate phenomena that we group together as "a world-wide religious revival" deal with questions about morality, politics, faith, and spirituality that lead in very different directions. They do not express a single movement, a single sensibility, a single existential orientation.

Perhaps they share only this: a rejection of the confident promises of classical secularism to which rationalist progress has been tied. But then many thoughtful "secularists" would also agree with this, and unlike other secularists, regard temporality as heterogeneous. At any rate, a consequence of these confrontations is that a new world seems to be emerging in which there is a multiplicity of self-styled "nonsecular" traditions. That world *is* changing fast. Whether this will lead to a greater sense of interdependence and care for others, a greater awareness of the finiteness of human life and its natural environment, or, on the contrary, to further hostile targeting of women, immigrants, unbelievers, possible terrorists, and so forth is something one cannot confidently predict. Nor can one be confident that future dangers will all issue from what we now call "religion." On the contrary, I think it unlikely that the greatest threats to our common world will come from the poorer, less-efficient nation-states, or from the less powerful immigrant populations in the rich world.

PART II

The Nation

Seeing Nationhood

Images of American Identity

David Morgan

Since the early days of the British colonies, the Anglo inhabitants of North America have been fond of claiming for themselves a sense of uniqueness. Whether a "city on a hill" or making the world "safe for democracy," this sense has often been expressed as a national mission or vocation.[1] Although scholars of American history and culture over the past twenty years have criticized "American exceptionalism" as uncritical and nationalistic, the idea is still powerful among many Americans today. But determining what the mission might be is no less conflicted than the question of whether there is one at all. Throughout their history, Americans have looked to geography, heroes, wars, political ideals, religion, public education, and the English language for a common, albeit uneven and inconsistent, culture as evidence of a shared identity. In sound, images, objects, and the built environment, Americans sought out the signs of nationhood. Though "nationhood" is an abstraction, these signs testified to its material promise; they evoked what many Americans fondly considered its inevitability, its historical destiny, and its looming imminence. For them, material representations of the nation were signs of Providence working out the favorable circumstances of nationhood in the manner conveyed by the all-seeing eye of God on the reverse side of the American Great Seal, created in 1782 at the request of the revolutionary Congress. The eye beams hermetically from the apex of a pyramid, where it floats confidently beneath the Latin incantation *annuit coeptis*, "He has favored (our) undertakings." Americans cling to the notion, even affixing the image in the form of a talisman to the backside of their currency.

The power of language to conjure nationhood was not lost on the founding generation. One of the first things that American educators did when the

FIGURE 1   James Trenchard, "The Reverse of the Great Seal of the United States," engraved for *The Columbian Magazine*, September 1786, facing p. 51. Courtesy of the Library of Congress.

new nation was founded was publish schoolbooks for the cultural formation of young American citizens. The young Noah Webster set out in 1783, even before America had signed a treaty to end its war with Britain, to revise educational practice and provide an authoritative textbook for teaching English in the schools, even stipulating how American English was to be spoken by including a "standard of pronunciation." Webster described in a letter to a Connecticut politician that year his hopes for his new book and nation:

> The more I look into our language and the methods of instruction practiced in this country, the more I am convinced of the necessity of improving one and correcting the other. . . . I must think that next to the sacred writings, those books which teach us the principles of science and lay the basis on which all our future improvements must be built, best deserve the patronage of the public. An attention to literature must be the principal bulwark against the encroachments of civil and ecclesiastical tyrants.[2]

Language, literature, and the Bible became vital parts of America's civic arsenal for the protection of democracy. Americans were nervous about the ability of democracy to work and were rather certain it would not unless education intervened to help make citizens capable of literacy and the liberal virtue of self-sacrifice. Teaching young Americans how to speak and write the English language was for Noah Webster a way of achieving national unity and stability. For later Whig Protestants from the Northeast and the western states, education was a way to assimilate the polyglot of the new nation and thereby to direct the rising influx of immigrants.

We get a snapshot of anxieties about the sounds of democracy in Washington Irving's well-known story "Rip Van Winkle," published in 1819. Irving contrasted the quiet soundscape of provincial village life in colonial America to the din of the early national period. Awakening from his enchanted sleep, the anachronistic Rip Van Winkle stumbles into town in the midst of a national election that pits Federalist against Democrat. The noise of the new democracy is almost unintelligible to him as he drifts into the clamoring marketplace: "There was a busy, bustling, disputatious tone about it, instead of the accustomed phlegm and drowsy tranquility" of his former life.[3] Van Winkle's old chums, the village sages who used to gather daily on the steps of the local inn to peruse old newspapers and exchange worn stories, have been replaced by a new discourse conducted by a "bilious-looking fellow, with his pockets full of handbills," who harangues listeners about such things as "rights of citizens—elections—members of congress—liberty—Bunker's Hill—heroes of seventy-six—and other words, which were a perfect Babylonish jargon to the bewildered Van Winkle." As Christopher Looby has noted, the reference to Babylon suggests a comparison of modern America to the biblical story of Babel, the looming tower to human vanity that precipitated the scatter of primitive humanity into a linguistic diaspora.[4] The story of Rip Van Winkle captures what must have seemed to many Americans a sudden loss of the slower pace and rooted social structures of colonial life as the press of a new political order unleashed a rush of print and a higher pitch of rhetorical assaults.

Teaching young people how to speak as Americans was not separated from teaching them what to see and revere as patriotic citizens. Primers and spellers were commonly illustrated, during the first half of the nineteenth century, with images of pious acts and national heroes such as George Washington at prayer on the eve of a battle during the Revolutionary War. This image illustrated a primer published in 1844, which considered prayer the American child's earliest form of speech and sought to demonstrate the power of that speech in the person of the nation's icon. Word and image were carefully combined to teach the lessons of citizenship.[5] The line between religion and national identity was never clearly defined, since the role of civil piety was considered important in securing a literate and loyal citizenry in the new republic. This lack of clarity has been a source of both endless controversy and robust self-determination, since it has refused to empower any single party in the ongoing debate over national identity. The history of American art and popular imagery provides a rich record of the attempt among American artists and viewers to visualize American identity. In prints, paintings, sculptures,

FIGURE 2   General Washington at prayer, *The Illuminated American Primer*
(New York: Turner & Hayden, 1844), 34. Courtesy of the American Antiquarian Society.

photographs, and drawings, we find diverse paths in the quest for national character. What are the memories and stories Americans treasure? What are the national rituals and ceremonies they preserve? What places capture the national imagination? What is sacred when they think about who Americans are? How do images make some people visible and others invisible in the interpretation of national character and mission?

One of the oldest, most traditional ways in which Americans have told themselves who they are is by erecting monuments to their heroes as a way of publicly remembering what they did and how the present is rooted in the achievements of the past. The head of George Washington is certainly the most widely recognized "American" image in our culture. From the earliest days of the American republic, first General and then President Washington was the "father" of the American nation.[6] It was his military leadership and republican wisdom that helped birth the nation and guide it through its first, perilous moments. In 1785, the French sculptor Jean Antoine Houdon came to Mt. Vernon, Virginia, to create a bust of Washington by taking a mold from life. Houdon then cast a clay model, which he retouched according to the neoclassical fashion of his day. Washington looks more like an ancient Roman senator or Greek hero than he does an eighteenth-century landowner. But the solemn expression, smooth complexion, square features, and prominent forehead conformed to the classical ideal of nobility. Washington's actual appearance was translated into the visual language of heroism. The international iconography of republicanism became the neoclassical style, which is evident in Thomas Jefferson's choice of architecture for his home as well as the campus of the University of Virginia. The same visual idiom shaped the design for Washington, D.C., and the buildings of the federal government from the mid-nineteenth century to the mid-twentieth.[7]

Houdon's sculpture became the prototype for thousands of public monuments placed in parks, museums, libraries, and schools. It even ended up on the quarter. The bronze bust carries on its verso a "certificate and oath" from the New York bronze founder who cast it in 1898, indicating that the work is a "perfect reproduction of the Life-Cast" by Houdon. This assurance of authenticity mattered to patriotic Americans because they wanted "the real thing," an icon of their country's father. This image, rivaled only by certain portraits of Abraham Lincoln, has been the official symbol of American identity for generations because it symbolizes the ideal of

FIGURE 3   After Jean Antoine Houdon, *Bust of George Washington*, 1898. Courtesy of the Brauer Museum of Art, Valparaiso University, Gift of the Class of 1898 in memory of Prof. Kinsey, 48.3.

85

heroic self-denial that many Americans have historically wished to serve as the origin of the nation. Washington avoids any expression of emotion because he represents a fusion of individual and type into the single figure of the archetypal national hero. He calls attention not to himself but to the nobility of virtuous deeds, those that create the national character that John F. Kennedy had in mind when he urged Americans to ask not what their country could do for them, but what they could do for their country.

Even if many Americans today are unmoved by the call for republican selflessness symbolized by the neoclassical severity of Houdon's portrait, Washington remains the most familiar president, in part because his image has presided over so many of the national rituals and ceremonies in which Americans have participated. The Fourth of July, Veterans Day, Memorial Day, Presidents Day, and any pilgrimage to the Mall in Washington, D.C., is incomplete without the face of Washington. His portrait was used in the early editions of Noah Webster's *American Speller* and by a host of American primers, the basic schoolbooks for generations of American youth from the late eighteenth century throughout the nineteenth century. This very public portrait quickly became the core of an American civil religion in antebellum America, a set of images, rites, places, and documents (such as the Declaration of Independence and the Constitution) that all Americans were thought to hold in common. As sectional tensions rose between North and South, common symbols such as Washington became a way of identifying uniform American values.

But the center could not hold. Moreover, it only contained white America. African Americans and Native Americans did not enjoy equality in the mythos of nationhood. It took the national travail of the Civil War to begin the march toward freedom, a development consecrated by the carnage of the war and commemorated by the Freedman's Monument by Thomas Ball, paid for largely by funds raised by former slaves and unveiled near the Capitol building on April 14, 1876. The date itself was significant. It was not the anniversary of Lincoln's signing of the Emancipation Proclamation (January 1, 1863) but the eve of his assassination, April 15, 1865, remembered in the year of the nation's centennial celebration, 1876. The image shows Lincoln granting freedom to a slave, who kneels at his feet, still bearing a manacle about his wrist. Lincoln stands beside a Roman altar, holding the presidential proclamation of freedom for slaves in the rebel states. His gesture bids the kneeling man arise a freed one, unburdened of the state of oppression. But the floating grace of the extended fingers and the stark contrast of standing and kneeling figures charge the gesture with something more. In fact, the grouping is not unlike the portrayal of Christ in the first American illustrated edition of Harriet Beecher Stowe's *Uncle Tom's Cabin* (1853), where a standing Christ raises an arm in an exalted gesture of deliverance as Tom kneels humbly before him, the darkness of his skin contrasting with the

FIGURE 4   Thomas Ball, Freedmen's Monument, 1876, National Mall, Washington, D.C.
Courtesy Library of Congress, Division of Prints and Photographs.

lily whiteness of the solemn savior.[8] It is the postresurrection Jesus, heavily robed, with a cruci-
form staff in his other hand, the traditional symbol of Christ's victory over death. The association resonates with the date of the unveiling of Thomas Ball's monument, as if the final deed
and purpose of Lincoln's life was to free slaves in an act of sacrificial redemption. Standing at
the altar of the republic's civil religion, the martyr–high priest–savior dispenses liberation, and
in doing so on the anniversary of the nation is inserted into the national *cultus* beside
Washington.[9]

   This visual re-remembering of Lincoln's legacy resonates in a literary remembrance that
drew from Ball's iconography without acknowledging it. In his *Incidents and Anecdotes of the
Civil War* (1885), Admiral David Porter enhanced the Christological hagiography that Ball's
sculpture affixed to Lincoln's memory by relating the account of Lincoln's encounter with an
aged slave when he visited the city of Richmond, Virginia, near the end of the war. Porter, who
accompanied Lincoln, told the story that, as the president's boat approached the river's shore,
the old slave saw him and exclaimed, "Dere is de great Messiah! I knowed him as soon as I seed

FIGURE 5   Jesus appears to Uncle Tom, illustration in chapter 38 of Harriet Beecher Stowe, *Uncle Tom's Cabin* (Philadelphia: John P. Jewett, 1853). Courtesy Library Company of Philadelphia.

him. He's bin in my heart fo'long yeahs, an' he's cum at las' to free his chillun from deir bondage! Glory, Hallelujah!" Porter then wrote that the old man "fell upon his knees before the President and kissed his feet."[10] As if to compound the Christological iconography, Porter then switched to another image familiar in Christian art, portraying Lincoln as the Man of Sorrows: "It was a touching sight—that aged negro kneeling at the feet of the tall, gaunt-looking man who seemed in himself to be bearing all the grief of the nation, and whose sad face seemed to say, 'I suffer for you all, but will do all I can to help you.'"[11]

Lincoln then looked down and implored the slave to cease the homage. "Don't kneel to me," he objected. "That is not right. You must kneel to God only, and thank him for the liberty you will hereafter enjoy." Porter ended his account by appearing to conceal its debt to Ball's statue: "What a fine picture it would have made—Mr. Lincoln landing from a ship-of-war's boat, an aged negro on his knees at his feet. . . . In the foreground should be the shackles he had broken when he issued his proclamation giving liberty to the slave."[12] Porter's coyness rubs thin here, for Ball's sculpture, as noted above, included a broken shackle about the kneeling man's arm.

The liturgical logic of American civil religion presents Lincoln as the Great Emancipator and quietly ignores the emancipated, as if the event were not about the millions of enslaved human beings who had been submitted to injustice for two centuries but about the white hero who gave his life to free them. The illogic of this view was challenged on the very day of the monument's unveiling by Frederick Douglass, who spoke on the occasion to the gathering of white citizens at the foot of the statue. "Abraham Lincoln was not, in the fullest sense of the word, either our man or our model. In his interests, in his associations, in his habits of thought, and in his prejudices, he was a white man." Douglass went on to point out that Lincoln was "the white man's President, entirely devoted to the welfare of the white man."[13] These words strike latter-day ears with considerable force, but in the Civil War era and after, Lincoln's reputation varied widely. The nation was in the process of sorting out its view of Lincoln, since the view of Lincoln became a way of viewing the nation, of determining the meaning of the Civil War and its legacy. It was not until the following generation's spate of biographies, in the context of the sacralization of the American flag and the formation of American nationalism, that Lincoln was recast in patriotic memory as a more consistently saintly figure. As for Douglass, his speech refused to pull punches. He correctly observed that, during the early years of his presidency, Lincoln asserted the priority of the Union over the fate of American slaves in matters relating to the war. "First, midst, and last, you and yours," he addressed his white audience, "were the objects of his deepest affection and his most earnest solicitude. . . . To you it especially belongs to sound his praises, to preserve and perpetuate his memory, to multiply his statues, to hang his pictures high upon your walls, and commend his example, for to you he was a great and glorious friend and benefactor."[14] Yet Douglass did not fail to recognize Lincoln's significance. He was a Moses to American Blacks rather than a white Jesus—"he saved for you a country, he delivered us from bondage." Flawed though this Moses was, attending first to political expediency and the pragmatic demands of statesmanship and only second to the abolition of slavery, Lincoln was nevertheless the agent of change that kept the country together and decisively ended slavery. By dwelling on the man's many failures and mixed motives, however, Douglass strained to remind his white fellow citizens that the monument's and nation's apotheosis of Lincoln missed the mark. But the move toward a nationalistic *cultus* of Lincoln prevailed, installing him beside Washington in popular imagination as a central figure in American civil religion.

Violence and suffering often establish the sacred spaces and saints of civil religion, such as battlegrounds or heroes like Lincoln and Martin Luther King, Jr. The power of civil religion is its broad public recognition and its centrality in government and government-sponsored activities, such as public school (think of the Pledge of Allegiance), national holidays, and the courtroom (where Washington's, Lincoln's, or King's portraits are likely to hang). A civil religion is a public and formal construction of memory and common purpose through an apparatus of rituals that rely on images, music, and other art forms to organize collective consciousness. Yet there is not one American civil religion but at least two, corresponding to rival totems: the Statue of Liberty with emphasis on individual rights and dissent, and the American flag, whose nationalistic adoration as a sacred object raised above blasphemous desecration stresses homogeneity and sometimes xenophobic intolerance of foreigners. The two civil religions may be named patriotism and nationalism. The one interprets the task of American democracy as to preserve liberty; the other, to safeguard national unity.

If many Anglo-Saxon Americans have wanted to believe that their nation is grounded in racial destiny and Christian providence, the reality is that the nation has resulted from immigration and colonization, a dense intermixture of racial and ethnic groups over many generations. But the influx of newcomers should not be allowed to conceal the important set of alliances that secured the American state internationally. Strongly identifying with Britain and Germany, to which the bulk of its citizens traced their ethnic and cultural heritage, Americans relied on a collective imagination of "civilization" to locate their national project within the global maze of mutual and conflicting interests. Imagining nationhood is never merely an internal affair. External moorings fix the nation within a larger context of mission or purpose. Intimately encoded in such imaginings are the deep stories of race and ethnicity that inform a people's identity. This becomes visible in what might be called the "liminal gaze" that a nation casts beyond its borders, demarcating the boundaries of its kin or kind from the threshold of the "other." An illustration from *Harper's Weekly*, for instance, drawn by Thomas Nast, no doubt captures what many Americans felt about the structure of their world in the last quarter of the nineteenth century. The image appeared in the summer of 1878, during the Congress of Berlin, which was hosted by Otto von Bismarck in order to mediate conflict surrounding the treaty that had recently ended the war between Russia and Turkey. The leading powers of Europe—Britain, France, Austria-Hungary, Germany, Italy, and Russia—met with the Ottoman Empire and several small Balkan states, all of which had their own and conflicting interests. Nast drew the confrontation between Western Europe and the pan-Slavic movement promoted by Slavophiles in Moscow, which gathered the energies of embattled and occupied nationalities in the Balkans. These are collectively represented by the "Cossack" centaur. The clash is between "civilization," dedicated to republican or constitutional government (symbolized by the Greek temple and Britannia-Athena), and the barbaric force of the creature. The centaur comes from ancient Greek iconography, where he embodied the unruly, libidinous forces that attacked civilization in the famous battle of the Centaurs and the Lapiths. "Halt, Cossack!" Britannia demands. "So far, but no farther!" In fact, Britain had been able to bring Russia to the table only by threatening war. Nast sees the conflict as Britannia thwarting the advance of pan-Slavism over the fragments of Turkish weaponry, remnants of the Russian and Turkish War. Fading in the distance, beyond the dark chasm that separates civilization from barbarism, is a Muslim

FIGURE 6   Thomas Nast, illustrator, "Halt, Cossack!--So far, but no farther!" *Harper's Weekly*
22, no. 1122 (June 29, 1878): 512-13. Courtesy Brauer Museum of Art.

mosque of Constantinople, marked by the crescent and prayer tower. If Europe had once been delimited by the threat of Islam at its borders, now it was Slavic nationalism and Russian imperialism that menaced the precinct of civilization. An article in the same issue of *Harper's* praised Bismarck for asserting "a strong Protestant impulse that places him far in advance of the reactionary faction."[15] It was Anglo-Saxon Protestant rule that would curb Slavic ambitions. But *Harper's* failed to note that the German emperor was no republican. Moreover, concealed by the nobility of Nast's Grecian imagery is the bald self-interest of Britain, which had sought to bolster Turkey in the Crimean War as well as in the aftermath of Turkey's war with Russia in order to protect its route to colonial India. Germany, for its part, wanted to isolate Russia from Western European alliance.[16] Liminal vision allows viewers to see only what it considers worthy of seeing. The power of images is sometimes their ability to dissemble.

Another example of the liminal gaze in American culture is one turned inward. In the cultural logic of Anglo national mythology, the Native American had to vanish or assimilate in order for the landscape to be appropriated to the mission providentially designated for it. Missionaries set to work to convert Indians, but many whites concluded that the Native race would not survive subjugation. As a result, the commonplace of the "vanishing Indian" arose.[17]

In 1827 a Baptist preacher named Samuel Eastman lauded the noble cause of God's "American Israel" and pointed to the West "as the grand theatre on which he intends to transact much of that preliminary business which must precede the universal reign of righteousness and peace in the world."[18] Eastman recounted the national narrative of Protestantism, beginning with the Pilgrims at Plymouth, who occupied a land that had hitherto been "a mere waste place in the creation of God" and "a hunting ground for heathen tribes of men."[19] In the course of the nineteenth century, the "vanishing Indian" became a familiar trope in the rhetoric of Anglo Protestant nationalism, constructing a view of national identity that endorsed the "manifest destiny" of one people at the expense of another. In 1855 Henry Wadsworth Longfellow published *The Song of Hiawatha*, a book-length epic poem that celebrates the culture of the Ojibwa, culminating in the departure of the poem's hero, Hiawatha, upon the arrival of Europeans, including a Jesuit missionary. The image of Hiawatha paddling his canoe into the sunset was a paradigmatic representation of the Native American for many Anglos, who regarded the American continent as a providential gift to the progress of *their* civilization. By marking the edge of the nation, the photograph of Hiawatha constructs a mythic center of nationhood as the point from which viewers watch Hiawatha limning the boundary.

But it is also true that many whites lamented the decline of Native American culture. Moreover, the photograph reproduced here was not created by nostalgic or triumphalist Anglo-Americans. It was created by a group of Ojibwa in the late nineteenth century who, though long converted to Christianity, enthusiastically used Longfellow's poem as the basis for staging an annual play in the round, recounting the legend of Hiawatha. The Ojibwa welcomed Longfellow's poem as a compelling record of their folkways. A woman who created an illustrated lecture on the saga of Hiawatha and incorporated the photographs by the Ojibwa, including Figure 7, in her presentation referred to the production as "the Oberammergau of North America," that is, the Passion play of Native Americans.[20] In this reading of the Ojibwa play, which was enacted on an island in Lake Huron just beyond the Canadian border, Hiawatha becomes a Christ figure who is crucified on the cross of cultural subjection for the sake of his people. The use of the Christian trope of the sacrificial savior conveys the intercultural complexity of Native American and Anglo relations. Even though the Ojibwa relied on a poem created by a white man and had themselves converted to Christianity, they were able to infuse the vanishing Indian motif with a religious and cultural significance that redeemed it from securing their doom and cultural acquiescence. The result was not a return to a precontact state of affairs, but neither was it mere subjugation to white culture or seamless assimilation.

The trope of Christ's passion transformed the travail of Native Americans into a redemptive suffering that tailored a special relationship between the oppressed culture and the god of the nation, making a place for the Indians within the national narrative. Something similar took

FIGURE 7   Hiawatha departing into the sunset, photographer unknown. Katherine Bowden Papers,
Christopher Center Library, Valparaiso University.

place in the Civil Rights movement of the mid-twentieth century when Martin Luther King, Jr., asserted that "unearned suffering is redemptive."[21] From that perspective, lynching, beating, threats of violence, and the deeds of bigots morphed into the abuses suffered by a righteous and innocent people in the manner of Christ's passion. The very religious motif of exceptionalism, of the American Israel, could be applied with equal force by groups long marginalized by whites. If exceptionalism could be used by the dominant culture to authorize American imperialism and a cult of nationalism, it could also be deployed by the oppressed within the nation to reinscribe their place within the national mythos.

The landscape has remained one of the most potent forms of collective imagination among Americans. The American frontier had been for generations a providential affirmation of American national destiny and had been captured in the sublime style of landscape painting by such painters as Frederic Church, Albert Bierstadt, and Jasper Cropsey. Each of these painters belonged to the so-called Hudson River School, following the example of Thomas Cole in seeking out the native power and appeal of the American landscape: in particular, the Hudson River

Valley in New York State, as well as such spectacular scenery as Niagara Falls and Lake George. When the New York art and literary critic Adam Badeau viewed Frederic Church's painting *Niagara* (1857), he considered it "perhaps the finest picture yet done by an American; at least, that which is fullest of feeling."[22] When Badeau looked at Church's painting, he saw the compelling traces of national character. The painting displayed:

> a true development of American mind; the result of democracy, of individuality, of the expansion of each, of the liberty allowed to all; of ineradicable and lofty qualities in human nature. It is inspired not only by the irresistible cataract, but by the mighty forest, by the thousand miles of river, by the broad continent we call our own, by the onward march of civilization, by the conquering savage areas; characteristic alike of the western back-woodsman, of the Arctic explorer, the southern filibuster, and the northern merchant. So, of course, it gets expression in our art.[23]

When Americans like Badeau looked at the sublime power of the American landscape as it was celebrated in paintings like Church's, they did not see the romantic past, the trackless wilderness of an unpopulated domain, but its conquest—the "march of civilization." They beheld the future, the raw materials fueling national progress. And they saw a deft match between national character and material landscape. Badeau and most of his contemporaries lamented the apprenticeship of American culture to its European superiors and longed to recognize indigenous genius. The landscape represented this as a kind of rough matrix bearing a new national culture. "Let us prefer Indian girls to Greek slaves," Badeau proclaimed, "American originals to copies of old and effete ideas."[24]

Looking back to his native land from the intimidating social hierarchies of London, painter Jasper Cropsey produced the largest landscape he'd yet attempted in 1860, *Autumn—on the Hudson River*. In it he sought to capture the emerging harmony of divinity, landscape, and human presence: the mid-afternoon sun illuminates a color-drenched scene overlooking the Hudson, shining down like the biblical star over an occidental Bethlehem (the town of New Windsor) on the shore of the river. The trees in the foreground part to frame the sun's epiphany, its luminous streams descending to form the sharp contours of a vast pyramid. The contemporary British poet William Cox Bennett published a poem on the painting, in which he contrasted the lesser "Nature" of England to the divine revelation envisioned in Cropsey's painting, which had roused a sensation when displayed in London in 1860:

> God, glorified in nature, fronts us there,
> In His transcendent works as heavenly fair

FIGURE 8   Jasper Francis Cropsey, *Autumn—on the Hudson River,* 1860. Courtesy of the National Gallery of Art, Washington, D.C. Gift of the Avalon Foundation 1963.9.1.

As when they first seemed good unto His eyes.
See, what a brightness on the canvas lies!
Hues, not seen here, flash on us everywhere;
Radiance that Nature here from us conceals;
Glory with which she beautifies decay
In your far world, this master's hand reveals,
Wafting our blest sight from dimmed streets away.[25]

The glory of Cropsey's landscape whisked the London-bound eyes of the poet to the rustic beauty of radiant America. Considering the bleakness of industrial London, it is not difficult to understand the poet's contrast of a divinely infused and luminous nature to the dimness and decay of urban England. But when many Americans looked appreciatively at rural America, it was also to look away from metropolitan America, which they linked to the loss of the national soul and its perversion in the nation's urban citizens. The city was regarded as a dangerous, degenerative place. One clergyman writing at mid-century conveyed the alarm of those who regarded the menace of city life to be a debilitating effect: "The unremitted cares of business, the rage of passions, the fury of politics, the restlessness of ambition, the thirst of gold, the struggles of competition, overtax the physical, intellectual, and nervous constitution, and doom it to the depressive horrors and enfeebled state of reaction; and fast wear out human life. . . .

The soul has too many points of contact with the human world, and is contaminated and degraded by it."[26] Humans were intended for village and farm, where rhythms were slower and life more consistent and homogeneous. And, Cropsey's painting would aver, exposure to the benevolent irradiation of the divine is a more constant source of spiritual nurture.

Yet the rise of national wealth and industrial productivity, fueled by the labor of immigrant workers and a vast landscape rich in natural resources, focused energy in the nation's major cities. Increasing numbers of people settled in or near cities, and a slow demographic shift from countryside to city was under way over the course of the century. By 1900, the American city had become a potent symbol of national power. If the wilderness landscape was the physical expression of divine promise, the city was proof of national productivity, America come of age, a dynamo of industrial achievement and financial growth. Reginald Marsh's *Skyline from Pier 10, Brooklyn* communicates the excitement that Americans old and new had come to feel about the urban landscape, with its towering heights and endless bustle, its hymns to technology and industry and the power of capitalism to transform the land into a modern metropolis. If the garden paradise had been the emblem of American ideals in the nineteenth century, the city captured many hopes in the twentieth as the promise of convenience, leisure, and opportunity. Marsh's image applies the visual formula of the sublime mountainscape of earlier painting to the energetic, irrepressible skyline of Manhattan. The work of humankind was replacing the handiwork of God. The crenellated building in the foreground and the looming skyscrapers

FIGURE 9   Reginald Marsh, *Skyline from Pier 10, Brooklyn*, 1931; reprint 1970.
Courtesy of the Brauer Museum of Art, Valparaiso University. Gift of Ester Sparks, 98.6.

suggest the proud edifices of a modern Babel. This is a powerful example of American optimism and pride, of boundless hope in what national industry and a robust economy can do. Anchored confidently in the foreground is a naval destroyer, symbol of American might.

But there were limits to this optimism, beyond which lurked a dark side to modern urban life. Edward Hopper's haunting paintings and prints of isolated city dwellers give dark glimpses into the psychological and social alienation that is the underbelly of voracious capitalist production. People, women and minorities in particular, are frequently isolated as the powerless and the victimized, as cogs in an immense economic apparatus that tends to reduce human beings to the exchange value of their labor. Hopper's subjects, lost in the urban night, peer desperately out of windows or emptily into coffee cups. Alienation also resounds in Thomas Hart Benton's retelling of the parable of a prodigal son, who has returned to the broken-down hovel of his childhood home. Victim of the dustbowl and the economic depression of the 1930s, Benton's prodigal may have left the failing homestead to find his fortune. He returns to his place of origin in search of something irreplaceable, but finds it destroyed. The wayward son is deprived of home, the place where the prodigal would secure the affirmation of his progress in the world, and is instead greeted by the sun-scorched skeleton of the fatted calf and the broken remains of his father's house. Home, this visual sermon seems to proclaim, is not a permanent feature of the American landscape.

FIGURE 10   Thomas Hart Benton, *The Prodigal Son*, 1936. Courtesy of Brauer Museum of Art, Valparaiso University.

The disastrous effects of the dustbowl and the Depression undermined the American dream and sent hundreds of thousands of impoverished laborers and farmers into a desperate migration westward, tragically captured in John Steinbeck's novel *The Grapes of Wrath* (1939) and in the film version of 1940. Adverse weather and the national banking crisis visited the Joad family in the form of the bank's foreclosure on the Oklahoma farm where they served as tenant farmers, resulting in their exodus to California, the American Promised Land since the Gold Rush in 1848, after the United States acquired the new territory in its war with Mexico. The exodus to find work in the fruit and vegetable farms of California is fraught with harassment and abuse by police, local residents, and farm owners, all of whom despise the itinerant masses—as one service-station worker said to another, watching the Joads' loaded jalopy pull away, "Them goddamn Okies got no sense and feeling. They ain't human. A human being wouldn't live like they do. A human being couldn't stand it to be so dirty and miserable. They ain't a hell of a lot better than gorillas."[27] Steinbeck's protagonists are encased throughout the novel in the economic injustice of capitalism. He used Christianity both to frame his critique of social inequity and to punctuate the desperation of refugees. Faced with dismal hunger and an endless line of migrants, Tom Joad and a lapsed preacher who accompanies him agree that prayer is useless: "Prayer never brought in no side-meat," Tom observes. "Yeah," the preacher replies, "An' Almighty God never raised no wages."[28] The preacher dies later, when he is hunted down by a band of vigilantes who regard the migrant workers as "reds." His death recalls the words of Jesus on the cross: "You fellas don' know what you're doin'," he addresses the mob, "You're helpin' to starve kids."[29] While Steinbeck portrayed an economic struggle in Marxist terms, chronicling the plight of the proletariat, the automobile in Benton's lithograph suggests that the returning prodigal was not the victim of economic oppression. Nevertheless, the grim message of the print comports with the systemic critique of Steinbeck's novel. The very infrastructure on which forgiveness relies in the biblical story of the prodigal son—the security of home and the enduring authority of patriarchy—has been crushed by climate change and financial disaster. As the preacher told Tom Joad, he "used to give all my fight against the devil 'cause I figgered the devil was the enemy. But they's somepin worse'n the devil got hold a the country, an' it ain't gonna let go till it's chopped loose."[30]

The Depression era and its art demonstrated that nature, the mythic stronghold of the nation's well-being, could fail in the manner of the dustbowl and that farm life could suffer capitalist exploitation. If that weren't dark enough, the older anxiety about life in the city has continued to haunt the American psyche. The dark side of the American city has received extensive treatment in a number of popular films, such as *The Out-of-Towners* (1970), *Escape from New York City* (1981), or the countless instantiations of Batman in film, animation, and comic books. The Gothic darkness of Tim Burton's *Batman* (1989) emulated the visual intricacy and sinister gloom of what has become a modern classic in the genre of the American urban wasteland, the sci-fi noir *Blade Runner* (1982). Los Angeles is a gritty, murky dystopia that seems to have devoured the rest of the nation. As a future city-state set in 2019, it bans all artificial life forms known as "replicants" from coming to earth. They are manufactured by the enormous commercial conglomerate Tyrell Corporation, whose corporate headquarters looms above the smoggy city as a giant *ziggurat*, a monstrous Tower of Babel reaching to the heavens. While Cropsey's sublime image of a solar pyramid channeled divine presence to the earth, incarnating a luminous architecture of benevolence, and Marsh's celebration of Manhattan's skyline praised the progressive good of technology, the pyramid of the Tyrell Corporation rises above Los Angeles with grim awe. The musical score used by director Ridley Scott invokes a precipitous decline, a decadent civilization steeped in exhaustion, a kind of splendid decay that promises impending demise. The moral capital compiled by Cropsey and invested by Marsh has long been spent. Judgment looms. The very idea is suggested by the fact that Tyrell provides the artificial forces for the colonization of other worlds, just as the "sons of God" interbred with the "daughters of men" to produce the antediluvian race of ancient giants that Yahweh angrily destroyed with the ancient flood (Genesis 6:1–8).

Replicants are regarded by the inhabitants of earth as subhuman slaves, who threaten revolt in much the same way that Frankenstein's monster in Mary Shelley's novel (1818) must avoid human contact because it is a botched and lethal form of human engineering. But *Blade Runner* suggests that the prohibition is motivated by a fear akin to white racist fear of Blacks, Latinos, and Asians. In the commercial release of the film, the police captain refers to replicants as "skin jobs," and Deckard, who narrates the film, compares him to the bigots of a former era. But the film makes clear that, by "othering" the replicants as nonhumans, earthlings bolster their uncertainty of their own humanity. The implication is that authenticity is a constructed affair, enforced by violence. There is no real difference between slave and master, replicant and human, black and white. The difference is merely perceived, socially constructed, and violently enforced.

Los Angeles is, of course, one of the most diverse and troubled major American cities for staging a story about race relations—the land of dreams, where films are made but where poverty and racial tension regularly erupt in urban chaos. In Philip K. Dick's novel *Do Androids Dream of Electric Sheep* (1968), on which the movie was based, androids (not called replicants) are described by one member of the police force as "murdering illegal *aliens* masquerading" as humans.[31] One thinks of the perennial anxiety of Americans regarding immigrants and the perceived need to fortify the national border with Mexico in order to keep out the Mexicans who slip into Southern California and Los Angeles seeking menial work that white Americans would rather not do. Ironically, what separates replicants from humans is their inability to empathize, which is determined by a technical apparatus. But it is the Blade Runners themselves who are unable to empathize, regarding the replicants, in the words of one enforcer, as "a barrier that keeps [replicants and humans] distinct."[32]

Images are a menace when they threaten to become real, to rival human beings as human, when the replicants are, in the Tyrell Corporation's slogan, "more human than human." Humans engineer the replicants in order to prevent them from becoming truly human. Human beings must be kept away from replicants because in them they will recognize the lie of their culture, the artifice of their own humanity, the fiction of whiteness, the myth of racial superiority. If you can't keep aliens out of the country, the country will become theirs, and your people will start to intermarry with their people. Perhaps this is one reason why so many Americans nowadays want to build a wall between the United States and Mexico. Female replicants are especially repellent and suffer graphic violation in the film because desire for them is overwhelming. Women represent the greatest danger of images, in the way that black women represented a great danger as slaves: miscegenation or interbreeding. So we watch the first termination occur to a scantily clad female replicant, falling in slow motion as Deckard hunts and assassinates her.

Deckard is redeemed from this racist ideology only when he falls in love with Rachel and is moved to feel compassion for her. Only by recognizing and embracing her humanity can he move from regarding her as a target and threat to engaging her as a moral equal, and in so doing become human himself, since, in the director's cut, he is himself a replicant. The final turn in his development occurs when the replicant Roy, whom Deckard has been hunting, suddenly saves Deckard rather than killing him. Like Frankenstein's monster, Roy seeks out his maker, Tyrell, who had made him a flawed creation, and asks for a better existence. When Tyrell is unable to comply, Roy kills him. Yet Roy spares Deckard, saving him with a hand punctured by a Christological nail.

Blade Runner argues that human beings can be redeemed in spite of their sins. Deckard goes from a hit-man mercenary and replicant himself to a compassionate lover; Rachel, from an unenlightened replicant to a genuine human being; Roy, from a Satanic murderer and rebellious angel (at one point he quotes the fall of Lucifer in Milton's *Paradise Lost*) to a genuine and compassionate human being. Roy and Deckard become human only when they each refuse to de-humanize others. Justice is the moral search for authenticity, discovered only in compassion toward others. *Blade Runner* recognizes two kinds of redemption: in the case of Deckard and Rachel, romantic love humanizes and redeems them; in the case of Roy, the film celebrates an Existentialist or even Buddhist self-mastery in the transformation of Roy (as he dies, he delivers a death poem that recalls a Japanese Zen tradition). Americans are like monsters that can be saved. The Armenian ideal of free will is far more attractive to the American myth of the self-made individual than the rigid Calvinist idea of predestination, which is much too tragic and fateful. If Darth Vader can be redeemed, so can Frankenstein's monster in the form of Roy. Though monsters must die for the evil they have committed, their death is redemptive.

Especially important to the American psyche are the geographic borders of oceans on each side of the continent, creating the illusion of an insular separation from the rest of the world. Americans prefer to wage war off native soil and rely on imagined projections of protective struggle like Figure 6 to nurture their sense of security. The war in Iraq is the latest example of exporting violence in order to prevent the homeland from suffering it. Taking the battle to the enemy means locating it off of native soil. Iraq quickly became a magnet for opponents of the United States, allowing them to fit into the mythic device of good versus evil that served the Bush Administration precisely because it is a powerful feature of the national imaginary. But this cultural logic encounters a complication in the case of Mexico, which shares a long border with the United States. The challenge of "invasion" by undocumented workers seeking employment renders the border porous and compromises the sense of security. Many Americans reject out of hand the demonstration that such workers actually contribute to the American economy and that they perform labor that most American citizens are not willing to undertake. The great majority of undocumented workers from Mexico and other countries do not intend to remain in the United States but plan to return to their homelands after making the money they came to seek. To date, places like Miami and Los Angeles have been border zones charged with violence, corruption, debauchery, and racial confusion. In some way, *Blade Runner* dramatizes the threat of the impurity of such places on the imagined map of the nation. But the film does not offer a satisfactory answer for most people. Compassion threatens the loss of personal as well as national sovereignty. As a way of closing the porous border with Mexico, many Americans support the construction of an impassable wall. The American Israel may become an image of contemporary Israel.

In spite of America's often bullish way with the world, people work out hybrid forms of identity, as the Ojibwa did with Hiawatha and the colonizer's Christianity. In the globalizing world of the present, though the myth of national sovereignty and cultural purity persists, Americans and Mexicans (like everyone else in the world) have come increasingly to live in one border zone or another. Graciela Iturbide's marvelous photograph *Angel/Woman* (1979) shows a Mexican woman in the Sonoran Desert fabricating her existence from a cultural past, a bleak landscape, and the consumerist world of American capitalism, represented by the ghetto blaster she totes through a difficult passage.[33] Cultural mythology notwithstanding, identity is not something one inherits intact or is destined to carry through life as a fixed burden. Character is the product of history, a shifting mix of cultures, and the choices that individual people make about the lives they wish to lead. Identity is negotiated between the present and the past. This

101

woman, a Seri Indian, whose face is hidden from view, walks in her traditional dress as if out of the magical space of a novel by Gabriel García Márquez. She is an anomaly but also a survivor, and more: she is a harbinger of a larger, future American identity. Walls notwithstanding, this mysterious Angel and Woman bears a message of what may come to pass as the border culture between Mexico and the United States broadens across North and Central America in a historical rhythm of change that we can now only begin to intuit.

The Visible and the Invisible in South Asia

Peter van der Veer

You may not have noticed it yet, but, according to some observers, democracy has arrived in the Middle East. It came as part of the shock and awe of the American invasion in Iraq and resulted in elections there that were declared a success. Now it is spreading all over the Middle East. Some years ago we saw a large anti-Syrian demonstration in Beirut on our television screens. Our commentators said that this was another sign of the coming of democracy, a process of transformation of the Middle East that was started by the American invasion of Iraq. No longer could the voice of the people be suppressed by corrupt elites. When the Shi'ite Hezbollah later organized an even larger pro-Syrian demonstration, our commentators were somewhat at loss whether this should also be interpreted as a sign of the coming of democracy. After the destruction of parts of Beirut by Israeli planes in a conflict with Hezbollah, nobody talked about the coming of democracy anymore.

Much of this representation follows the narrative and imagery of the fall of the Berlin Wall and ultimately of that primal scene, the storming of the Bastille in the French Revolution: the people finally get rid of dictatorship and take power in their own hands. Whether the facts on the ground are the same or even similar is doubtful, but the representation is the same for East Germany, Romania, Georgia, Kyrgyzstan, Iraq, and Lebanon. These are just a few instances of the worldwide soap opera of democracy we are enjoying daily on our televisions. It is hard to tell whether we are better informed about the world because of the availability of these images, are just better entertained, or are amused to death, as Neil Postman put it. However, there is little doubt that, with an increasing visibility of locales in a world market of images, there is no decrease in invisibility of practices and institutions in those locales. We see more, but we know perhaps not less but just as little. A good example of this is the representation of the Tiananmen demonstrations of 1989 in Beijing, which fits neatly into the narrative of the coming of democracy and its suppression and thus has been widely televised and circulated. Images of demonstrations by tens of thousands of members of Falun Gong in 1999 on the same square against the suppression of their so-called sect have scarcely been televised or circulated, since that story cannot be easily represented as a narrative of democracy. The actions of Falun Gong and the response by the Communist Party escape from this narrative frame, and one needs quite a bit of extra information to be able to interpret why breathing meditation is threatening to Communist rule in China. This dialectic of the seen and the unseen, of the visible and the invisible, occurs in many ways, and I will try in this presentation to make some of it visible. My main suggestion is that a focus on the visual register should involve a strong awareness of both what is made visible in state practices and what is made invisible, as well as a sense of the counterfactual nature of liberal claims of openness, transparency, and full accountability.

The nation form is a modern social configuration. Its modernity is shown in the emergence of a range of institutions and practices, including visual ones. Modernity is also shown in the disappearance of visual practices that are stigmatized as nonmodern or traditional. Foucault gives a famous European example when he speaks about the disappearance of the public execution, the spectacle of the auto-da-fé, the stake, and the gallows. This is such a good example because it connects the disappearance of the public execution to the rise of a number of other modern practices, such as new ideas of the person, of crime and punishment, and of mental health, which are part of new perceptions of the possibilities of the nation-state. It is also such a good example since it implicitly makes one think of the variability of modern arrangements existing today, since, indeed, public executions have not disappeared in China and Saudi Arabia, while in the United States witnesses are invited when the death penalty is carried out. One needs comparative work, as in this volume, to counter claims of a singular, universal modernity. While capital punishment is an ultimate sign of the power of the state to give and take life, it is only one in a repertoire of visual practices—such as flags, public commemorations, tombs of the unknown soldier, uniforms, and so on and so forth—that evoke the power of the state to symbolize the immortality of the nation in relation to the death of individual citizens.

A focus on the visual practices of the modern nation-state also brings to the fore the opposite of the visible, namely, the secret, hidden practices of the state. The modern state not only shows, it also hides. Spectators see only a part of reality and may say later that they did not know what happened, although it happened under their very eyes. Jews in Germany were not massacred in large-scale public executions but secretly in concentration camps. Prisoners are not flogged in public to be an example to others, but they are secretly tortured in order to find the truth they are hiding or just to humiliate them. When these practices are found out and made public, the discussion often turns to whether they belong to the formal side of the state or the informal one, like the economy.

One of the oldest state institutions dealing with the security of the state is indeed secret. The secret service is a central institution not only in undemocratic societies but also in democratic ones. That fact in itself is already very productive in creating collective fantasies of conspiracy, rumors, metaphysics of invisible presences, the romanticism of adventure in Kipling, Ian Fleming, and all the spy novelists. Intelligence and security deal not only with foreign powers that threaten the sovereignty of the state but also with internal forces of dissent and disloyalty. The difference between outward appearance and inward truth seems to be crucial here. People may appear to be loyal, law-abiding citizens, but behind their mask may be a loyalty to a foreign power and a secrecy about their true motives. It is striking how much this narrative of loyalty to the nation resembles the domestic narrative of spousal loyalty. In both cases, the indeterminacy of visibility and true motives fuels the drama of betrayal and punishment. Since anxiety about security has been heightened after 9/11, there is a strong sense in Europe that immigrants are loyal not to the nation-state but to foreign powers, such as global terrorism. This question of loyalty is as old as the Protestant Reformation in Western Europe, when it was raised mostly in relation to Catholic loyalty to Rome. It has received a new lease on life, however, with Muslim immigration to the West, so that now people have become anxious about whether there is even a clear Pope or Rome or Church. Visible signs of the difference of these immigrants, such as the famous headscarves in Europe, are interpreted as symbols of disloyalty to the nation-state that receives immigrants. But even in India, where Muslims have been living for a millennium, or, for that matter, in China there is a widespread feeling that Muslims are not loyal to the nation-state but secretly put their religion first. In that sense, they are a security issue for the institutions of the state. To follow out the metaphor of the domestic drama, this may lead to divorce, ethnic cleansing, or elimination.

Christian Europe seems to offer an example of this in early modern Spain's banishment of Jews and Muslims. On the very day in 1492 that Columbus set sail to what turned out to be the New World, he noted in his log the shiploads of Jews leaving their Old World home of a millennium under threat of death. Spain also offers a good example of the modern state's emphasis on making true motives visible, given that the Inquisition developed methods to find out the true loyalty of Spanish Jews and Muslims who were forcibly converted to Catholicism. In the seventeenth century, the Spanish state decided that true loyalty could not be determined, and a law was passed decreeing that the Moriscos be eliminated or deported, since they formed a different *nacion*."[1] One of the most interesting issues for my argument is that both the visibility of outward signs of difference and their invisibility can be interpreted as symbols of disloyalty to the state. One can show oneself to the outside world as a completely assimilated citizen and

105

still be suspected of having a different orientation in one's heart. And, like jealousy, such anxiety can take over bureaucratic rationality and lead to genocide, as we have seen over and over again, starting from the time when modern ideas of the nation emerged.

Not only the political power of the state but also its economic power is often invisible and deals with the invisible,. Money is an ultimate sign of a nation's sovereignty, as the word for the coin itself indicates and as the portraits and symbols and inscriptions on money signify. Moreover, the state's power depends on its tax base. Indeed, the welfare of the nation, as well as the effectiveness of the state, depends upon monetary value. Inflation, devaluation, revaluation, exchange value, the value of one's labor—all are signs of the health of the polity and the trust-worthiness of political leaders. The state guarantees the value of its money, and people hold a strong belief in the invisible power of the state when they hold visible coinage in their hands. The state is held accountable for the functioning of the market, and this is, in effect, more important for people's political judgment than most other fields of political action. Neverthe-less, the value of money depends on invisible market forces that are not controlled or are only partly controlled by the nation-state. So here again, as in espionage, the foreign hand comes in to explain sudden changes in the fortunes of the nation, and internally that foreign hand is helped by the disloyalty of marginal economic groups like Jews or Lebanese or Indians or Chinese, who connect the local to the global via trade and money lending. Since money signifies exchange and thus the basis of society itself, it attracts moral thought concerning the possibili-ties and limits of exchange. Money, then, is the source of evil, the province of the devil. And indeed much religious thought is focused on banking and interest. Islamic thought about sharia is only one instance of this. Through its fetishism and circularity, money transcends purity and opens social life up to corruption. Corruption is often considered to be the aspect of economic action that takes place behind the scenes, in the dark, but what about the invisible hand of the market itself? This is, again, a field of great fantasies of conspiracy and great, unfulfilled de-mands of transparency. And it immediately concerns the central institutions of the modern nation-state.

Not only the practices of the institutions of the state are made visible or invisible in particu-lar ways. It is also interesting to look at the visibility or invisibility of practices that are, as it were, conceived to be outside of the state, in civil society or in a sphere that is called "open" or "public": the public sphere. Not only are communication and "openness" crucial to civil society and the public sphere, as has been most prominently argued by Jürgen Habermas, but their opposite, secrecy, is also key. Reinhart Koselleck has argued that the emergence of the secret societies of Freemasonry was essential to the development of the Enlightenment critique of the Absolutist state.[2] The important point here is that in the eighteenth century the Masonic lodges were able to erect a wall protecting their debates and rituals from intrusion both by the state and by the profane world. It is precisely a moving away from state institutions and official politics that enables a fundamental moral critique of power. It should be clear, however, that this critique can take an unpleasant and terrorist form, as it did in the Jacobin theory of the French Revolution. This uncomfortable dialectic between secrecy and critique troubled German theorists like Habermas and Koselleck after the Second World War. Both in civil society and in the state, there is a constant creative tension between what is made visible and what is made invisible.

The changing nature of technologies of publicity and secrecy, such as nowadays the Internet, is of crucial importance in understanding both state power and its critique in the public sphere. It is certainly not true that one gets better informed with the growth of media, such as television, that produce more and more images of the world. Behind that growing visibility is a growing invisibility. However, the development of technologies of communication, including the visual, is important in the transformation of society into the nation form. Benedict Anderson focuses on the print revolution of early capitalism for understanding the rise of the national imaginary.[3] In his view, the modern public of the nation is a reading public. I would think, however, that the story of the nation in many areas is also a story of the uneven spread of literacy. The public sphere may, in Habermas's terms, be bourgeois and thus literate, but in the formation of the nation an illiterate mass has to be mobilized not by texts but by images and sounds. In South Asia, as elsewhere, starting in the second half of the nineteenth century, the mass production of images fostered an imagination of the nation. To this was added radio, with all the implications of which language would be chosen for broadcasts, Hindi, Urdu, or the mixed Hindustani. Before Partition, a Hindi poet (S. H. Vatsyayan, or Agyeya) and an Urdu essayist (Chaudhuri Hassan Hazrat) together made a concerted attempt to create a lexicon for Hindustani broadcast, but this effort was immediately aborted after Partition. Yet the language of *Bollywood* films is still Hindustani, showing how far the popular ear extends beyond the limits of the nation.

Liberal theorists often understand the modern nation-state to be secular. That is somewhat strange, since religious movements have played such an important role in the rise of nationalism everywhere. Nevertheless, there is a widespread ideal among liberals and socialists alike that religion should be a private matter and not a public affair. We can only conclude that this ideal has not been realized in many nation-states that appear to be modern, such as the United States, Poland, and Ireland. For me, religion is one of the most important fields of social practice and is constitutive of the modern nation-state. In my view, Anderson downplays the importance of religion in the emergence of the modern national consciousness, although he shows an awareness of the connection between print capitalism and the Protestant Reformation. It is, however, not primarily the novel but the printed Bible and religious tracts that were crucial in the rise of a modern consciousness. Religion was nationalized in the various discourses of modernity throughout the nineteenth-century world and had a productive and necessary dialectic with secular nationalism. During this period, religious movements all over the world make ample use of new visual technologies to produce a visual culture for the masses that became crucial for their understanding not only of their religious beliefs but also of the connection between religion and nation. In the United States, already in the nineteenth century the evangelical movement for a Christian America was built on that. And there is nothing nonmodern about it, although it is not secular.

Religious ritual is certainly a spectacle and a theater productive of strongly held beliefs. It is also a source of secular rituals of the nation-state and of its ideology, or, as Carl Schmitt puts it, its political theology. Many authors have pointed out that secular nationalism has a religious origin. I would, rather, argue that what we understand as the religious and the secular are mutually dependent. Moreover, the structural opposition of the secular and the religious is transformed in the rise of the nation-state. Secular nationalism must find its legitimacy in the culture, the language, and the history of a people, and religion is always part of that. Religious nationalism always has to come to terms with the secularization of the law, the market, and science. Under colonial conditions modern education arrives under the flag of missionary Christianity, as it does in the Syrian Protestant College, renamed the American University of Beirut, where the plaque on the main gate bears the biblical words "That they may have life, and have it more abundantly." "This College is for all conditions and classes of men without regard to color, nationality, race or religion," its founder Daniel Bliss argued in 1871: "A man, white, black or yellow: Christian, Jew, Mohammedan or heathen, may enter and enjoy all the advantages of this institution for three, four or eight years; and go out believing in one God, in many Gods, or in no God. But it will be impossible for any one to continue with us long without knowing what we believe to be the truth and our reasons for that belief." The dialectic of the secular and the religious is so deeply intertwined in defining social life that it is hard to disentangle, and perhaps it is not always useful to do so.

Religious practices and institutions, such as rituals, processions, churches, temples, and images, have an abundance of visual richness, so much so that secularists often deplore the visual poverty of secular rituals of marriage and death. Nevertheless, religion seems to be primarily concerned with the invisible, with the afterlife, with God, with the soul, with spirits. According to William James, religion is founded on the subjective experience of an invisible presence. This may be true, but we have only access to that subjective experience through the mediation of concrete, visible practices, such as speaking, writing, and acts of worship. At the same time, these acts may be considered to produce an experience of the invisible. There is a whole range of activities that induce religious dispositions and concern the relation between human subjects and the invisible. Crucial in that mediation is, precisely, invisibility or virtuality. There is always uncertainty and indeterminacy about the addressee and the success of communication. I would suggest that this is also true for the relation between subject and state, and I do not find it surprising that interpreters of that brilliant novel about modernity, Kafka's *The Trial*, hesitate between the state and religion when discussing invisible power. There seems to be a secularity to the spiritual and a spirituality to the secular that are totally neglected by liberal theorists of the state.

Given the fragmentary nature of nationalism, allow me to give you now a few snapshots of the visual imagery that is part of the wide array of practices involved in producing the nation-as-space. First of all, let us enter a country. One has to cross a border, which is often not very visible. The arbitrary nature of the border is made clear in border conflicts. In South Asia, the border between Pakistan and India is particularly a site of dispute and ultimately armed conflict. A good example of this is the Kargil conflict in 1999. India and Pakistan share a 740-kilometer line of control along the Jammu-Srinagar and Srinagar-Leh roads. We are talking here about an uninhabitable area of ice and snow. There are a number of outposts that get snowbound and must be "abandoned" by both sides until the snow melts. This leads to a game in which both parties try to seize "unoccupied" posts. In 1999, Pakistan infiltrated across a frontier of 100 kilometers or so in the Kargil area. In reply, the Indian army conducted what it called "one of the biggest anti-militancy operations in recent years." Highly successful air strikes by India were followed by the shooting down of two Indian jet fighters and an armed helicopter. An open war seemed unavoidable, but Pakistan decided, after a number of skirmishes, to withdraw.

Two things about this conflict have made a lasting impression on me. The first is the visual imagery of soldiers in a landscape that may have seemed attractive from the 50-degrees-centigrade heat of Delhi and Lahore but that is, in fact, completely uninhabitable, impenetrable and forbidding. This kind of military effort to control such an unattractive area shows the importance of the idea of the nation-as-space. Long before the Kargil conflict, in 1962 the Indians had suffered defeat in another forbidding part of the Himalaya Mountains in a conflict with China. This continued to be a major source of national humiliation, as if one had not been able to protect one's house against intruders. Second, I had seldom seen Indians in such a frenzy of patriotic emotions as during the Kargil crisis. Let us listen to the language of patriotism:

With unrelenting courage and fierce determination, our brave soldiers are guarding the country from the enemy's clutches. Facing danger at every step and hostile weather conditions, they put their lives at risk. Forsaking the comforts of home and family life for a life of hardship and danger, it's their unwavering love for their motherland that spurs them on. This is dedicated to the brave men of our soil who embrace danger and even death willingly for the sake of the country. This is the tribute to their indomitable will, their stoic courage, and their intense love for nation.

The impenetrable mountain range is an excellent backdrop for this narrative of masculine heroism and hero-worship. In the end it is not territory as such that counts but the way the landscape as a background for heroism functions to represent the honor and sovereignty of the nation. Nation-as-space is made real by the representational theater of the Kargil conflict. This is a secular space, although the roots of the conflict between India and Pakistan are communal or religious. Much of that spatial imagination of the nation is based on imperial mapping, and one of the nationalists projects is to provide a precolonial mapping that can offer deeper roots for the nation as space. For Savarkar, the ideologue of Hindutva, the basis of a Hindu nation is the sacred geography of India. *Pitrbhhumi*, or Fatherland, is *punyabhumi*, sacred land. Modern discourse on the nation as a territorially based community is connected to religious discourse on sacred space. Sacred space is constructed through ritual. In the classical Durkheimian formulation, the crucial ritual act divides space into sacred and profane, but anyone who has tried to use this opposition gets into empirical trouble. I think that ritual as a spatial performance provides an arena of several mapping strategies that make some spaces visible and others invisible. In India pilgrimage has always been a major ritual of trans-locality. In the nineteenth century, pilgrimage networks greatly benefited from improvement in communications, such as the railways, and they have become increasingly important for growing parts of the population up to the present day. It is, then, not surprising that Savarkar's ideology of a sacred fatherland of Hindus was made visible in the 1980s in rituals derived from pilgrimage.

The VHP (Vishva Hindu Parishad; The World Hindu Organization) experimented on a large scale with ritual in what is called "a sacrifice for unity" (*ekatmatayajna*) in 1983.[4] Sacrifice, in this case, referred to an extremely complex and well-organized cluster of processions that reached, according to the VHP's estimate, some sixty million people. Three large processions (*yatra*) traversed India in November and December 1993. The first started in Hardwar in the North and reached Kanyakumari (India's southernmost point). The second, inaugurated by the King of Nepal (a Hindu kingdom that is not part of India), started in Katmandu and reached Rameshwaram in Tamil Nadu. The third started in Gangasagar in the east and reached Somanatha in the west. Significantly, the three processions crossed in the middle of the country in Nagpur, which is not a pilgrimage center but the headquarters of the RSS (Rashtriya Swayamsevak Sangh; National Volunteer Organization). At least forty-seven small processions (*upayatra*) traversed other parts of the country, connecting up at appointed meeting places with one of the three larger processions. The processions followed well-known pilgrimage routes that link major religious centers, suggesting the geographical unity of India as a sacred space (*kshetra*) of

Hindus. In this sense, pilgrimage was transformed into a ritual of national integration for Hindus. Processions of temple chariots (*rathas*) are an important part of temple rituals in India. An image of the god is taken for a ride in his domain, during which he confirms his territorial sovereignty and extends his blessings. The processions of the VHP made use of *rathas* in the form of brand-new trucks—some critics called this Toyota-Hinduism. Each of the three main processions was named after its "chariot": Mahadevaratha, Pashupatiratha, and Kapilaratha, names that refer to gods and saints worshiped in the places from which the processions started out. The chariots carried an image of Bharat Mata. The political use of the mother goddess in India is also known from regional parties, such as Telugu Desam, but Mother India was here projected onto the map of India. The chariots also carried waterpots (*kalasha*) filled with local sacred water mixed with Ganges water, the most sacred of all. Waterpots are among the most potent symbols in Hindu ritual, signifying power and auspiciousness.

This nationalist ritual is thus an assemblage of several important elements in Hindu ritual, and one has to be an anthropologist to say that this is just an invention of tradition. What is made invisible by this ritual of unity is that through its mappings it makes invisible other possible mappings, in which Christians and Muslims would have a place. Christians and Muslims are shown to be outside the fold. Being a pilgrimage, it makes invisible all the other ways to understand the sacred geography of India—in terms of non-Brahmanic sites, Sufi shrines in which Hindus and Muslims come together, Christian shrines in which everyone appears, etc. Indeed, the reason for putting this ritual together was to launch a protest against a much-publicized mass conversion of Untouchables to Islam in Meenakshipuram in South India.

This particular ritual was later followed by a number of similar rituals, of which the campaign to liberate the birthplace of Ram in Ayodhya has been the most important. One element in this campaign was particularly successful, namely, the making of special bricks, inscribed with the words *Shri Rama*, for building the Ram Janmabhumi temple on Ram's birthplace after the destruction of the mosque that had been erected on that birthplace in the sixteenth century by a general of the Mughal Emperor Babar. These bricks were consecrated in a ceremony called Ram Shilan Puja, then collected and transported to Ayodhya. The processions that brought these bricks to Ayodhya often went through Muslim areas and created communal violence according to an age-old pattern in which rituals create riots. These bricks came not only from India but also from abroad, wherever persons of Indian origins lived. Rama was pictured on some posters as a warlike hero but on others as a baby, like baby Krishna, addressing the wide spectrum of national sentiments and devotional emotions. This campaign contributed to the electoral victory of the BJP (Bharatiya Janata Party) in India and the destruction of the Babar mosque in Ayodhya, as well as to communal carnage in many places in India, such as Gujarat and Bombay. Since the issue can never be solved (*sub iudice aeternitatis*), it continues to be a wonderful political tool for Hindu nationalists.

One often hears that such Hindu nationalist rituals show the politicization of ritual and are a travesty of true religion. Hindutva is viewed as a fake religion, a simple sleight of hand to gain political power. There is no doubt that the rituals I have described are to be understood as nationalist, but does that make them fake? I would not know how observers and interpreters who stand outside of a tradition could justify such a claim about true and fake religion, although clearly those who stand within a tradition may argue that some rituals are heterodox or a travesty. The question ultimately seems to boil down to who has the authority to interpret rituals and decide what their symbolic meaning is. One therefore has to examine the power of an institution such as a church or the state, of a movement like the VHP, or of discourses such as that of nationalism. If we go back to the example of Falun Gong with which we began, the Chinese government decided to interpret this movement's breathing techniques and medita-tions not as genuine but as a political threat to the state. According to the *People's Daily* of June 15, 2000, the government has never forbidden the practice of normal exercises: "people have the freedom to believe in and practice any method of qigong, except when they . . . use the banner of exercises . . . to spread superstition, create chaos, and organize large-scale gatherings that disturb social order and influence social stability." Whatever people say they are doing, their practices are interpreted in a political arena. Similarly, women wearing headscarves in Holland or France may think that such a practice is part of virtuous conduct, but the state and liberal opinion may decide that it signifies disloyalty and extremism and/or the unjustifiable subjection of woman to man.

The problem with analyzing rituals as symbolic texts that can be read by anthropologists or by the state is that such an analysis makes a symbol the vehicle of a meaning that can be decoded. However, as Talal Asad has argued, one may define a symbol not as an object or an event that serves to carry a meaning but as a set of relationships between objects or events uniquely brought together as complexes or as concepts, having an at once intellectual, instru-mental, and emotional significance.[5] This allows us to raise questions about the conditions under which such complexes or concepts are formed and how their formation is related to varieties of practice. The conditions (discursive and nondiscursive) that explain how symbols come to be constructed and become natural and authoritative then become the object of in-quiry. Of course, Hindu nationalism reconceptualizes tradition as part of a Hindu modernity and, indeed, history writing is a major element in this conceptualization. Certainly this has been going on for more than a century, and it cannot explain the rise of the Sangh Parivar (the allied forces of Hindu nationalism) in the 1980s. That must be related to the decline of the Congress patronage system. These are major long-term and short-term conditions for the naturalness and authority of the Hindutva ritual campaigns. Another major condition, however, is a shift in the Indian mediascape: the rise of television and the success of the televised *Ramayana*.

A major element in Hindu ritual is visuality. Central to worship is the concept of *darshan*, which means "seeing." Seeing a divine image brings one into the presence of the supernatural. Certainly some images are more powerful than others, so Hindus go on pilgrimage to see them. They do so at certain moments in the calendar, since some moments are more auspicious than others. The mechanical reproduction of images—in calendar art, for example—has increased the reach and the mobility of images but has not really damaged the authentic power of the original image. Actually, more people participate in pilgrimages to more distant destinations, and the popularity of divine images is enhanced by reproduction. It is important to see that these sacred journeys are completely intertwined with secular consumption patterns, especially the development of tourism. The popularity of a particular cult is further enhanced by itinerant preachers, who spread the story and embellish it as storytellers, drawing huge crowds and making it into a contemporary moral tale. Devotional theater has also for a long time played a role in spreading the popularity of a cult. All these elements were in place in the story of the god Rama, which was well known all over India in different regional versions, including a classical Sanskrit text and a hugely popular Hindu rendition, *Tulsidas's Ramcaritmanas*.

Mass communication via television (seeing form afar, *durdarshan*) is a part of the ongoing transformation of this mediascape, but a major part. It does not replace the elements I have just mentioned, but it changes them. It is hard to underestimate the influence of the televising of the *Ramayan*, the story of Rama, on Indian television in 1987. It drew record audiences, which were surpassed only by the subsequent televising of the other major religious story of India, the *Mahabharata*. Part of its success lay in promoting a moral utopia of sacrifice for the community and a rejection of the shallowness of secular individualism. At least that was what the Hindutva ideologues capitalized on. More concretely, the televised *Ramayan* transformed the birthplace of Rama from a mythical place in a sacred text into a site in Ayodhya that was simultaneously superreal, decontextualized, and dehistoricized. Certainly, pilgrims to Ayodhya had been doing something like that for centuries, but pilgrimage to Ayodhya had always been a regional, limited affair. Central to this pilgrimage is *darshan*, sacred seeing, and this raises the crucial question of mediation between the viewer and the sacred. To transform the streets of Ayodhya into the sacred streets of heavenly Ayodhya (or Saket) depends on a deliberate, meditative effort by the viewer, assisted by a priest or a monk who takes him around to see, among other things, the birthplace of Rama. On television, however, viewing is not guided by theologically inspired meditative practice. Its melodramatic conventions may derive from the older practices of the Ramlila performances, but television's virtuality relates in new ways to religion's virtuality by making *darshan* superreal but theologically undisciplined. Traveling to Ayodhya in an actual pilgrimage transforms a person into a pilgrim, but traveling to it by way of television transforms a person into someone who may have an opinion. In the end, these transformations of the mediascape, both religious and secular, enable the political projects that we have witnessed in India over the last two decades.

Coming to my conclusion, I want to suggest that to look at the visual implies a simultaneous concern with the invisible, the unseen, the secret, as well as with the conditions of seeing. The assumptions of liberal theorists that the modern democratic state is open, transparent, and accountable must be criticized, since it is a utopia that legitimates imperial politics. We have to confront the magic of the state and its occult powers to represent itself as stable, as controlled by rationality, bureaucratic or otherwise. And we have to confront its pomposity, its excess of uniforms, military drill, weapon shows, and statues and portraits of the great leaders. This is an area of mimicry, of illusions of grandeur, of the violence of fantasy in state terror, as in Saddam Hussain's Iraq, the Shah's Iran, Mussolini's Italy. We also should examine the ways in which this is ridiculed and criticized in cartoons, such as those of Laxman in India, in rumors, in exposures as part of a complex public sphere—but we also need to look for radical moral critiques of the state that are hidden and secret.

A comparative exercise allows one to see, beyond images that have been made natural and unquestionable, not so much reality or truth as the conditions under which certain images are produced as authoritative. Comparison allows one to see that similar elements, like the capitalist market, state bureaucracy, and religious movements, make up different configurations and trajectories. This is always very clear in discussions about the religious and the secular. The interdependence of the religious and the secular develops differently in different contexts. The argument that secular modernity comes from the West and/or from Christianity is based on the historical fact that some major Enlightenment arguments for secularity have indeed originated in Dutch, French, and American societies. In all these societies, these arguments have been taken up, discussed, and, to a greater or lesser extent, accepted. Nevertheless, none of these societies is a simple instance of a universal, secular modernity. Indeed, there are great differences between French *laicité*, the American wall of separation, and Dutch pillarization. This makes comparative work on the interdependence of the religious and the secular of great importance for political theory.

If there is one political leader who truly exemplifies this interdependence, it is Gandhi. Gandhi found himself confronted with two major problems. First, Hindu-Muslim antagonism was a major threat to the creation of an Indian nation. This problem became more and more crucial in the struggle for Independence. Second, Indian society was marked by one of the most pervasive systems of inequality in the world, which was religiously sanctioned by Hindu tradition. Gandhi made a major argument for developing Indian secularism when he pleaded for nonviolence and tolerance. Gandhi's argument was based on a moral reasoning quite different from Western Enlightenment arguments. His notions of nonviolence and tolerance did not emerge from a perspective like that of John Stuart Mill, according to which one must be tolerant because one can never be sure one has attained a universal truth.

In Gandhi's view, one does attain truth through one's experiments with truth (*satyagraha*), but this truth is a moral truth, which must be experienced and indeed shown to others through one's own example. One should not criticize those who have not realized such truth and, given that criticism is already a kind of violence, one should in general avoid violently imposing truth upon others who are not convinced by one's example. Truth, then, is moral, though cognitive truth is important in helping us to realize our moral goals rather than being destroyed by materialism. This kind of religious reasoning makes tolerance possible and thus can be the basis of nonviolent coexistence in a multicultural and multireligious society with a secular state. The visual image of the Hindu ascetic was used by Gandhi to fight imperialism and construct a vision not of a Hindu India but of a multicultural India. Our methodologies and theories should enable us to make such practices visible.

The Power of Mary in Secessionist Warfare

Catholicism and Political Crisis in Bougainville, Papua New Guinea

Anna-Karina Hermkens

From 1988 until the late 1990s, people on Bougainville Island were immersed in a vicious war that destroyed nearly all infrastructure and social services. Foreign reports almost unanimously analyzed the crisis as a sociopolitical conflict. However, religion, particularly Catholicism, played a major role during and after the crisis. Catholic devotions and revelations were deeply intertwined with "traditional" concepts and beliefs, as well as with the politics of the crisis. Furthermore, people believe that peace was achieved through prayers, especially pleas directed to Mary, the mother of Jesus Christ. Indeed, the Bougainville crisis was conceptualized as a Holy War, and by examining it we can see how religion legitimizes sovereignty and violence, supports charismatic leadership, and inspires people to fight simultaneously against oppression and for peace.

Bougainville is a small island group in the South Pacific, belonging to Papua New Guinea. It comprises two main islands: Buka (circa 50 km long) in the north and, separated by a small sea channel, Bougainville Island (circa 200 km long) in the south. In addition, there are many small islands and atolls. Bougainville is often referred to as one of the most beautiful island groups in the world due to its beaches of white sand, its blue waters, and the long, lush green mountain spine that runs through Bougainville Island. It was also known as one of the most developed provinces of Papua New Guinea because it contained a large copper mine.

A walk through Arawa town in Central Bougainville, however, reveals the devastation that has resulted from nearly a decade of warfare. Bushes have overgrown the once prestigious air-conditioned supermarket of Arawa and the former provincial office. A rampant growth of weeds preys upon the concrete skeletons of the once-thriving businesses along the main southern road to Kieta, giving a sinister border to the town. The ruins and weeds form a fitting backdrop for the rough looks of the young city-dwellers lounging at the edge of town, often dressed in army pants, with bandanas tied around their foreheads and biceps, and wearing T-shirts displaying photographs of Jean Claude van Damme, Bruce Lee, and other Rambo-like "heroes." While many Bougainvilleans are striving to recover from the crisis and to rebuild their lives, these young men appear eager to cultivate the years of warfare.

During the war, almost all roads, hospitals, schools, banks, private businesses, and government buildings on Bougainville were destroyed. Many houses and churches met with a similar fate. The conflict resulted in immense human suffering. The number of people who died in the crisis is estimated to be about fifteen thousand, which amounts to about 10 percent of the entire population.[1] According to Marilyn Taleo Havini, "no one has escaped the twists and turns of fighting zones, having families trapped in opposite camps."[2] Beyond those killed in the fighting, many people lost loved ones because of the interruption in basic services, such as medicine. To grief is added the trauma that follows in the wake of torture and rape. A generation of new Bougainvilleans has grown up in a context of combat and has not received adequate schooling.[3] Some were born in the bush while their parents were fleeing the colliding forces. Others spent their childhood in one of the many "care centers" spread across Bougainville. It should therefore come as no surprise that many find it hard to let go of the war, both in their physical appearance and mentally, given how deeply ingrained experiences of grief and trauma have come to be in people's lives.

Faced with the negative peace and stability that characterizes Bougainville today, many people turn to religion in search of meaningful structures, peace, comfort, and aid. But in Bougainville religion—specifically Catholicism and above all a cult of Mary—is hardly a matter only of consolation and peace. It played a major role in the crisis, and it was during the decade-long war that people's spirituality reached unprecedented heights and that Marian devotion in particular became ascendent in many parts of Bougainville. In this essay, which is based on anthropological fieldwork conducted in the Koromira district in Bougainville in 2005,[4] I will analyze the role of religion during the Bougainville crisis. I will focus not on official doctrines but on "lived religion,"[5] that is, on people's religious conceptualizations, practices, experiences, and strategies.

I will organize my insights around three key principles, showing how nationalism, custom, and religion are intertwined and how they mutually enforced an ideology of warfare. We will then be able to see how religion can legitimize sovereignty and violence, support charismatic leadership, and inspire people to fight simultaneously against oppression and for peace. Let me begin by introducing the main actors and elucidating the supposed causes and historical context of the Bougainville crisis.

The Bougainville Crisis

Two of the major actors in the crisis were the Bougainville Revolutionary Army (BRA) and the secessionist movement of Me'ekamui Pontoko Onoring. The name of the latter roughly translates as "government of the guardians of the sacred [or holy] land." It is also called the "Fifty Toea Movement," referring to the monetary contributions required of its members. *Me'ekamui* is also used to refer to Bougainville as a holy island, *me'eka* meaning "holy or sacred" and *mui*, "island or land." Both groups fought for justice and independence, and both engaged in often brutal combat with the Papua New Guinea Defence Force (PNGDF) and the Bougainville Resistance Forces (BRF). The latter consisted of Bougainvilleans who sided with the Papua New Guinea government, which, according to its own account, was attempting to prevent the political fragmentation of the Papua New Guinea nation-state. According to the secessionists, however, the government was seeking to control Bougainville's natural resources, in particular, the world's largest copper mine, located at the center of Bougainville Island.

The Panguna mining project, which is run by Conzinc Rio Tinto Australia (CRA) and Bougainville Copper Ltd (BCL), commenced its operations in 1972. In the course of time, the project faced increasing local resistance and demonstrations by landowners.[6] Led by popular leader Francis Ona, himself an alleged Panguna landowner and a former BCL employee, the landowners demanded a payment of ten billion kina as compensation for past damage to their land and the environment.[7] Angry with the mining company, which refused to meet their terms, Francis Ona and his group (first referred to as "Rambos," taking the protagonist of the popular Sylvester Stallone films as their role model, but later known as the BRA) sabotaged a power-line pylon, causing a power failure at the Panguna mine.[8] Following this militant action, which occurred in November 1988, the BRA embarked on a campaign of sabotage that effectively shut down the mining operations.

The protest against the Panguna mining project became linked to the demand that Bougainville secede from Papua New Guinea. Hiding in the mountains, Ona's group united with Damien Dameng's Me'ekamui secessionist movement. This union transformed Ona's Rambo party from a militant anti-BCL sabotage faction into part of a coalition striving for independence from Papua New Guinea.[9]

The Panguna mine conflict catalyzed a latent yet long-standing desire for freedom and self-governance. Since colonial times, Bougainvilleans had been dominated by various oppressive regimes, which had often bred feelings of resentment and resistance among the islanders.[10] In particular, the fact that, by fiat of the colonial administration, Bougainville had become part of the Australian mandate area of Papua New Guinea had resulted in protest. After having been under foreign rule for over fifty years, Bougainvilleans were not very eager to become a province of an independent Papua New Guinea.[11] Since 1964, the Bougainvillean secession movement had become stronger and more organized with the emergence of the Napidakoe Navitu movement.[12] (*Napidakoe* is an anagram of the names of ethnic groups in the Kieta subdistrict of Bougainville Island, and *Navitu* means "united people" or "grouping.") In May 1975, the urge for independence was so strong that the Bougainville Provincial Government actually voted to secede from Papua New Guinea.[13] Three months later, the Bougainville Provincial Assembly announced its decision to declare the independence of the Republic of North Solomons. This declaration came into effect on September 1, when the flag of the North Solomons was raised at the Arawa market.

Despite these efforts to gain autonomy, Bougainville became part of an independent Papua New Guinea on September 16, 1975. Starting in January 1976, antinationalist riots on Bougainville Island protested the annexation, and they ended only after negotiations with the national government.[14] These negotiations, however, could not fully subdue feelings of disappointment and resentment against Papua New Guinea. Many Bougainvilleans share the notion that they are "the neglected district" of Papua New Guinea.[15] Islanders frequently complain about the fact that only 2 percent of the Panguna mine's revenues are ploughed back into Bougainville, with Papua New Guinea taking the largest share of the profits and denying Bougainville any substantial infrastructure development. Moreover, Bougainville's people and politicians started blaming those affiliated with the mine not only for environmental damage but also for the violence and criminality of Papua New Guinea laborers (termed redskins, in contrast to the Bougainville blackskins), unemployment among the local population, and other societal ills.[16] These sentiments resulted in Bougainvilleans taking up arms and killing or driving out redskins—men, women, and children—from Arawa and Bougainville Island. As a result, by the early 1990s most non-Bougainvilleans had left Bougainville in fear of their lives. This "ethnic cleansing" was, however, not the end. *Raskols* (bands of roving criminals) from Kieta village began to turn on Bougainvilleans from other parts of the island working and living in the Kieta area and demand that they too return home.[17]

In the meantime, anti-BCL sabotage and civilian violence against redskins triggered a tough response from the Papua New Guinea government, which, after first sending a police riot squad, mobilized its defense forces to protect the mine, seize control over the area, suppress the BRA insurrection, and eliminate the terrorizing *raskols*. This, however, created even more local violence and animosity against the Papua New Guinea Government, given that the army used excessive violence against Bougainvilleans whom they suspected of being affiliated with the BRA. Since they were in unknown territory, the PNGDF seems to have suspected everyone and to have chosen suspects at random: beating, torturing, burning houses, and killing domestic animals. In consequence, to the Bougainvilleans it seemed that the army regarded the entire population as an enemy and many more men joined the BRA.[18]

In August 1989, Catholic priests in Bougainville issued a statement in favor of reconciliation. This was followed by a public meeting of fifteen hundred people in Arawa, including the prime minister, national government ministers, church leaders, and traditional leaders, in support of peace and reconciliation. However, Ona rejected the national government's "peace package," and as a result violence escalated.[19]

In March 1990, the Bougainville Ceasefire Initiative was signed between Papua New Guinea and the BRA. The latter were to hand in their arms, and the PNGDF was to withdraw from Bougainville. However, although the PNGDF withdrew and some BRA arms were handed in, the ceasefire was broken before early May, leaving the BRA in control of the entire island. The Bougainville Interim Government (BIG) was established as the legitimate authority on Bougainville. Ona was appointed president, with Joseph Kabui as chairman of BIG. On May 17, 1990, the BIG declared independence from Papua New Guinea. The Papua New Guinea government responded by imposing a total economic blockade on the island, which stopped all services, including humanitarian aid.

In August 1990, the Endeavour Accord was signed, allowing some NGO services access to Bougainville, but it was broken a few months later. This second breakdown deepened the conflict, as more groups began to oppose the BRA regime and Ona, who stayed in his hideout in the Panguna Mountains, refused to participate in peace negotiations and failed to establish control over gangs and BRA members who were killing, stealing, and torturing Bougainvilleans suspected of siding with Papua New Guinea. As a result, the Bougainville Resistance Forces (BRF) and the Buka Liberation Front (BLF) were formed, working together with the PNGDF, whom Bougainvilleans asked to return to the island to stop the violence. The result was a civil war characterized by anarchy, terror, and violence, in which various opposing groups, including *raskols* claiming to be BRA, language groups within the BRA, villagers, and released prisoners robbed, looted, destroyed, raped, killed, and tortured seemingly at will.[20]

After almost ten years of violence, warfare, and numerous broken peace agreements, the crisis officially ended in 1998 with the signing of a ceasefire and the August 2001 peace agreement.[21] It was agreed that all government functions (except those of defense, foreign affairs, international shipping and aviation, and the supreme court) would be transferred to the Autonomous Region of Bougainville. Furthermore, the participating parties agreed that the Panguna mine would not be reopened and that within the course of a few years elections for an Autonomous Bougainville Government (ABG) should be called.[22] Ona and his Me'ekamui followers, however, did not partake in these negotiations and agreements, arguing that Bougainville was independent and had its own government already, the Government of Me'ekamui, with Ona as its president. One month before former BRA member Joseph Kabui was elected president of the ABG in June 2005, Ona proclaimed himself "King of Bougainville"—His Royal Highness King Francis Dominic Dateransy Domanaa, King of the Royal Kingdom of Me'ekamui—in protest.

Today, Bougainville is in a process of postconflict peace building, which includes trauma counseling and traditional reconciliation ceremonies between the BRA and the BRF, and between these excombatants and their victims' relatives. It will take many more years, if not generations, to overcome the traumas people have suffered. As part of the same effort, Bougainville is gradually rebuilding its infrastructure and sociopolitical and economic services. Nonetheless, the earlier issues of dispute and the roles played by influential leaders such as Ona are still very much at the political forefront, challenging the legitimacy of official bodies.

This account could make it sound as though the conflict mainly concerned environmental, economic, and political resentments and aspirations. However, one should not overlook the fact that the crisis developed within a particular cultural context: a number of cultural principles and beliefs, which are intertwined with local Christian logics, bolstered the conflict's particular dynamics and politics. Obviously, the various groups involved differed about how to interpret these principles and beliefs, as did members within particular groups. Yet the most important constitutive elements of Bougainville's religious and political landscape during the crisis included strong notions of *kastom* ("tradition"), Christianity, and nationalism. Let us examine these elements in the context of the concept of *Me'ekamui*.

Bougainville as a Holy Island

The interrelatedness of nationalism and religion within Bougainville's secessionist movement has its root in the concept of *Me'ekamui* and can be traced back to Damien Dameng's ideology of the Me'ekamui movement.

Me'ekamui, meaning "sacred or holy island," refers to sacred sites at which ancestors are believed to reside. These are located all over Bougainville. In the past, each village appointed a caretaker of sacred places. These sites included stones, trees, and rivers, and they were visited to make offerings and to pray for a good harvest, to give thanks, to pray for a return of health, etc. As elder John Bovora, born in 1942 in Berasinau village, Koromira parish, related: "The early Christians, our *tumbuna*, had sacred places they would use for making offerings on stones in preparation for the harvest, for example. What was asked for during the offerings would come to pass." As is apparent in this quote, the concept of Bougainville as a holy land has come to be infused with Christian rhetoric. According to Bovora and my other informants, however, their ancestors knew God before the missionaries came. Bovora said: "Our *tumbuna* knew God exists. They knew how to pray to *Kumponi*, to God. If the missionaries had known this, they could have built Churches at these places. Now there is confusion: we have our churches and we have our sacred places. If they had built churches at these sites, it would have been clear." This notion of Bougainville as a holy island and its inhabitants as precolonial Christians reso-nates with Dameng's ideology, which champions customary Bougainvillean culture while strongly opposing the presence and influence of the outside world. However, despite Dameng's opposition to outsiders, the ideology of Me'ekamui contains Christian elements as well as con-ceptualizations of indigenous religious practices and beliefs. As Anthony Regan describes it:

> From around 1959, Dameng built support among several thousand people around ideas of rebuilding customary social structures. In the process, however, they built something new, rejecting "bad" aspects of custom, and building in some "good" aspects of the changes brought by the missions and the colonial administration. The movement's adherents, how-ever, believed that their social structure was built mainly upon custom, and saw it as supe-rior to the colonial administration and the Christian missions, both of which Dameng opposed.[23]

This feature of combining notions of custom, Christianity, and nationalism while rejecting colonial and Western influences becomes apparent in the manner in which adherents of the Me'ekamui movement have conceptualized their situation. A Me'ekamui leader in the village of Buin in south Bougainville, for example, told me that the Bougainvilleans were waiting for other monarchies, such as the United Kingdom and the Netherlands, to offer their services to what he called "the Kingdom of Me'ekamui." It is believed that these services do not reach the island because the ABG, the Papua New Guinea government, and Australia have put an em-bargo on all transnational relations, as they did during the crisis. The same leader urged me to reveal Jesus' true name to him. He explained: "Jesus is only listening to you white people, giving you factories and goods, while he does not hear the prayers of us, Bougainvilleans. This is because we do not know his true, Bougainvillean name." This example illustrates how outsiders are accused of blocking services and are held responsible for the destruction of sacred powers. Concurrently, however, these outsiders are believed to hold the divine key to power.

Key Elements in the Secessionist Movement

The interrelatedness of nationalism and religion within the Me'ekamui movement becomes all the more clear when one disentangles the principles that structured Ona's and his followers' ideology and actions. According to James Tanis, who is a former BRA member, secretary of the BIG, and the current president of the Autonomous Province of Bougainville, three main principles guided the BRA's efforts during the war, as well as in the reconciliation process. These are *Osikaiang* ("indigenous"), *Me'ekamui* ("Holy Island") and *Sipungeta* ("roots").[24]

The first principle, *Osikaiang*, denotes people's indigenous Bougainvilllean identity.[25] In the lingua franca of Papua New Guinea, *tok pisin*, it also means *as ples*, signifying one's place of origin or birth. In the context of the crisis, it referred to the notion that Bougainvilleans are the customary owners of the land, as opposed to outsiders, who have no spiritual and ancestral attachment to it. *Osikaiang*, or rather, the concept of Bougainvillean identity, constituted a crucial element in the crisis. Dark skin color was and has remained the most distinctive marker of Bougainvillean identity. The term *redskins*, with which Bougainvilleans refer to the lighter-skinned people of other parts of Papua New Guinea, is generally used in a derogatory sense, to contend that these people have had a damaging influence on Bougainville society and culture. Along with an antiwhite attitude, which developed under colonial rule, the emphasis on *Osikaiang* fueled Bougainvilleans' nationalistic and secessionist sentiments. As a Koromira church worker and Eucharist minister put it: "Before the crisis, these redskins and Europeans, they were coming to Bougainville, bringing their customs. During the crisis, we got rid of all of them. All the squatters [settlers from Papua New Guinea in the cities of Kieta and Arawa] are gone now. The crisis has straightened all this. God gave us the crisis, so now a new Bougainville must arise." Thus, Me'ekamui nationalism entails local conceptualizations of tradition, identity, ethnicity, and racism. Not only does this quote illustrate how a lot of locals feel toward "redskins" and "whites," it also displays how, for reasons of self-empowerment and a legitimization of the war effort, God was appropriated as "an ideology of resistance."[26] As elder John Bovora expressed it: "We asked God: 'You provided us with this land. Is it for outsiders to destroy our land?' Our prayers were heard, so now this is our chance. We must maintain the peace given by God, and then we will get freedom!"

In addition to the conceptualization of indigenous identity and custom, the principle of *Me'ekamui*, especially the notion of holiness, was a second constitutive element of the BRA ideology. According to Ona and his followers, only through holiness could the fight both against oppression and for peace be won. For them, as President Tanis has said: "Holiness, peace, and reconciliation must start from the roots [*sipungeta*]. From one's inner self to families, clans, and later to the nation. The spirits of the dead must be put to rest. If this can be done our homeland is truly *Me'ekamui*—a holy place where the creator dwells amongst His people."[27] The deep-seated notion that holiness is a prerequisite for the creation of a holy nation directed the BRA combatants' war efforts. Indeed, the struggle to deliver the land to its rightful owners was perceived as a "holy war."[28] Furthermore, the principle of *Me'ekamui* required that soldiers to stay holy before, during, and after battle. Especially in the Koromira area of central Bougainville, the pursuit of holiness was held in high esteem. As Paul Kaanama, an elder of one of the mountain villages in the Koramira area, explained: "During the war, none of our BRA boys died, because they fought with holiness. They did not kill unarmed men—only PNGDF. It was a holy war. So before they went into action, they prayed. And God protected them."

Ex–BRA combatant and prayer leader (chaplain) Albert Natee narrated:

Francis Ona said this land must become holy again, *Me'ekamui*. We prayed to God and he gave us strength. This directed us to engage in a clean battle. We were fighting for our rights, to get rid of all these bad companies and their effects. All BRA and all Bougainvilleans—everybody practiced this holiness. We had to stay with the Church. Our spirits had to be holy, so God would get rid of Satan [the mining companies]. We had to stay holy to get rid of it. And God helped us. How? His power worked through the rosary.

Before we would go on patrol or go into battle, we would pray the three most powerful decades: the Lord's Prayer and three Hail Mary's. This we did collectively, as a group. The mysteries we would pray in private. We would pray for protection and for guidance. I would get them [the BRA] all together and read bible passages and explain how to stay holy in combat. We stayed holy by not gossiping, not swearing, and not getting angry. When somebody caused trouble in the camp, we would send him away. We had to stay holy! As a group we should stay holy, and one man could not be allowed to destroy this. He would have to make some kind of sacrifice and could return after some weeks. He had to apologize to God, to us, to those to whom he had wronged. If he refused, he would jeopardize our safety. God will not protect us when we have done wrong. Also, when I die, I must go to heaven. So before and during the battles, I had to stay holy so that in case I got shot, I would go straight to heaven.

Because they were waging a "clean" war, they believed God was on their side. As Koromira people I spoke to put it, "God was with us during the crisis. Nobody died of sickness or was killed." In the Koromira area, people have a general conviction that those who were killed in combat were nonbelievers or headstrong boys who had done something wrong.

Thus, *Me'ekamui* ideology promoted the BRA's struggle for independence from an exploitative Papua New Guinea and outside interference. Deeply informed by a strongly localized

Catholic discourse, this ideology constituted a form of ethno-nationalism with fierce antifor-
eigner or anti-"redskin" sentiments, as well as the notion of a traditional customary society. Yet
paradoxically the war was legitimized by appropriating nonindigenous elements of Catholicism
into the Bougainvillean ideology of resistance, thereby conceptualizing the struggle against
Papua New Guinea and Australian hegemony as a holy war to restore Bougainville to the status
of the unblemished holy island it once was.

Francis Ona: A Holy Leader?

The task of saving Bougainville had befallen the BRA, who, especially in the Koromira area,
acted as a holy army, guided by Francis Ona and supported by Mary and by God. As several of
his followers explained, Ona's idea was that, through devotion to Mary, the mother of God,
Bougainville would get faithful leaders who were connected with the land and lore of the island.
Since Bougainville was perceived to be a holy land, the people, and especially its leaders, would
have to become holy as well. In Ona's vision of *Me'ekamui*, the Catholic faith, in particular, the
veneration of Mary, played an important role.

The majority (69 percent) of the circa 180,000 Bougainvilleans are Catholic, followed by
United Church (15 percent), Seventh Day Adventists (7 percent), and Pentecostals (6 percent).[29]
Beginning in 1901 European, and subsequently American and Australian, missionaries of the
society of Mary, referred to as Marists, introduced the Catholic faith.[30] The society derives its
name from its members' attempt to imitate the Virgin Mary in their spirituality and daily work.
Marists act out of love for Mary and with the compassion of Mary, aiming to bring others
closer to God through their teachings of faith and practical skills. As John Mauro, a sixty-seven-
year-old Marist brother from Bougainville, explained: 'For me personally, Mary is my mother.
Through Mary, we try to become close to God. In fact, our motto is: All to Jesus through Mary,
all to Mary for Jesus. So Mary is our first superior."

Due to the zealous efforts of the Marist missionaries, the Marist spirit spread all over
Bougainville. The importance of Mary in the lives of many Bougainvilleans, both before, during,
and after the crisis, can be seen as among the influences Marist fathers, brothers, and sisters
had on peoples' spiritual and mental mindsets. On the other hand, more recent Marist teachings
have inspired many influential Bougainvilleans to act against the successive acts of oppression
that had faced Bougainville.[31] They taught their students not to accept colonial or postcolonial
oppression but instead to promote self-determination and strive for political leadership
positions.

In order to assert himself as a holy leader, Ona turned to Mary for inspiration. According
to the Dutch bishop of Bougainville, Henk Kronenburg, Ona sought Mary's advice on a daily

basis by addressing Her statue. Ona would carry out his plans for the day only after he received a confirming message from Her. As token of his devotion to Mary, Ona initiated the Marian Mercy Mission. According to a female member of this movement, its devotees have a particular way of saying the rosary and regularly engage in fasting and prayer sessions. Father Bernard Unabali, a Bougainvillean Catholic priest in Arawa, described it as a very strong movement, with a strict emphasis on morality, and said that it urges the conversion of all Bougainvilleans.[32] Since this Marian movement has been led by Ona and is connected with his secessionist struggle, it obviously has political and nationalistic traits, however.

The interplay between Ona's nationalism and his devotion to Mary came to the fore markedly in the warm welcome he extended to the pilgrimage of the international Pilgrim Virgin Statue of Our Lady of Fatima to Panguna in 1997. Those who witnessed the pilgrimage claim that Ona was convinced by Mary to end the fighting.[33] The proceedings were captured on film at the time by Catholic missionaries. On these never-released recordings, Ona can be seen and heard praying in front of the statue, making a vow to Our Lady to work toward peace. More significantly, he also consecrates the island of Bougainville to Mary. Thus, in addition to devoting his own life to Mama Maria, he appropriated the whole of Bougainville in Her name.

Ona's strategy of obtaining political influence through religion became most apparent in his attempts to enhance his leadership of the holy island of Bougainville with a sense of personal divinity. Although many Bougainvilleans viewed Ona's crowning with dismay and irony, many of his followers—especially those calling themselves Me'ekamui—perceived Ona to be their king. As the president and subsequent king of Me'ekamui, Ona sought political legitimacy through an adherence to religious doctrines and an appropriation of biblical powers. Above all, Ona's crowning can be seen as an act to reaffirm his power and influence against the ABG. When Ona went to Buin in anticipation of the upcoming elections, one man asked him: "Shouldn't you step down now we have the ABG?" Ona answered: "I am not a King of the government; I am the King of all grasshoppers, trees, oil, minerals, of everything that is on this island. When I step down, our island will go down [it will be destroyed by the mining activities of Papua New Guinea and the whites]." Moreover, Ona maintained that a monarchy would open up the isolated and largely ignored area of Me'ekamui and its king to the outer world. As he stated: "I've got people all over the world supporting me as a monarch. We've got a monarchical system in which different kingdoms support each other, so all the monarchies are willing to give me our much-needed aid."[34]

Significantly, Ona's crowning as the King of Me'ekamui appeared to resonate with the kings of the Old Testament. In the Bible, both God and humans are referred to as king. Biblical kings had unlimited control over their followers, with their God-given title denoting independence, unrestricted power, and extensive dominion. This link between divinity and political

leadership was effectively disseminated when Ona's followers and sympathizers in the secessionist struggle began referring to him in terms of divine leadership. In fact, on the occasion of the
first anniversary of his death, Father Bernard Unabali described Ona as "a Savior of Bougainville" who, just like Moses in the Bible, led the Bougainvilleans to freedom.[35]

This short overview makes clear that Ona's identity as a leader oscillated between that of a
hero of the Bougainvillean uprising and a divine leader. From a alleged landowner and rebel,
he initially turned into a patriot-hero, inspiring and mobilizing people to fight against "occupying" forces. Subsequently, probably in an attempt to elevate his status and increase his influence,
he contrived to be crowned king—an at once worldly and divine king on a quest to save the
holy island and kingdom of Bougainville. In short, Ona and the people close to him actively
sought to build a Kingdom of Me'ekamui, whose theocratic power base was largely founded on
Ona's capacity to convince his followers of his divine leadership. By claiming to hear Mary's
voice, Ona assumed the gift of prophecy, which, as Thomas Csordas has argued, is a vital
component of charismatic leadership.[36] Having access to Mary and experiencing the immediacy
of her divine presence and voice is, obviously, a key element in having social and religious
authority.

However, it seems that Ona's authority was only perceptible to those living close to him or
to those having unlimited belief and faith in his abilities. Outside Ona's realm, his kingship was
met with criticism and even laughter. During the crisis, Ona had failed to achieve a strong
leadership position. Although early on he had publicly denounced the criminal and violent
activities of *raskols* via a radio broadcast, he could not control vigilante groups both within and
outside the BRA. His refusal to come down from of his hideout in the Panguna Mountains and
his continued refusal to partake in peace negotiations also contributed to his fading support
and lack of political power in the wider region. Only weeks before the elections for the ABG
government were held in 2005, Ona decided to come down from his mountain, surprising both
followers and opponents by his strong public performance. We will never know to what extend
Ona would have been able to contest the "secular" ABG government, since his unexpected
death a mere two months after his crowning abruptly ended his career as the king of Me'ekamui.

When comparing Ona with other leaders of religious movements, such as Joseph Kony of
the Lord's Resistance Army (LRA) in northern Uganda, differences stand out more than similarities do. Similarities include the fact that both leaders assumed religious or divine authority.
Whereas Ona was proclaimed King of Me'ekamui and assumed the gift of prophecy, Kony
proclaimed himself the spokesperson of God and a spirit medium, primarily of the Christian
Holy Spirit.[37] Moreover, like the BRA, the LRA, which was formed in 1987, is a self-proclaimed
Christian rebellious guerrilla army, operating against the government and claiming to fight for

127

a theocratic state, which the LRA wishes to base on the Ten Commandments and their local (Acholi) tradition.[38]

However, the transgressions for which Kony and his LRA are held responsible—such as widespread human rights violations, including murder, mutilation, abduction, sexual slavery of women and children, and the military use of children—did not occur in Bougainville. This is primarily because Ona did not advocate a "war of terror" in "the name of God," as Kony does. In fact, Ona condemned the violence, looting, and destruction by vigilante groups, whom he could not control. Unlike Kony, Ona failed to be a strong political leader who could have both prevented and instigated more violence. Moreover, although at one point the BRA did start to violate human rights, their initial struggle was against outsiders: the foreign mining company and the Papua New Guinea government. Moreover, the emphasis placed by Ona and several of his BRA followers in the Koromira area upon "holiness" may have also prevented large-scale transgressions like those in Uganda. Only by fighting a holy war, in which combatants should be pure and there should be no innocent victims, could Ona's goal of creating a holy island with holy leaders be achieved.

The intriguing question that remains is: Why did Ona and his followers have this urge to re-create a holy land, led by holy leaders, and what did they expect this theocracy to bring?

The Crisis as a Holy War

According to Mircea Eliade, it is a profound human nostalgia, a longing to inhabit a "divine world," that motivates people to re-create a holy land.[39] This religious nostalgia is an expression of the desire to live in a pure and holy cosmos, as at the beginning of time. In BRA and Me'ekamui people's perception, this beginning referred not to the time of creation but to the time before the missionaries and other whites came, a time identified as paradisiacal. However, the desire to reestablish a "prelapsarian" world was not just a matter of religious nostalgia; it also resounded strongly within the realm of politics. A statement by Paul John Kaanama, of Koromira parish, reveals how strongly a sense of nostalgia was combined with powerful nation- alist sentiments: "We had a divine right to be free! Political and economic salvation was what we prayed for. Papua New Guinea and others dictated to us. We had no say in it. They misused their powers, using our resources against our will. God has given us this land!" A holy war was deemed necessary to recover and purify the holy island of Bougainville, because it had been polluted, desecrated, and destroyed by outsiders.

When one analyzes in more detail the concept of the holy war and the reasons it was deemed necessary, two aspects come to the fore. First, the war was believed to redefine moral and ethnic boundaries. Second, the rhetoric of a holy war was used to mobilize and legitimize the crisis as a struggle to regain spiritual, economic, and political control.

The aspect of redefining boundaries, of recreating and maintaining divisions between Bougainvilleans and others (outsiders), was important in legitimizing the crisis. It was perceived as a necessary evil to counteract the decline of sociality and morality that Bougainvilleans were facing. Bougainvilleans blamed this decline on Papua New Guinea "redskins" and "whites," who had brought their own customs to Bougainville, thus contributing to a disintegration of Bougainville culture. In addition, Bougainvilleans claimed the right to avenge cruelties and killings allegedly committed by "outsiders," such as the rape of Bougainvillean women. Stories of these horrors, which purportedly occurred in the years leading up to the crisis, circulated widely. In consequence, cleansing Bougainville from menacing foreign elements became part of the ideology that constituted the crisis, legitimizing the urge to reclaim Bougainvillean culture and land and the assertion of a Bougainvillean group identity. As Ona put it: "This war is to protect the environment and social/cultural system on Bougainville. It was something that every Bougainvillean wanted, in terms of the rights for Bougainville."[40]

Intertwined with this urge to purify Bougainville and circumvent social and moral decline was the impulse to redefine ethnic boundaries. Bougainvilleans used skin color as a political symbol before, during, and after the war. In fact, skin color had become synonymous with cultural identity. While Papua New Guinea highlanders were classified as violent redskins, Bougainvilleans were termed peaceful blackskins. People had created a Bougainville ethnic identity that sustained collective cooperative efforts against the outside forces, such as Papua New Guinea redskins and Australian whiteskins, that overwhelmed them.[41]

The second main aspect of why and how the crisis was conceptualized and legitimized as a holy war was the battle for control. Using rhetorical references to God and Satan to describe the crisis, Bougainvillean leaders implied that their holy war resembled an Old Testament conflict between good and evil. The contending parties were increasingly depicted as God's chosen people versus the enemies of the holy land. While in America similar rhetorics led to a representation of the United States as God's chosen nation to combat evil and to establish good—"namely American hegemonic power and its economic, cultural and political 'way of life' over the rest of the world"[42]—in Bougainville the ideology of the holy war was directed against such hegemonic powers and initially targeted a mining company, Papua New Guinea, and outside capitalist interests. A reporter said of Ona's role in the crisis: "A small, black, people, on a far-off island in the Pacific, have shown that 'we can win' against the combined forces of world capital, New Flag Imperialist Australia, and their local servants."[43]

The ideology of Bougainville as a divinely chosen nation derives, I will argue, from a deeply felt loss of control and power. In fact, many people felt that the powerful capitalistic West and the Australians had taken over the spiritual powers of Bougainvilleans along with their environment. They objected to the fact that these foreign powers had come to dominate both local economy and local politics.

Several Me'ekamui adherents and ex–BRA members claimed that spiritual control was taken from Bougainvilleans via the spread of Christianity. Missionaries and other foreigners were blamed for having prohibited ancestral practices of worship and offering at Bougainville's sacred sites. Moreover, because natural resources are traditionally conceptualized as being part of the holy land, extensive logging, fishing, mining, and other (foreign) activities that did not acknowledge these sacred sites and the sanctity of the land were blamed for desecrating both sites and land. They argued that both disrupting the sacredness of the land and taking too much of its resources were offences against God, who created the land. In addition, land is perceived as being an intrinsic part of Bougainvillean culture and people. As young Bougainville leader Raphael Bele argued against the mining company BCL during land negotiations: "Land is like the skin on the back of my hand. You inherit it and it is your duty to pass it on to your children. You would not expect us to sell our skin, would you?"[44] In short, it was hoped and believed that the war would recover the sacred sites and protect the holy land of Bougainville against foreign exploitation.

Obviously, the urge for spiritual control over resources and land entails the pursuit of economic control. Starting in the 1960s, Bougainvilleans have protested the enforced acquisition of land for mining purposes by the Australian administration. This protest led to the establishment of the Napidakoe Navitu movement. Its activities initially focused on putting a halt to the land problem emerging around the mining area.[45] In the 1980s, these protests evolved into a strong sense of dissatisfaction among local landowners with the unfair distribution of the mine's revenues. Tensions between Papua New Guinea and Bougainville ensued, as only a fraction of the Panguna mine's revenues flowed back to Bougainville. Ona and his fellow landowners demanded monetary compensation for the impact of the mine, a 50 percent share of mine revenues, and a transfer of ownership to Bougainville. As many Bougainvilleans shared the discontent regarding this lack of control over Bougainville's revenues, the militant actions of Ona and his followers against the mine and Papua New Guinea initially met with general approval and support from the Bougainvillean population.

Ultimately, after having been confronted with oppressive regimes since colonial times, Bougainvilleans were eager to obtain political control and autonomy. As a result of the crisis, Bougainville now has a large degree of autonomy. Many responsibilities and powers have by now been transferred from the national government to the ABG. Ten to fifteen years from now, the ABG will be granted a referendum to decide whether Bougainville should remain a province of Papua New Guinea or should seek some form of political independence. Many Bougainvilleans to whom I spoke believed that God not only gave the island its crisis but also put an end to it, thereby offering Bougainvilleans the opportunity to better their own and their island's position. For many, this implied that independence from Papua New Guinea should be the next step.

The Power of Religion

The holy war of Bougainville shows how the power of religion revolves around its intimate relationship with nationalism, custom, ethnicity and racism, charismatic leadership, violence, and peace. The nationalist movement of Me'ekamui and the BRA—indeed, nationalism in general—appropriated symbols and meanings from cultural contexts that are important in people's everyday experience.[46] One of these cultural contexts is religion, in particular, Catholic teachings. Other symbols and meanings were derived from local myths and traditions, such as the notion of the sacrality of the land of Bougainville.

Although Catholicism is a globally institutionalized practice and part of transnational discourse, the Bougainville case shows that Catholic elements and symbols can be appropriated into local secessionist protests and practices of resistance,[47] as well as into local peace efforts. In Bougainville, these symbols and meanings revolve around Mary's holiness and Marian devotion, with the rosary playing an important part, as well as around people's connection with their land and customs. Some religious prerequisites for Marian devotion happen to be present in Bougainville's culture, which may help explain why Mary could have become so popular there.[48] For some islanders, the matrilineal system and traditional gender relations may have facilitated the acceptance of Mary. Traditionally, mothers have an important role in Bougainville societies. They are the caretakers of the land, which is inherited via the female line, and they are the ones children turn to when they need something from their fathers. Just like Mary, the mother has a mediating role in Bougainville culture, Others conceptualized Mary in terms of local cosmologies, for example, by claiming that local mythological female figures and their sons were actually Mary and Jesus. The past is thereby reinterpreted to give it a viable and inclusive future while simultaneously rereading the future as it was shown to them by Europeans to perceive a past that is their own.[49]

Thus nationalist conceptualizations of Bougainville tradition and identity came to be supported by a Christian rhetoric in which the power of God as both creator of Bougainville and facilitator of the crisis took center stage. This infusion of Christian teachings into both nationalism and custom can also be witnessed in emergent nationalisms in other parts of the Pacific,[50] such as the Solomon Islands and Fiji, as well as in Africa and other parts of the world. In the Bougainville example, we thus see how nationalism and religion can be closely intertwined. As

Anthony Smith argues: "what is vital for nationalism and the nation . . . is the very core of traditional religions, their conception of the sacred and their rites of salvation. This is what the nationalists must rediscover and draw upon in forming their own ideals of community, history and destiny."[51] And this is exactly what Ona and his followers did. In fact, their nationalism took the shape of what Bruce Kapferer labels an ontology, a doctrine about the essence of reality, drawing upon myth, custom, and religion for its symbolism.[52]

The rhetoric of Bougainville's holy war exhibits the need to reclaim sovereignty, as well as spiritual, economic, and political control, from the hegemony of foreigners. This supports Margaret Jolly's claim that Pacific nationalism implies the negotiation of:

> the Western origin of Enlightenment and progressionist values—the promise of enfranchisement, emancipation and, more recently, development. But at the same time, nationalist political elites have to establish their credentials as anti-colonial and anti-Western, by denying the cultural hegemony of the West and by legitimations based on claims of authentic cultural difference and past identities.[53]

This tension between what Jolly labels the modernist project of freedom and nationalist recuperation in the name of original traditions is clearly visible in Bougainville. Here, the secessionist movement of Me'ekamui claimed Bougainville to be a sovereign nation in terms of shared cultural traditions, ethnicity, and the belief in God, rejecting foreigners and colonial influences.

The significant role of Ona as both a political and a spiritual leader during and after the crisis brought to light the power of religion in supporting leadership. Charismatic leadership and the notion of charismatic authority have become increasingly significant in the context of new religious movements.[54] The Bougainville case shows that such leadership may also be related to secessionist movements like Me'ekamui and, moreover, that the emergence of such leadership is related not only to religion but also to crisis. By appropriating a Christian rhetoric and using devotion to Mary as a means of obtaining holiness, Ona successfully infused religion with political strategies and ambitions. By institutionalizing himself as the leader, the president, and subsequently the king of Me'ekamui, he managed to stabilize and more or less maintain the power base of his leadership, despite attempts by the ABG to annul his influence and control in Bougainville. Without the crisis, Ona's political career would probably never have developed in the first place.

In their study of charismatic leadership, D. Madsen and P. Snow take the existence of crisis as their point of departure. According to their analysis, crisis weakens people's feeling of "self-efficacy" and their ability to handle challenges successfully. As a result, people seek security in what is called "proxy-control."[55] Ona's popularity was initially great, because people sought in him a hero and a potential savior. However, as soon as "his" BRA committed brutalities against Bougainvillean civilians and it became clear that he could not control vigilante groups within and outside the BRA, many people lost faith in his abilities. In consequence, Ona lost his charismatic power, especially in areas outside his direct influence. This shows that charismatic leadership is to a large extent dependent upon the ability to use force and exercise control, both over one's opponents and over one's followers. Charisma and divine inspiration do not suffice to make a successful leader.

Unfortunately, Bougainvilleans have not been able to maintain the holiness adhered to and experienced during the crisis. Many complain that Bougainvilleans have lost God again. There is a lot of violence on the island, and alcohol and substance abuse abound, amid growing tensions between the ABG and the Me'ekamui governments. This all endangers the fragile peace that people so desperately prayed for. Again people turn to Mary for help, this time no longer to request that She direct the fight against oppression or to seek protection against the violence of the crisis but to maintain peace and evict the evils that autonomy has brought. A truly liberating autonomy and the presence of God are still beyond the horizon for Bougainvilleans.

The Mourid Brotherhood at the Center of Senegalese Political Life

A Dialectic of State and Religious Power

Cheikh Guèye and Olivia Gervasoni

The complexity of ongoing political moves and a strong overlap between religious and political powers in Senegal, a country where democracy and secularism are being reinvented from day to day by various actors, is an excellent example of the dynamic interplay between religious and political power. This dynamism has been especially interesting since Adboulaye Wade, who claims membership in the Mourids, the largest of the religious Sufi brotherhoods in Senegal, was elected president in March 2000. Indeed, it threatens to create a new paradigm for the relationship between religious and state power in Senegalese politics.

In Senegal, with its strong Muslim majority, the brotherhoods have a specific relationship with the state. Foremost among these is the Mourid Brotherhood, which was founded at the end of the nineteenth century by Sheikh Ahmadou Bamba, a mystic and an ascetic *marabout*, or spiritual leader and religious dignitary, who sought in this founding to renew the spiritual force of Islam. The word *Mourid* means "aspirant" or "one who desires." About a third of all Senegalese Muslims belong to this brotherhood. Mourids are well known for their spirit of enterprise and work ethic, their solidarity, and their dynamic role in the economic life of Senegal. Their economic role extends outside the boundaries of the country, since they constitute the majority of Senegalese emigrants. The Mourid Brotherhood is organized as a caliphate, with a Caliph General that is hereditary and has authority over a hierarchy of other marabouts, each with a regional following, and their disciples, or *taalibes*. One becomes a Mourid by declaring a profession of faith and entering into a close relationship with a marabout through a special ceremony.

Since its creation, the Mourid Brotherhood, thanks to its form of organization and how it functions, has coexisted with the authorities in a system of service-exchange. The population's attachment to the marabouts, who exercise considerable authority over their devotees and who are highly respected for their religious scholarship, socio-economic success, and political capabilities, has contributed to this situation. At its founding, the Senegalese state drew upon the Mourids to reinforce its legitimacy, and, in return, it bestows favors on them.

This situation shifted somewhat when Abdoulaye Wade came to power in March 2000. His membership in the Mourid Brotherhood gives him symbolic prestige among the faithful, who see a concrete manifestation of their political aspirations in his accession to power. He can draw on the celebrity of Amadou Bamba—and all that comes with it. The relationship between the state and the brotherhood oscillates between a desire by the president to reinforce his power by drawing on symbolic religious association with the Mourids and Mourid attempts to appropriate the political symbolism of the head of state. The current Caliph General's entourage identifies strongly with the rule of A. Wade, who, in his turn, plays this card endlessly, multiplying his visits to Touba, the holy city of the Mourids, and promising to contribute decisively to the construction of the town.[1] This strategy may pay off for the president and also for the caliphate, but it carries with it a risk of confusion, of conflating the roles the president creates for himself by the ways he draws upon his membership in the brotherhood. The present Caliph General has declared his political neutrality, but might he or his successor one day send out a *ndigël*, the order given by a marabout to his taalibes, on behalf of a single party? And what if Mourids come to feel that the state belongs to them, so that they can do what they please with it? Needless to say, other Senegalese seem somewhat vexed by these possibilities, especially since the election of A. Wade had been regarded as a moment of reconciliation for most of the nation. Won't the Caliph General's entourage, not to mention future caliphs, continue to insinuate their institution into the political game, in order to further the autonomy of the brotherhood?

Part of the brotherhood perceived the election of A. Wade as a concrete expression of old messianic dreams, foretold by Sheikh Ahmadou Bamba. This seems to be at the root of a new order of rapprochement between the state and the Mourid Brotherhood. What significance should be attributed to this development? Does it really constitute a new relationship between the state and the Mourid Brotherhood, moving it beyond spiritual and material dimensions to give rise to new symbolic forms? Does the election of a Mourid president herald a new order, and is it likely to alter the behavior of the Senegalese population vis-à-vis religious forces?

The Mourid Brotherhood in Relation to the State: A Regulatory Symbiotic Relationship

The early persecution of the Mourid Brotherhood by the French colonial government, which actively opposed the brotherhood and exiled Amadou Bamba from 1895 to 1907, had the ironic effect of making the brotherhood a product of the centralized colonial authority by enabling it to grow in numbers and strength through reports of its founder's miraculous survivals of torture and to detach itself from the affairs of the city of Touba. Thus to analyze the evolution of the Mourid Brotherhood is essentially to analyze its position vis-à-vis the colonial state. To protect its members, it had to construct solid internal bases, both within the colonial state but also in opposition to it. The process of autonomization in which it engaged bestowed on its marabouts a function like that of the tribunes in ancient Rome, that of protecting the populace from arbitrary or harmful actions by magistrates. Paradoxically, if the brotherhood evolved in part as a response to government authorities, the contemporary Senegalese state has come to bear the mark of its relationship with the brotherhood.

A Dialectic of Autonomy and Articulation

The Mourid Brotherhood was formed against the centralized colonial authority as well as by it, in a permanent dialectic movement. After their initial opposition, by 1910 the colonial authorities had found the brotherhood quite helpful in their own need to secure their economic interests in the region. The colonial authorities thus became involved in the economic development of the brotherhood and in its internal life, particularly in the succession of caliphs. These interventions did not, however, prevent the brotherhood from concretizing its wish for autonomy through a social and political organization that asserted its distinctness.

The Mourid doctrine translates Sheikh Ahmadou Bamba's conception of the world. A Mourid pledges his allegiance to and agrees to participate in a society-based project of considerable dimension, integrating into his behavior the principles of humility, moderation, and, above all, disregard for power and all that is worldly. The Sheikh recommended to the elite among his taalibe a positive neutrality with regard to "power," so long as this power does not go against religion. Indeed, his teaching clearly reveals a distrust of power. "As to the pursuit of grandeur or power for the purpose of acceding to a position of authority or preeminence, or in order to set oneself above one's fellow men, this is a thing which distances the believer from God," he wrote.[2]

The Sheikh's undertaking merged a variety of aspirations in a religious Islamic renewal designed to preserve the society of the Wolof people, who constitute 40 percent of all Senegalese, from disintegration and ensure its cohesion. The colonial authorities, by contrast, considered the brotherhood as a means toward fulfilling its own politico-religious objectives. Despite this dissonance in aims, even the mystic work of the Sheikh thus became partly linked to the intervention of the colonial state, since without the state's encouragement Mouridism could not have developed so successfully by the time its founder died. By intervening in its evolution, the authorities facilitated the achievement of the ambitions and projects of Serigne Touba, as Sheikh Ahmadou Bamba was later called.

After Senegal's independence in 1960, the postcolonial state set the tone for the evolution of the brotherhood by involving itself in Mourid affairs on various levels, especially with regard to succession in the caliphate. When fears linked to the succession reemerged, each marabout would mobilize his political allies. Politicians even set off infighting among the young marabouts to reinforce political alliances. This happened in 1997, for example, when rioting in Touba contested the excessive control exercised by the *dahira* of the Mourid Students (Hizbut Tarqiyya) over the affairs of the caliphal institution.[3] This conflict exposed the principal line of fracture within the brotherhood, that separating the founder's biological heirs from his spiritual heirs. The internal divisions brought about by conflict over the successions have somewhat eroded the power of the marabouts. In a situation such as this, the brotherhood withdraws, giving priority to its autonomy.

Thus Mouridism, initially based on religious experience, became an "institution" of a social, economic, and political order, both homogeneous and coherent. The inability of the state fully to integrate into the social fabric and to become universally recognized gave further vigor to the brotherhood. The latter's strength lies in part in its capacity to resist integration into the state and to constitute alternative forms of social and political organization. Its objective is not to destroy the state but to confront it from within an autonomous space. Because Mouridism grafted itself onto the structures of traditional society and created a place essential to sustaining the links of human dependency, it has succeeded in significantly limiting the state's ability to intervene in its domain. This alternative social and political structure finds expression in the relationship between marabout and taalibe and in the system of organization that results, based on the strength of that relationship and on the *ndigël*.

Birth of an Opposition Force: The Marabout's Function as Tribune

During the colonial period, there at first appeared to be a distinct separation between the brotherhood's authority at the "periphery" and state authority at the "center." Yet when state authorities intruded in the internal affairs of the brotherhood during successions, a politico-religious alliance resulted, based on an exchange of services. From then on, a marabout assumed a political role, entrusted with the duty of negotiating with the state on behalf of the interests of the brotherhood and its community. The brotherhood and the marabouts soon came to play the role of social stabilizers. While giving priority to its own interests, the Mourid Brotherhood became a channel of communication between the state and the taalibe. By retaining its autonomy, it could also appear to challenge state authority, for though the marabout becomes the "tribune" of his community, he has at his command a whole flock of taalibe ready to express themselves on the political scene, whether under the banner of Mouridism or not. In June 1980, for example, the Mourid marabout Serigne Abdou Lahat intervened with the authorities on behalf of his community over low peanut prices and government policies concerning drought.

Nevertheless, the Caliph General should be distinguished from other Mourid dignitaries. The line taken by the Caliph is highly variable, everything depending on economic circumstances, the political evolution of the brotherhood, and its wish for autonomy. There was a perceptible change after the advent in 1990 of the last Caliph General, Serigne Saliou Mbacké. Much more reserved than his predecessors vis-à-vis the government, he refuses to appear to be a lackey of the state. He is always silent during elections, thus putting an end to the practice of issuing electoral *ndigël* from the center of caliphal authority, Touba. But when the Caliph General avoids appearing to be a political leader, other important marabouts take it upon themselves to fulfill this function, as did Serigne Modou Makhtar, the late Serigne Kosso, and even the late Serigne Modou Bousso Dieng.

The Mourid Brotherhood and Islam in general constitute in themselves a political code and a distinctive language, in which the marabout holds power over his followers. Most often, the marabouts position themselves as the representatives and spokespersons of a group. In Senegal, the Mourid Brotherhood embodies both a temporal and a spiritual power. This protection offered by the marabout as tribune is part of what unites the community. It materializes as intervention and influence peddling in the political and social field. The marabout's positions are complementary: by operating in the temporal sphere, he strengthens his appeal among the taalibe, yet his power, his *baraka*, is "supernatural," opening for him an area having real sense for Senegalese where the state is powerless. The capacity to cross from one field to another confers on marabouts the right to issue *ndigël* in both political and societal domains.

The political extent of these electoral *ndigël* has always been exaggerated by analysts, however.[4] It is within the brotherhoods that the limits of the *ndigël* must be determined. It first lost some of its power and impact within the marabout-disciple relationship itself. Contact between the contracting parties of this relationship has lessened in the urban anonymity of Touba, and the value of spiritual instruction has diminished. In consequence, the *ndigël* has lost some of its sacred significance. Several bans imposed by the Caliph in the town of Touba, for example, are completely ignored: depigmentation of the skin, traffic rules, etc. The marabout clientele also seems to have fragmented, though in reality what seems to have been reshaped is not the brotherhood itself but its relation with the state. The advent of Serigne Saliou Mbacké and his attitude to politics constitute a veritable new order, even as in marabout lineages and matrilineages individuals have gained more power of economic and political determination. The current Caliph adopts a position of neutrality, and political demonstrations within the precincts of

Touba are prohibited. "I would like those who are called upon to run our country to be the best," he declared in April 1998, at the festival of Eid (the end of Ramadan), in order to halt the stream of politicians coming to him to "solicit his blessings and prayers" or even "in the guise of taalibe." The Caliph's declaration marks his intention to keep his distance from representatives of the state and to reaffirm his supremacy in his own territory.

In response to this disengagement of the Caliph, the state's relationship with the brotherhood fragmented. Many resources were mobilized to solicit other marabouts from the brotherhood's central administration, according to their respective influence on the Caliph or on the taalibe, as circumstances dictated. This change in strategy on the part of the state triggered new behavioral patterns within the brotherhood and shattered the foundations of its internal power plays. Religious legitimacies, political power, and economic success now mutually nurture one another more than they did in the past. The state, through the pressure it brought to bear in political and economic domains, created or consolidated religious legitimacies. This is not a new state strategy, but it was implemented more generally before the presidential elections of 1993. Marabouts fit into the political game in different ways. If up until the 1980s they were to an extent "kingmakers," between 1990 and 2000 they became politicians, often elected representatives, present at the National Assembly and in certain local administrations.

"The Will to Be King," or Mourid Figures in Politics

The Mourids' appetite for political power can be analyzed from two aspects. The first concerns diverse methods of investiture in the political domain, and the second, individual Mourids' perceptions of the connection between their identity and politics. The Mourids gained possession of the political sphere in several ways. The 1990s saw marabouts enter politics via the electoral tickets of the country's large parties. Serigne Dame Mbacké de Darou Mousty became the first when he registered as a candidate for the PDS (Democratic Party of Senegal) on the eve of the controversial 1988 elections. Several others followed, and today there are several Mbacké-Mbackés in the National Assembly. Mourid lobby groups were formed and gravitate around influential political figures with a view to receiving benefits or even procuring positions of authority. This is the case with the *dahira* RAMOU (Mourid Gatherings), whose members have close ties to A. Wade's authority and whose president, Madické Niang, became the Minister of Energy and Mining. Finally, the involvement of marabouts in electoral campaigns is still evident, though this is a matter of less important marabouts acting as spokespersons, often aided in their task by their influence with one or more *dahiras*. Serigne Modou Kara Mbacké is one such figure. President of the MMUD (World Movement for the Unicity of God), he estimates that he is at the head of approximately five hundred thousand taalibe. For several years, he has declared himself to be a "kingmaker," openly supporting certain candidates and rejecting others. But what does this mean to ordinary Senegalese in light of their own power as citizens? Modou Kara Mbacké was booed during a demonstration for having uttered the name of Ousmane Tanor Dieng (protégé of Abdou Diouf in 2000 and currently the Permanent Secretary of the Socialist Party), who has a record for being "the man most reviled by the people."

More and more marabouts enter the political scene by means of their own, openly declared, Mourid political parties, despite Constitutional law 81.16, dated May 6, 1981, prohibiting the creation of a political party on a religious basis. This is the case of Serigne Ousseynou Fall, brother of the current caliph of the Baye-Fall Mourid movement (a subgroup of the brotherhood, characterized by its sacerdotal devotion and eccentricity). During the last presidential elections in 2000, when A. Wade came to power, religious views sometimes replaced political programs. The marabouts involved in the campaign consider their role to be the same as that of all Senegalese citizens. Serigne Ousseynou Fall, for example, broaches religious topics in his platform.[5] By creating his party, the MDC (Citizens' Movement), in 1999, he sought to advocate work, solidarity, and loyalty, major virtues of Mouridism. He wants an ideology suitable for his land, capable of pulling the country out of a state of underdevelopment. Apart from being a descendant of the founder of the Baye-Fall Mourid group, Serigne Ousseynou Fall has had an educational and professional career, which helps him communicate with his electorate. After serving in the Ministries of the Interior, Communications, and Senegalese Abroad, he now devotes himself to the brotherhood "to improve the lot of the Mourids." He declares: "I have examined and reviewed all the governments and have discovered no authentic Mourids like myself."[6] He intends Mourid ideology to prevail even within state institutions, since "in Sheikh Ahmadou Bamba's teaching there is social organization, and running a society involves politics."[7] Ousseynou Fall wants to put an end to "the exclusion" of Mourids from government.

However, religious parties do not yet seem to operate in Senegal. To judge from election results, democracy and secularism have not been attacked through religious intervention in political matters. Nevertheless, political commitment by religious leaders could result in the emergence of a category of marabouts (the grandsons) and influential figures within the brotherhood who will attempt to bring more members of the brotherhood into the political field. For that to happen, the existing socioeconomic and political compromises would have to be renegotiated to enable Mourids to increase their level of intervention. Indeed, the post of politico-religious leader may already have come into existence.

Other marabouts (Serigne Dame Mbacké and Serigne Bara Mbacké for the PDS) prefer to appear on the tickets of the large political parties instead of entering the political game on their own. This also benefits the parties, for whom having a representative of the brotherhood on their tickets is an important pledge of support. The PDS has long understood this, and A. Wade has always considered the brotherhoods to be a sociological force to be reckoned with.

"Interest groups" illustrate this method of investiture in the political game by endeavoring to appropriate the political symbolism of a Mourid president. The election of a Mourid to the presidency was occasion for Mourid messianism to take stock of itself. Had Sheikh Ahmadou Bamba predicted that the brotherhood would one day take over power? In more than twenty interviews with Mourids involved, or seeking to be involved, in political life, we could distinguish three large groups.

In the first group are Mourids who are convinced that Mouridism alone is the way to salvation and that, as Ibrahima Sall states, "Mourids have always been kingmakers and it is time for them to be kings."[8] Among those who believe this are: Serigne Ousseynou Fall; one of the members of his party, Madické Wade;[9] and even Atou Diagne, president of the Hizbut Tarqiyya.[10] These men are all from Mourid families and have had a Western-style education. For them, to be a Mourid in politics is to achieve the country's economic and political advancement, ensuring that the Mourid ideology triumphs over all others. Furthermore, they are motivated less by a desire to ensure the country's development in line with Mourid values than by the frustration of having felt excluded from running the city's affairs, a frustration that is not borne out in fact. Being a Mourid in politics means enabling the brotherhood to increase its power as well as securing posts of influence as individuals, using the reputation of the brotherhood.

The difference between the second group and the first may lie in the offices that its members hold. All are in the government and in the National Assembly. Their political rise has been effected. Representatives of this group whom we interviewed include: Madické Niang, Vice President of RAMOU and new Minister for the Habitat (now Minister of Energy and Mining); Souleymane Ndéné Ndiaye, spokesman for the President of the Republic; Moustapha Sourang, Minister of State Education and Higher Education; Modou Diagne Fada, Minister of the Environment, Youth, and Health; Kansoumbaly Ndiaye, former Minister of State Education; Oumar Sarr, deputy for the PDS (Mbacké); and Ablaye Faye, Executive Vice-President of the National Assembly.[11] Apart from K. Ndiaye and A. Faye, all are from Mourid families, and all are members of the PDS except M. Sourang, who is from "civil society." To be a Mourid in politics for them no longer involves a focus on acquiring power, since they have already done so; the challenge lies in handling this identity so that Mouridism can serve the country and retain its supremacy in relation to the multiplicity of Senegalese brotherhoods.

Finally, in the last group are Mourids who are occupied in the political game but for whom religion must remain distant from the political field. Four whom we interviewed are members of RAMOU but have distanced themselves from the *dahira*: Serigne Abdou Fatah, Honorary

President of RAMOU; Madior Bouna Niang, member of RAMOU and President of the Functional Commission; Sheikh Bamba Sall, Executive Vice-President of RAMOU; and Modou Amar, deputy for the URD (Union for Democratic Revival).[12] Two men who have no ties with RAMOU have just joined them: Boubakar Thioube, member of the URD, and Talla Sylla, leader of the *Jëf Jël* (a party he created in 1998, whose acronym means "reap what you have sown" and which is the fruit of a rupture with the PDS).[13] These men are from traditional Mourid families and have long educational and political careers. For them, Mouridism and politics are incompatible. Mourid doctrine cannot be at the base of a political program, only of a societal program furthering development. To be Mourid in politics means knowing how to respect one's beliefs and putting the spiritual and the temporal in perspective, even in explaining Sheikh Amadou Bamba's precepts. The internalization of Mourid principles does not imply their use for political purposes.

Today the state can no longer ignore the dynamism of Mouridism. It must acknowledge that the brotherhood has established new modes of social regulation and that it represents, at least at a symbolic level, a parallel society that escapes state control. The growing involvement of the Mourids in the political domain, as well as their ever-stronger demands for recognition, oblige state authorities to accommodate this new force. This forces the state to interfere in the religious domain. It vacillates between attempts to prevent the religious legitimacy of Mouridism from forwarding Mourid ends and a desire to monopolize that legitimacy in order to equip itself with a sort of official Islam. The relationship between the state and the brotherhood lies, therefore, somewhere between an exchange of services and a desire for symbolic domination.

Symbolism, a Topos in the Relationship Between the State and the Mourid Brotherhood

The state's need for an alliance with religious power results from the fact that it is a graft onto Senegalese society that did not take well. Citizens are poorly assimilated into the state, and politicians would like to improve the state's image, which is sullied, in the eyes of a large section of the population, by the sin of secularism. This secularism functions as a paradox. The historical and cultural substratum that created it has no bearing on Islamic societal realities. However, within the context of Senegalese brotherhoods, secularism offers a guarantee of stability. The participation of marabouts in political life is not contrary to the principles of secularism.

Senegalese legislation followed the French example of separation between church and state until January 7, 2001, when a referendum permitted President Abdoulaye Wade to modify the constitution in a few small points. Though the Senegalese state still recognizes secularism as a fundamental principle of the country, at present every new head of state has to swear an oath to God. The plurality of religions is not questioned, but the oath challenges the concept of secularism as it was understood in Senegal as far back as 1983. With the revision of the constitution, A. Wade has reassociated the spiritual and the temporal. In fact, he is the best example of the new form of quest for the political support of the marabouts; he attempts to appropriate the spiritual within the temporal via symbolic language. Making use of both his Mourid affiliation and his marabout-taalibe relationship with Serigne Saliou, he demonstrates his faith and interest in the brotherhood to the entire body of taalibe. The prayers that the Caliph General accords A. Wade have a different meaning for certain Mourids, inasmuch as A. Wade is both President of the Republic and a Mourid taalibe. Moreover, promises of a material nature (a heliport already completed in Touba, the Khelcom Road, etc.) have been made to the brotherhood, causing the president's adversaries to say that his faith is merely a matter of political calculation. Within the sphere of the exchange of services, these political calculations have turned the state into the brotherhood's material protector.

By appropriating the symbols of the brotherhood and associating them with the symbols of the state, of which he is the representative, the president has assumed a double identity, which is transparent even within the state. But he is not the only one to use the symbolic weight manifested in his affiliation to the brotherhood. A part of the Mourid population now identifies with him, and therefore with the state.

The State Cleanses Itself of the Sin of Secularism: Abdoulaye Wade, or the Political Appropriation of Mouridism

The legitimacy of the authority of the state institution and its representatives must constantly be reaffirmed. Despite the polls, every president must be accepted by the spiritual powers. It is not sufficient for the state to handle its affairs successfully; the political, economic, and societal actions of its leaders must seek legitimization. Today the state continues to keep the marabouts informed of its actions. In 2001, A. Wade declared that he "would undertake nothing for Touba without the Caliph's approval." A change is perceptible: given the Caliph General's withdrawal from political matters, Touba controls national politics less than it has in the past; but everything to do with Touba must receive the consent of the marabout authority, so that the brotherhood remains "the master of the place."

Moreover, it is standard practice to justify the political game to the marabouts. After dismissing his prime minister, Moustapha Niasse, A. Wade made a point of explaining to Caliph Serigne Saliou Mbacké the reasons for his decision. Likewise, Moustapha Niasse, who is on good terms with the religious heads of the country, visited Touba with the same purpose in mind. It seems that politicians need to justify their unpopular acts to the marabouts, not to receive their benediction but so that the population can be informed of them. Symbolism again becomes the essential element in the legitimization of the state.

The arrival of A. Wade in the presidency only reinforced what already existed. After his election he made several promises to the brotherhood, the first being the construction of an airport in Touba, considered to be the second most important town in the country economically. If this proposal delighted the Mourids, the reactions of those outside the brotherhood were different, and certain people considered absurd the construction of an airport that would really be used only once a year (for the "grand *Magal*"). During his first year as president, A. Wade persevered in this type of initiative: he renamed the fortnight dedicated to women "Mame Diarra Bousso Week," after Sheikh Ahmadou Bamba's mother, considered to be the model of a pious, devoted woman; he also declared that he would not undertake anything for the country that was contrary to the recommendation of his marabout, the Caliph General of the Mourids. In addition to these declarations, he publicly visited Touba before each of his undertakings, like preparing for elections or visiting foreign heads of state. The state's material and spiritual protection of the brotherhood has increased with the accession of a Mourid to the presidency.

Previously, symbolism resided in the religious language politicians addressed to the brotherhood and the actions they undertook for Touba. At present the head of the state monopolizes this symbolism, under cover of a desire to penetrate and dominate the religious sphere. In fact, to be recognized by the members of one's brotherhood is important from a political point of view. Even should the Caliph give no more electoral orders, A. Wade can count on the Mourids' perception of him. In allowing them to identify with him and hence with the state, A. Wade is shaping an image as "President of the Mourids."

A. Wade's accession to the presidency and his affiliation with the Mourid Brotherhood marks a further step in the intensification and personalization of the relationship between the state and Mouridism. A new paradigm is being put into place, backed by a logic of collaboration and support for the Mourid project, muting a logic of confrontation. This new order was already signaled when A. Wade declared, some time ago, that the new credentials for control of the state and civil religious society, by one and the same authority, would be possessed "by he who best interprets religion," thus, by a religious leader.[14] A. Wade seems to intend to position himself in the guise of such a leader. By constantly demonstrating his faith and belief in the blessings of Mouridism, he is succeeding in becoming the spokesman for the brotherhood and its staunchest representative in the state. Without stating it as an objective, he appropriates the symbols of the brotherhood and evidence of interest shown in him by others, which all tends to replace the authority necessary for issuing *ndigël*.

By choosing that his first visit after his election as head of the state would be to the Caliph General of the Mourids, he was positioning himself to be the legitimate depository for the vote of Ahmadou Bamba's descendants and taalibe, who pass for "kingmakers." The Caliph General's esteem for A. Wade is considered by some to be a *ndigël*, without being called that. However, this situation does not discourage the other political parties, who regularly visit Touba. On each of his visits, the President of the Republic engenders a wave of popularity. Not only does he acquire, by virtue of his office as head of state, the status of an important taalibe, but he reinforces the symbolic weight of the Caliph General.

In the relations being formed between the new authorities and the leadership of Touba, political power is taking on a divine quality and is giving religious Mourid legitimacy to the man holding the state's highest public office. If A. Wade's principal objective is to be in favor with Serigne Saliou, behind this lies the desire to be considered by the Mourids as their representative and their ally. The technique is clever but is not without danger for the president's credibility. In addition to material manifestations and state promises to the brotherhood, the president appropriates religious symbolism politically by publicly displaying his affiliation to Mouridism and by multiplying his visits to the Caliph General.

Although the manner in which these actions are calculated and their objective are not clearly expressed, they get results. The president has become a point of reference for the Mourids, and during the last legislative elections, in April 2001, he got a record number of votes in the region of Touba. In the town of Mbacké, the ticket of Oumar Sarr won more than 80 percent of the valid votes. (Oumar Sarr is Mbacké's deputy for the PDS in the legislative elections of 2001 and former technical adviser to Kansoumbaly Ndiaye in the Ministry of State Education.) During the electoral campaign, the president's *Sopi* coalition (a term he revived from the 1880s and 1890s, when it expressed the will to change) also managed to gain a *ndigël* in Touba Belel through Serigne Sidy Mbacké, the eldest son of the late Serigne Abdou Lahat Mbacké, third Caliph General. These results must, however, be qualified, for the numbers of votes cannot be attributed solely to the Mourids. The decline of the Socialist Party (PS) has played a role in the increase in power of the PDS. The networks of brotherhood support for the PS, like those for other political parties, are disintegrating. The PDS has the advantage of having a member of the Mourid Brotherhood as its leader. The legislative elections that followed the presidential elections also showed the population's confidence in A. Wade. In them, the Senegalese chose to give the president the means to govern.

The new order has affected not only authoritative power but also the chances for certain Mourids to appropriate it. Many now feel that the power of the state belongs to them. One witnesses certain groups attempting to "hijack" the political symbolism of the President of the Republic, who has become for awhile the "President of the Mourids," providing a route through which the rest of the brotherhood can take possession of institutions.

The Mourids, or the Appropriation of the Political Symbolism of the President of the Republic

The effects of this "hijacking" are felt especially within the first and second groups of Mourids involved in politics. Members of the second group, who feel that the issue at stake "in being Mourid" lies in ensuring both that Mouridism continues to support development and that the Mourid Brotherhood remains in accord with the other brotherhoods, use the symbolism of the president only for political ends. They are often members of the PDS, and having the same religious convictions as the party representative increases their cohesion. The loyalty of these party supporters to the PDS and to their president is illustrated, therefore, not only in their political actions but also through their common adherence to the philosophy of Sheikh Ahmadou Bamba. This symbolism seems to be effective in the Mourid basin, the geographical area around Touba and Diourbel, where the electorate, already won over by A. Wade, voted overwhelmingly for Oumar Sarr, who until then was unknown in the region. The first group represents what, in fact, in Senegal and even within the brotherhood are called "political opportunists." If being Mourid means enabling the brotherhood to increase its power and individually securing posts of influence, then having a Mourid president is a chance to claim the right to power and to put in place strategies for domination.

What is therefore probably at stake is the representation of the Mourids by the head of the state. Those who sympathized with this project grouped together around Maître Madické Niang or backed the movement of support, created one year after the election of A. Wade, called the ADA, or *And Diapalé Abdoulaye Wade Nguir Serigne Touba*, which means "together support Abdoulaye Wade around Serigne Touba." Though this type of grouping may have existed in the past, the reference to the holy founder is a novelty. Not only does the ADA link Sheikh Ahmadou Bamba to authoritative power, but it also assimilates the entire brotherhood, irrespective of any possible alternative opinion, to A. Wade and to the PDS.

In the press, the ADA was very quickly likened to a "Mourid stranglehold" tightening around the president. In an interview, Maître Madické Niang reexamines the *ndigël*.[15] In the case of the ADA, so far as he was concerned, it was no longer a question of calling for the *ndigël* but of "managing to convince on an objective basis,"[16] the apparent motivation being not to take up a position but to give the head of state the institutional means to govern. Journalists considered that the collective of the ADA constituted a decisive step in the strategy of enmeshing the "president-taalibe" alignment undertaken by the Mourids, whose aim was both to reap the benefits of the power recently acquired by one of their own kind and, equally, to manifest their intention to have an impact on future elections.

As such comments increased, the Caliph General interceded, asking the Mourids to distinguish "futile things" attached to politics and this world from matters relating to Sheikh Ahmadou Bamba. The ADA movement was thereby stifled. Despite the brevity of its existence, it manifested a new move by the Mourids, who rapidly seized the opportunity to make themselves heard by means of the brotherhood, using the symbol of A. Wade as their relay channel. The absence of this type of support movement when A. Wade was in the opposition casts doubt on the altruism of the participants. This symbolic appropriation not only served the president's supporters grouped together in the ADA; its detractors also play on the president's Mourid identity and the use he makes of it in order to stymie him. Mourids who belong to other political parties are especially quick to accuse the president of using his affiliation to Mouridism for political ends, saying that before he was elected to power no one knew that he belonged to the brotherhood. Others, equally opposed to the PDS, protest the practice of Mouridism in the highest echelons of the state, as this does not conform to the fundamental principles of Sheikh Ahmadou Bamba.

In making use of Mourid symbolism, A. Wade appears to have emerged a grand winner today. By claiming his affiliation, he has reaped the fruits of his investments and has set the symbol ablaze with the help of those who also wish to benefit from it. However, one should be aware of the risks taken by the president in doing so, specifically the possibility that a prevalent Mourid dominance in the Senegalese state may evolve, based on the president-taalibe dialectic and latent risks of instability, both at that national level and between the brotherhoods.

The President-Taalibe Dialectic

The idea of a "president-taalibe" dialectic corresponds to the possibility of conflating A. Wade's two roles. His role as president and his capacity as taalibe are supposed to be radically different, according to the secularism of the state. It is not a question of preventing presidents from living their faith to the full but rather of controlling the use they make of it. The danger lies in associating the head of state with the brotherhood rather than with his political party. The symbolic use of Mouridism contributes to this risk of confusion. If A. Wade becomes, in the eyes of the population, the President of the Mourids, the threshold to a state associated with them will be quickly crossed. The authority of the state and its legitimacy vis-à-vis the population and the other brotherhoods could well suffer in consequence.

The confusion of the two notions poses the problem of the place occupied by the president vis-à-vis the brotherhood. In his role as head of state, A. Wade theoretically holds a power superior to that of the brotherhood and of the Caliph General, but when he assumes the role of taalibe, he must comply with the orders of his marabout. The president-taalibe dialectic, by conflating the head of state and Mouridism, leads to a matter that directly affects the population because it heightens the risk of instability, both nationally and between the brotherhoods.

Rivalry within the brotherhoods now becomes important. The state has long been accused of fostering dissension among the chief Mourid marabouts to prevent the formation of too powerful a union. Nowadays, the brotherhood seems divided between those who want to support A. Wade and perhaps benefit from his favors, and those who, distinguishing religion from politics, refuse to have him associated with Mouridism. This competition within the brotherhoods could also take hold in the political parties. In Senegal, all political groupings gather up Mourid activists. Certain members refuse to acknowledge the alleged preference of the Caliph General for A. Wade and declare that Serigne Saliou is there for everyone. The opposition most to be feared is the one that could arise between the country's diverse brotherhoods. Promises made by the head of state to the Mourids could certainly cause the other brotherhoods, in particular the Tidianes, to think that the Mourids are favored.

Conclusion

It seems that the Islamic brotherhoods, which have existed in Senegal for over a century, have always had mutually beneficial relationships with the state authorities. The degree of Islam's mutual use of and instrumentalization by political power has varied according to context, as has, likewise, the use of political power in consolidating the position of Islam. The fact remains, however, that those holding political power have never agreed to total domination by religious leaders, and the latter have often been defenders of groups opposing those in power.

Nevertheless, the perceived risks of this situation, such as instability within the brotherhoods, between the brotherhoods, or at the national level, may be contained. The President of the Republic is managing to handle the sensibilities of other religious leaders and continues to treat them as key political figures. Several examples can be given. The demise of the Caliph General of the Layennes, early in 2001, gave A. Wade the opportunity to show his interest in the members of this brotherhood, who are numerous in the region of Dakar.

A. Wade has succeeded in controlling Senegal's multiplicity of religions and brotherhoods, at least insofar as can be judged after the second year of his term of office. At the same time, he has pushed to the fore his attachment to Sheikh Ahmadou Bamba, thus awakening a feeling of identification with the authorities among certain Mourids. The symbolism expresses the new issue at stake involving the political influence of the Senegalese Brotherhood of the Mourids and its relationship with the authorities through the person of the head of state.

Sharia and State in the Sudan

From Late Colonialism to Late Islamism

Shamil Jeppie

Sharia has been a complex and powerful symbol throughout the modern history of the Sudan. Centered on the place of Islamic law, or *sharia*, in the legal system are a series of issues concerning the complex relations between religion and politics.[1] Sharia has disrupted any boundaries between religion and politics that colonial or modern secular/ist actors have attempted to construct or elaborate. It has refused to become a "religious law" for the private sphere only. In the postcolonial period, sharia has always to some extent been used by some political grouping or other to advance its cause. Since law is so integral to the historical development of Islam and its practice by Muslims, even though interpretations vary vastly, some sections of the population of a Muslim country would always be open to persuasion through the call to "implement full sharia." In the Sudan there has been tremendous variation and much debate and political struggle about sharia as a protected sphere, from regulating Muslim personal law (marriage, divorce, inheritance, custody, etc.) in the colonial period to the calls for and experimentation with a "sharia state" starting in the 1970s. Even today, though the issue attracts less attention—partly because a peace agreement is in place between the previously warring north and south, and because of the crisis in Darfur—in the Sudan sharia and its current implementation as a system of private and public law suitable for a multireligious, multicultural country in the twenty-first century remains a question.

In the first quarter of the twentieth century, the colonial state instituted sharia as a separate legal subsystem dealing especially with matters of personal law. By the last quarter of the century, the dominant political forces inside the country promoted sharia as a comprehensive system of personal, commercial, criminal, and public law. In the first period, colonial power kept sharia in a subordinate place; in the last, the postcolonial state was increasingly forced to give sharia preeminence at the expense of other legal traditions. At the start of the century, it was marginal under colonialism; by the end, it was dominant under an "Islamic state." Furthermore, various parties asserted it as the basis of the country's constitution, attempting to turn the Sudan into a "sharia state" amidst ongoing civil war in the south of the country.

From the beginning to the end of these periods, sharia was used in various ways by the state and those outside it to register divergent projects of political transformation. The British colonial administrators sought progressively to decrease its role, while in the postcolonial state key political actors willingly or tactically pronounced their support for sharia as the foundation of the constitution and legal system. Sharia was not only officially recognized, it was part of the structure of rule. But this was different from demands in the last quarter of the twentieth century for a state explicitly devoted to the implementation of sharia as the dominant body of law.

This essay traces some of the significant issues involved in the use of sharia as a body of law in the legal and political history of the Sudan. Of special concern is the chequered history of the relationship between sharia and the state in the Sudan. Sharia cannot be studied without looking at the state and its judicial preferences. The colonial state imposed its policies and laws, and the independent state inherited these judicial traditions and a good deal of the colonial state's political practices. When exponents of a highly modernist interpretation of the aims and scope of sharia emerged, they firmly focused their ambitions on capturing the state. Furthermore, the repressed Islamic heritage of sharia returned to take pride of place in the pantheon of laws fairly soon after the foreigners departed.

Because English Common Law was a sign of British colonial domination, Sudanese independence brought with it the notion that an indigenous legal culture ought to replace the foreign one. A hybrid legal tradition was, in fact, the legacy of the postcolonial state. Instead of accepting or developing this mixture of legal traditions, certain sections of the Sudanese elite progressively called for less of the British legacy and more of the Islamic one. There were glimmers of a "Sudanese Common Law" in the making by the late 1960s, but this process was cut short by the increasing claims for sharia as the only authoritative legal discourse.[2] Such demands were part of broader political and ideological struggles within and about the postcolonial state. In postcolonial Sudanese politics, sharia has thus been fought over as a symbol. The intensity of this struggle, however, may have led to a reduction in the level of sophistication of the thinking and interpretation of the centuries-old, rich scholarly traditions that went into the making of sharia.[3]

Sharia from Early to Late Colonialism

In the words of one of the "holy trinity" of the Sudan Political Service, the South African–educated Legal Secretary C. C. G. Cumings:

> There is nothing so forceful, not even language, in shaping the thoughts and habits of a nation as the law. Examples innumerable can be cited. I need mention one. India for all her political intransigence has yet received from England in the law a seal which is likely to remain. Many of her political leaders are lawyers trained in the English law and betray their upbringing even in their most rebellious moods. Egypt on the other hand was lost to English influence when the [Civil] Codes were promulgated.[4]

Until independence in 1956, sharia courts, and judges to run them, with a "Grand Qadi" at the head, were a part of the colonial machinery. Sharia was a key part of a three-pronged judicial system of rule, the two others being the "Civil courts" and "Native courts." Although sharia was not codified, since it was part of a modernizing colonial bureaucracy it was given a "modern" shape and to an extent "modern" content, as reflected in certain of the reforms.

The dominant *madhhab* ("school" of legal interpretation) in the Sudan has been Maliki, but the Egyptian Grand Qadis often ignored this fact and based their decisions on the *Hanafi madhhab*, dominant in Egypt.[5] But the Qadis also made innovations in their application of the sharia, especially in the area of "personal law." Thus many of their judgments were based on both Hanafi and Maliki opinions, as well as mixing earlier jurisprudential decisions of each school.[6] Furthermore, they brought certain pioneering legal opinions from the leading Egyptian "reformist" scholars at al-Azhar University. Whereas Qadis in Cairo may have been hesitant to apply these views, in Khartum they could give the views unhindered expression and application.[7]

The modern career of sharia begins in the colonial period, when it is turned into a parochial, half-dead legal apparatus meant only for what the colonial masters defined as appropriate spheres of application. In the *madhhab* of the colonial state, sharia was restricted to personal matters. Yet, as I will show, in this restricted area the senior practitioners of sharia exercised a good deal of independence.

At the apex of colonial authority was the governor-general, in "supreme military and civilian command of the Sudan," and the colonial bureaucracy under him, staffed by British citizens. The civil courts served the British, Europeans, and other "non-Mohammedans" in the country. It is telling that these courts were called "ordinary courts." Muslims could also bring their cases to these courts. Indeed, the "ordinary courts" had jurisdiction in all areas not covered by the sharia courts.

Muslims, who were the majority in the northern regions and the country as a whole, primarily had recourse to the sharia courts. In the south, and among the nomadic Muslim peoples in the north, native or tribal courts practicing "customary law" had authority. But each sphere of authority was ultimately subject to the approval of the British governor-general. Egypt was supposed to be a *co-domini* of the Sudan, but Egyptians played a secondary role in running the colony. In the 1920s, their presence was even further reduced.[8] Insofar as the law went, the Egyptians were sent to Khartum to oversee the operation of the sharia courts. Thus, before independence the "Grand Qadi" was always an Egyptian.[9]

The British clearly regarded the civil courts, their methods, and their precepts to be the superior system. The three-tired legal structure was not one of equally valid components. The civil courts effectively applied English Common Law, and this legal tradition, through the sheer weight of British colonial dominance, became the preeminent tradition in the country. The Civil Justice Ordinance of 1929 had a "justice, equity and good conscience" clause for cases in which there was no clear-cut legislation. This clause, however, was interpreted to mean English Common Law, and thus colonial chief justices and judges drew extensively on English precedents, legal (Latin) terminology, and treatises.[10] Section 5 of the Civil Justice Ordinance of 1929 gives custom and "Mohammedan law" preference in personal-law matters unless contrary to "justice, equity and good conscience."[11] A separate Sudan Penal Code was promulgated based on the Indian Penal Code drawn up in British India.

Sharia was seen as substantially less significant, but it had to be tolerated to some degree because of the Muslim population and especially the fear of offending the "traditional" Muslim elite. After the conquest of the Sudan late in 1898, Lord Cromer, British agent and consul-general in Cairo, traveled from Cairo to Khartum to proclaim the new authority and the government's respect for "Mohammedan Law" to the religious notables he met. The Mohammedan Law Courts Ordinance of 1902 and subsequently the Mohammedan Law Courts Procedure Act of 1915 governed the administration of sharia.[12] The first act (section D) provided for the Grand Qadi to issue regulations relating to sharia for the courts to apply. These circulars of the Grand Qadis of course had to have the approval of the governor-general. In due course, judicial circulars were regularly published reflecting respective qadis' close interaction with Sudanese realities.[13]

The "native courts" were officially recognized twenty years after the conquest, immediately after the 1920 report by Lord Milner, which recommended the use of "native authorities" and decentralization. In the north the British promoted these courts' judicial functions, largely to displace the sharia courts. In the south they fostered the courts' administrative role in such matters as collecting taxes.

This was the end of direct rule and the beginning of indirect rule. Thereafter, in the north native courts were gradually used to attempt to displace sharia courts. On personal status issues, for instance, the native courts were given concurrent jurisdiction with sharia courts. There were attempts to halt the work of the Qadi College established in 1902 to train sharia judges. By April 1929, more than eighteen sharia courts had been abolished, while thirty-eight "native" *Shaykhs*' courts were established. In the same year one-third of the sharia judges were pensioned off, and twenty of the forty-two sharia courts were abolished.[14] But the efforts completely to displace the role of sharia were never successful. Sharia remained, but as a poor relation in the family of laws applicable in the Sudan.

It is significant that the British entertained sharia at all. They could have further restricted its legal space or worked harder to reduce its operation, as they did starting in the 1920s. The recognition of sharia was strategic. Its sphere of jurisdiction was also slowly but substantially narrowed. Primary considerations in this were fear that the Mahdist movement, which had captured much of the Sudan in the 1880s and 1890s, would be revived and the need to placate the religious elite to prevent their being mobilized against the new infidels running the country. By allowing the courts to operate, the British incorporated Egyptians and a handful of locals in the structure of authority. Egyptians were, after all, supposed to be co-partners in ruling the Sudan and served in numerous positions throughout the country. But they never held positions above the British.[15]

In the legal structure the Egyptians were given preeminent positions in the sharia courts. However, the Sudan Political Service and the Civil Service, staffed by an Oxbridge-educated elite, had ultimate authority. In the provinces the district commissioners often also took on the role of judges, although few of them had legal training. The district commissioner was "judge, administrator, chief surveyor, inspector of education, chief of police, and military ruler all in one."[16] The number of senior British administrators was small. Between 1899 and 1959 they numbered no more than four hundred in all, "rarely reaching one hundred and twenty-five officials on the ground to administer almost a million square miles."[17] Indirect rule, through the native authorities but also to an extent the sharia courts, was therefore absolutely necessary to the apparatus of rule, especially starting in the 1920s.

Mahmood Mamdani has argued that the late colonial state was bifurcated between a small, urbanized civil society and a vast rural domain dominated by despotic native chiefs and tribal authorities.[18] The Sudan, especially after 1920, is a model example. Mamdani argues that urban civil society was nonracial but open only to those with "civilized" standards of education. This opening of civil society to the Sudanese happened in the 1920s, as graduates of Gordon Memorial College found employment in the lower ranks of the civil service. This group was also the first to agitate for independence. But this movement remained small even at independence. The native chiefs and traditional religious figures maintained their dominance over most people in rural areas. The sharia courts were in a curious, in-between position: they were neither English nor customary, and they often conflicted with both. Sharia judges were not hereditary chiefs but educated in specialized colleges. But these colleges were not the Western institutions that would admit them to a privileged status in civil society.

After the First World War, a number of factors led to attempts to weaken the sharia courts while giving native administration more influence. Anticolonial protests in Cairo, fears that they would spread to the Sudan, and glimmers of nationalist agitation in Khartum made the British acutely concerned about their position in the Nile Valley. In March 1919, thousands of Egyptians took to the streets in what was to become a sustained period of protest against the British presence. Nationalist mobilization against the British in Cairo resonated in Khartum. The governor-general of the Sudan, Sir Lee Stack, was assassinated while on a visit to Cairo during the nationalist protests. In 1924, there was a pro-Egyptian uprising in Khartum. Many of the Egyptian military and civilian staff of the Anglo-Egyptian Condominium were then immediately evacuated from the Sudan. Such staff had not cost the regime much, and until 1913 the Egyptians had borne most of the costs of the Condominium.

As a result of these developments, the state drastically slowed its efforts to "Sudanize" the bureaucracy. Thus in the 1920s native administration was given great weight; it started off as pragmatic policy and became a creed after 1924. Native authorities were one way to displace the emerging Sudanese educated elite. The Power of Nomad Sheikhs Ordinance was passed in 1922 and the Village Courts Ordinance in 1925 (the former was repealed in 1928 and replaced by the Power of Sheikhs Ordinance; the latter was amended in 1930). By 1929 there were seventy-two such courts, and they had tried over ten thousand cases by the end of that year.[19] It is clear that one of the reasons for "recognising and organising native administration in the North was to minimize reliance upon the Sudanese educated class . . . (and) judicial and administrative powers were transferred from the Sudan civil servants and judicial staff to the native authorities."[20] Everything was done to hinder the development of a modern educated elite. Education in the north did not expand, most definitely not legal education in either sharia or Common Law.

Nationalism, Sharia, and Islam

Around the time of the "birth" of anti-British agitation in the Sudan, in November 1920 a pamphlet circulated saying (among other things) that: "They [the British] have blocked the way of advancement and education. If the Government were a Mohammedan one, it would not enforce regulations which are against the Mohammedan law."[21] There seems to have been no elaboration of what was meant by "Mohammedan law." Such sentiments could merely have expressed an antipathy to everything British—especially, of course, their laws. Thus, "We do not want to be governed by a foreign ruler" was the movement's call, as articulated in a pamphlet by Ali 'Abd al-Latif, one of the founders of the White Flag League in May 1924.[22] The movement against the British was split between those who were pro-Egyptian and those with the slogan "Sudan for the Sudanese." The positive content of the nationalist movement emerged through its campaign against the British.

Even after the revolt of 1924, which involved Egyptian and Sudanese troops, colonial officials continued to dismiss the actions and demands of the nationalists as either originating in Cairo or the result of immaturity.[23] As one official put it: "Many hands plied the shuttle of nationalism: as often as not they were Egyptian." In February 1938, the Graduates' General Congress was established. One of its first public statements contained a clause calling for the separation of the judiciary from the executive, but it did not call for either to be "Islamic."[24]

The British feared that the sharia courts and their personnel—who could in certain circumstances have been serving as imams at mosques—would be potential sources of anti-British activity. If not openly antistate, these courts would at least offer alternative structures of legitimacy. A judicial circular (number 32) was issued by the Grand Qadi in 1931 reminding the imams of mosques that they were government employees. Furthermore, it stated, the local sharia judge should carefully supervise speakers in the mosques and "should forbid them to misuse the floor for things not connected with religious guidance." The reduction of these courts' role after 1920 partly ensured their acquiescence. Recognizing and organizing the native authorities was a way to minimize reliance upon the small and potentially growing group of Sudanese-educated people. Thus judicial and administrative powers were transferred from the Sudanese civil servants and judicial staff to the native authorities.[25] The sharia courts were located in between the modern, educated sector and the "traditional" authorities; they were less "reliable" than the latter but were not the immediate threat presented by secular educated Sudanese.

Although Islam was implicit in northern Sudanese nationalist discourse, sharia was not. Islam was seen as the unifying culture, at least in the north. Sharia was not a demand that either the British had to deal with or the nationalists 9ad to explain to themselves. Islam was taken to be a sign of local culture, distinct from the culture of the colonizers. The content of this "Islam" is far from clear, whether it referred to the popular Sufi tradition or the strictly legal or broadly meant Arabic Islamic civilization—but it certainly reflected elements of the nationalists' own urban and educated understanding of Islam.

The Sudanese wing of the Egyptian Islamic movement, al-Ikhwan al-Muslimun (The Muslim Brothers), was born in April 1949. In August 1954, a Unified Sudanese Muslim Brotherhood Organization was founded. It combined three separate groups. Comprising educated activists, al-Ikhwan had only limited success with the urban middle class and was unknown among the rural population.[26] In the nationalist movement the Sudanese al-Ikhwan made no impact.

In the vast countryside the "tribal" chiefs and *shaykhs* felt threatened by the nationalists. Indeed, when self-government came, the chiefs and *shaykhs* combined to form a curiously named Socialist Republican Party, which the British favored because they opposed all the leading parties and expressed sentiments favorable to the old order.[27]

By the time the British departed, sharia had become an inherent but subordinate part of the legal system of the country. When a constitution for the new state was written, sharia was not in the language of the dominant political parties. The Grand Qadi of the sharia courts issued a plea, however, for sharia to become the basis of the constitution.

English law was adopted as the primary legal system because most members of both the bar and the bench were trained in this legal tradition. Indeed, reliance on English law greatly increased in the immediate postindependence years.[28] The scope of English law expanded despite indications that its application was becoming more local. However, the "justice, equity, and good conscience" provision was never seriously interpreted to mean either the letter or the spirit of sharia.

Yet two decades after independence sharia became a major political issue. It became a symbol intimately tied to the nature of the state and the character of the country's constitution for proponents of an "Islamic state." For the opponents of Islamic parties, sharia became an object of attack. Thus at the end of the twentieth and the beginning of the twenty-first centuries the debate about sharia became an inherent part of the constitutional debate in the Sudan.

Sharia's champions claimed that it reflected the character and customs of the Sudanese people. Many northern Muslims definitely felt this way, and custom was largely viewed by them as being static and already Islamic anyway. Moreover, the northern Muslim elite involved in running the state apparently believed, at least in theory, that they could further consolidate their control if the constitution were explicitly Islamic. The urban-based elite, which had the greatest interest in the state, strove to demonstrate the modernity of sharia and to argue that it was compatible with the workings of a modern state. Their proposals for and interventions to enact sharia took place in the context of the growth of the state bureaucracy. However, the sign *sharia* was seldom given substance. Its complexities were only slightly explored, its diversity ignored.[29]

Self-government, Independence, and Sharia

Self-government came to the Sudan very much as a surprise, both to the Sudan Political Service and to the nationalists. Martin Daly, the historian of the Condominium, claims that as late as "1945 a target date of 1965 was presumed for independence, even after which a sustained British role was expected."[30] Egyptian independence, which came about through a coup d'état by Gamal 'Abd al-Nasr in 1952, played a tremendous role in forcing the British to give the Sudan self-government. After the Second World War, the British return to Sudanizing the civil service had been extremely slow, even though "advisory" bodies and a legislature were created to bring Sudanese into selected positions of authority.

In 1953 a Self-Government Statute was promulgated. At the end of December 1955, a transitional constitution, a modified version of the Self-Government Statute of 1953, was passed by the National Assembly. It named the country a sovereign democratic republic and asserted for the first time parliament's independence in international matters. The transitional constitution, as indicated by its title, was a temporary arrangement hurriedly contrived in order to facilitate the country's orderly passage to independence. The constitution's makers intended to replace it, at an early date, with a permanent constitution that would adequately reflect the character, needs, and aspirations of "Sudan and the Sudanese."[31]

The Postcolonial State

Nicholas Rose has captured well the problem that faced the postcolonial state:

> To govern, one may say, is to be condemned to seek an authority for one's authority. It is also that, in order to govern, one needs some "intellectual technology" for trying to work out what on earth one should do next—which involves criteria as to what one wants to do, what has succeeded in the past, what is the problem to be addressed and so forth.[32]

The values of rationality, efficiency, and progress have been staples in the thought of new rulers of postcolonial states. The new political order also demands new instruments for the conduct of government. The constitution functions both as a foundational text and as a symbol, and thus as a reference in actual political life. Most importantly, and in practical terms, constitutional states provide for equality before the law, the separation of the judiciary from the executive, and independence for the former. The Sudan's first constitution enshrined these values.

157

The judiciary was theoretically free from executive interference. This was a major change from the authoritarian colonial tradition, which had rolled the judiciary and executive into one, at least in the provinces. The first Sudanese chief justice, Sayed Muhammad Ahmed Abu Rannat, was appointed in 1955. The legal system remained bifurcated, with the legacy of the British "ordinary courts" dominant over the others. Little thought was given to transforming various levels of the legal system so as to reflect the new values of the state or the diverse aspirations of the people. This lack of full attention to the law would become a long-term problem. The malaise can be seen in the way in which legal education and the law profession were organized.

Even though Khartum University now had a single faculty of law, it offered two types of legal education: one based in the Common Law and the other in sharia. The faculty therefore had a "sharia Division."[33] Common Law lecturers were almost all the same personnel as before independence. Despite the best intentions, they continued to teach a law that was foreign, using source materials that were equally foreign. How to "localize" the law was a major issue in the faculty. There was little in the way of law reports, case material, or law journals to report or discuss local problems or ones similar to them.

The bar association had at least three divisions. First, it was broadly divided into sharia and civil (which further divided into a section for those trained at the Khartum branch of Cairo University and those at Khartum University). There was yet a further distinction between those qualified at Khartum University who could appear before only the civil courts and those qualified—having taken additional courses and examinations—to appear before both the civil and the sharia courts.[34] Given these divisions, in time legal differences became "associated with political ideologies and programs, complicating the search for a national legal profession."[35] The advocates trained in sharia, for instance, demanded and indeed established their own bar association, but it was not recognized and was disbanded within a year of its establishment. In later years, conflicts in the association between Islamists and others increased. There were parallel conflicts between nationalists and socialists in the bar association. In 1975, there were only 8 "sharia" advocates but 248 "civil" advocates, of whom 50 could also practice in the sharia courts.[36]

Customary law remained outside these struggles, but its "advocates" strove to maintain their relatively autonomous position. With self-government, the tribal leaders established a political party—the Socialist Republican Party—but it did not survive independence. The first military regime, in 1958, hailed the role of the native leaders. By 1964 there were 950 native courts in Sudan.[37]

The country's first experience of military rule, in 1958, did not "seriously undermine the country's basic commitment and rule of law," according to Abdullah Ahmed Al Na'im.[38] It was the ensuing civilian government under Sadiq al-Mahdi (who became prime minister in 1966) that eroded the independence of the judiciary. In December 1966, the Supreme Court over-turned the banning of the Sudanese Communist Party and the expulsion of its members from the National Assembly, which had happened a year earlier, in November 1965. Prime Minister al-Mahdi rejected the court's ruling, arguing its decisions were not binding and thereby violat-ing Article 99 of the 1964 constitution. His disregard for the Supreme Court led Chief Justice Awadallah Babiker to resign.[39]

When left intellectuals and activists mobilized against this action, the Umma Party, the National Unionist Party, and the Islamic Charter Front (ICF) decided to respond with a call for an "Islamic constitution."[40] Al-Mahdi then went on to propose that sharia be the basis of a new constitution. The National Committee for the Constitution had as a member Hasan al-Turabi, a stalwart of al-Ikhwan al-Muslimun. Al-Turabi's first law degree was from Khartum University, from which he graduated in 1955, and he had additional degrees from the University of London and the Sorbonne. In later years, he would become the leading champion of an "Islamic consti-tution" and an "Islamic state."[41] He participated in the writing of Pakistan's constitution and would later serve as member of parliament and as attorney general of the Sudan.

The compromise constitution eventually proposed by the drafting committee contained a clause stating that it was derived from "the principles and spirit of Islam." Al-Turabi had led a group from al-Ikhwan who stressed participation in the political process against an apolitical group that emphasized moral reform.[42] Al-Turabi's ICF continued to lead a campaign for an Islamic constitution. Southerners and Communists critiqued the ICF proposal. The Communist Party noted that "those who advocate an Islamic constitution do not clarify how they are going to apply Islamic *sharia*," while a southern lawyer asked whether the Sudan "would be turned into a theocracy."[43] Sharia and the constitution were from then on firmly linked in national debates. But before these debates could unfold and parties could contest one another, the mili-tary stepped into politics once again.

In May 1969, Major General Ja'afar Numayri seized power in a coup d'état. By May 1971, he was President of the Council of the Revolution and leader of the newly created Sudan Social-ist Union. His government instituted a series of legal and administrative changes to reflect the new "socialist" character of the state.[44] The Civil Code Act of 1971 effectively replaced the English Common Law. The sources of the Civil Code Act were the Egyptian civil code, sharia, and the laws of other Arab states.

In a major move to streamline the justice system, the Judicial Authority Act of 1972 was passed, and with it the sharia and other courts were merged into a single system. Only four types of courts would exist: the Supreme Court, the Court of Appeal, the provincial courts, and district courts. In a further attempt to unify the system, all laws would be drafted in Arabic, and the Arabic text of all laws enacted since independence be considered the original.[45] Despite these changes, however, no "suggestions as to how to bridge the gap of legal knowledge between each division were considered. It was simplistically assumed that since the new codes would be in Arabic then sharia judges would easily apprehend and apply them. Nothing was done to unify legal education at the law faculties in order to guarantee the success of the attempted merger."[46]

In 1973, Numayri issued the country's first permanent constitution, a document that expresses the marriage of socialist language, positive sentiments concerning Islam, and all the modern virtues of equality and democracy.[47] But it also in effect gave him absolute power. It is explicit about the role of Islam in public life. Article 9 of this constitution says: "The Islamic law and custom shall be the main sources of legislation. Personal matters of non-Muslims shall be governed by their personal laws."[48] The constitution also contained several clauses ensuring the equality between men and women, such as Article 38, which says: "The Sudanese have equal rights and duties irrespective of origin, race, locality, sex, language or religion."[49]

But these constitutional changes were not enough to satisfy all the constituencies Numayri was trying to address. Therefore in April 1977 he established "The Committee to revise the laws of the Sudan so as to conform to the sharia rules and principles." A number of factors led Numayri to favor an Islamic social and political program.[50] By September 1983, he declared the imposition of all the penal aspects of sharia, superimposed on the existing criminal code.[51] This took everyone by surprise, including supporters of sharia and those in al-Ikhwan who were close to him. Al-Turabi recalls: "We were not concerned with Numayri's motives. We were aware that official initiatives towards Islam were a response to the growth of Islam towards which we had been working for a long time."[52] To enforce the new laws, Numayri declared a state of emergency in April 1984 and authorized the establishment of new courts to try cases under the new laws. "The legal profession and large sections of the intelligentsia were horrified by the conduct of these new courts," comments Abdelwahab El-Affendi.[53]

By 1984, Numayri had effected a thorough transformation of the laws and legal structures of the country. Substantive and procedural laws, as well as criminal and civil legislation, were affected, putting considerable pressure on the judiciary and government officials to keep pace. There are five broad categories under which the legal changes can be grouped: (1) statutes regulating the operation of courts; (2) statutes reorganizing courts and regulating legal personnel; (3) statutes related to taxation; (4) a mixture of important substantive laws, such as the penal code, and (5) "The order of *ma'arouf* and prohibition of *munkar* Act of 1983."[54]

The Civil Transactions Act of 1984 was the most extensive piece of legislation passed since August 1983. It covered contracts, sales, torts, gifts, and insurance, altogether amounting to 819 separate sections divided into 95 chapters. In 1984 the courts heard the first case of a person accused of handling *riba* (bank interest).[55]

According to the Civil Procedure Act of 1983, customary law was one of the sources of law. The definition of customary law excludes ecclesiastical rules of the church and the civil laws of foreign countries. Family and land laws are the two major areas covered by customary law in the Sudan.[56]

Constitutionalism and Sharia

For a postcolonial state, a constitution is a sign of its modernity. It is at once a symbol and a means of constructing the nation-state, given its claim to be a single document uniting all members of the state as equals. Sudanese politicians have engaged in endless constitutional struggles. "Islamists" have been as obsessive about it as any secular "constitutionalist." The debates over sharia have been at the heart of constitutional debates in independent Sudan.

In September 1956, a national committee was established by the Council of Ministers for the purpose of drafting a "permanent constitution." The Grand Qadi, Hasan Muddathir (the last Egyptian to hold the position), immediately submitted a memorandum urging the adoption of sharia principles for the country's new founding document. He wrote: "the laws governing its people should be enacted from the principles of an Islamic constitution and in accordance with Islamic ideals out of which such a community has been shaped."[57] The national drafting committee also had representatives of al-Ikhwan and like-minded men who submitted a motion for an "Islamic constitution." They argued that it was just, resonated with the Islamic culture of the Sudan, linked the country to its "Arabic-Islamic tradition" and the Islamic world, and, finally, was in accord with the commands of the Qu'ran. Yet when a motion was made to propose an "Islamic constitution," the committee voted it down by twenty-one to eight votes.[58] The motion's sponsors did not entirely lose, however, for clauses favorable to sharia and Islam were included.

Sharia was specified as a basic source of law, and Islam was stated to be the official religion of the country. Yet the proponents of an "Islamic constitution" still walked out of the committee meeting. When they returned later for a revote, they lost again. Abdel Salam Sidahmed argues that: "The nature of the Islamists' arguments . . . reflects a rather simplified outlook that presents Islam and the thesis of an 'Islamic constitution' as something to be taken for granted rather than a comprehensive new view of politics and society."[59] The Umma and the People's Democratic Party apparently demonstrated no support for an "Islamic constitution."

The 1973 "permanent constitution" states that "Islamic law and custom shall be the main source of legislation. Personal matters of non-Muslims shall be governed by their personal laws." Under Article 16, Islam, Christianity, and "heavenly religions" are given equal protection.[60] In January 1987, the National Islamic Front produced its "Sudan Charter," which stated that "Islamic jurisprudence shall be the general source of law, [as] it is the expression of the will of the democratic majority." Sharia would be applicable to Muslims; to members of "scriptural religions" their respective church laws would apply, just as for followers of "local cults" their "special customs" would apply.[61]

The constitution issued in 1998 was the most recent attempt, before the 2005 Comprehensive Peace Agreement between the north and the south, to produce a foundational document to regulate the political affairs of the Sudan. Sharia does not occupy a prominent place in this document. The central question, however, is the ease with which the constitution can be ignored. Hardly twelve months after being issued, it was suspended, and the president declared a comprehensive "state of emergency," a move allowed by the constitution. Despite this action, which makes clear that a constitution can easily be shelved, discussions in opposition circles and various factions inside the state continue to emphasize the need for constitutional talks in order to restore democratic rule to the Sudan.[62] This was achieved in 2005, when an interim national constitution was adopted. Sharia is only applicable in the northern states of the Sudan under this constitution.

State, Sharia, and Late Islamism

Numayri's rule is a major turning point in the postcolonial history of the Sudan. Any discussion of sharia and the state must return to his role in forcing sharia onto the judiciary, the legislature, and, of course, the executive. If he had not "returned to Islam" and the NIF had not made an alliance with him, the history of the Sudan would have been very different.

In 1969, he came to power through a military coup d'état supported by the Sudan Communist Party (SCP). Soon afterward, he eliminated the SCP after an attempted coup and established the Sudan Socialist Union (SSU), which would become the country's only legal political party until 1985. Through the SSU he ran the state.

In the 1950s, al-Ikhwan was ineffectual, though it promoted the notion of an "Islamic constitution." Yet this did not contradict its support for democratic politics, in theory and in practice. In the 1960s, Al-Ikhwan expanded its membership among university students, and in the middle of the decade it transformed itself under the umbrella name of the ICF. It remained on the margins of the political system but was effective at promoting its causes.[63] It threw all its energies into ensuring that the SCP was banned as a legal political party and remained proscribed as an organization. Left-wing activism in the Middle East in the 1960s made al-Ikhwan fear to lose its influence and position.[64] Al-Ikhwan went underground when Numayri came to power in May 1969. By the end of his regime, al-Ikhwan had become a mass political movement. It had infiltrated the structures of the official SSU and was concentrating on expanding its student base.

Al-Ikhwan's rapprochement with Numayri coincided with his increasing enthusiasm for Islam in his personal life. The apogee of this was his declaration of sharia, especially its penal law, in September 1983. He had moved from being a secular socialist to being a staunch champion of sharia. However, discontent with him did not subside, and after the popular uprising against Numayri's regime that led to his overthrow in April 1985, al-Ikhwan established the NIF in May.

At the beginning of Numayri's regime, the state was presented as a progressive secular entity. Sharia courts were essentially left alone. Four women judges were appointed to the highest level of the sharia courts between 1970 and 1975. These appointments were a significant response to pressures from women's groups, and they seem not to have evoked strong opposition from more conservative elements. The period between 1973 and 1979 "represents one of the more enlightened periods in the modern history of the sharia in the Sudan," according to one student of the sharia courts.[65] The Grand Qadi during this period was Shaykh Muhammad al-Gizouli, and when he retired in 1980 the position was not filled. Instead, the sharia and civil courts were incorporated into a single system, with a chief justice at its head and two deputies, one each from the previous sharia and civil divisions.[66]

There were a number of significant sharia decisions relating to family law during this period. Judicial Circular 54, requiring the consent of women in marriage, and Circular 61, recognizing the right to divorce of women who had suffered from beatings, were major reforms in the sharia affecting women.[67] Related to the latter is Circular 59, giving full recognition to divorce on the grounds of cruelty to the wife, drawing on Maliki sources. Circular 62 instructs judges to issue maintenance orders in child-custody cases at the outset of such cases, to prevent hardship to the child or children.

In the area of custodianship, an important reform had already been set in place in the 1930s. Then, according to Circular 32 (of 1932), the Qadi adopted Maliki instead of Hanafi views, advocating that the mother may retain custody of her son until puberty and her daughter until her marriage if good reason is shown that this is in the interest of the children.[68] During the 1970s, under Numyari's rule, "A number of reforms affecting the status of women were introduced, among them equal pay for equal work, improved maternity leave benefits and a controversial move which allowed *nafaqa*, maintenance, payments up to half of a man's salary to support a wife so entitled."[69] But, as so often, the practical expression of these reforms was constrained by available resources, education of the legal personnel, and the uneven education of the population. The *ma'zuns* (the religious officials who perform marriage ceremonies), for instance, were often not fully aware that the consent of the bride should be given and were ill informed about the new rights and responsibilities of marital partners.[70]

One-party rule under the leadership of a single strong man managed to enact a "progressive" constitution and also to bring the civil war with the south, which had begun in 1955, to an end. In 1972, Numayri and the southern rebels signed the Addis Abba Accord, ending the civil war—until 1983, when it began again. This was to be the longest period of peace in independent Sudan.[71]

Numayri's ability to sign a workable peace was equaled by his ability to turn in other directions as well. Thus in 1977 he made his opening moves to win over opposition leaders, including "Islamists." Former Prime Minister Sadiq al-Mahdi and Hasan al-Turbai were released from prison and invited to join Numayri's government. "The Committee to revise Sudanese law" was then formed, working closely with the president. As we saw earlier, a legal revolution was effected in the ensuing months and years. Abduallahi An-Naim, a Sudanese lawyer and legal scholar, has observed that "the basic structure and fundamental principles of the Sudanese legal system, which had been gradually developed over the preceding 80 years, were completely changed within weeks."[72] By 1984, Numayri overtly declared Islamization, expressed most clearly in the September 1983 decrees entailing the imposition of sharia punishments.

When Numayri's government fell in April 1985, the transitional constitution of 1956 was called into use once again. The return of democratic government in 1986 was short-lived, however. In the elections for that government, the NIF won only 17 percent of the vote.[73] Although the sharia clauses in the constitution were not removed, they were not implemented. The place of sharia was one of the central points of dispute for the political parties, and it deflected them away from other pressing social and economic crises. At least five cabinets ("Councils of Ministers") were formed, reflecting numerous coalitions in government in the short period between 1986 and 1989.[74]

A constitutional conference was scheduled for September 1989, at which all parties would once again debate the future of the country. The established traditionalist parties—the Umma and Democratic Unionist Party—had by then come close to explicitly and unambiguously declaring their preference for an "Islamic constitution." But before ideas could be contested at a conference, the military stepped in at the end of June 1989. This time it was supported by the NIF, whose leaders saw themselves as the purest Muslims in the land. Of the NIF and similar groups, Abdul Wahhab El-Affendi notes "the self-righteousness of most modern Islamic groups which, even more than some secularist groups, looked down on their less "Islamic" compatriots and sought to impose their version of Islam on them. The aggressive style of most Islamists, their rigidity and uncompromising attitudes made them the worst politicians."[75] As a vanguard party, they combined arrogance with a disregard for democratic procedures to ensure their hegemony.

Late Islamism

The way in which Islam's public and political role came to be defined by an elite within an Islamic political movement resembles the parody by Leon Trotsky of Lenin's mode of organization during the Russian Revolution: "Lenin's methods lead to this: the party organisation at first substitutes itself for the party as a whole; then the Central Committee substitutes itself for the organisation; and finally a single 'dictator' substitutes himself for the Central Committee."[76] In twentieth-century Sudan, Islam was what the "Islamists" said it was, and in their structures and procedures they attempted to shape the character of sharia and Islam. The quote from Trotsky sums up what happened in the Sudan under the NIF, except that the contest between party leader Hasan al-Turabi (whose position in the government was attorney general) and head of the armed forces Umar al-Bashir was a persistent feature of the regime. The Revolutionary Command Council under Brigadier al-Bashir suspended the transitional constitution of 1985 and issued decrees banning all nongovernmental political activity and publications. It also declared a comprehensive state of emergency.

In the 1990s, a number of officially recognized Islamic universities produced a good number of lawyers in their sharia departments. These students were qualified to operate in the new legal environment being created under the NIF. Yet, as could be expected, these young lawyers and judges lacked experience in legal practice and their decisions were highly driven by ideology.

In June 1998, the country was given a new constitution. Only in Chapter 2(4) does it say that "*sharia* and custom are sources of legislation." However, it opens with prayers and "principles guiding the state," which affirm that "governance belongs to God." The constitution identifies Islam as the major religion of the country and then, in Article 10, specifies *zakat*, tithing, as a duty for citizens, without specifying to whom it would be applied, thus implying that non-Muslim citizens would also be liable to *zakat* taxation. The constitution does not declare the state or the constitution itself to be Islamic. However, it repeals none of the earlier legislation promulgated by the present regime. In attempting to identify the religious tone of this document, critics may overlook its generous grant to the president of the right to declare a state of emergency.[77]

The National Committee asked to write the constitution was not required to produce an Islamic constitution. However, it had to respect "Islamic principles" and be sensitive to the "divergent views and aspirations of a pluralistic society that has to live and work in one place." In the end, the members agreed that "the sources of legislation were to be Islamic law and custom. Custom was not defined, though the general principle of law is that custom should not be repugnant to the law and morality."[78] But the draft constitution that the committee submitted to the president was subjected to scrupulous scrutiny and finally changed. One critic notes that "what came out was almost identical to the 1987 Sudan Charter of the NIF."[79]

Conclusion

Sharia is presently the dominant "legal system" in the Sudan. It is legitimized by the ruling party of the north and by the constitution, even though the latter is not explicit about that. The heritage of Numayri's "legal revolution" and the policies of the NIF regime make Sudan one of the only African states to apply all aspects of sharia, at least in theory or at the level of ambition. Certain "controversial" aspects of sharia that contradict current international conventions and standards of human rights, such as *hudud* punishments, which entail amputation, or the death penalty, have, conveniently, been relaxed or not implemented in practice. Thus a contradiction exists between the declared application of sharia and the actual fulfillment of this declaration.

The state has been central to the place of sharia in the modern Sudan. The relative autonomy of the judiciary at certain moments in the postcolonial period has been almost completely obliterated. The state has imposed sharia and made the whole sharia apparatus and other judicial structures subservient to the state. Sharia is therefore, in a sense, at the service of the state. It is not independent in the Sudan.

But historically sharia is not easily susceptible to control and centralization. Qadis and muftis have been fairly autonomous and have often opposed the state in historical Islamic experience. It remains to be seen how long the Sudanese judiciary will remain subjected so thoroughly to the political agenda of the ruling party, unless there is fundamental political transformation. But this situation is typical of contemporary Islamic and African politics.

"Bolivarian" Anti-Semitism

Claudio Lomnitz and Rafael Sánchez

On January 30, 2009, fifteen heavily armed individuals stormed the Tiferet Israel Synagogue in the Mariperez neighborhood of Caracas, Venezuela. They held down the two guards, robbed the premises, and proceeded to desecrate the temple, throwing the Torah to the floor, along with other religious paraphernalia, and painting anti-Semitic slogans on the walls. Among the signs, one could read: "Out, Death to All"; "Damned Israel, Death"; "666" (the Mark of the Beast in Revelation), together with a drawing of the devil; "Out Jews"; "We don't want you, assassins"; a Star of David indicated as equal to a swastika, etc.

This event, though extreme, was neither isolated nor unprecedented. In the previous four years, there had been alarming signs of state-directed anti-Jewish manifestations, including a 2005 Christmas declaration by Hugo Chávez himself: "The World has enough for everybody, but some minorities, the descendants of the same people that crucified Christ, and of those that expelled Bolívar from here and in their own way crucified him. . . . have taken control of the riches of the world."[1]

On November 29, 2004, the police had stormed the social, educational and sports center Hebraica with the excuse of searching for guns and explosives. As in the case of the preemptive strike by Chávez's nemesis, George W. Bush, the weapons of mass destruction never materialized. But finding them may never have been the purpose of this bizarre incursion: the event was carefully timed to coincide with Chávez's arrival in Teheran on an official visit. Thus, Sammy Eppel, director of the Human Rights Commission of the Venezuelan Hebrew fraternity, poignantly interpreted the event: "Chávez was showing Iran: 'This is how I deal with my Jews.'"[2]

According to the World Conference Against Anti-Semitism, which took place in London in February 2009, between October and December of that year the Chavista media became noticeably more aggressive: *Aporrea*, the main pro-Chávez Internet website in Venezuela, published 136 anti-Jewish texts; since the start of the year, an average of 45 pieces had appeared per month. In the thirty days between December 28, 2008, and January 27, 2009, coinciding with the Israeli invasion of Gaza, the number of pieces increased to an average of more than 5 per day. *Vea*, a government-owned daily newspaper, according to the organization, went from publishing a single anti-Semitic article in October 2008 to 13 in November and 16 in December. During the period between late December and late January, they, too, averaged over 5 pieces per day.[3]

Even though this kind of tally can blur the distinction between criticism of Israeli policies vis-à-vis the Palestinians and sheer anti-Semitism, the prominence of classically anti-Semitic themes, tonalities, and sentiments is staggering and undeniable. Indeed, at least since the war in Lebanon of 2006, anti-Semitic comments have become commonplace in communications media that are either controlled by the Venezuelan government or ideologically close to it, such as *Vea*, aporrea.org, Cadena Venezolana de Television (VTV), especially its program *La Hojilla*, and on publicly and community-owned radio stations. So, for instance, Mario Silva, the anchor of *La Hojilla*, which is the main television outlet of Chavismo, declared on November 28, 2007, at a time when a student movement against Chávez was consolidating, that the Cohen family, owners of the Sambil chain of malls, "are financing all that is happening. I have said for a long time that those Jewish businessmen who are not in the conspiracy should publicly come forth. . . . And many of those in the student movement that is currently activated have a lot to do with that group."[4]

Chávez himself has been at the forefront of an effort to equate Israel with Hitler and then to retroject Jewish conspiracy onto the Venezuelan opposition. Thus, on August 26, 2006, while on a state visit to China, Chávez declared that "Israel criticizes Hitler a lot. So do we. But they have done something similar to what Hitler did, possibly worse, against half the world."[5] As recently as January 10, 2009, in the days leading up to the plebiscite to validate Chávez's permanent reelection, the Venezuelan leader conflated the Jews, the Empire, and his internal opposition: "The owners of Israel, in other words, the Empire, are the owners of the opposition."[6]

These invectives from the upper echelons of government are echoed in the Chavista media and in public demonstrations of animosity, vandalism, intimidation, and graffiti.[7] Regarding the media, an egregious and sadly symptomatic example is a January 20, 2009, article by Emilio Silva in aporrea.org, titled "How to Support Palestine Against the Artificial State of Israel." In that piece, Silva calls for a set of measures geared to isolating the Jewish population inside Venezuela as well as its supposed allies, ultimately the Venezuelan opposition tout court; it also calls for international measures to support the Palestinian struggle against Israel, advocates the destruction of the state of Israel, and associates Judaism with "Euro-Gringo" imperial interests in such disparate places as Afghanistan, Congo, and Colombia. Beyond the specifics of his political program, the tonality of the critique, which resonates broadly in the Chavista press, is coined in the idiom of modern anti-Semitism. Thus, Silva characterizes the enemy as "those Zionist Hebrews [who] care more for their pocket-books than for anything else, including Jehovah" and calls on his readers to "publicly interpellate any Jew in any street, mall, square, etc., to take a position [with respect to Israel] by yelling slogans in favor of Palestine and against the miscarried and disfigured [*estado aborto*] state of Israel."[8] The overall effect of this anti-Semitic rhetoric is to crystallize, in the figure of the Jew, the internal and external enemy of Chavismo, which can then either be expelled from the body of the nation as a foreign element or publicly subjected to the will of the people.

Chavismo's Other

Anti-Semitism plays a key role in the ideology of Chavismo, best synthesized in the writings of Argentine ultra-nationalist and Holocaust denier Norberto Ceresole.[9] Ceresole had a long history of close links with national-popular military elements throughout Latin America, notably the Peruvian president Luis Velasco Alvarado, to whom he served as adviser, and the putchist faction of the Argentine army known as the *carapintadas*. It was through the latter group that Chávez met Ceresole, who first appeared on the Venezuelan scene in 1994 and served as his adviser. Ceresole was expelled from Venezuela in June 1995 by Venezuelan intelligence as a propagandist for Chávez's failed 1992 coup against President Carlos Andrés Pérez. He reappeared on the local scene after Chávez came into power in 1999, and he enjoyed close relations with senior members of the government. He died in 2003.

In that year he published *Caudillo, ejército, pueblo: La Venezuela del Comandante Chávez* (*Caudillo, Army, People: The Venezuela of Commander Chávez*), a book that outlines Chávez's political ideas and strategies, much more closely than the writings of the *Libertador* Simón Bolívar, who is routinely carted out as Chávez's source of ideological inspiration. Chávez has repeatedly defended Ceresole's thought, despite his controversial position within the Chavista movement—particularly among the more moderate wing, which rejected Ceresole, not least on account of his anti-Semitic positions. Thus, as recently as May 2006, in his weekly radio and TV program *Aló Presidente*, Chávez referred to Ceresole as a "great friend" and an "intellectual deserving great respect."[10]

Ceresole's blueprint for Chavismo is based on the triangulation between the leader, the people, and the army, where what is fundamental is the physical, bodily relationship between these three elements, articulated by the figure of Chávez. Thus, Ceresole interpreted Chávez's mandate in the wake of his first electoral triumph in the following terms: "The order that the people of Venezuela emitted on December 6, 1998, is clear and final. A physical person, and not an abstract idea or a generic party, was 'delegated' by that very people to exercise Power."[11]

Ceresole differentiates Chavismo from fascism, which he disingenuously refers to as "the European nationalisms of the post-WWI period," on the basis of the fact that in the former there is no predominant party structure.[12] Instead, what is crucial is the immediate physical relationship between the leader and the people, with every other political instance figuring merely as a channel of transmission between them. It is no coincidence that Human Rights Watch recently declared that a "defining feature of the Chávez presidency has been an open disregard for the principle of separation of powers enshrined in the 1999 Constitution—and, specifically, the notion that an independent judiciary is indispensable for protecting fundamental rights."[13] The Chavista corporealization of politics seeks to obviate all representative instances in favor of an immediate, visceral relationship between the leader and his followers. Within such a figuration of politics, any alternative vision is expelled from the body of the nation and reduced to an alien and monstrous element that must be annihilated.

In such a scheme, the figure of the Jew comes in handy, and, indeed, Ceresole indulges in traditional anti-Semitic paranoia. It is no coincidence that the first heading in the introduction of Ceresole's book on Chávez is "The Jewish Question and the State of Israel." The place of anti-Semitism in such a book might seem puzzling, but Ceresole explains his reasons clearly enough:

> The first time that I perceived the "Jewish problem" was when I discovered, empirically, that the so-called "terrorist attacks of Buenos Aires" [in 1992 and 1994] . . . corresponded to an internal crisis of the State of Israel and not to the action of a supposed "Islamic terrorism." From that time onward, the Jews erupted in my life. I suddenly discovered them not as I had known them until then, that is, as individuals distinct from one another, but rather as elements for whom individuation is impossible, a group united by hatred, and, to use a term that they like, by ire.[14]

Thus, Ceresole attributed the bombing of Buenos Aires's Jewish Center, which killed eighty-seven people and wounded over a hundred, to the Jews themselves. Interestingly, Chávez's immediate reaction to the looting of the Tiferet Israel Synagogue was not much different: it could only be an attack perpetrated by the opposition against his regime.[15] Similarly, Chávez has been a proponent of the idea that the attacks of September 11, 2001, were the result of a conspiracy orchestrated by the Bush government in order to blame Islamic militants and thereby justify his plans to invade Iraq.[16]

More generally, despite the romance between Chávez and a string of intellectual superstars (from Toni Negri to Oliver Stone), the lack of regard for representative instances ultimately makes ideology and even ideas generally into squalid reflections of the robust gestures and gesticulations of the leader. As Ceresole puts it: "The Venezuelan model is not a theoretical construction—it springs directly from reality. It is the result of a convergence of factors that we could define as 'physical,' therefore, that have not been conceived beforehand (in opposition to the so-called 'ideological' factors)."[17] Instead of political parties, representative institutions, and, above all, ideologies, Chavismo thinks of itself as a physical relationship between the people and Chávez, with love as the potent glue connecting them, and shit as the substance of the opposition.

The Political Vocabulary of Chavismo

Much in line with Ceresole's blueprint, ten years of Chavista rule have indeed undermined the autonomy of the representative institutions of political mediation. This process has been amply documented by Human Rights Watch, which states, among many other things, that "in 2004 Chávez signed legislation that made it possible for his supporters in the National Assembly to both pack and purge the Supreme Court. . . . Since this takeover occurred, the court's response to government measures that threaten fundamental rights has typically been one of passivity and acquiescence."[18] There is rampant discrimination against opposition members in government hiring practices, the issuing of identity documents, the use of government agencies as an electoral base, etc. Instead of independent institutions of representation, the regime has offered unremitting love between the leader and the masses.

Thus, for instance, in the recent campaign for the referendum on abolishing limits to presidential reelection, the principal motto was "Amor con amor se paga [Love must be repaid with love]," a saying that put forward the notion that Chávez's spontaneous and overwhelming love for the people comes with an obligation that must correspond. An election poster celebrating Chavez puts this quite graphically:

> A Message of Love to the People of my Venezuela; I have always done everything for love.
> For love of the tree and of the river, I became a painter.
> For love of knowledge and study, I left my beloved hometown to study.

For love of sport, I played baseball.

For love of country, I became a soldier.

For love of the people, I made myself President, you made me President.

These years I have governed because of love.

Because of love we built the Barrio Adentro program.

Because of love we built the Misión Robinson.

Because of love we instituted Mercal.

We have done everything because of love.

There is still very much to do

I need more time.

I need your vote.

Your vote because of love.

The problem with substituting a language of love for the institutional protection of rights is that any sign of disenchantment can be read as a lack of love, as ingratitude, or as a hidden affiliation with the designs of a foreign enemy: capitalism, "Euro-Gringo imperialism," or, better yet, Zionist-Fascist-Euro-Gringo imperialism.

Appearances notwithstanding, Chavismo has chronic difficulties in fixing a stable enemy. Despite constant attempts to reduce all opposition to a miniscule internal oligarchy backed by imperialism, societal frictions multiply and enemies proliferate, from workers' unions to the student movement, the church, civil society organizations, etc. These difficulties are reflected in Chávez's institutionalized verbal incontinence (with weekly performances in his show, *Aló Presidente*), as well as in a risky but calculated media strategy based on gaining a profile by way of a combination of unexpected measures, dramatic gestures, threats, and insults. In this regard, Chávez's media persona is consistent with the fascist strategy of casting aside all forms of protocol and substituting for them the excessive antics of the clown. Chávez is Venezuela's Ubu Roi: constantly shifting the rules of the game to disorient his opponents.

The difficulty in fixing a stable enemy is the obverse of Chavismo's inability to stabilize itself. Chavismo's instability is endemic and in part originates in the excessive attempt to implant a Jacobin revolution, with all that this entails in the way of state centralization, under intensely globalized circumstances. The last either continuously derail such an attempt or otherwise bring it to a screeching halt. The instability also springs at least in part from Chavismo's deliberate policy, itself to a large extent symptomatic of these same globalized circumstances, of weakening the state's representative instances and replacing them with "love" and a political calculus that allows the leader to publicly indulge his own viscerality against his enemies. The most immediate result of such passionate, sentimental premises is a view of politics and political life as an agonistic, hand-to-hand combat between the "people," held together by "love," and a series of proliferating enemies, united solely by hatred—by the all too biblical "ire" that Ceresole imputes to the Jews.

The role of evil as the opposition's agglutinating force is at the heart of Chávez's political vocabulary. Chávez represents his enemies as inherently weak and contemptible. They need evil if they are to congeal as a political force. Chávez refers to his opponents as *escuálidos* ("squalids"), a term that in Spanish connotes not only dirtiness and abjection but also flimsiness, wimpiness, and scrawnyness. Not surprisingly, the figures that are canonically associated with degradation in reactionary lore lurk as undertones in this discourse. As with his admired "father" Fidel Castro, homophobia forms part of that repertoire, although unlike Cuba, where homosexuality was banned and homosexuals were persecuted, Chavismo relies on homophobia as invective rather than institutionalizing it as state policy.

Homophobic sentiments and images are most commonly mobilized around the figure of the *escuálido*. So, for instance, the Chavista theme in the so-called Battle of Santa Inés—against the opposition's 2004 campaign to revoke Chávez's mandate—was "Florentino y el Diablo," a story about a handsome and very masculine Creole cowboy who wins a duel with the devil. Florentino, who in the campaign is identified with Chávez, appeared in a set of posters as a wholesome rider on a tall horse, overwhelming, lance in hand, a squeamish, stereotypically gay devil, who stands for the *escuálidos*. Florentino's lance points to the devil's bottom, in a gesture of penetration that Chávez has himself enacted verbally. Thus, in the TV program *La Hojilla*, Chávez used sodomy as his metaphor for dominating the opposition (*vamos a jugar el juego del rojo . . . tu te agachas y yo te cojo*; a nonrhyming translation of which is "let's play the game of red, you bend down and I fuck you"). This verbal game does not jeopardize Chávez's own gender identity, since in much of Latin America the male sodomizer is not regarded as being a homosexual.[19]

Perhaps the most glaring and sad example of official homophobia occurred in the context of one of the skirmishes with the Catholic Church, which, along with the opposition-owned media, is the main institutionalized opponent of the regime. On the occasion of the assassination of a prominent priest in a Caracas hotel room, Venezuela's attorney general sought to dispel criticisms of the government's incapacity to combat crime by claiming that the priest "had participated in his own death."[20] Proof of this was that "we found excrement and also injuries in his anus."[21] Another telling example is from Silva, the anchor of *La Hojilla*, who, after calling a gay social columnist who criticized the bad taste of a military parade *pato* ("queer"), jabbed: "You would probably want our armed forces to dress in pink or wear silk uniforms. I can picture you leading the parade all wrapped in feathers. I'm not homophobic, by the way. But each of us should assume his own condition. You have no right to talk about the army, the army is very foreign to what you are. You have to show respect."[22] Pronouncements such as these are often followed by proclamations of the speakers' alleged love for gays and their tender commitment to multiculturalism.

The substance that all opponents have in common, be they *escuálidos*, *patos*, or Gringo-Zionist-imperialists, is shit. This association extends also to Jews, as two graffiti that appeared in Caracas in 2008 and 2009 can testify. One read "David, I shit on your star"; the other showed a swastika and a Star of David, both with the fetor of shit steaming off them, joined by an equal sign. Thus, in an aggressive speech surrounded by the highest-ranking military and dressed in military garb, Chávez referred to the opposition's victory the day after a key referendum as a "Victory of Shit."[23] Chávez routinely calls his opponents *plastas* ("lumps of shit"), so their victories must also be victories of shit; in consequence, the army was publicly made present as a force of containment. This metaphor is perhaps symptomatic of Chavista hysteria about the opposition: it is never easy to keep shit in its place. Thus, Lina Ron, the leader of the radical wing of the Bolivarian movement, wrote in her weekly column that "we Chavistas are like the Guaire River, the more shit that the opposition hurls at us the more we swell up, when we finally burst our banks we will turn them all into flood victims."[24] Once upon a time a crystalline river, nowadays the "Guaire" is an open sewer that divides Caracas into two roughly equivalent segments. Unlike Chávez's more frequent usage, here "shit" is not a term of abuse reserved for opponents but rather a form of self-description employed by Ron to refer to her own Bolivarian forces, swelling like a tumultuous river of feces to overwhelm its opponents. In sum, if we can claim quite literally that "Bolivarian" political vocabulary is full of shit, this is due to the regime's inability to stabilize the political enemy, which explains the Bolivarian obsession with physically identifying it: the enemy as shit, the enemy as queer, or the enemy as Jew.

Duality of Power

One of the key features of Chávez's regime from its inception has been its inability either to bend the inherited state apparatus fully to its will or to abolish it and replace it with its own revolutionary design. After all, the regime has an ambiguous status, since it strives to conduct a revolution—conceived as a refoundation of the nation—within the constraints of electoral processes, constitutional conventions, and the expectations of preexisting internal and external actors. In other words, the "Bolivarian Revolution" has developed within a framework where certain democratic practices are expected and where the entitlements of consumers, labor unions, governmental bureaucracies, community organizations, and property owners must be taken into account, if not necessarily respected. One strategy to deal with this situation is constantly to rewrite the rules of the game, redefining what is and is not legal, criminalizing the opposition, and changing the purview of state institutions.

More broadly, however, Venezuela has tended to develop a dual institutional structure: the old, increasingly decrepit framework of schools, hospitals, roads, etc. coexists and competes with a parallel government, beholden directly to Chávez, which manages petrodollars in a more flexible and discretionary fashion. Confronted with the difficulty of consolidating a stable regime, Chavismo has often opted for letting institutions of the "bourgeois order" rot, while importing state functions as so many franchises—intelligence, education, health, sports, public works—mostly from Cuba. Thus, Jorge Castañeda has persuasively countered the notion that the Venezuelan state gives to Cuba while receiving nothing in return. Instead, he insists that the exchange between the two states is crucial to the survival of each: if Venezuela gives cheap oil to Cuba, it receives in exchange an intelligence and a security apparatus that is fundamental to Chávez's personal and political survival.[25]

In classic Leninist theory, the duality of power between old regime structures and emerging revolutionary institutions was meant to last only for a brief transitional period. In Chávez's Venezuela, on the contrary, this duality has become endemic. As a result, state accountability has been compromised and uncertainty is rampant. Paramilitary groups, drug mafias, high crime rates, death squads, and corruption thrive in such a situation. Responding to the outcry of the press and the international community over the sacking of the Tiferet Israel Synagogue, the government produced a set of culprits, which included eight heavily armed members of a municipal police force. Given the structures of dual government and the diffusion of weapons among societal groupings of various stripes, the significance of such a finding is hard to assess. The question of whether a group of this kind operated following instructions from above or were merely vandals hiding behind the diffuse anti-Semitic rhetoric that the government has made its own is to a degree irrelevant. When gangs are on the loose to such an extent, the state itself increasingly behaves like a gang.

Chávez's War of Religions

The sacking of the Tiferet Israel Synagogue produced an outcry in the local and the international media. As criticism became louder, Chávez's initial position became untenable. His first reaction had been to blame the opposition for the attack. Given his tendency to conflate opposition, imperialism, and Jews, the possibility of a Jewish plot suggested itself. But confronted with the clamor, Chávez did not pursue that course and instructed his minister to find the culprits, which he did within a week. Alongside the prosecution of justice, Chávez insisted that freedom of religion was and would continue to be respected in Venezuela, as if freedom of religion were somehow the issue.

The reduction of anti-Semitism to a modality of religious intolerance is a subterfuge. It allows Chávez to focus on matters of religious pluralism, while drawing attention away from his unrepentant attacks on Jews and more broadly on the figure of the Jew as the supreme incarnation of abjection. These are his real targets. From the time of the Dreyfus Affair, modern anti-Semitism has been connected to anxieties related to national integrity, not to religious pluralism per se. Chávez may dislike Venezuela's fifteen thousand Jews, but the bigger issue is that he has chosen to characterize his opposition as antinational. This is where the *figure* of the Jew comes in. Freedom of religion has never been an issue in Venezuela—there are too many Protestants, too many Catholics, and even enough Jews and Muslims to make abolishing freedom of religion politically unviable and utterly unpopular. In this regard, Chávez's "guarantee" of freedom of religion is a red herring.

However, neither can it be said that religion is unimportant. In the war between "the people of love" and "the people of shit," religious symbolism comes in handy. Thus, Venezuelan leftist opposition leader and editor Teodoro Petkoff has pointed out that Chávez has reduced the Israeli-Palestinian conflict to a war of religion. After Israel's disproportionate and deadly attacks on Gaza, he severed diplomatic ties with Israel. Less remarked in the international media was the government's provocative mode of expressing solidarity with Palestine: the foreign minister led an official legation, all members donning a keffiah, to a Caracas mosque. By expressing his solidarity in a mosque rather than in an official building, Chávez identified the Palestinian cause with the cause of Islam (implicitly siding with Hamas over the Palestinian Authority) and identified the Venezuelan nation with Islam, just as he has identified Judaism with the Empire.[26] Chavista graffiti ties the Star of David to the swastika; it also proclaims that "Islam is our Patrimony." Paradoxically, this move turns Chávez's vaunted religious pluralism into a war of religion, of sorts.

The Costs of Bolivarian Anti-Semitism

It is clear that Bolivarian anti-Semitism has broad implications and effects in Venezuelan society. For the Jewish community, the immediate effect is to cast doubt on Venezuelan Jews' national belonging. After the synagogue incident, the Jewish community got the message, and protesters marched, showing their national identity cards. In recent years, the Jewish community in Venezuela has shrunk from fifteen thousand to around twelve thousand, and it is possible, ironically, that by intimidating and discriminating against Venezuelan Jews, Chávez has increased emigration to Israel. The Venezuelan government's posture poisons the discussion of the Palestinian/Israeli question with the venom of anti-Semitism, inhibiting a just and productive argument from the left. Finally, presidential indulgence in a politics of denigration pilfers the promise of the Venezuelan progressive movement by making open discussion of classism and racism impossible. Like its distant cousin, Peronism, Chavez's reliance on confrontation and brinkmanship can only produce retrenchment.

Yet the costs of Bolivarian anti-Semitism are at least as heavy for the broader society as they are for the Jewish community. When a regime combines populism, military uniforms, homophobia, and anti-Semitism, it is time to worry.

PART III

The Individual:
Between Powerlessness and Empowerment

The Power of the Less Powerful

Making Memory on a Pilgrimage to Lourdes

Catrien Notermans

The small town of Lourdes, nestling among the lovely foothills of the French Pyrenees, is the site of the world's most famous Marian sanctuary, receiving an estimated six million visitors every year. Bernadette's visions of Mary in 1858 are formally given as the principal reason for this "site of memory."[1] Though remembrance is certainly a major motive for undertaking a pilgrimage to Lourdes, often the official remembrance of Mary's appearances to Bernadette is not the primary focus of the pilgrims' devotions. Lourdes evokes and answers different kinds of memories and appears to be especially helpful for remembering pain in personal life history.

In this essay I describe how a pilgrimage to Lourdes enables sick pilgrims to narrate and act out different kinds of memories, both painful and nostalgic, related to intimate family history. Through remembering painful events as well as good health and happy moments in their lives, pilgrims are able to connect past, present, and future and to experience continuity and wholeness after periods of powerlessness, discontinuity, and loss. Whereas dominant power structures in both the biomedical domain and the private sphere of the family often suppress and ignore the narration and recollection of emotional pain, a Lourdes pilgrimage enables one to articulate it. I will argue that pilgrimage provides ailing and aged pilgrims with a stage for powerful performances and symbols, in which they narrate and experience painful memories that would otherwise remain undisclosed, submerged under secrecy and shame. Experiencing pain enables the pilgrims to cope with it and gain power and control over their situations.

Though religion is often characterized by institutional regulations, enforced restrictions, and submission to both these restrictions and supernatural powers, it should not be seen as purely restrictive or oppressive. Religion may also include various strategic possibilities that people can use to improve their day-to-day circumstances.[2] From this perspective, religion is not only a means for the dominant to coerce and impose submission on the subdominant but also a means for the subdominant to contest dominant power structures. Though in most cases religious action does not effect a structural power reversal, it may enable people to challenge dominant power structures and exercise power in order "to renew their faith that the world is within their grasp."[3]

Social scientists who focus on social suffering confirm that the dominant power structures under which people suffer often prevent them from speaking out.[4] I challenge the hypothesis that people in pain have no words to express their suffering and argue that, when pain or suffering destroys one's capacity to communicate, it can be publicly articulated through religious practice. Ailing pilgrims who travel to Lourdes aim mainly to turn their pain into bearable memories rather than to eliminate it. Throughout the pilgrimage process, they feel enabled to fully experience and even celebrate their pain by remembering it in religious narratives and performances.

Following Mieke Bal, I see memory as the action of telling or performing a story, an action that is potentially healing because it generates narratives that integrate painful and traumatizing past events.[5] I also join recent anthropological studies of pilgrimage that emphasize its aspect as remembrance. Challenging the narrow definition of pilgrimage as a journey to venerate a particular saint in a specific sacred place, scholars of pilgrimage have recently argued that sites or journeys become sacred when pilgrimage fulfils the need to construct and reconstruct particularly painful periods of (inter)national and personal history and thus heals pilgrims' physical and emotional wounds.[6] Whereas the pilgrimage studies of Jill Dubisch and Katharina Schramm focus on traumatic memories of public events—the Vietnam War and transatlantic slavery, respectively[7]—my study of the Lourdes pilgrimage deals with pilgrims' narration of painful memories from private family history. Ailing pilgrims travel to Lourdes, not to ask Mary for miraculous healing, but to share with her the hardships of family life, to remember their pain and the loss of much-loved persons. Both male and female pilgrims easily identify with Mary as the suffering mother, and she mirrors the excessive pain they experience in everyday life.[8]

I will analyze the power of religion to overcome the difficulty of narrating and remembering pain as a dialectical process. Indeed, I will show that religious power has two aspects: those who activate religious symbols, and the symbols themselves. On the pilgrims' side, power is manifested primarily in personal narratives; the power of symbols is more evident in performances at the sacred site. In ritual practice, religious symbols may evoke emotions and memories not anticipated before or even during the religious experience, inducing a feeling of physical or mental improvement.[9] Not only visual symbols but also symbols that communicate through music, sound, smell, taste, and bodily gestures may evoke emotions that give religion the power to transform human experience.

A case study of ailing Dutch pilgrims who went on a six-day pilgrimage to Lourdes in 2004 can provide a good illustration of these dimensions of religious power. As an anthropologist, I interviewed participants before, during, and after the pilgrimage. I accompanied the pilgrims to Lourdes and saw how traumatic memories were articulated and healed throughout the whole process of looking forward to, participating in, and looking back on the pilgrimage. For reasons of privacy, I will use pseudonyms for the pilgrims.

The Pilgrimage to Lourdes

In June 2004, I participated in a six-day pilgrimage by 265 pilgrims. The journey was organized by VGZ, a Dutch medical insurance company that each year facilitates three pilgrimages to Lourdes for about six hundred pilgrims in all.[10] The group included both chronically ill pilgrims and many solicitous volunteers, who cared for the pilgrims' minds, bodies, and wheelchairs. We traveled by plane and lodged in five top hotels in Lourdes so the pilgrims would feel freed from the sickroom atmosphere of everyday life. The pilgrimage coordinator was an inspired and devoted businesswoman, who attached more importance to the personal relief of old and ailing pilgrims than to Christian notions of sin and redemption. Her two goals in organizing the pilgrimage were to give the sick pilgrims a relaxed and unforgettable pilgrimage to Mary's shrine and to involve VGZ bureaucrats as volunteer assistants so they could become acquainted with the sorrows and needs of insured persons, with whom they never communicate in their daily working life. Among the volunteers that assisted the pilgrims in each hotel were VGZ managers, VGZ employees, priests, medical doctors, nurses, trainee nurses, and me, an anthropologist.

Though it was impossible to get to know all 265 pilgrims, I closely followed the ones with whom I shared a hotel and, as a result, the daily ritual program. Our group consisted of 34 sick pilgrims and 14 volunteers. The pilgrims ranged in age from fifty to eighty-six (with the exception of one thirty-four-year-old pilgrim), and most of them were women (28 women, 6 men). They all came from the city of Venlo and its surroundings. Before the pilgrimage I selected a group of 21 pilgrims, with whom I had in-depth interviews before and after the pilgrimage. Among them were five married couples, two mothers and daughters who planned to travel together, two friends (women), and five women journeying alone. With only six exceptions, all of them were visiting Lourdes for the first time.

Consistent with the general trend toward secularization in Dutch society, the pilgrims claimed to be religious people, including Catholics, but not churchgoers. Many said that they could not attend church regularly because there are not enough priests to celebrate mass every week. What priests there are were said to be so old that they often fall ill and consequently do not show up for services. It has become common, moreover, for just one priest to minister to several parishes concurrently and to celebrate mass in each church only once every few weeks. More directly, they described their nonattendance as a criticism of practices and ideologies prevalent in the church. Besides the complaint that most priests are old, they often claimed to have problems with the authority of young conservative Dutch priests, who celebrate mass with an air of superiority.

This attitude toward the churches, however, does not mean that the pilgrims ceased considering themselves to be religious or even Catholics. They said that they felt very much at home with the Catholic liturgy and ceremonies and recalled longingly the time when churches were full, numerous, and able to meet their needs. As they described their everyday religious practice, its main features were frequent visits to Marian chapels in the neighborhood, the lighting of candles in both local chapels and their own homes, and regular prayers to Mary.

VGZ subsidizes the pilgrimage only for insured people suffering from chronic illnesses. All the sick pilgrims presented complex clinical pictures, combining different major and minor diseases with social isolation, problematic mobility, and the prospect of continuing physical deterioration. All described a pathological process of ten years or longer. VGZ permits sick pilgrims to be accompanied by close relatives, who have to pay the full fare.

The pilgrimage was organized in collaboration with an experienced Dutch pilgrimage organization (for transport and accommodation) and the Lourdes sanctuary organization (for the ritual program). The pilgrims participated partly in mass rituals organized by the sanctuary, partly in the more intimate, exclusive rituals that VGZ organized for the whole group, and partly in still more private rituals separately in each hotel. This alternation of mass rituals, more exclusive rituals, and private rituals appeared to be very important for the rhythm of the pilgrimage and the way the pilgrims experienced it.

On the first day we traveled by plane, settled in the hotel rooms, and started our pilgrimage with an opening ceremony for the VGZ pilgrims in one of the smaller churches at the sanctuary. On the morning of the second day, we had our own closed mass at the grotto, and in the evening we joined in the great torchlight Marian procession organized by the sanctuary. On the third day, we went on a day trip to the Pyrenees to distance ourselves from the sanctuary, rethink and deal with emotions that had been released during the previous days, get a breath of fresh air, and celebrate a mass with laying on of hands in a small Romanesque church in a Pyrenean village. On the fourth day, a Sunday, we participated in the international morning mass organized by the Lourdes sanctuary in the huge underground basilica. That afternoon our hotel group participated in the blessed sacrament procession, also organized by the Lourdes sanctuary. On the fifth day, we had our most intimate ritual with the hotel group when we performed the stations of the cross, guided by the priest for our group. That same evening the pilgrimage concluded with a final VGZ ceremony in the church where we had started our pilgrimage. The next day everybody flew back home, exhausted, confused, but satisfied.

The ritual program planned by VGZ and the Lourdes sanctuary left sufficient scope for individual devotions at the sanctuary, shopping at the souvenir market, coffee breaks on the Lourdes terraces, and conversation among pilgrims and between pilgrims and volunteers. This blend of collective and individual activities ensured a unique experience for each pilgrim.

The Less Powerful

When I asked the pilgrims a week before our departure why they were going on a pilgrimage to Mary in Lourdes, they never answered concisely, nor were their answers focused on Lourdes or Mary. They started by narrating their medical histories and, connected to this, the most distressing episodes in their life histories. In the course of their illness and frequent visits to specialists in various hospitals, they had become expert in explaining their maladies in clinical terms. They were so used to explaining their conditions to doctors, neighbors, friends, and relatives in this medical idiom that they had less difficulty finding the names of all kinds of scans, tests, diagnoses, medication, therapy, and medical specialists than the words to express the emotional world underlying these clinical experiences. The most life-threatening episodes of falling ill, searching for a diagnosis, and rehabilitation were carefully narrated, with detailed memories of almost every hour and every doctor. Throughout the interviews I observed them repeating their medical stories in the same pattern, choosing the same storyline and the same anecdotes, and effortlessly resuming the thread when I interrupted them for explanations. These stories already existed before I confronted them with questions about a Marian pilgrimage.

Storytelling in biomedical terminology is, as Michael Jackson points out, "a vital human strategy for sustaining a sense of agency in the face of disempowering circumstances."[11] In their medical stories the pilgrims described how they had to struggle with medical authorities who do not take their reports seriously. Such authorities sent them from pillar to post, approached them impersonally, and did not take pains to communicate diagnoses and decisions intelligibly. Rather than taking their patients' needs, emotions, and opinions seriously, medical authorities imposed their own conclusions, which left patients feeling that they were often wrong. The pilgrims had little confidence in doctors and were constantly on the alert for incorrect judgments or treatments. They felt humiliated and marginalized, and they complained that there was no communication between equals, only arrogance, indifference, and power inequality. At the same time, they came across as tough fighters, people who would not give up and would not be defeated.

Along with these medical stories, the pilgrims also narrated crucial episodes in their life histories: how they met their spouses, how many children they had, what paid labor they had done, how many grandchildren they had, as well as troubles or illnesses in their extended kin network. Many pilgrims portrayed their lives, even before they fell ill, as one long struggle. Physical pain is so intimately connected with feelings of being marginalized and not taken seriously in society that expressions of pain reflect much more than just the biomedical diseases from which people suffer.

Many pilgrims attributed their cancer, lung disease, or other physical damage to dangerous machines, air pollution, or harmful substances in their work environments. In particular, they blamed their superiors for not taking it seriously when they began to display physical symptoms. They told how powerless they felt because they had no alternative job opportunities and because their complaints were systematically ignored. Health problems finally forced them to give up their work, but no one took their side or worried about them.

The pilgrims also mentioned their age as a source of humiliation and marginalization. They must deal with medical and religious authorities who, although much younger than they, are in a position to dictate to sick old people what they must do. At their age, loss of health and disrespectful treatment in hospitals and churches go together with the loss of beloved friends and relatives. When needed most, their dear ones are lost through ill health or death. Age confronts the pilgrims with their own finitude and strengthens their feeling that there is no social support, that everything and everyone falls away, and that they are on their own.

The complex medical situations of the pilgrims do not fully account for their motives in making the pilgrimage. Pilgrims do not hope for a cure or miraculous healing. After so many years of treatment and surgery, they have accepted the prospect of never regaining their health. The journey to Lourdes is, rather, meant to close a particularly painful phase in their life—like a dangerous operation or a long period of rehabilitation—or to celebrate, say, a marriage that has lasted forty years. They want to break out, leave their everyday life behind, and start life anew.

Making Memory

Throughout the pilgrimage, storytelling changed as the medical framework ceased to dominate the shape of narratives. What mattered now was the interaction between volunteers and pilgrims. The moment we arrived in France, each pilgrim was given a wheelchair, whether she used one in everyday life or not. During the days that followed, the sick pilgrims were constantly surrounded by helpful volunteers, who were instructed by the pilgrimage organization that their primary task was to listen to the pilgrims: "Push their wheelchairs, be patient, and listen!" In contrast to relations with doctors in everyday life, there was no distance between the pilgrims' emotional world and the clinical world of medical authorities. The doctor in our group was constantly among the pilgrims. He intervened when they needed medical treatment, but he also pushed wheelchairs and listened to intimate stories about their illnesses. Not only the doctor but also the priest—likewise missing from everyday life—helped to ensure an extraordinary pilgrimage. He stayed in the same hotel and was ready to listen whenever he was solicited by the pilgrims. The pilgrims greatly appreciated having both a medical and a religious specialist near at hand.

For each new item on the program, the volunteers took charge of a different pilgrim. This gave the pilgrims the opportunity to tell and retell their stories time after time. Storytelling was mainly confined to one-on-one relationships with volunteers. Sitting in wheelchairs with volunteers behind them, they felt safe to confide sorrows they must keep to themselves in everyday life. The pilgrims preferred talking to volunteers, whom they would probably never meet again, rather than to fellow pilgrims from their own neighborhoods. Having enough problems of their own, they had little need to listen to other people's suffering. The volunteers, for their part, gladly listened to all stories. The nursing volunteers actually complained that in their ordinary working lives they never have time to listen to their patients. Now they got to listen to sick people rather than just nursing them, and they found that satisfying. The pilgrimage thus created a narrative community composed of pilgrims speaking out about their secret suffering and willing volunteers listening to them. In this pattern our group moved between the hotel, the sanctuary, and the shopping area of Lourdes, and between the different ritual events in the pilgrimage program.

The first day, pilgrims wanted to shop for souvenirs. Some wanted to find small gifts for relatives; others looked for statues or headstones to be placed on the graves of deceased relatives. All bought candles to light at the sanctuary in remembrance of loved ones. This search for mementos prompted stories about memories of Lourdes that are kept alive in the family. The pilgrims told how their pilgrimage linked up with past pilgrimages by relatives. Both male and female pilgrims claimed that their pilgrimage was in remembrance of loved family members, often fathers or mothers, who were real worshippers of Mary and had been to Lourdes.

After we had visited the sanctuary and the shops on the first day, our emotions began to flow on the second day, when we had our VGZ celebration at the grotto. Pilgrims declared that it felt as if "the pain fixed inside the body begins to move." Roos, a fifty-nine-year-old woman who has been rheumatic for ten years, grieved for a dead child. "When I applied for the VGZ pilgrimage," she said, "I wrote down my rheumatism and the difficulties I have in walking, but here I don't even think about it anymore. I am here to remember my son. The pain came when I saw Mary in the grotto; I felt the pain passing through my body, from my toes through my belly to my head, and I immediately realized that pain—that is Wouter."

Her youngest son had died in an industrial accident five years earlier. "It was so sad," Roos told me. "We had celebrated his wedding just three months before the accident; we hardly had time to see the photos and video recordings made that day. Then, at the age of twenty-six, he died suddenly of nitrogen poisoning. There was a leak in the lab where he worked, always giving it his heart and soul." Roos complained that people would not allow her "to tell her story," while in her mind she constantly dwelt on her son's death: "From morning to evening I think of him, and I miss him so much." The statue of Mary in the grotto evoked these memories because Roos had first come to Lourdes just after giving birth to Wouter. "When I was in pain, just before the delivery, a friend from the women's movement came to see me and told me I had won a pilgrimage to Lourdes. Now I have come back to Lourdes to part with him again."

Her emotions vacillated between grief for her son, anger toward his superior, who was never adequately punished for his negligence, and jealousy of her daughter-in-law and her son's colleagues, who were given all possible support in their mourning process. Her husband and oldest son never spoke about their mourning, as they dealt with their sorrow in a totally different manner, by silently visiting Wouter's grave in the cemetery. Given that they mourned in silence, they told Roos to silence her pain and forget about it. "But I cannot forget this pain," Roos told me. "People are quick to think that after a year of mourning you must stop crying and start life again. But this pain will stay with me forever. One never forgets the death of a child." Roos's memories of pain mingled with nostalgia for her son: his jokes, his hugs, the way he stroked her hair when he entered the house and greeted her. These nostalgic memories also hurt, but "it feels good," said Roos, "to remember all those precious moments."

From private conversations with different pilgrims, I learned that many of them were struggling with the invisible wound of having lost a child. Almost all pilgrims in our group had had to cope with the death of a child or with seriously ill children. Pilgrims also told shameful secrets that they had always bottled up, like the shame of having children who had run away from home, committed suicide, or turned out to be homosexual. The pilgrimage enabled them to remember these children and to experience their own pain about their loss.

In addition to the loss of loved ones, pilgrims grieved because of trouble in their family relationships. While we were waiting for the afternoon program to begin, another woman, Hanneke, told me about her trouble with her husband. Hanneke is fifty-eight years old. She began to suffer from arthritis and heart disorders twelve years ago. She can hardly walk, and throughout the pilgrimage her physical condition visibly deteriorated. With a smiling face, she mentioned that she had undergone fourteen operations during the past sixteen years. The pain she told me about, however, was not associated with her own body but with her husband's illness and her marriage. Seven years ago her husband fell ill, was diagnosed with a rare hereditary lung disease, and was told he had only three years to live. He had to give up work, and he labors so hard for breath that he can only sit in a chair and watch what is going on in the home. "Now that he can no longer order his staff around," Hanneke told me, "he has begun to dictate to me what to do. He has changed into a totally different man—domineering, disrespectful, always quarreling, and treating me like dirt. He makes me so miserable and angry that I often smash coffee cups against the wall, but only when he can't see me." Once Hanneke left home, but she came back. "Of course," she told me, "how can I abandon my husband? We had a very good life together. We've got a son and a grandchild; how can I leave him now when he has only a few years to live? I have put on a mask, and now I totally efface myself and my pain in order to care for him."

At home Hanneke has to be strong. She never cries, and she devotes all her attention to her husband. Here in Lourdes she has time to cry, to feel her own pain, and to enjoy the care of the volunteers. It is she, not her sick husband, who is the center of attention. This enables her to distance herself from him and all the trouble that his illness has caused in the private sphere of the family: "I take off my mask and give in to my own feelings and emotions. I start to recognize that I am ill, too, that it is not only my husband who is suffering." Hanneke told the priest about her suffering, and he repeated it during the ceremony of the laying on of hands. "At that moment, he appreciated and recognized my suffering," she said. "I felt that my pain is worth suffering and that I am allowed to show my pain."

Like Roos and many other pilgrims, Hanneke mingles painful and nostalgic memories. She recounts how she used to enjoy life with her husband, how much she liked his attentive gestures, the love letters he wrote, and the small presents he still offers her. The narration of painful memories also creates openings for positive and joyful memories, which cannot surface so long as pain remains trapped in the body.

Painful memories not only give rise to nostalgic memories, they also trigger memories of pain that pilgrims thought had gone away. Pilgrims kept saying that "unexpected pain, held in the depths of my body, suddenly surfaces and makes me feel sad." Suppressed memories of the Second World War, memories of a first husband or a miscarriage more than fifty years ago, saddened them but also enabled them to enjoy the pilgrimage fully. Gradually they started to cry and then had difficulty in stopping as the remembrance of one painful event triggered other painful memories. Through crying and storytelling, bottled-up grief and anger started to flow. They left the body, bringing emotional relief. The pilgrims felt healed as they settled these restless memories. Recollecting their pain enabled them to distance themselves from it.

The pilgrimage program, comprising a carefully considered sequence of ritual and symbolism, facilitated this process of emotional release. It nurtured self-confidence, which enabled pilgrims "to speak out loud." In all public rituals, they were invited to perform duties and to participate actively in the world's most famous Marian ceremonies. During mass at the grotto, pilgrims joined the choir. In the torchlight procession, they again joined the choir and carried the VGZ banner and the Dutch flag. Some pilgrims even sang Mary's Seven Sorrows solo outside the rosary basilica. Microphones carried their voices all over the sanctuary. The pilgrim who carried the VGZ banner led the procession, with thousands of pilgrims following her. Singing the rosary, moving their wheelchairs, and raising burning torches to the rhythm of the Ave Maria, the pilgrims performed on the public stage of Lourdes and gradually got a feeling for what it is to be seen, heard, and recognized. In all the rituals, they played an active role—singing, carrying candles, praying aloud, or reading the Bible in public. This shift from their marginal position in everyday life to center stage in Marian ceremonies was in itself a form of therapy and empowerment.

Nostalgic memories were particularly prevalent during the international mass on the third day of our pilgrimage. In the huge underground basilica, which accommodates up to twenty-five thousand pilgrims, we celebrated mass with pilgrims of all nationalities and ages, with dozens of priests and bishops, and with a huge choir, which our pilgrims were invited to join. The basilica is so colossal that, in order to involve all pilgrims, the main ritual actions in the center of the basilica are recorded and displayed on several big screens. The pilgrims were delighted to see so many children and priests at the mass. The well-known liturgy, the familiar smell of incense, and the Latin chants, which they still know by heart but never sing in church anymore, were eagerly absorbed. They were pleased to experience the church in all its glory and to rediscover things that they thought were lost. In experiencing a living church, they also experienced earlier happy moments of good health and life when everybody they loved was still there.

During the performance of the stations of the cross on the fourth day, the emotional intensity reached a climax. The priest guided our group along the stations and invited the pilgrims to compare their own suffering with the suffering of Christ. As this was the end of the pilgrimage, they felt completely at ease in the group, though they did not expect much from this last ritual, which they had often performed "automatically" in the past. However, given that the priest, who had listened to all the pilgrims' stories over the past few days, discreetly integrated each pilgrim's personal sorrow into his reflections at the stations, the pilgrims were so moved that emotions resurfaced and they could not refrain from crying. Everybody identified with the priest's reflections when he recounted how suffering people often fall down, scramble to their feet, then fall down again; how little by little everything is taken away from them; how incomprehension and loneliness make things worse; and how most people only watch, so that only a few join in and stick together. At the station of Mary crying over her son's corpse, the priest repeatedly said, "A child has been lost." Thus he managed to encapsulate all the pilgrims' suffering in one single, powerful image of the sorrowful mother mourning her lost child. This Marian image now symbolized all the kin-related suffering that had been narrated, performed, and accepted during the pilgrimage. It also empowered the pilgrims to remember that their own pain was on a par with Mary's widely celebrated and everlasting pain. This last ceremony "transformed individual suffering into meaningful shared experience."[12]

The pilgrims then returned home, emotionally and physically exhausted. The pilgrimage appeared to have been a journey of profound transformation. It not only entailed physical movement in space, from home to the sanctuary and from one ritual space to another, but also emotional movement: a movement that brought what was previously hidden to the surface, with marked therapeutic effects. No pilgrim saw the journey as a holiday, because it was painful and arduous. They set out with a story, remade their existing stories, and constructed new ones. Now they were going home with a story that was worth telling: a story in which private pain is no longer silenced but considered equal to the suffering of Mary and Christ; a powerful story that would enable them to take up everyday life again.

Powerful Action

One week after the pilgrimage, the pilgrims told me how tired they were. After their return, they secluded themselves and slept for days. Some even disconnected the telephone to rest and recover. Others actually fell ill. The pilgrims were surprised that so much could have happened in just a few days, in which so many memories surfaced and so much pain was experienced. They described it as an overwhelming experience, a journey that confused them but simultaneously felt good. Some pilgrims, who had been to Lourdes before, concluded that it was "a real pilgrimage" rather than a holiday because of the pain they felt and the emotional change they had undergone. It was not holiday but "therapy."

The pilgrims also remembered the pleasant relationship with fellow pilgrims and volunteers, the safe, warm atmosphere in which everything could be told, the nice hotel, the good care, and the well-organized program. However, none of them has contacted the other pilgrims in the region, nor do they intend to do so. The narrative community has fallen apart, and pain has become private again. As the Lourdes experience was filled with painful memories, people hesitated to recount it. Retelling would imply going through the pain again, and that is not what the pilgrims aim to do. The articulation of pain was contextually bound to the sacred space of Lourdes and to the temporary community of volunteers and pilgrims. For now, the pilgrimage has satisfied their need to narrate their pain. Having undergone it, they want to distance themselves and enjoy inner rest and relief until the moment comes when they need the experience again. "I am sure I'll go back to Lourdes," many pilgrims affirm, "but it won't be next year, at the earliest in five years' time or so."

When I interviewed the pilgrims three weeks after the journey, the experience had already resulted in new and powerful actions. Roos fished out all the documents about her son's death that she had collected: photographs of his wedding and his burial, newspaper cuttings about the accident, his obituary, and letters with the court's judgment of her son's employer. She had never organized the documents before, but now she had started to arrange them in an album and had even selected a wedding photo to be displayed in the living room.

Since her return home, Hanneke had had "terrible dreams" again every night. She hardly dared to share them. She dreamt of being dead herself. "It's so strange," she told me. "I see myself being placed in the coffin, wearing my wedding dress, with my husband and son standing next to me. It is so beautiful." When I asked her how she interpreted these dreams, she said: "It is so amazing that my husband is alive and cares for me, that he puts me in my wedding dress. I feel quiet now, as I am not sure anymore that he will die first. I always thought that my illness would not kill me, that I only had to care for him. Now I recognize that I feel a wreck and could die myself." Hanneke has told her dreams to her husband, as well. She said that it feels as though their roles have been reversed. She worries less about him, and both worry much more about her.

These examples of how the pilgrims pick up their lives again after the pilgrimage show that they have made fundamental changes and are able to do what feels good for them. While they can hardly intervene in the biomedical cure of their diseases, they feel empowered to maintain the emotional healing that began during the pilgrimage. The painful events that overwhelmed them before are now under their control.

Conclusion

This study of the pilgrimage to Lourdes from the perspective of the pilgrims and the power relations in which they are involved shows how the journey facilitates the making of painful and nostalgic memories and brings about emotional healing and empowerment. I have focused on sick pilgrims who feel marginalized and constrained by dominant power structures, such as arrogant employers, church authorities, and physicians. Suffering from chronic illnesses and multiple biomedical diseases, these pilgrims feel that their greatest need is less to be healed than to make public their marginalization and humiliation in dominant structures of inequality, as well as their private pain, which is often denied by these power structures.

In the process of pilgrimage, pilgrims overcome the difficulty of remembering and feel enabled to make their stories heard, shared, and recognized. Before the pilgrimage they were overwhelmed by losses that they were unable to communicate, either in the biomedical domain or in the private sphere of home and family. Lourdes emerges as an outstanding place for making pain into memories and for simultaneously experiencing and enjoying pain. These findings challenge the theory that people in pain have no words to express their pain and confirm findings that religious practice offers a language to articulate emotional experiences of pain.[13]

During the pilgrimage, the sanctuary unfolds as a "landscape of memory,"[14] evoking stories about how Marian devotion has been passed on in the family and how certain kin relationships are filled with pain. The commemoration of dead relatives in different generations emerges as an important aspect of memory work during the pilgrimage. The remembrance of dead children, especially, is narrated, experienced, and performed with great intensity. In addition to mourning, relational troubles—both marital and family problems—that in everyday life often remain shrouded in secrecy and shame are frequently expressed during the pilgrimage. In Lourdes all these painful memories are triggered by the sacred scene, the rituals and their powerful symbols, and an audience willing to listen to the pilgrims' tales of suffering.

As a ritual of remembrance, the journey to Lourdes is also a pilgrimage of connection. Through recalling and experiencing painful historical events, pilgrims are able to connect past, present, and future, and to discern continuity and wholeness in stages of life that had been dominated by feelings of discontinuity and loss. Through recollecting and reorganizing their past, the pilgrims are able to resume the present and to envision a new future. Commemoration of deceased relatives ensures continuity in both family history and individual life history. Thus the pilgrimage to Lourdes is a practice of making memory, meant to maintain continuity when discontinuity seems to predominate.

"Without my headscarf I feel naked"

"Veiling," *Laïcité*, Politics, and Islamist Discourse in North Cameroon

José C. M. van Santen

Discourse about the Muslim "veil" and the wearing of headscarves in public places in Western countries has made its way into the heart of contemporary Western history and identity. However, as Markha Valenta argues, the arguments are hardly about the "veil" itself.[1] She beautifully reveals that at the heart of the debate is the West's own current crisis of identity and historical destiny. The most urgent and contested discussions are in fact located in Continental Western Europe. [2] Though English-speaking nations in the West share the same prejudices, "this has not generated the same level of distressed debate, which is part of the as yet unresolved problem of minorities in representative democracies, whereby the case of Islam stands out at this moment by virtue of the urgency with which it is experienced as an issue in need of immediate and drastic attention."[3]

The debate about the "veil" is not only a debate about Islam in the West, the future of the Western nation-state, or the nature of the West and its democracy. In this essay, I will investigate the prohibition on wearing headscarves at state-subsidized schools in Cameroon and its relation to fundamentalism and the foundation of Islamic private schools.[4] France, the former colonizer of Cameroon, provides a striking example of the crisis of secularism that is central to the European discourse on the "veil." Since 1905, there has been a strong separation between "church" and state, religion and politics, as a result of a historical struggle between Catholicism and Republicanism during the first decades of the Third Republic (1870–1905). Due to the arrival in France of many Muslim immigrants, who are there to stay and have become French citizens, many French intellectuals and politicians, on the left as well as the right, believe that the secular character of the Republic is under threat and that the headscarf symbolizes this threat. Nevertheless, the same intellectuals and politicians have no difficulty in speaking of their "Judeo-Christian legacy," as Talal Asad remarks.[5] In the context of the March 2004 law that prohibits pupils at public schools from wearing conspicuous religious symbols—*signes religieux ostensibles*—the debate concerning *laïcité* in connection with the "veil" regularly makes the front pages of internationally renowned newspapers.

The notion of the "veil" is tied up with religious experience and beliefs, and in the Islamic world its sense is disputed: some wonder whether the Arab word *hijab* should be translated as "veil," since "curtain" would be just as accurate. "Veil" is closer to *nikab* or *khimar*, because both, like "veil," signify a piece of cloth that covers the face.

In Cameroonian popular discourse, the ban on the wearing of headscarves by girls in public schools is cited as a reason for the establishment of many private Islamic schools, primary as well as secondary. They are built with money from NGOs, most of them based in Saudi Arabia, and that places the discussion in the context of a struggle for international influence and sovereignty.[6] The Islamic faith reached the northern parts of Cameroon centuries ago, and its arrival is a good example of the way religion and political power go together: together with Islam came political subjugation by Islamic invaders, who settled in this area and built their own communities. However, the past, in which the Islamic faith could not be detached from the political situation, is still very much part of the present, and relations between religious and political leaders are still quite strong.

Following the Islamic faith, accepting Islam as a religion, being a Muslim, deepening one's knowledge of the faith, becoming literate by studying the Qur'an, and, in former days, invading other areas all contribute to constructing an identity, especially among the Fulbe, the largest group of the original invaders. So getting educated was and is important. Until recently, this meant Qur'anic education, because secular education was associated with the later colonial invaders. Refusing secular (colonial) education is, retrospectively, considered an act of resistance against the colonizers and their policies. As a result, non-Islamic ethnic groups have gained a lead in secular education: they were keen on attending missionary schools and in this way getting rid of their inferior status as "unbelievers" and uneducated people.

The fact that the Islamic population—far fewer of whom have received "secular" education than Christian or "pagan" citizens—need to catch up with secular education is given as a reason for founding new Islamic schools in an Islamic environment. However, an important argument that accompanies this reasoning is that a space needs to be created where women in particular can obtain a secular education while being able to hold onto their Islamic identity. Here the "veil" or headscarf enters in, given that in public, state-subsidized schools children have to attend classes bareheaded due to the state's *laïcité*—an inheritance from the colonial government, as prescribed in constitutional law.

In this essay, I will explore how these aspects of new Islamic discourse interrelate around the topic of the headscarf, which has become an integral part of concerns about schooling and education. Michel-Rolph Trouillot remarks that, behind the banality of millions of encounters between individuals or groups and governments, we discover how deeply government is present in our lives, regardless of regimes and particulars of the social formation.[7] Yet nowadays, he argues, images of governmental power are also challenged, diverted, or simply forced to give way to infra- or supranational institutions. In addition, we must theorize the state beyond what is obvious about it. As an avenue of approach to these questions, let us look at the case of Maimouna, an Islamic girl of Fulbe ethnic background. Already in her first years of secondary school, she has expressed a wish to continue her education at the university level.[8]

She lives amid the new youth cultures that are emerging, especially in urban areas, among young women and men whose prospects of securing a better future through work or study have been diminished by economic, political, and social problems on both a national and an international scale. Some of them are very open to Islamist discourses, while others are eager to incorporate Western images into their projections of a modern Muslim identity. Islamist discourses thus manage to influence local notions of Muslim identity, in particular with respect to gender.

Veiling, the Laical State, and Cameroon

In the Western media, people from of all walks of life regularly assert the negative impact they believe the "veil" or headscarf worn by Islamic women has on liberal, progressive, secular, and, above all, enlightened society.[9] As Valenta states: "It is the conjunction between, on the one hand, an essentialist narrative of Europe's history and, on the other hand, an ahistorical account of Europe's present that explains why Islam, and the veil as its symbol, today are widely represented as simultaneously *alien* intrusions on Western ground, *premodern* holdovers, and *antimodern* threats to what we have achieved today."[10] The "veil," once a valued symbol in many religions, became a symbol of fundamentalist Islam, read as synonymous with extremism or even terrorism. Some people automatically pair "Islam, fundamentalism, and the debate on veiling": fundamentalism is easily confused with the issue of the standing of women, with the "veil" signifying "the low legal status of women in Muslim society,"[11] though gender relations there are seldom thoroughly analyzed, and the voices of Muslim women are not often heard. A contrasting view holds that Muslim women see wearing the headscarf as part of their identity.[12]

Since 9/11, the political implications of the "veil" have further increased. In many European countries, more women are "veiling" and ready to defend this choice. Structural discrimination against Muslims has led to stronger identification with a belief system and, for immigrants, with the society from which they have come.[13] Books whose titles include the word *veil* are imagined to sell well, so the word is used even in the titles of works that do consider women as agents, as in *Veiled Sentiments, Beyond the Veil, La révolution sous le voile*, and *The Hidden Face of Eve*.[14]

Cameroon, like its former colonizer, France, is a laical state. The term *laical* originally denoted members of the Christian church who did not receive clerical orders. Later it referred to Christian communities that did not have ecclesiastic functions in the heart of the church. Only during the early Middle Ages, in a complex history of relations between the temporal and the spiritual, did the term come to acquire new, antireligious connotations.[15] After centuries of struggle between the French state and the Catholic church, the conviction that only a laical, secular, state is compatible with all forms of religious life and is the only rational framework for guaranteeing freedom of expression has become a staple of French political life.[16]

The Cameroonian constitution mandates an official division between state and religion. According to Cameroonian constitutional law, "no person shall be harassed on grounds of his origin, religious, philosophical or political opinions or beliefs, subject to respect for public policy;—the State shall be secular [*L'État est laïc*]. The neutrality and independence of the State in respect of all religions shall be guaranteed;—freedom of religion and worship shall be guaranteed."[17] A consequence of this law is that, as in France, no overt symbols of religion may be brought into school, given that school is a public space.[18]

This returns us to the issue of "veiling." In most Cameroonian communities, whether Christian or Islamic, women (and often also men) use various types of head covering, in pointed contrast to the official policy that forbids wearing headgear in the classroom. This holds in the southern, Christian parts of the country as well as in the north, where the majority of the population is Islamic.

In North Cameroonian Islamic communities, people draw a distinction between various forms of headgear. The ordinary turban, which nearly all women of whatever ethnic and religious origins wear is called in Fulfulde (the local lingua franca) *hadiko*. Islamic women add a cloth around their heads and shoulders in the color of the rest of their outfits, called *kudel*. A recent fashion is to place on top of this a shawl of a thin material, called *lafaay*. New, but still rare, is a colored veil, called the *tope*, as in Sudan and Chad; women may wear it when they are going out and when they wear Western-style clothes, which the *tope* can more easily cover up. Even more uncommon is the black Arab dress called *hijab* or *hidjâb*—a word derived from the Arab verb *hadjaba*, "to cover up."[19] As a rule only Mousgoum women, who live near the Logone River, on the border with Chad, wear the *hijab* and thereby cover the face with a black cloth.[20]

In Cameroon, the wearing of the headscarf or *lafaay* in public has in general not been a matter of debate. In the north, most women who work in public institutions such as town halls, prefectures, or banks are Muslim; they wear a headscarf and also a *kudel* and/or *lafaay*. But men performing public functions also wear Islamic outfits. Until the 1990s nobody ever talked about this. However, with the wave of fundamentalist movements has come the establishment of private Islamic schools, whose number is rapidly increasing. The issue of veiling has suddenly come to the fore as a reason for establishing these schools. As the male director of one of them—in the company of an Islamic director of an ordinary public school—explained:

To understand the new movements, knowledge of Fulbe culture is essential. When the French arrived, they met little resistance except here in Maroua, because the population here refused to be dominated.[21] Afterward the Fulbe considered the creation of Western schools to be a threat. What use was it to our own culture, which is Arab-Islamic and by definition antioccidental? There is a *point qui ne convient pas*. The French pressed us to go to school and with that we lost touch with the roots of our own culture, the reason why many fathers did not want to send their children to school, especially their daughters. Public schools did not have the right spirit.

Because we did not want to lose another generation, to remain without a secular school education, and because there is this obvious division between the East and the West, we got together and founded Islamic schools. Parents have fewer objections to sending their daughters to school, because in the Islamic schools they learn about the Qur'an and they are allowed to wear their headscarves, the *lafaay*, whereas this is forbidden at public schools.

Of course, this is a good example of what Olivier Roy means when he speaks of the relation between Muslim intellectuals—and I consider this man to be one—and the West: there is a constant struggle among many Islamic intellectuals to historicize Western culture in order to debunk its claim to be universal.[22] But the critique of Western cultural hegemony is sustained less by a valorization of existing traditional cultures than by modern reconstructions of new identities, even if they resort to historical themes. In this context Arabization—whatever may be meant by that—appears to be a rejection of the nation-state—and with it the West—replacing it with better Islams (in the plural).[23]

Concerning girls' participation in the school, the director remarked:

We are very happy with these new developments, the fact that we have nearly as many girls as boys. What use is "development" without the participation of women? Isn't it true that "the state occurs through the mediation of women" [literally, *La nation passe par les femmes*]? Don't children spend half of their lives with women, especially their mothers? In Fulbe culture women are respected; that is why they need not till the land. Islam, however, does not forbid women to work; women need to be as active as men in the development of a state. We therefore need to create the right conditions, and Islamic schools are a start. They get the normal curriculum, as in other schools, but in addition knowledge of the Qur'an [in Fulfulde translation] and the Arabic script. Girls can wear their veils in these schools, whereas they must take them off in state-run public schools. That fact makes it harder for them to go to school—not only because their fathers may fear improper behavior but also because they feel ashamed themselves. Those who founded the Cameroonian state and made the rules [*status*] were all Christians from the south, and they never took our [Islamic] culture into account.

The director of the state-subsidized public school, who agreed with these words, added: "They had forgotten that, at the time the French arrived, Islamic culture was deeply rooted in our culture, and that we always have been learned and educated, women as well as men. With the arrival of Western influence, they forced a culture upon us that is not ours. A school should be embedded in a culture, not the other way around." To relate these words to the practical situation, we need only note that in 1998 this particular Islamic school had as its students 312 girls and 430 boys; in 2006, 387 girls and 348 boys.

Indeed, until recently all children "marched the *defilé*" bareheaded during state-organized festivities such as *la fête national* and *la journée de la jeunesse*. It is therefore remarkable that in 1999 in Mokolo, a town in North Cameroon, the children from the state-subsidized Franco-Arab school (a school system that had existed since colonial times), for the first time wore black veils that covered their shoulders when they marched in the *defilé*.[24] By 2005, in the *defilé* one could observe hundreds of pupils of the Islamic primary as well as secondary schools in their school uniforms, which cover the legs, as they consist of trousers underneath skirts, and a *hijab*, covering the head and shoulders.[25] When asked about their dress, these children answered that it was a natural consequence of their Islamic faith and that they wanted to be good Muslims. However, many girls who do not cover their heads in school are also convinced that they are good Muslims. Obviously divergent discourses are at work here.

In daily discourses some believers, as well as imams and *mallum'en* (religious teachers, called *marabouts* in French), consider the introduction of the *hijab* as an unnecessary influence from the "white Pakistani," who since the new waves of fundamentalism, which started around 1992, act as itinerant preachers, accompanied by local imams and religious leaders. Depicted as "Western whites" who bring in "Wah'abian" influences, they are not necessarily well regarded.[26] As the imam of village *X* stated, relating these preachers to the introduction of the black *hijab*:

"We are not in need of those black crows. We do not need them in our streets. Fulbe women have always dressed correctly, with a cloth, *kudel*, around their head. Where in the Qur'an should I read that this cloth ought to be black?"

Another woman, literate in Arabic, regarded the new black *hijab*, which also covers the face, as an achievement, as part of a new freedom, a modern life, though she would not wear it herself:

> I wished they had invented it much earlier. It gives us so much freedom; we can go wherever we want without men staring at us. Once I met a man in the street whom I thought to be a good friend of my husband. He spoke of indecent things. Never had I felt more humiliated in my life. Had I worn the *hijab* he would not even have recognized me!

In the 1980s the "veil" was not yet an issue. Nobody in the region ever mentioned it, and it was not yet a topic of a general debate, as it is today. However, in retrospect it seems to have been an issue after all: people now explain that Islamic girls often were not sent to school because they had to take off their headscarves in the classroom. It was primarily fathers who objected to sending their daughters to school, as they—being males—had the responsibility, in this particular Muslim society, of ensuring that their children were educated within the Islamic faith. If children grow up to be "bad" Muslims, the fathers will be blamed. Many men did not and do not want the community to gossip about their daughters going to school bareheaded, not least since it may then be difficult to find proper marriage partners for them.

Official state statistics and various state documents simply say that the north is still very "backward" and that the *taux scolaire*, the number of children going to school, is still very low. However, for Muslim fathers getting girls "properly" married is an important issue, one that comes up over and over again when one discusses "modern" life with Muslim men.[27] They feel that Muslim girls have always been well educated, as Qur'anic education in Arabic has never been denied them and it continues to be what is most important.

Indeed, Islamic men do seem to be the driving force behind the creation of an "Islamic private school system." To give an example, in Boula, a small village fifty kilometers from Maroua, a meeting took place in August 1999 between the local chief, the imam, and some councilors in the company of people "from abroad." The purpose of the gathering, as I found out during my visit to the village, proved to be the foundation of an Islamic school. Political as well as religious leaders are involved in the foundation of these schools because in North Cameroon educational and political institutions are closely connected. Even when wearing the headscarf is given as a reason for the founding of these schools, they can also be interpreted as a political move, an act of resistance against the government in the south, given that the Islamic

Fulbe in the north recently lost political hegemony when a Christian southerner was installed as president. By the same token, Islamization and fundamentalism(s) as global forces are about restructuring the state, even in secular countries such as Cameroon.

North Cameroon: A Symbiosis of Politics and Religion

Islamic kingdoms have been a political force in West Africa for more than six centuries. From 1200 to 1700, the Mandara sultan controlled the region at the northern base of the Mandara Mountains (on the present border with Nigeria, with Mora as a capital), while further north lay the wealthy Bornu Empire, near Lake Chad, with Magari as its most important town. On the eastern Logone riverbank was situated the kingdom of Barghuirmi. These empires regularly clashed with one another.[28]

Somewhat later, the Sokoto Empire arose further south, founded by Uthman dan Fodio in the area that is now northern Nigeria. Starting in 1800, the Fulbe, originally a nomadic people, invaded the Diamara region and subjugated acephalous ethnic groups like the Guiziga,[29] while struggling with hierarchically organized populations like the Mundang.[30] The Sokoto rulers granted them the *tutawal*, the right to install Fulbe chiefs in the conquered areas, so after a victory a Fulbe chief would be installed there. Competence in matters concerning the Qur'an was the main qualification for becoming a "chief."[31] Evidently an imam had to play a role in these matters or even appoint a "chief." The imam under the first Islamic ruler in Maroua, installed in 1801, had more power than the chief himself.

All these hierarchically organized provinces were occupied by the Germans when they marched north in 1900 to conquer the area. The German colonial system was taken over by the French after the defeat of the Germans during the First World War. The French colonial system used the hierarchically organized empires of northern Cameroon to govern the local populations.[32]

Here we may bear in mind Mahmoud Mamdani's remark that in Africa indirect rule came to be the mode of colonial rule, and that indirect and direct rule, like customary and civil power, ceased to be thought of as alternatives. The countryside was governed by indirect rule, while towns were subject to direct rule. This meant that colonial rule was experienced by the vast majority of the colonized as rule by one's own people.[33] In North Cameroon regional varieties appear. During the colonial period, acephalous ethnic groups were at first ruled by Islamic chiefs of the hierarchically organized Fulbe people. In due course—and here the mountain population of the Mafa may serve as an example—they no longer accepted rule by the Fulbe chiefs, insisting upon their own—though also Islamic—chief.[34] Only in the 1950s did a

Christian alternative become available, when missionaries settled and started to convert local non-Islamic populations.[35] Thus, for the majority of the population, for a long time the authority of the chief resided in a single person, who exercised all aspects of power—judicial, legislative, executive, administrative, and also religious. Ethnicity, at first a form of colonial control, became in the long run a form of revolt against it; according to Mamdani, this power system still has a strong impact on processes of democratization.[36] In North Cameroon, a way to escape "being a 'native' subject"—that is, an "unbeliever" of one of the non-Fulbe ethnic groups—lay in the option of converting to Islam. That has been taking place on a large scale, especially in urban centers.

Local rulers were able to hold onto their power for a very long time. Since independence, a traditional chief has in reality become the adjunct of a *maire*, a burgomaster, but even today many citizens pay more respect to "local chiefs," who are still installed and inaugurated by the state, than to administrators of the "modern" political system.

Education

Qur'anic education has always enjoyed a high status in the Muslim society of North Cameroon.[37] It has long been a criterion in choosing traditional chiefs. For a long time, men as well as women refused French secular education. The director of the Islamic school and many other "intellectuals" nowadays interpret this refusal as an act of resistance against the French colonials. Even the smallest settlement in North Cameroon has a Qur'an school. In fact, it is the first thing that is installed when a nomadic group settles, and even when they are traveling nomads will create a place, by making a half circle with pebbles—to pray and read the Qur'an when they put up their temporary homes.[38] They thereby draw a distinction between *mallum* and *Moddibo*. The former have written down, one by one, every *surah* of the Qur'an on their wooden boards, *alluuha*, memorized it, washed it off, and written a new one. Nevertheless, memorization does not imply that they understand the meaning of the Arab texts they can recite. The latter are scholars in Qur'anic sciences, those who do understand the Arab meaning.[39] Renaud Santerre, who researched Qur'anic schools in Maroua in the 1960s, mentions that these scholars usually studied documents dating from the twelfth to the sixteenth centuries.[40] Nowadays many books are brought in from elsewhere, especially Saudi Arabia.

Eighty-five per cent of the Islamic children who do not attend secular schools go to "traditional" Qur'anic schools. Most children who go to secular schools also go to traditional Qur'anic schools at dawn or after sunset. In 1993—thus, before the installation of the new private Islamic schools—7,750 children in Maroua had modern and Qur'anic schooling, of whom 3,133 were girls and 4,617 boys.[41] In North Cameroon, French schools were established much later than in South Cameroon. The first one was started in Maroua in 1918, and it faced much opposition, especially from the Muslim population. The *lamido*, chief, of Maroua pretended to promote education at the secular school, thereby winning much credit with the French administration. In reality, he paid parents, who later withdrew their children from the school, and parents who wanted their children to continue their education had to pay tribute to him.[42] When missions arrived in the 1950s, secular education became a real issue, but it attracted mainly non-Islamic children, from what Mamdani calls the "ethnicized tribal groups."[43] For them it was a way of becoming "citizens" without converting to Islam.

The first private Islamic school in Maroua opened in the school year 1993–94. Such schools are not financed by the state, and teachers must be paid privately. In 1987, the proportion of children attending school in a town like Maroua was 59 percent (children aged eight scored the highest percentage); in 1993, 70.6 percent of the boys and 58 percent of the girls went to school. Many Muslim parents still object to modern education because they fear that it will lead youth to stray from the path to God, though this fear is less when they attend Islamic schools, where the children receive a religious education, girls and boys are segregated, and girls are allowed to wear the headscarf.[44] In 2007, in the province Extrême Nord Islamic private schools had 4,439 pupils, of which 2,430 were girls.

Due to the dominance of Western-educated southerners and the fact that the non-Muslim population of the north is better educated, the Muslim population has realized that, if they want an alternative "development" not based on the West, they must appeal to secular education, after all. In addition, as the director of the Islamic school put it, this development ought to include women.[45]

Education also came to the fore when a European NGO organized gender-sensitivity training for imams, local chiefs, and preachers in Maroua.[46] One of the dilemmas the NGO asked them to discuss among themselves was the following:

You have a boy and a girl, both of whom went to primary school. You now need to send them to secondary school, but you realize that you do not have the money to send them both. Whom will you send? All but one of the participants answered that they were more likely to send the boy to secondary school, as he would have to provide for his family when he grew up.

Then another element was added: At primary school the girl turned out to be far more intelligent . . . so whom would they send to school?

They had to discuss the matter in small groups. It was the imam of the largest mosque in Maroua who from the beginning had a dissenting view and stated that, if you had two children, you had to send to school the one who was more intelligent, regardless of sex, that is, of whether it was a girl or a boy.

Discussion of the matter in small groups finally led to a point where at least 80 percent of the participants were in favor of sending the brighter child to school. The outcome of the whole workshop, which lasted several days, was that much needs to be done to better women's position, that their bad position in society is due to ethnic residues from pre-Islamic times, and that education for women needs to be encouraged. Again, people who were jointly political and religious leaders were appointed to disseminate this message, rather than agents from the state-governed institutions (such as schoolteachers or prefects).[47]

Education for women is part of the historical Islamic context, however: training for girls is a well-established and integrated aspect of Islamic culture in North Cameroon. At the beginning of the nineteenth century, Uthman dan Fodio, the ruler of the Sokoto Empire who instigated the jihad that led to Islamization in large parts of North Cameroon, underlined women's right to education.[48] He stated:

> Oh Muslim women, do not listen to the words of the misguided ones who seek to lead you astray by ordering you to obey your husbands instead of telling you to obey Allah and his Messenger. They tell you that a woman's happiness lies in obeying her husband. This is no more than a camouflage to make you satisfy their needs. They impose on you duties which neither Allah nor his Messenger imposed on you. They make you cook, wash clothes and do other things which they desire while they fail to teach you what Allah and His Prophet have prescribed for you. Neither Allah nor His Prophet charges you with such duties.[49]

Uthman dan Fodio also claimed that a woman ought to be allowed to go in search of knowledge if her husband cannot teach her.[50] He not only advocated religious education for women but also emphasized the importance of giving them secular instruction in business transactions.[51] His writings are still part of present-day Islamic discourse, and the women within his own family serve as good examples of the position women can attain. One of his daughters, Nana Asmaou, was a scholar of poetry, and, as Jean Boyd and Alhadju Shaku Shagari state, "In the Fodio family the intellectualism of five generations of women can be traced."[52]

The importance of educating women is acquiring new content, as the foundation of Islamic schools indicates, in the new fundamentalist discourse. In addition to these Islamic private schools, illiterate women as well as men regularly assemble—separately, of course—to study the Qur'an under the guidance of a marabout. This may not seem unusual, because Islamic teachers always have many students. However, these cases involve large groups of adults, and the women assemble when their children are at school to learn how to write and read the Qur'an in Arabic. Peripatetic marabouts from different regions and countries have many new followers.

The example of Maimouna, a young Islamic girl who is highly motivated to obtain a good education yet also wants to be and remain a good Muslim, encapsulates the relationships between veiling, modernity, politics, religion, and faith.

Maimouna

I have known Maimouna since she was six months old. She is ethnically a Fulbe, a member of the nomadic cattle-raising group that originally spread Islam throughout North Cameroon at the beginning of the nineteenth century. The Fulbe have produced many religious scholars, and in Fulbe society an educated person has high status: Maimouna's grandfather was a learned scholar—though he lacked a French education—and a highly respected marabout. He had sent his boys to school but not his girls, so Maimouna's mother remains without a secular education and does not speak French. But her mother is skilled in Arabic and is also a marabout. Maimouna's father was related to the chief of a village forty miles away, so he carried the title "prince"; he went to primary school but quit due to a bad experience with the local teacher. He marketed peanuts, the local cash crop. He was a pious, quiet man with a strong sense of justice; he married her mother when she was thirteen years of age. The children adored him, and every day he brought something special home for them from the market, like sweets or fruit. The parents had a warm relationship, which they never showed in public. No matter who entered the compound, they immediately split up and went to their separate spaces within it: according to Fulbe custom, men's and women's activities are highly segregated. All the children—three boys and three girls—can write and read Arabic and had finished reading the Qur'an by the age of twelve.

Maimouna's parents have sent all their children to primary as well as secondary school, so all of them received a secular education. Maimouna is third in line, behind an older brother and sister, but she is the brightest in secondary school—the lycée—where she surpasses her eldest brother and her elder sister, as I have observed throughout the years. In an interview I conducted with her at the age of fifteen, in which we discussed the issue of veiling, she explained that she considered the veil to be a relic of an archaic African past; at that time she also expressed her wish to continue on to the university and to study social science (anthropology or law). Her view is that it was uncommon in former days to send girls to school; in this context she refers to her grandfather, who denied his daughters access to secular education. She wants to be independent in her later life: she says that she wants never to be financially dependent on a husband, which is remarkable if we take into consideration that she lives in an environment where men's obligation to provide for their wives and children—in accordance with Islamic law, thus financially as well as concerning nonmaterial matters such as access to education—is repeatedly emphasized. She stresses that her parents support her but that she never knows exactly what her father feels about her going to school. He sometimes pities her because she has to study hard. When his friends point out that she has already reached the age to be married—in Cameroon, girls still often marry at the age of fourteen—he may still say that he will marry her off, but his tacit support for her school education is revealed in the small sums of money he gives her in the morning before she goes to school so that she will be able to buy an extra snack during the long day. Her mother, on the contrary, encourages her overtly in all that she does. She gives her time to study at home and hardly ever asks her to do household tasks.

During our interview Maimouna—who casually played with her headscarf, which fell onto her shoulders during the conversation—also blamed African "tradition" for girls' not being allowed to pursue a secular education. In her opinion, Islam is not to be blamed. She has deduced this from itinerant preachers from outside the region, called Pakistanis, who are part of the new Islamic fundamentalist wave, and she is sure that their women are all literate, have jobs, and so on, unlike the women in her own "African Islamic" surroundings.

During the interview, her elder sister, bareheaded, was busy cooking. Her mother, wearing a simple headgear, came and went, supervising the cooking and everything else going on within the compound. I reminded Maimouna that some years earlier she said that she always hated to take off the headscarf—a rather simple one—when she entered the classroom. At that time she had commented: "Without my headscarf I feel naked." She now attributes these words to the ignorance of a young girl and to reminiscence of her ethnic "traditional African" practice. As a researcher and good friend of her mother, I had treasured the image of her entering the school and walking toward the classroom, where at the very last minute she would take off her head-scarf, her *lafaay*. In 2003, at the age of sixteen she attended her final class at the lycée and prepared to move fifteen hundred miles away, to continue her studies at the university in the capital city of Yaoundé.

So what was the end of Maimouna's story? Stories embedded in society do not have endings but are like a perpetual motion machine: Maimouna's father became ill in December 2004 and, after having Maimouna close to him during his illness, passed away in January 2005. She passed her exams in July 2005 with good results; she traveled to the south and started university in September 2005, at the age of eighteen. Had he still been alive, her father would have been worried sick to think of his "little girl" all by herself in the huge capital, but he would have been very proud of her, too. In September 2008 she will start studying for her Master's degree. Her mother has all the confidence in her that an adolescent could hope from a parent, and she keeps in contact via the modern device of a mobile phone.

Conclusion

How do politics, the laical state, the issue of veiling, and modernity come together in the story of Maimouna's life and its cultural context? Her life and her interpretation of what she considers to be the new Islamic messages can help us understand what is going on in her society. For her the Saudi Arabians ("Pakistani") bring a right to secular education; for her the "veil" is no longer an issue. She regards it as a relic of an archaic past, a relic from her grandfather's century, from a period when most men—including her grandfather—did not send their daughters to school.

Her gesture of removing the headscarf just before entering the classroom encapsulates the whole discussion of the relationship between the nation-state, modernity, Islamic discourse, and the "veil" as a symbol of the Islamic faith. Men treat the "veil" as a sign of proper conduct on the part of women and thus the foundation of the new type of private schooling. In earlier times, fathers decided not to send their daughters to school, afraid that improper behavior— going bareheaded into a classroom together with boys—would ruin their chances of finding a good husband, while in retrospect they explained their refusal to send their children to school as an act of resistance to the colonial state. Nowadays men with political and religious power initiate the foundation of private Islamic schools because in these new institutions of education women can wear the headscarf in the classroom, where they can be educated to contribute to "development" and/or modernity in a way that is not dictated by "Western" society.

However sympathetic (or correct from a feminist point of view) this emphasis on women's right to education may seem, the reality is much more political. The councils of traditional chiefs, local politicians, and religious local and provincial leaders make decisions about an issue that seems to be in the interest of women. While they cite the education of "their daughters" as a reason for founding the new private schools, in reality they are "throwing out the state" (with its rules decided upon in the political center, the capital, where the ban on wearing the veil at school is considered part of the laical character of the state) and "getting their own" culture, which they call "Arab-oriented." Thus in North Cameroon, as everywhere else in the world, though donning or rejecting the "veil" may seem an autonomous act by individual girls, behind it are institutions, politics, and discourses concerning what it means to be a good Muslim in this laical, modern society in which one needs education. In this discourse we see that Maimouna has changed her understanding of "veiling" as an aspect of proper conduct for a Muslim woman: a couple of years ago she thought it important; now it is of minor significance. She views it as an ethnic leftover and thinks that when people Islamized they did not understand that other things are much more important. So she takes up her society's distinction between ethnic and Islamic consciousness, and she maps it onto her understanding of the Islamic faith so as to align it with her wishes and views concerning her own future. After she went to the "Christian" south of the country to attend university, she continued to think the headscarf of minor importance, though she also continued to wear it most of the time.

The story of Maimouna also indicates that modernity is gendered. Men choose the kind of school where the "veil" is allowed; women choose education. Modernity for Maimouna means being able to go to school, to university, and she justifies this by referring to the process of re-Islamization going on around her. For her, the itinerant preachers—the "Pakistanis" from Saudi Arabia—have brought the message of entitlement to education. She now attaches less significance to wearing or not wearing a "veil." Does this mean that modernity for Maimouna also means secularization? That question only the remaining course of her particular life can answer.

Religion and Powerlessness

Elena in *Nothing Is Missing*

Mieke Bal

"Elena" is an episode from my video work *Nothing Is Missing,* a multiple-screen video installation (2006–7). Briefly, visitors are invited to sit in armchairs or on sofas around them a number of women speak to someone else. The women have been filmed in their own homes, in a number of different countries from which currently migrants frequently come to what is called "the West": the Near or Middle East, Africa, Middle or Eastern Europe. The interlocutors are people close to them, intimates, the

relationship with whom has been interrupted due to the migration of the women's children: a grandchild she didn't see grow up; a child-in-law she didn't choose or approve of; the emigrated child; in one case, three generations. Intimacy, but sometimes a slight uneasiness, is characteristic of the situation. Sometimes you hear the other voice, sometimes not. In this piece I single out Elena, a woman living in northeastern Romania whose only surviving son, Simion, works in an investment bank in Toronto, Canada. He visits twice a year, using up all his vacation days to do so, and our visit took place during his annual summer visit to help with the haying.

Communication unfolds between the older woman, in this case Elena, and her relative, but when the work is installed, due to the installation setup, also between the women, and between the women and the visitors, all at once. The performative aspect on all these levels brings about a merging of these communications. The armchairs can be moved or turned, as if one were visiting the women on the screen, concentrating on one or alternating attention among them.

The women are filmed in consistent close-up, as portraits. The relentlessly permanent image of their faces provides a modest monument to the women who suffered these profound losses. It also forces viewers to look these women in the face, in the eyes, and listen to what they have to say, in a language that is foreign, using expressions that seem strange, but in a discourse we can all, affectively, relate to.

Thus, this work pertains to what I call "migratory aesthetic." This term refers to the aesthetic impact of the cultural mixture in the contemporary West.[1] This is not a project of anthropology, nor the construction of a tourist attraction. One of the many issues of the project is the attempt to go beyond the acknowledgment in, for example, ethnography of the researcher's presence "in the field." Instead, the people affected by migratory culture speak for themselves. For this reason, in my installation there is no narrative voice; only the mothers do the talking. Any sense of tourism is also carefully avoided: while intensely visual, the films show neither monumentality nor picturesque scenery; no spectacle is offered to gratify a desire for beauty; instead, the films engage intimately with the individuals concerned. All sound is diegetic. Indirectly, the installation constitutes a monument to those mothers who were left behind, bereft of those they most loved.

Most of the women invoke God, Allah, or other deities and saints. It is safe to assume that they are, and consider themselves to be, religious. I am interested in the role their belief plays in the way they deal with their plight: the loss of their cherished child.

But how can a written text do justice both to the voice of the (m)other to whom I, as the writer of this text, supposedly listen and to the situation recorded, where that other person speaks in a language inaccessible to me? Instead of looking only at these women's statements of their relationship to religion, therefore, I present here the full transcript of the half-hour conversation one of these women held in the summer of 2006 with her only surviving child, her son Simion, who had left the rural area in northern Romania where he was brought up for Canada.

In order to retain a sense of the presentation of these speeches in the video installation, I present this transcript with line breaks according to the subtitled video. A dash indicates a change of speaker. Sometimes the line breaks are suggestive of Elena's speech—as opposed to writing. At other times, the breaking has a poetic effect. The line breaks are a constant reminder of the artificial and derivative nature of a translated conversation. But, even if ever so subliminally, they also remind the reader of the video portrait, which allows, indeed, forces the visitor to look the woman in the face. The lack of punctuation and capitals in the video, which I maintain here, is meant to render the sense of a flow of speech instead of a written text.

The following is from "Elena," one element in this installation. It is, in my estimation, the most characteristic conversation, between the most impressive woman and her only son who left. It is also the most haunting image. Ever since the recording revealed its full content during the translation process, I was struck by the literary nature of the text—or should I say, event? Elena speaks beautifully, in imaginative words and with narrative devices. In her manner of speaking I saw a struggle between emotions of love and anger, pride, disappointment, and resentment, and the fatal sense of reaching the end of a life that was never fulfilled. God and Holy Mary are frequently invoked in the course of Elena's talk.

I am offering the transcript, in sections but without deleting anything. To each section I juxtapose my own response. This response is belated; I could not communicate with Elena other than by using her son as interpreter, and with body language. Only after the translation was done did the full impact of her speeches hit me. This belated response, then, is also a way of acknowledging her priority as a speaker over my effort to "give her voice" in my writing.

This running commentary is an attempt to understand what happened, that afternoon in August 2006, between a bereft mother and the son who had left her for a better life, an uncertain future, and also, I presume, a never-ending loneliness and regret. In the texture of this conversation, Elena's religion is woven in and out. My question—one I will refrain from answering—is whether her religion either empowers or disempowers this woman.

Prelude

(In the installation, this is accompanied by images of the travel to and the encounter with Elena and her son.)

after a bumpy ride
through the hills of bucovina
in north-eastern romania
we reached the house of elena candrea

211

elena was busy haying
with the help of her son simion
her only child who comes every august
from canada to visit his parents
when the farm work is at its busiest

we reached the house
of elena candrea

elena talks to simion
about her life
and how she misses him
those long months
when he is far away

The landscape was breathtaking. It was 7:30
A.M. when we finally arrived; the sun was trying to pierce through the mist of early morning, the fields were an intense green only

possible at certain brief hours. It was the
middle of summer, toward the end. Simion
(Simi) had just arrived from Toronto. The
haying was overdue. The discrepancy between the beauty of the landscape and the
grim unhappiness of the people—only temporarily suspended because of Simi's presence—was painful to bear. The second pain
point was our total lack of any knowledge of
the language. It wouldn't have helped to
know some Romanian. Elena speaks a dialect
few out of the direct area would understand.
A third painful moment occurred when,
after I had cheerfully participated in the haying, my bad knee began to make further participation impossible. From now on, filming
and photographing were the only things I
could do during my stay.

Conversation between Elena and her son
Simion:

SIMION: *just say something about me*
what kind of child I was

ELENA: *you were a good boy, you listened to*
me

you listened to me

you studied well
you earned your own bread

you must take care and
come back to me

as long as I have days to live

SIMION:—*you still have*

ELENA: *yes*

SIMION: *like now?*

ELENA:—*indeed*
—*yeah*

with the help of her son simion

There is always that moment when I set the camera, test the sound, leave the room, and hope for the best. How do two people separated so drastically after a life together speak to each other about just that? I can't imagine. My retrospective access to the conversation happens in my studio, when Simion is long gone back to Toronto and Elena is back to her lonely, cold, and extremely simple life. Simi clearly started with the first question on my emergency list. Sometimes the interlocutors of the mother are a bit shy and think they won't know what to say. To reassure them I give them this short list of questions, all simple and general. The first one is: what kind of a child was she, he, or, in this case, I? He asks it, she answers, then takes over and so, within seconds of the beginning,

manages to give him an order: you must take care and come back to me.

ELENA: *now my life goes away*
as I wouldn't like anyone to have it

SIMION: *why?*

ELENA: —*why because at home*
I am sad and I work hard . . .

I ran with the bulls through the forest

everyone was sad, with the war
everyone ran through the forest

they took us with all that hunger

we were going and going for food
we were many . . .

we were going and going for food
we were many ...

it was mother who looked after us
not father

she took us to school for four years
because this is how it was

It took a bit of persuasion to get Elena to sit down. The haying was more important to her than this film. Rain could start at any moment, and what then? You can see the haste in the quick, economic use of language. Every line says something important. Her life is passing while her precious boy is far away. She is aware of other people, other mothers. She doesn't mince her words: I am sad, it's only work, no play. Next line: back to the past, without transition. Of course, Simi knows all these stories of his mother's childhood, but the viewer of the installation doesn't. There was war, hunger, many children sent out for food. Good mother, bad father. Just a bit of elementary schooling. Elena can read and write, but how literate can you be after four years?

> then we worked from day to day
> hardship and poverty settled down on us
>
> because we wanted land
> so we worked and worked . . .
>
> until we saw that everything was all right
>
> our mother relied on us
> she asked all of us to work
>
> she didn't have any other choice
>
> we were many at home
> we were ten
>
> she asked us to work
> we worked in the field
>
> when I was about fourteen, fifteen years old
>
> I took the bulls
> through the forest for two years

Despite that sparing use of words, the narrative logic is amazingly sophisticated. That poverty and hardship go together cuts right through the romantic idealization culturally instilled in us through the aesthetics of the picturesque. But poverty just makes for hard, difficult lives. The only way to turn a form of slavery into a modest but autonomous life is to buy land. And as Elena tells us, this is the trap: your life wastes away before you get anywhere. As a young girl, the tiny woman we see in the video had to master bulls and brave the dark forest to take them to graze. Poverty cannot afford to shirk considerations of danger. It strikes me, though, that in this film that, she knows, is about and for her as a mother, she spends more words on justifying her mother than on any other topic.

> and I transported things everywhere
>
> every day, for two years
>
> through the forest
> and we had to do a lot of work
>
> and in the fields and everywhere
> to earn for my dowry
>
> I needed it because father didn't give it
> to me, he didn't buy me even a needle
>
> can you imagine?
>
> he didn't give me a penny!
>
> that's how my life was

She presents us with a visual picture: a young girl heavily burdened—with things, with life. Carrying things is a metaphor for carrying the burden of this tough life. With ten children at home, lots of food had to be gathered. But then, how many were girls, in need of a dowry? Here, the system breaks down. The father, who is to make his daughter marriageable by endowing her with enough property to make it worth some young man's while, refuses to invest in her. She needed to earn it herself. This is not how it was supposed to be. You can see the misery of the next generation coming, bred by avarice. The last line of this fragment rounds off the short description of Elena's childhood, triggered by her evocation of her misery now: my life goes away.

> *I liked playing theater*
> *and dancing*
>
> *he didn't allow me to lead my life*
>
> SIMION:—*where did you want*
> *to go with the theater?*

ELENA: *where? they took me to act*
that's what the theater was in those times

long ago, we were kids
I was a girl, you know, a little girl

there was a theater in dorna

ciocanita and prisecaru used to come

they were all saying "come with us"

because I play well, I was playing well

This episode is stunningly at odds with the evocation we just heard. This is a narrative proper: after a situation description, something happens that breaks up the monotony of the situation. This girl that spent her best years slaving away to make a future escape into marriage possible did have a life of culture, pleasure, and talent. In the villages of the hills, ambulant theater groups passed by, scouted for talent, and noticed Elena. What has been many young girls' dream happened to her. They said, "Come with us!" They offered instant escape, a new life of camaraderie and glamour—even if glamour might not have been what she thought it was. And the stricken woman knows she owed this brilliant opportunity to herself. Her pride in that talent touches me deeply.

I could memorize
I acted very well

also the dancing and everything else

and she didn't let me do it

mother said "if you go
you should not call me mother again"

because I am soft-hearted . . .

once I started to go but when
I reached the bridge I returned home

I cried for a while there
and I returned home

I regret it a lot today that I didn't do it

but what did I know in those times?

Even old and wasted by the hardship of her life, Elena is beautiful. It is, therefore, easy to imagine her as a beautiful young girl, wanted and courted because she was also able, cheerful, and willing. But motherhood is a sharp-cutting knife. If you go, you lose your mother. This will resonate all through the conversation. When, later, her own child wants to leave, she does not stop him. A short episode further refines the narrative. Once I started: something specific happens. She was going to go, we hold our breath, and she gives up. The bridge of no return, to be

burned behind her, she cannot muster the courage to cross. But braver, perhaps, is that she tells her son that she regrets it. She regrets the life, that is, of which her son who sits in front of her is the fruit. Verging on cynicism but not quite, Elena braves the convention that prescribes self-sacrifice to mothers.

if I can't say mother again . . .

it's over!
what can I do?

there is no one to come here
and do the work

say something if you can!

so I didn't say anything

then I continued to work with the bulls
every day

I don't want to say anything else

She went back home because she needed a mother. The mother alleges the need to get the work done, but that doesn't sound right. It doesn't compensate for the loss of the mother with which the daughter was bullied into returning. The discrepancy strikes young Elena dumb, and so she says nothing. And the life of routine, of misery and hardship, resumes, the memory of the window of opportunity and the glamour that shone through it slowly fading away. This is Madame Bovary after the party at the Château de la Vaubyessard. From that life story we learn that a miserable life after a glimmering of hope becomes worse than it was before. To Simi, in the present, Elena says that she doesn't want to say more. We are barely a few minutes into the film.

every time someone would come
to ask for my hand

father would start arguing
saying whatever came to his mind

he would say
"keep your mouth shut, you stupid girl, stay
*   out of it"*

that's how it was for me

after I came here it was the same

with your father I still had a hard life

SIMION:—*can you talk a bit about me?*

So, candidates for Elena's hand did show up, in spite of the pittance she had for a dowry. Looking at her now, I am not surprised. But the stingy father is also irrational and a bully.

Stay out of it—of her own future, her life. This man who probably felt a near-slave makes his daughter a slave. But isn't parenthood about trying to give your children a better life than you have had? I feel revolt. Of the man she ends up with, Simi's father, we hear nothing. This is also a sophisticated narrative strategy. The main event is skipped, elided. This speaks volumes about how eager she was (not) to marry this one. And the moment becomes uneasy. Before Elena gets a chance to complain about her husband, Simi asks the next question. Interviewing is not just about making people talk, but also about shutting them up. That is what he does here.

ELENA:—*as a child, as a pupil in school*
things like these

when you were a little boy

you wouldn't leave my side at all
you didn't want to sleep with anyone

until you went to high school

you were sleeping just with me
you were with me all the time

I would carry you for a while,
then the luggage, then climb the hill

next to the corn fields
with you in my arms

But the mother takes her revenge on her son's refusal to hear her out. He wants to hear about himself? Look at this! All she gives him are memories of his dependence on her. She depicts him as another piece of luggage, or an extension of herself. You have to imagine the big guy he is now, almost twice the size of tiny Elena. The pronoun *you* recurs, like a litany: you this, you that, and all that accompanies that pronoun are descriptions of dependence. The temporal qualifier "until you went to high school" is slightly embarrassing for the big guy, and probably an exaggeration. Well, he cut her life story off, didn't he? Translating this I felt the tension in the air, of which I had had no clue at the time of filming. This is the kind of moment I hope for, moments that turn narrative into drama. This is why I don't stay present during the conversation.

> *then you went to school*
> *you wanted to go since you were five*
>
> *that's how much you liked it*
>
> *you would stay in the house*
> *while I was in the field*
>
> *you'd stay in the house I remember*
>
> *you'd say "stay, I'll sleep"*
> *when you heard me coming you'd be up*
>
> *grandma would give you*
> *an alphabet book*
>
> *and you'd read everything in it*
>
> *you were drawing, writing, everything . . .*

This is a topos that recurs in all the elements of my project: the child is always premature,

eager to learn, the best student. This child was literate when he started school, probably as literate as Elena was when she left school. But even so, it is the mother figure who was instrumental in this early learning. This goes against the misconception running through culture in the wake of psychoanalysis. The idea, there, is that the mother nurtures but the father teaches. This grandmother was probably the father's mother, not hers. The father's parents lived in the ancestral house, next to the one they had built for the young family. We stayed in that ancestral house, where the walls were covered with tapestries woven during the long winter months. We saw the same patterns in the fantastic museum of folk art in Bucharest, on our way back.

> *when you went to school*
>
> *you could read everything in the paper*
>
> *you would say "what is this, what is this*
> *this is a, this is b" etc., etc.*
>
> *that's how you studied*
> *you were a good student*
>
> *the holy mother helped you*
>
> *holy mary, mother of god*
> *helped you study*
>
> *because god and holy mary helped you*
> *because she is all powerful*
>
> *if you believe in her*
>
> *. . . in god*

Behind the proud mention of the child's premature capacity to read lurks the attraction of the big wide world. If the child can read the paper, he is lost to innocence. The idyllic country life is interrupted by knowledge. I remember the slave narratives, such as Fredrick Douglass's autobiography, and the romanticized version that was so influential, Harriet Beecher Stowe's *Uncle Tom's Cabin*. Slaves were not allowed to learn to read. Knowledge is dangerous, fears the censor. Books are weapons, reply the freedom fighters. And they learn it. The invocation of Holy Mary as the force behind Simi's talents is the first of a long string of appeals to religion. Later on in the conversation this appeal will function in less positive ways. Note that Elena did not invoke the help of the Holy Virgin to describe her own talent as an actress and a dancer.

after all this, you left

I cried enough and I thought of you
you were among foreigners

you were small and slim

I was concerned about you

. . . and I still am

SIMION:—*but now I am no longer small and slim*

ELENA: *no you are not small, you are ok but not fat, you are still slim*

I don't know what you eat among those foreigners

whatever you eat, oh my god!

only I know what you need

After is a tricky word. Does it signify temporality only, or causality? It suggests regret: such a gifted child, I lost him! But here the viewer might go in a direction different from the speaker: of course he would leave, with baggage that would open doors for him in the wide world. But before we get there, Elena takes us back to her emotions. She doesn't elaborate; she just says that she cried. "Who wouldn't?" is the response such spare use of words earns the speaker. But right after this, we reach the most hilarious point of the film. Seeing in the near-giant Simi Elena's concern for her small, slim boy strikes a humorous note. How can she be so out of touch with reality? My guess is that because he is, as she says in a phrase that sounds biblical, "among foreigners." This is repeated: "I don't know what you eat among those foreigners." And then she reappropriates her motherly power over him.

219

you would say sometimes

they don't give you much food . . .

well that's how it is
it will change

there is nothing we can do

that's how it is

you went out into the world

often I have no one to utter a word to
no one to tell stories to

I miss hearing words do you know that?

especially when . . .

that's how it was

In a glimpse, we see something of the difficulty of newly arrived immigrants. Despite his current good situation, he must have suffered a real form of hardship, and perhaps even, at least in his mother's anxious imagination, hunger. The repetition of resignation—"that's how it is"—is the first explicit expression of powerlessness, resonating with the story about her own missed opportunity. He went away, so you have to take the consequences. But the mother who just before worried about his food among foreigners cannot be as stoic as she here seems to be. Stoicism is not the same as powerlessness, but here we see how fine the line between the two can be. Remarkably and movingly, immediately after evoking Simi's misery, she comes up with her own, and instead of food, words are what is lacking. She has no one to

talk to, to tell stories to. This is a need as real as the need to eat.

in the beginning it was really hard
. . . I really don't know how I could stand
*   it*

often I think "was I really stupid?" or . . .

SIMION:—*can you tell the story of my*
departure?

ELENA: *about your departure?*
. . . you just went away

you always liked traveling
to other countries, you just left

that's what you liked
climbing mountains visiting other countries

that's what you liked, to travel all the time

since you were a child

We reach the heart of the project here. The mother bearing the loss is what I wanted to get into the picture. Not to commiserate and indulge in sentimental feel-gooding, but simply so that we realize no one voluntarily leaves such deep grief behind; not if there is no need. Elena starts to blame herself, and this theme will return later. But here, Simi interrupts her again. A pattern begins to emerge: whenever emotions become the subject of the conversation, he diverts his mother's attention. When I first asked him to participate in the project, he was very protective of his mother. He wanted to see all the films made so far, the installation, and talk to me. I thought highly of him for it. Here, he seems to protect her from effusive crying. Now I also see the other side, however. Perhaps he, her son, doesn't want to hear it. The departure is another topos in the films.

"You just left," she says here. This happens often. Sometimes the mother just receives a call from the airport.

once you left with your father

you almost didn't come back

when you were five

when you were five, you know
when you carried the corn on the hill

you went to vatra dornei, to 12 apostoli
to negrişoara

then when you came back
you came in the evening with your father

and you slept for two days

you didn't wake up

you wanted to go

what can I do?

The woman who just said she misses telling stories to someone as among the worst consequences of his departure now tells another story. More will follow. This is another one of her great talents. This is a story of the son's tendency, desire, to leave. At five, the age when he learned to read, he also learned

to escape. And lest we forget, he was also escaping the same kind of work: carrying stuff up the hill. Yes, reading is dangerous. Here he was still safe, with his father, but clearly the latter made him walk too much. Was he trying to discourage the boy, or just careless, or unaware? The story ends in resignation. Now it is Elena not against fate but against the boy's desire. Confronted with desire, she is powerless.

that's what you liked

traveling just like your father

your father liked going through all forests
he'd just go and you are the same

and now the same from canada
I can hear you saying . . .

that you went there, that you went there
that you went there

yes . . .

SIMION: *do you know where I am?*

ELENA: *how can I know? do I see you?*
you just say that

I'm in london
I am in . . .

I don't remember
where you've been

in america you went . . .
I don't know where else

The child clung to his mother; the adult follows in the footsteps of his father. In light of the earlier remark on her married life that Simion cut off so effectively, this link between his leaving and being like his father strikes me as a bit aggressive, as well. "He'd just go" sounds very much like the resigned powerlessness that so many of the mothers express. Clearly, he didn't consult his wife; nor, she intimates, did Simion consult her. The son is aware of his mother's incapacity to find comfort in imagining his new dwelling. She has no clue where he is. For this, too, she blames him. For her, all the cities he visits with so much gusto are just names. Instead of her telling him stories, he cites foreign names to her.

to bezas and somewhere else
where else have you been?

huh?

SIMION:*—it's las vegas*

ELENA: *and where else have you been*
with the daughter of viorela cuclu

and chicago

SIMION: *—yes chicago*

ELENA: *I don't remember where else you've*
been
you've been everywhere

where haven't you been?

and here to slovakia
to bratislava, to . . .

where else, can I remember
where you've said you've been?

This effect of name dropping continues. It is almost as if her difficulty in remembering names she has no way of recognizing is an attempt to ridicule his travel craze. What is the point, if one name is confused with another and she cannot even pronounce them correctly? The discrepancy between a real visit to Las Vegas and the name turned unrecognizable in Elena's memory represents the painful discrepancy between the life world of the mother and that of the son. But before one might laugh at her ignorance, she says "here": in a region many Western visitors don't know any better than Elena knows America. Slovakia, we know, is a post-Soviet country, but Bratislava—do all visitors know whether that is a city or a country, and where exactly it is located? Thus, many of us may share Elena's ignorance. Already earlier, when she mentioned all those cities and towns in her own region, I felt geographically lost.

for your courses you walked everywhere
you went to see everything

on all the mountains around iaşi
you climbed all of them, ceahlău, to . . .

where else? here in câmpulung to the
monasteries, you've been everywhere

you'd mention only afterwards
that you've been there

SIMION:*— I'd say that only afterwards?*

ELENA: *yes, only afterwards*

Elena is now speaking of the period when Simion was still in Rumania but had to go places for his studies. This would have been a relatively happy time: his successes as a student would compensate for his frequent absences, and there was always the possibility that he would find a job close to home. Yet the way she describes the excursions sounds more like athletic tourism than like boarding school or other forms of distant learning. Mountains and monasteries feed our imagination of the natural and cultural attractions of a beautiful country. Hence, I feel the tension, already present in what precedes, between Elena's support of her son's intellectual needs, of which she is proud, and his strong-willed independence, which led him ever farther away, until he crossed the ocean forever. That tension accompanies the emotional tension between her love and her anger. It remains the key to the effect of the films in this project. Is this theater, or are we undesired voyeurs?

*you would say you've been
everywhere*

*that's how you enjoyed it
to walk and hike . . .*

and you still travel

SIMION: —*ah, and this is not good?*

ELENA: *yeah, it's good it's good*

*that you travel so much
I just hope god guards you*

*I hope god and holy mary guard you
that's all I can say*

it's good

*you liked traveling like this
may god bless you and I hope you take a
wife*

When she goes on about his desire to travel Simion interrupts her again, this time not to divert her attention from the abyss of misery she is about to plunge into but to defend himself. There is nothing wrong with the desire to travel. And what can Elena say to that? She adjusts, and confirms that this desire is a good thing. In a conversational predicament, there is always the possibility of falling back on God. May God and Holy Mary guard you. It is as if she dared not say, "Yes, but . . .," as if contradicting her son were not possible. Yes, it's good, but you are in danger. Instead, she invokes the deity for protection . . . until, at the end of this passage, she lets slip out what she has up her sleeve. The result is another moment of humorous tenderness for the visitor: "I wish you take a wife" connected to "may God bless you" by the simple and devastating conjunction "and." Devastating, because the power of the deity is now equalized with that of the son. There is nothing so strange about the two wishes. It is the "and" that makes this sentence funny.

*I cried for you, I have cried a lot
there is a piece of each day that I cry*

when I'm alone especially

I'm thinking . . .

god what a life I have had

if only my son were next to me
how good it would be

if this is what god gave me
just one son, one of them died

maybe I've been sinful
what did I do wrong? I don't know

if I had five or six children
maybe one would have been next to me

I would have had something

From a moment of mild laughter we move straight into the heart of the tragic, of the tragedy of migration. Elena is left with nothing after a life of hardship. At the age of seventy-one, she is as alone as she has always been. It comes as no surprise that God is needed again at this moment. Resignation— "this is what god gave me"—is inflected into a beginning of revolt by the small word *if.* Could God not have been a little more generous? But a nuance in the story reveals a more complex emotion. She had two sons; one of them died. It is not only that God has been pretty stingy; he has been cruel as well. But religion is a heavy weapon. Rather than revolting too strongly, so that she might lose the comfort of belief, she blames herself. "What did I do wrong?" I am sharply aware that the target of this self-blame is sitting in front of Elena. How is she not to make Simion feel he is the guilty one, rather than God or his mother?

at least one child

now I have to take the cow
from the hill to the house by myself

if only I didn't loose that child so young . . .

what can I do?

that's how god made things happen
I don't know

I've been sinful, who knows how I have
sinned and what I have done

god has beaten me

SIMION: —*you've said you want to get a passport*
to visit me, what will you do?

The "something" is one child—not too much to ask, is it? That one child is further burdened when his mother depicts what she has to do in her old age, when other people can enjoy some rest. She says this at the moment when her son has come from Canada to help with the haying. I know he is very caring and responsible. Not he himself is to blame but the situation in which economic inequality, just as much as his desire to broaden his horizon, has made it impossible for him to stay. Perhaps aware of the injustice of burdening Simion with all her misery, she becomes more aggressive to God, who has "beaten" her, and to herself, who has "sinned." After the strongest expression of her powerlessness—"God has beaten me," Simion interrupts her again, trying to bring up a more positive subject. She can, in fact, visit him.

yeah but I don't think I will
come to you, I am weak . . .

it's hard, far away, and I'm alone

if I had someone to keep me company
I would come, but like this . . .

I have no one to come with

SIMION: *—I'll find you someone*

ELENA: *who shall I find?*

I don't have a passport
and I won't get one

SIMION: *—you can get one*

ELENA: *what shall I do at home?*
he has this problem with his leg

what can I do?

SIMION: *—that's how it is*

The illusion of resolution is quickly dissipated, however. The idea of a visit is "too little too late." She finds reasons of different kinds: she is old; her husband cannot be left alone; and she has no passport. When her son contradicts the finality of the latter argument, she quickly comes up with the pretext of the father. But at the heart of her reluctance is the feature that, we now know, characterizes her life: she is alone. This is a very reasonable objection. But loneliness is more than being on her own. It is also feeling the

inaptitude for braving a world of crowds without having acquired the skills for it. Most of all, it is resignation that holds Elena back. The last two lines of this fragment put it into words; her body, at this moment in the film, puts it into gesture, body language. "What can I do?" is her most frequently used phrase.

ELENA: *if only he wouldn't drink so much*
but you see he drinks a lot

SIMION: *he likes it don't you see that?*

ELENA: *he was told not to drink beer and*
wine and the like

he says, he was saying at that time . . .

"I don't get drunk when
it comes to drinking"

SIMION: *—how is it with the others in the*
village?

Elena has an agenda for this conversation. She won't let the assignment to talk about the migration of her son come in the way of her unique opportunity for self-expression. The structure of this conversation is remarkably consistent. Whenever she goes off into complaints about her life, her son tries to divert her attention. But he has to be very alert. How could he know that an encouragement to visit him would end in a complaint about his father's drinking habits? The total disconnection between her topic and his next question—a question that surely didn't come from my generic list!—betrays his desperate wish to keep the conversation halfway decent. But this time, as we see in her next speech, she doesn't surrender so easily. She simply fails to understand the question.

—*how is it with the others in the village?*

ELENA: *with whom? the others?*

SIMION: —*how do you feel in the community . . .*

—*in the village because your son is away?*

ELENA: *ah, it's so good, everyone*
praises me and they all say, all of them

lucky me, I have such a good son . . .
it's so good he left . . .

he earns a lot, he is a big man now . . .

there's nothing for me to complain about
everything is just fine

there's nothing for me to complain about
everything is just fine

but what's the use of it
if I can't stop crying?

lucky me, that he left
I have such a good and dear son

He simply repeats the question; she continues to refuse it. He is forced to rephrase it. And thus he gives her an opportunity for biting sarcasm. Yet his question is quite relevant. Is her position as a mother of a migrant a more lonely one than before, or does she get some comfort out of it? "Lucky me" to have a son who made it in the world. This is not strange at all. We will soon hear about others who don't manage that. The irony of the repeated word *good* is partly generated by the different meanings the qualifier acquires. A "good son" is the desire of every parent. But the same word *good* with "that he left" takes that positivity away. The features that constitute goodness are clearly totally irrelevant for Elena. Money, power, reputation? It only makes the situation worse for her, because she is even denied the right to complain. Explicitly, she points out the uselessness of those successes. As a result, the last two lines of this fragment become almost unbearably sarcastic.

a good son!

because god is great and powerful
I have prayed, I keep on praying for him

for the rest of my days

when I'm gone
god will pray for me

everyone praises me

no one pities me

everyone . . .

you had everything
god gave you good luck

As before, Elena seamlessly moves her aggression between her son and her deity. The
God who has beaten her is still the only one
she can turn to. But after the previous sarcastic summing up of her son's "goodness"
this "because" that establishes the link between her reasons for gratitude and her
anger about her fate is risky in its transfer of
irony. The image of God that emerges from
these words is more than stingy and cruel;
now he is judged to be worthless and almost
dismissed through the irony. Great and powerful—it sounds like the divine version of
making money and being a big guy in the
world. But Elena bides her time. After her
death God will have second thoughts about
the way he has treated her. The "lucky me"
of the previous fragment returns here, indirectly cited through the words of the people
in the village.

you didn't resemble those
from your father's side

you resembled those from our side

that's what they say

it's good that you're as
a man should be

god gave you this gift

he made you like this
your father says

"I spent a lot, what would he be like
if I didn't give him money?"

you could give him all the money in
the world . . .

if it was not for god
he would have nothing right

The child is torn between the three parties
vying to possess him. The mother claims he
is hers; he doesn't resemble his father. Yet we
have just heard that his worst feature—his
desire for travel—came from his father. God,
by contrast, has more of a say in how Simion
turned out. The father contests this. Elena's
own father had refused to invest in his
daughter, but Simion is a male, and therefore his father did invest in him. The father
takes pride in the result and wants to claim
credit for it. The mother objects, using one
male figure—God—against the other. Traditional wisdom—money cannot buy happiness—is integrated into a theater of rivalry
among males. Cruel and unusual as Elena's
god is, he is more useful to her than her
drinking husband, who wants to take away
her credit as a mother.

it's god who gives

you didn't take care of him
god did

that's what I tell him
god and holy mother took care of him

227

and showed him the way
and gave him the good path

and this mind
god enlightened his mind

not him nor anyone else
that's how it is

To say that without God's help your efforts are vain is one thing; to deny that the father took care of his son is quite another. I wonder why God is so often invoked along with Mary. The phrasing here suggests that the latter's status as a fellow mother might have something to do with that. All this is spoken to Simion, but in an indirect quotation of what Elena said to her husband, his father, for she speaks about the man in front of her—her "you"—in the third person, as a "he." This strikes a chord for me. Conversation is a constant swapping of the positions of "I" and "you." Only an "I" is in a position to speak. But without that "you," without an interlocutor, speaking serves no purpose. In light of this theory of language, it is even possible to consider this linguistic form of indirect quotation a bit aggressive. It is as if she denies Simion access to her speech.

you see that I didn't listen . . .

that I listened and I didn't go

I was a good student, they allowed me to
    attend four classes

I was with a guy lazar ursu at school

we would both get first prize

this guy went away
his father allowed him

he had two sons. . . .

they both became engineers
they went away

and me . . . I remained . . .

with the sheep and the cows
and the hard work . . .

The story of Elena's ruined career as a glamorous actress returns with a vengeance. It is now complicated by references to a comparison between her and her son. Like him, she had a good set of brains. But she was a girl. The boy with whom she was first in her class went on to study and have a career. She didn't. But then, the two boys left. Like Simion. Here, Elena is not lamenting her son's departure but her own lack of mobility: "and me . . . I remained." Being a woman, she got stuck. The key to this passage is the verb *to listen*. The first occurrence refers to listening to the call of the sirens, the theater group who enticed her to join, and to the voice of her own desire. This listening would have empowered her. The second refers to a totally different sense of listening. Now, she listened in abject surrender to the voice of authority. She remains with—perhaps intimating an "as"—the cattle.

with taking the sheep to the hills

with making hay, mowing

and making fences

and lots of throwing and in the house
my god! I'm still mowing grass

I've made so many fences
on this hill

I remember well . . .

how many fences I made and raised on
the ground, now I can't do it anymore . . .

I can't do it anymore
these legs of mine hurt me

I can't do it anymore
I'm weak . . .

and this leg, I didn't look into it in time

that's the way it is, what can we do?

thank god I can still move

and I'm not stuck to the bed that's the
hard part to be stuck to the bed

god should make it that I die quickly

god should make it that I die quickly

so that no one has to take care of me
I don't bother anyone

it's so hard to look after an old person

The lament about her fate lingers in a description of the daily chores that constituted her life. The details of the description put forward the monotony of that existence, as well as the heaviness that weighs her down more and more with age. Why would she allude to memory? The memory of all her work is stronger, more adequate, than her memory of all the names of the places to which Simion traveled. Again, the situation in which this conversation took place is relevant. Elena has just been doing the things she describes here. Between building haystacks, Elena, somewhat reluctantly, quickly washed her hands, dressed up, and wasted half an hour of her precious working time to tell her life's story, express her emotions, shovel quite a bit of anger toward her son, and bad-mouth his father. And, as she narrated the beginning of this hard life, she now announces its end.

Elena has severe arthritis. I do, too. Hence, I had to give up helping with the haying after the first few hours. Elena just put a leather strap around her knee and climbed the haystack, where she reigned over the landscape and the men like a queen. I have beautiful pictures of her standing there. But she wouldn't even take time to look around her at the rolling green hills and the distant valleys. The second half of this passage conveys

229

the typical predicament of old age, female version. Women are particularly sensitive to the fear of impotence. All their lives they care for others. And that is precisely why they fear that dependency. They know from experience that self-sacrifice is not such a great way of life. People who haven't had to care for others wouldn't know this. I have heard that this gender difference makes women more prone to be talked into euthanasia.

> SIMION:—*how is it with the people in the village who*
> *have left for foreign countries?*
>
> ELENA: *well they go and work for three months*
> *and they come back*
>
> *they don't go so long as you*
>
> SIMION: —*what do their parents say?*
>
> ELENA: *what can they say?*
> *they are happy that they leave*
>
> *they are many, they should stay and make money, they can't look after them*
>
> *there is nothing they can earn here*
>
> *there is nothing, how can they live if there is no work here?*
>
> *they don't have enough*
> *that's why they go*

Reaching this painful point, Simion feels it's time for another distraction. He must have felt implicated in his mother's despair. For,

he asks her about his peers, the others who left, intimating that he is not the only defector. This time the strategy works quite well. Elena's answer demonstrates that not everyone who leaves is as successful as Simion and hence that she does have reasons for satisfaction after all. Simion rubs it in when he asks what the parents say. And yes, those parents are happy that they leave. But subtly and implicitly, Elena points out the limits of the comparison's validity. Those parents have many children, too many, as her own parents had. And then the larger picture looms, always present around the corner. Economic need is the rational for migration. Not having enough to eat is as life threatening as being harassed by a dictatorial regime. There is no absolute distinction to be made between economic and political asylum.

> *they all go my god, if they could all go like you, my god, it would be so good*
>
> *but they can't go, you see*
>
> *they go just for three months and . . .*
>
> *they don't allow them to stay*
>
> *they went and they were caught*
> *they were prohibited to go for five years*
>
> *malanca's son, he went to germany then I don't know where else*
>
> *she said he went last winter, no last autumn he went to hungary, she says*
>
> *how would I know?*
> *they don't allow him anywhere*

he even changed his passport
but they still don't allow him

This, then, is how politics affects, invades lives. Once this context dawns, Elena is able to see something positive in her own son's departure. The others are pushed back. They don't manage to get their residence permits and work permits. They remain "illegals" (*aber kein Mensch ist illegal*) and must return to poverty. They were "caught": it sounds like runaway cattle or criminals, when all they wanted was survival. The borders are shut behind them when they are expelled. They can try only so many times; after that, they become prisoners in their own place. This sad situation is the only site of comfort for Elena. Compared to those people, she is lucky indeed. This paradox recurs in all the films of the project. The mothers lament their loss and feel lucky at the same time.

things like this, they all go

I know that they go but they
don't stay so many years like you

they don't cry like me

SIMION: —*I've told you not to cry*
you have no reason to cry

ELENA: *oh my god*

I cry because you are far away
I'm worried

I hear about so many wars
strange things and bombs

the americans meddled where it's
not their business

they shouldn't have done it
they should have left them in peace

everybody should take care
of his own country

that's how it should be

Her relief is short-lived, however. Immediately she reverts to the other side of the coin. But politics has entered her field of vision and is not easily dislodged. Not only is she crying for her loss: his absence, her loneliness. And his attempt to comfort her is not adequate. She laments the dangers of the world. The relief that he has enough to eat—although what is he eating among those foreigners?—is overruled by her fear for his safety. While she lives on the top of that faraway hill in rural Romania, America is ruining her trust in a safe world. She doesn't specify much, but she doesn't need to. I realize how the world is, indeed, governed by the Iraq war and the other elements of the aftermath of that first time the United States was attacked instead of attacking and waging war away from home. No need to say more than "meddle" and "leave them in peace" and we all know what she is talking about.

what can we do? that's how it is

that's how god makes things
everything is from god

if god doesn't help

then we can't do anything

*we go with god, if he helps us it's good
if not it's also good*

well . . .

ok, what else shall I tell you?

I can still tell you something, but what?

*that my feet and hands hurt
what else can I tell you?*

The conversation reaches a point of stagnation. Elena has some trouble reconciling her revolt against world politics with the resignation that, after that incident on the bridge in her childhood, has become her most useful tool in life. This is why God remains a helpful ploy, in spite of his cruel lack of justice. If God helps, fine. But the usefulness of religion is that if he doesn't help, it's also OK because resignation is always a backup option. For me, this is why religion is not helpful. But I learn from Elena that some situations call for such an invention. In her situation, she knows only too well, she cannot do a single thing to make the world safer for Simion, the way she could when he was small enough to carry him on her hip. So the conversation falters. She is out of topics. Except to revert once again to her own suffering.

SIMION:—*do you think that if I were closer
to you
they would hurt less?*

ELENA: *huh?*

SIMION:—*do you think that if I were closer
to you
they would hurt less?*

ELENA: *yes they would hurt less because I
would
have stayed with you in Bucharest*

and somewhere else I don't know where

*I don't know what I would have
been doing*

I don't know . . .

but like this I can't go anywhere

SIMION:—*you can, of course you can
why can't you?*

ELENA: *you can, but if you don't know
anyone
nothing . . .*

what can we do?

Now it is Simion's turn for aggressive irony. Clearly, he is expecting that his mother will see the obviously nonsensical nature of her complaint. He cannot help that her feet hurt. Or can he? Elena is not easy to catch out on nonsense. She imagines a fictional scenario of another outcome to the story. What if . . . If Simion had had the same talents, the same capable personality, but had stayed in the country, she could have joined him in some place with better opportunities, yet not beyond her linguistic and cultural horizon.

Simion retorts that she can still go somewhere else and blames her for her lack of
knowledge. I imagine her crushed by this
somewhat contemptuous severity. All she
can do, in reply, is express her mantra of resignation: "What can we do?"

as a mother I want god to guard you
and I want you to go away

I want god to give you a good wife
as good as you

that's what god should give you

everyone must praise her, they should
say good words just as they praise you

that's all

what else shall I tell you?

SIMION:—*ok, now I want you to tell*
about the funny things I did as a child

ELENA: *what funny things, when did you do*
that?

you did one funny thing at school

Although she has been alleging her motherhood many times, this is the first time that
Elena demonstrates an awareness of the paradox of being the mother of a migrant. Being
a mother, hence inherently desiring the best
for her child, she must willingly wish that he
will leave her behind. It sounds ironic, but
this is, in a sense, an assertion of freedom.
Spinozist freedom, that is: the freedom to
endorse the destiny that otherwise crushes

the life out of your subjectivity. That freedom is limited is a commonplace of the
worst kind. But Spinoza argued that it is possible, within the small margins that destiny—or politics, or other forms of bossiness
that limit your freedom—leaves you, to re-
strict the degree of passive, even abject resignation that you accept and freely *will* the
situation you are in. The point is not that
you are less limited. The point is that such
an endorsement encourages you to be active
within the limitations. This allows Elena to
do two things here. First, she no longer just
wants Simion to marry but to find a "good"
wife, not just to provide offspring but to be
happy. Second, she is now not at a loss for
topics of conversation but is willing to listen
to Simion's wishes for topics. This is an opportunity he eagerly grabs.

SIMION: —*ok*

ELENA: *together with burlui's son*

when you went together
I don't know exactly what you did

burlui's son hit something
I don't know what, some carrots maybe

then he came to ioana's daughter
and said it was him

I realized it was you and burlui's son

burlui's son took him with you
otherwise . . .

he said he would hang you if
you didn't go with him

Elena accepts his suggestion and shifts a bit in her seat, as if to be more comfortable. Then she sets out on a course of animated anecdotes, none of which makes any sense to the outsider I am. We don't know who the characters are, but since Simion does, it would be artificial if Elena explained the stories. The stories are all about children's mischief: petty theft, small fights, inconsequential lies. All that is a domain of innocence, of happiness, at least in retrospect and in comparison with later developments. The children have no names; they are named as the children of Elena's contemporaries. This, too, makes sense. The last sentence suggests some bullying, the child's version of social strife and politics. But in the end, these are the moments in the conversation when understanding becomes impossible; this is inside talk, family idiosyncrasy.

SIMION:—*and in poiana?*
how was it?

ELENA: *in poiana you went to the plantations*

you think I know where
you went through the forest

directly from school and you
did what you did

then you went somewhere
you played with the ball . . .

and the principal caught you
he took your clothes

and you ran, where did you run?
I don't know where

then you came home crying
with no clothes on

and the next day I came with you

the principal said that you shouldn't
have run away

you should have stayed there
not run with the others

This story seems at first nonsensical; one of those stories only insiders can understand and, together, remember. On the other hand, it may be a bit more serious, perhaps less innocent. On one level, the child may have just cut school. Caught in his truancy, he was left without clothes—probably, if probability is a standard here, just his coat was taken. Coming home without a coat, for a child of such a modest family, is, of course, terrible. No wonder the child cries. The mother is indispensable again—oh happy times!—and helps him out. On another level, for me this coat story resonates with a long tradition of what can be called material morality. Joseph, who in Genesis was twice deprived of his coat, first by his brothers, then by the wicked woman who first tried to seduce him, then accused him of assault, infuses this anecdote with a bit less innocent but more gripping intertextuality. Is little Simi the guilty truant or the innocent party, harassed by a wicked principal? All nonsense, of course; but then the fabric of cultural circulating texts does tend to produce nonsense.

he gave them to you
that's how it was

you didn't go back to school
you came home directly

you were afraid to go back to school
he said he would have given them to you

but like this, I had to go with you
the next day

SIMION: —*and what did you do?*
you took me out of the shit

ELENA: *I took you out of it*
and he gave you the clothes

he said that you shouldn't have run
to follow the others

he was right, you should have gone back
he would have given them to you

you shouldn't have come home

you were afraid
or I don't know what you did

I don't know what you thought
you were afraid

The story is spun out. Perhaps Elena needs to make it longer to be able to insert her own role, so that she can get some recognition out of it. Simion is happy to oblige. Like a good parent, she confirms the principal's authority. Simi was a bad boy; the adult knew

best. But the poison is in the tail. The moral of the story is not that Simion shouldn't have run away, but that he was afraid. The judgment of cowardice is not far away. The fear alluded to is double. First he runs with the others, afraid of his peers and social ostracism. That is what the principal condemns, and that is the judgment with which Elena concurs. The second fear is what made him come home, the fear of the principal, the authority figure. Both forms of fear are somewhat problematic; at least, that is what Elena's insistence on it suggests.

SIMION: —*me? was I afraid?*

ELENA: *yes, you were afraid of the principal*
if you ran away with all the other boys

that's all, you didn't do any
other funny things

everyone at school praised you
the principal and everyone else

you could see, he said . . .

if you weren't a good student he
wouldn't have taken your file to suceava

he wouldn't have taken you
and said those good things

you had to take care, even if you're
the last to be accepted, still honor him

be an honor for the village
and the school

Simion's surprise demonstrates that Elena has hit a nerve. She seems to realize it, too, and tries to mitigate the effect. Ending the anecdotes of naughtiness—told at his request, no less—she now moves to more serious and positive memories. The praise for the good student he was goes hand in hand with reaffirmation of the principal's authority. Elena has a stake in this authority. Without it, Simion's scholastic success would have been worthless. The principal got him into high school, a school far enough away to make it necessary for Simion to be boarded somewhere else. The loss of him commences here. But at this point there is still hope that he might do well *and* stay close enough for his mother to join him. And close enough to be an honor to the entire village. Honor is a key feature of economically deprived or depressed cultures. Honor doesn't cost money. It is easy to call it an empty value if you live in a culture where other values, more costly, are close at hand. But for Simion's mother on her way to losing her only child, honor is the mode of exercising her Spinozist freedom.

and your class teacher said the same

SIMION:— *and the people from suceava?*

ELENA: *they also praised you, the landlord too*
even now they praise you

the people from the high school as well

they treated you as if you were silly
for a while, I don't know exactly how

when you became a student

then they realized . . .

the headmistress said "why didn't you stay in dorna? why did you come here?"

there was a teacher
he had been headmaster once

he said "let him come don't contest the result, don't do anything

if he is a good student, it will work
I will watch out"

But nothing comes easy when you are poor and from a rural area. Everyone praises the good student, but they also mock the boy from the farm, the country boor with different manners. Even the headmistress does not refrain from that kind of cruelty to children. Stay in Dorna—know your place. This is not an appeal to resignation but an oppressive classism. In all her appeals to God, Elena never practices this "know your place" ideology. Her mode of resignation is very different. It never comes without either revolt or willful abandon. If she accepts her fate, that is not because she belongs to a class where you have no choice. It is because she can derive a (modest) measure of subjectivity from that endorsement. The teacher who shows both greater wisdom and more generosity offers an alternative. He warns against revolt and does not come to the child's rescue, but instead encourages him to prove himself. That, too, is Spinozist freedom: work hard to overcome the limitations that burden you.

you were a good student
and you managed well

the headmistress started shouting
and everyone felt sorry afterwards

but you managed well
with the exam and everything else

in iași and everywhere else
you managed well, god helped you

SIMION:—*how about those from the*
faculty that have still visited you

my ex-colleagues, andrei . . .

ELENA: *they were all good students*
all of you lived in the same room

no drinking or smoking, they studied well
they were very good students

they all praise you as well
all of them

Elena revels in memories of how well her son managed in overcoming his setbacks. I find it funny that so often mothers blame other women for the ills of the world. Even this woman, who has suffered so much at the hands of men, has found a rival she loves to hate. She mentions the nasty woman twice. Something else happens here, as well. Simion is clearly getting into the mood of reminiscing. He asks about his former friends and teachers. This is the first time I hear a tone of nostalgia in his questions. It takes Elena a while to be able to share that mood. Instead of reminiscing about Simion's friends, she

continues to sing his praise. Studying well and not drinking and smoking are familiar topoi of mothers of migrants. It's OK for children to make mischief, but adolescents must refrain from these costly worldly pleasures.

SIMION:—*how do you like it when they*
visit?

ELENA: *I like it, they are dear to me, I told*
you

I like it but I'm more fragile, I can't
cook or do as much as before, I can't

I like it, I find them so dear

I like it because I can see others
and I can utter words to them

I tell stories and I like it so much

if only they could come when I don't
have to work the grass and the hay

you know, so I have time for them

not when you don't have a minute
even to sit

This fragment evokes astounding smells and tastes in me. Hospitality is a great Romanian value, as I have experienced firsthand. Between bouts of haying and chopping wood, Elena spends a lot of time behind the huge wood stove in the single room of her house. Two double beds, a small table, and then that enormous stove: that is the furniture of the

237

combined living room, kitchen, and bed-
room of the family. And there Elena cooks
what she can. She likes to receive visitors,
which is doubtless a rather rare occurrence.
Simion's question offers her yet another opportunity to lament her declining forces and
her existence of constant physical labor. But
the most poignant element in this evocation
for me is the reiterated mention of uttering
words. Elena loves language. Not having
anyone to talk to, she said earlier, is the
worst of it. She loves to tell stories. Speaking,
and especially telling stories, brings back a
glimpse of that gifted girl who could have
become an actress.

I like it when they come
but you see, they haven't come lately

only andrei is still coming
catalin and dascalu stopped coming

that guy, where was he from?
from botonani, I don't remember

SIMION:—*bordianu*

ELENA:—*bordianu*
bordianu also stopped coming

yes, people like this

SIMION:—*how about the foreigners?*

ELENA: *I like them too*
but I can't understand them

Elena comes up with two negatives here.
First, the people who used to visit, Simion's
friends from high school, slowly stopped

coming. This is a normal way in which time
catches up with aging people. The past in
which Simion was still present slowly fades
away. Second, at some risk, he evokes a very
different kind of visitor, perhaps in an attempt to comfort his mother for the loss of
the old guard: the foreigners who come in
the wake of Simion's international life.
Elena, thinking on her feet, declines the
comfort. I admire her relentless realism.
Never in the conversation has she been willing to be seduced by false consolations. She
cannot communicate with the foreigners. I,
who am counted among these, feel the same
frustration. It is hard to spend days in a
household that turns around this woman
without being able to communicate.

SIMION:—*yes you can, I translate for you*

ELENA: *yes you translate*
but if they come when you're not there?

then I don't understand anything

you translate only
when you are at home . . .

I don't have knowledge of
any language other than this

SIMION:—*at least you know it very well*

ELENA: *only this language*

I just yawned as if I'm sleepy
but that's how I do it

but I don't know why

SIMION:—*why would you be sleepy?*
ok, in general all things are fine, yes?

In light of Elena's craving for storytelling and language use, this retort to her son's attempt to be cheerful hits the nail of her predicament on the head. Now that he is gone, the only friends he can bring or send to the parental home are foreigners. But if he isn't there, there is no one to translate for her. And if he had not left, there would be no need for foreigners at all. Elena knows the limits of her linguistic skills. The prizewinning primary school student knows no other language than her own. Again, Simion attempts to cheer her up, acknowledging her talent with language. She repeats: "only this language." Then she yawns, signaling that the conversation is over. Aware of the eventual public nature of this recorded conversation, Simion doesn't want to give up without spinning a happy ending to this very sad tale.

> ELENA: *how can I know if things are fine? it's god's will . . .*
>
> *if only god keeps the weather fine to work the hay!*
>
> SIMION:—*ok, are you satisfied?*
>
> ELENA: *yes I'm satisfied*
>
> SIMION:—*with me I mean*
>
> ELENA: *I'm satisfied with you thank god*
>
> *god keep you healthy, look after you and holy mother bring you peace*
>
> *you returned, I could see you are fine*

> *god takes care of your days*
>
> *god help us! it's good we've seen each other*

But Elena refuses to play the pretend game. "Fine" is a relative concept. How fine can life be? The haying beckons. For rain threatens. The time spent on this conversation was spent at the risk of a failure of the haying. God, rather than happiness, has the last word. Simion, always the son, wants to get, at the end of this conversation of a kind he never before had with his mother, recognition of his success as a son. Being a true mother, Elena wishes her son well, and she ends by acknowledging the solace his temporary return has given her. This ending strikes the right tone for me. No excess of emotional outburst, just a version of "good to have seen you again," but with just that little more seriousness to it: it is good. This is Elena's version of the "nothing is missing" of one of the other mothers in the project, from which the title of the installation was derived.

239

PART IV

Religion and Power:
Artistic Representations

Music, Religion, and Power

Qawwali as Empowering Disempowerment

Rokus de Groot

What happens to a musical genre when it moves from local Pakistani and Indian Sufi shrines to global venues and media? What happens to the notions of surrender and powerlessness that are connected with this genre in its original Sufi context when it enters the world music scene? What happens to the submission of the participant musicians to strict religious supervision when they become divas on national and international platforms? What happens to the belief in spiritual power transmission at shrine rituals when it is used as an idea in the construction of national identity and as a selling point in a global market of commodities? What were the key ideas that enabled Western cultural entrepreneurs and publics to receive and modify this musical genre, which originated in an Islamic context?

This essay raises these questions in relation to the musical genre called *qawwali* and the various practices and transformations associated with it. *Qawwali* comes from the Arabic *qaul* ("utterance"). It originally referred to a genre of ritual music and to its performance in front of the shrines (*dargahs*) of Muslim saints, in auspicious buildings connected to such shrines or in the former dwellings of saints. Religious veneration of human beings is not allowed in orthodox Islam, as only Allah is deemed worthy of it. However, we do find widespread heterodox Islamic practices, especially in Pakistan and India, in which the physical remains of (mainly) men are worshipped as possessing spiritual blessing power (*baraka*), which is traced back to Ali, Muhammad, and ultimately Allah. These men are considered saintly because they are believed to have transmitted *baraka* during their lifetimes in exceptional ways, for example, as Sufi masters and missionaries. *Qawwals* are the professional, hereditary musicians involved in the genre. They perform in all-male groups led by one or two solo singers, with the body of the group acting as a chorus. The singing is accompanied instrumentally by harmonium, drums, and hand-clapping. *Qawwali* exhibits features of the light classical music of Pakistan and northern India; however, its religious ritual function has given it unique characteristics. The powerful playing on the *dholak* (a barrel-shaped drum) or *tabla* (a pair of drums) and the emphatic rendering of texts are a trademark of *qawwali*. The texts are in Farsi, Hindi, Urdu, or local languages. The singers-musicians traditionally perform *qawwali* without using a raised platform. *Qawwals* generally have a very low social and spiritual status.[1]

Belief in the transmission of spiritual power plays a key role in *qawwali*; the transmission is held to take place through the complete disempowerment of the subject. Music, with its supposed power to lead the participants "out of their minds" into ecstasy, is believed to facilitate this transmission. However, music is also seen as a possible hindrance, as it may attract attention to itself if it is not tutored by spiritual experts.[2]

During the twentieth century, new practices of *qawwali* developed alongside the existing ones, notably on the concert stage and, in the last quarter of the century, in popular music and film. This was mainly thanks to Nusrat Fateh Ali Khan (1948–97). *Qawwali* music became popular in the West in the mid 1980s through the "world music" industry.[3]

I will examine various forms of *qawwali*, paying special attention to changes in concepts of spiritual disempowerment and the transmission of spiritual power, the seemingly paradoxical relationship between the two, and the role of music in both. In the various *qawwali* practices, is a distinction made between spiritual and musical power? If so, is the relation between music and spirituality one of tension or of support? Which serves or dominates the other? Are there any shifts in this respect in present-day *qawwali* practices? The relevance of the last question will become evident in relation to the move of *qawwali* practices from shrine to concert stage, which has important consequences for the spiritual role of music and musicians.

Qawwali Performances in Lahore, in Chicago, in Pâkpattan, and on CD

Dam mast mast
In each breath intoxicated, intoxicated, in each breath intoxicated, look, they whirl around, in each breath intoxicated, Ali, Ali, the one who is intoxicated in each breath, Qalandar, intoxicated, the generous, intoxicated Lal Qalandar, intoxicated, intoxicated.[4]

This Urdu text was sung by Nusrat and his group of vocalists and instrumentalists at a concert in Lahore in 1996. The documentary *Le dernier Prophète* (*The Last Prophet*), by Jérôme de

Missolz,[5] shows Nusrat going on stage, while the audience is told that "This man has made Pakistan shine in the eyes of the world!"[6] The audience—a hall full of men, and men only—responds readily, with applause and pulsating arm movements; quite a few rise from their chairs. When Nusrat greets the audience, many more get to their feet. One of them forcefully moves the ends of his shawl up and down, alternately left and right, as though in a trance. The singers and musicians sit down. When the first tones of *Dam mast mast* are sung and played, the audience reacts with great enthusiasm. Many more stand up; most either clap to the beat or move in more individual ways. Some sway their arms and torsos, or their heads.

Nusrat, too, moves his arms and head while singing. At the multiple repetitions of the words *Qalandar mast mast*, he raises and lowers both arms with outstretched index fingers or open hands to emphasize the beat, and nods his head up and down with it. He sings loudly, as do the others in his group; his voice and those of the other lead singers are electronically amplified.

The energetic emphasis on the beat and the elated performance by Nusrat and his group are characteristic features of *qawwali*. His solo episodes alternate with group refrains. Overall, they accelerate the tempo and intensify the delivery of the text. As for the musical style, the main references are *dargah* ("shrine") *qawwali* and, to some extent. light classical Indo-Pakistani music.

Mast (which is also spelled *musth* and *mustt*) is a Persian and Urdu word for an altered mental state and is usually translated as "intoxicated," "possessed," or "mad." It is a key Sufi term for being intoxicated by God's love. *Mast* implies disempowerment: having sacrificed all separate individuality, one has lost control of oneself and become completely available to—and consequently drunk with—the "Divine Beloved" or "Friend." In Islamic mysticism, this sacrifice is called *fanâ'* ("annihilation of the self").[7]

The Last Prophet contains a fragment of another performance by Nusrat and his group, this time at a Western music venue, Bismarck Theater in Chicago. In musical style, this time the emphasis is on the Indo-Pakistani classical vocal tradition—called *khayal*—and light classical music with, between the choruses, virtuoso solmization episodes on *Sa-Re-Ga* etc. (the Indian note names) performed by Nusrat, who makes increasingly strong movements with his head and arms.[8] The solo episodes also contain lengthy, drawn-out, and ornamented virtuoso vocalizations by his nephew Rahat. The tempo is steadily increased. Nusrat makes sweeping gestures with his right hand, sometimes palm upward, sometimes palm sideways, as in *khayal*. One virtuoso solmization episode ends with a complex cadenza figure characteristic of classical Indian-Pakistani music (*tihai*).[9] The final refrain ensues, with the recurring words *Allah-hoo*.

The audience responds as enthusiastically as it did in Lahore, many with arms raised, moving in a more or less individual way; others clap forcefully to the beat. Some exhibit the same extremes of trancelike movement as at the Lahore concert. At the end, all burst into loud applause and cheering. The public seems mainly composed of people of Indian or Pakistani descent, although some white Americans can be seen. This time quite a few women are present, participating in the movements, though in a less extreme way than the men.[10]

A third event presented in the documentary is a *qawwali* performance near the tomb (*dargah*) of Sufi saint Farîduddîn Ganj-e-Shakar—who is popularly called "Bâbâ Farîd"—at Pâkpattan, in Pakistan. The lead singer, who is playing the harmonium, sits on a rug in the front row of his group along with the other singers, some of whom are clapping their hands to the beat; behind them is a second row of performers, including a tabla player. They sing the same text line over and over again in responsorial manner;[11] at some point they change to a new melodic line, rising to a higher pitch. The beat is emphasized strongly; the way of singing is exalted. The lead singer renders the text in an emphatic way, sometimes moving his head to the beat, and incidentally raises his left hand and arm at the onset of a melodic line. His movements and gestures are generally far more restricted than Nusrat's. The *qawwals* are surrounded by people; some are standing, some are sitting. This almost exclusively male audience behaves in a much more restrained way than the concert publics in Lahore and Chicago. Sitting to the right of the group is a man with a red head-covering. He is a Sufi spiritual guide—a sheikh—and he watches the musicians closely. A man from the audience starts to sway his head in what appears to be a state of trance. His eyes are half-closed; he does not seem to pay any attention to his environment and gives the impression of being disoriented. The singers gradually increase their tempo and volume. After some time, the man in trance is cautiously led away. The singers change to another line and further increase their tempo. Shortly afterward, money is showered on the main singer.[12]

A final episode in the documentary shows Peter Gabriel at his Real World Studio in Wiltshire, listening motionless to a recording of *Musst mustt* by Nusrat—the title song of the CD that was produced at this studio.[13] It is *Dam mast mast*. It has a much slower tempo than the other performances, is heavily edited and electronically modified, and is set to an unchanging, mechanically produced beat.[14] There is no acceleration. This is followed by an interview in which Gabriel states that shortly after 1980, the year in which he established WOMAD (World of Music, Arts and Dance),[15] Peter Townsend drew his attention to *qawwali* as music that greatly moved him. This is Gabriel's response to that music:

> my experience when I first heard Nusrat was very much the same [as Townsend's]. It was very powerful, a sort of spiritual feeling. And I get tingles in the back of my neck when I

hear the music. And he has a masterful control of, if you like, the spiritual volume. . . . with Nusrat it is more designed [than with other singers]. . . . he can build up an improvisation till it climbs up to a peak and you know when he gets there that it is gonna enter people's hearts.[16]

In discriminating among these four performances, I will designate the first two "concert," the third *dargah*, and the fourth "CD."

Qawwali apparently evokes strong physical responses. In the *dargah* fragment, this is restricted to an individual, who appears to enter into a state of trance.[17] The concert *qawwali* fragments show a public that as a whole reacts enthusiastically, even before the lead singer starts to sing. The verbal response from Gabriel is also quite strong, in both physical and emotional terms.

The musical performance to which these expressions are a response is characterized by a powerful emphasis on the beat, an emphatic rendering of text underlined by rhetorical gestures, exalted singing by both lead singer and group, ecstatically sung solo episodes, and (except for the CD) intensification, mainly in volume and the acceleration of delivery.

These four cases show that *qawwali* is a complex phenomenon, made up of musical, poetical, physical, emotional, and spiritual components:

Musical events and processes: the powerful musical rendering.
Poetical texts: notions of powerlessness (*fanâ'*), intoxication (*mast*), submission.
Physical and emotional responses: elated or trancelike behavior.
Spiritual setting and effect: localization near tombs of Sufi saints; references to the saints' names and mental states; possibly mystical experiences; for Western listeners, a general "spiritual feeling."

How are these components related to one another? How can one understand *qawwali* practices as references to—if not arousals of—an intimate, mystic state of love and at the same time as public events? Do notions of powerlessness and submission also play a role in the modification and commodification of *qawwali* into staged Pakistani popular music variants, which often have nationalistic overtones, and into Western world music variants? If so, are these notions modified from the *dargah* situation—and again, if so, how and why?

Mysticism in Islam

In her study *Mystical Dimensions of Islam*, Annemarie Schimmel states that "The goal of the [Muslim] mystic . . . is *fanâ'*, annihilation, and subsequent perseverance in God [*baqâ*]. This final experience is always regarded as a free act of divine grace, which might enrapture man and take him out of himself, often in an experience described as ecstatic."[18] The Sufi term for this ecstasy is *wajd*, literally, "finding."[19] In her seminal *Sufi Music of India and Pakistan*, Regula Qureshi specifies Sufis' mystical dimension:

> Sufi ideology is a response to orthodox Islam, at the same time emanating from its very tenets. Thus, while affirming the unity of God (*tauhîd*) and the absolute distinction between Creator and created, Sufism also assumes an inner kinship between God and man and strives to bridge the gulf between them through the dynamic force of love (*muhabbat*). Mystical love, the central concept of Sufism, has two complementary dimensions essential to the sphere of Sufi thought and experience. One comprises man's deliberate conscious striving toward God by following the Way (*tarîqa*), under the direction of a spiritual guide, to achieve "stages" or "situations" (*maqamât*, pl. of *maqâm*) of nearness to God. The other dimension comprises ecstatic intuitive fulfillment through God's illumination of man, His gift of "states" (*ahwâl*, pl. of *hâl*) of nearness, leading ultimately to union (*wisâl*) with God.[20]

Sufis generally do not approach the mystical states (*maqamât*) and stages (*ahwâl*) as a doctrine or as an object of learned discussion or contemplation but strive to achieve immediate experience of them.[21] The vehicle for this experience is the dynamics of emotion, in particular, the emotion of love. Given the Islamic view of the relation between God and humanity, man is not on the same level as his Creator. This is expressed concisely by Rumi, who writes in his *Mathnawî*: "The Beloved is all and the lover [but] a veil. The Beloved is living and the lover a dead thing."[22] This expression is actually a paraphrase, in terms of love, of the fundament of Islam: "There is no God but Allah." Therefore the lover's (man's) part in divine love is to make himself into nothing before his Beloved (in *fanâ'*), by stages, hoping to be given the grace of actually experiencing Him. The basic love emotion is thus connected with complete submission. Submission, again, is a translation of the word *Islam* itself.

The very expression *mast* is symptomatic in this respect. It means that one is out of one's own mind, overpowered by the Beloved. This is how Amir Khusrau expresses this:

Chahm-e maste-'ajabe zulf tarâze 'ajabe
O wondrous ecstatic eyes, o wondrous long locks
O wondrous wine worshipper . . .

As he draws the sword, I bow my head so as to be killed,
O wondrous is his beneficence, o wondrous my submission.

In the spasm of being killed my eyes beheld your face.[23]

Mystic Method, The Role of the Aesthetic, Submission

Certain schools of Sufism maintain that man can prepare himself for *maqamât* by cultivating mystical love submission, even without expecting to be given *ahwâl* and final illumination by God. This spiritual development is undertaken by means of ritual and devotional practices. One of them is *zikr* (also spelled *dhikr*)—the "recollection" of God in silent or voiced repetition of his names or of religious formulas. However, in the Indian and Pakistani Sufi Chishtiyya school, the aesthetic element is especially valued for expressing mystical thought and arousing the emotion of love submission, particularly by combining poetry, music, and movement in the ritual of *samâ'* ("spiritual hearing"). *Qawwali* is the musical practice connected with this.[24] The Chishtiyya school has applied music in its missionary exploits, feeling that this would appeal to the masses, who are attracted by an emotional kind of worship.[25]

At first sight, *samâ'* seems a mystical practice of therapeutic reversal from symptom to cause. While the Beloved has allegedly put the saint into the altered state of being possessed by Him, the listener's altered state, induced by the musical transformation of the possessed saint's words, is intended in turn to lead this listener back to the Beloved.

This makes for a rather complex process. At every step, there is a risk of idolizing emotional states or means (music and poetry). Idolatry, being the effect of the seeker's own willfulness, leads to the isolation of components of the process, thereby obstructing it. In Sufi tradition, however, one dynamic factor is held to keep everything performing its proper function: the belief in spiritual power (*baraka*).

Transmission of Spiritual Power

A striking aspect of Sufi *samâ'* is that the lover does not directly submit to Allah Himself. This is how Qureshi describes the ritual:

> Through the act of listening—*samâ'*—the Sufi seeks to activate his link with his living spiritual guide, with saints departed, and ultimately with God. At the same time, in opening himself to the powerful medium of mystical songs (Qawwali) performed by professional functionaries, he hopes for a spiritual experience of intensity and immediacy that transcends conscious striving [that is, attaining *wajd*, the ecstasy of "finding" God].[26]

The spiritual master (*sheikh, pir*) is held to be completely disempowered by the Beloved, who, ultimately, is Allah, but who is represented by the master's master, the master's master's master, etc., up to the Prophet's son-in-law Ali and Muhammad. In turn, the master—who is believed to be completely filled with the Beloved's power—helps his disciple to achieve the same state.[27]

This love-power transmission through a chain of masters, with constant, often public, assessment by the master of the disciple's stages and states, constitutes what Qureshi calls "the structural dimension of mystical love."[28] It is what V. S. Naipaul encountered when he visited shrines during his travels in Pakistan. A caretaker of a shrine near Allahabad explained to him: "I want to meet Allah. You can do that only through a medium. My *murshid* [master] is my medium. I want to love my *murshid*. I want my *murshid* to enter my heart. Allah is with my *murshid*. And when my *murshid* enters my heart, Allah is with me."[29] Upon enquiring, Naipaul learned that the *murshid* was not the living *pir* of that particular community at that time but the saint who was buried in the tomb. However, the *dargah* caretaker considered the present *pir* to be the representative of the saint. To clarify his point, he gave a political analogy, in which Jinnah, the founder of Pakistan, figured as *murshid*, the ruling president Zia ul-Haq as *pir*, and he himself as the latter's subject.

The genealogy of spiritual power is reflected in the hierarchy of subjects found in the order of *qawwali* songs for *samâ'*: it opens with the praise of God (*hamd*), is continued in praise of the Prophet (*na't*), and is followed by praise of the saints (*manqabat*).[30]

Apart from the structural dimension of power transmission, there is also the formal dimension of expressing mystical states. Though each listener responds to *qawwali* in his or her own way, according to his or her spiritual needs and emotional state at the moment, this is not an entirely spontaneous affair. As Qureshi explains, *qawwali* is an institutional framework resting upon two premises: "inner reality is confirmed in outward manifestation" and "formal rules are required to govern individual expression." *Samâ'* rituals have a more or less public nature, during which participants are assessed by the spiritual leaders.[31]

Places of Spiritual Power

For Sufis in India and Pakistan, this spiritual power is spatially concentrated in the tombs (*dargahs*) of the saints, as well as in places where they spent time in contemplation, such as *chillas*. The saint is not viewed as a historical figure. On the contrary, his power of grace is held to be present in the *dargah* as a mediation of divine grace, since this place is viewed as the abode of the saint's final union with God.[32] It may therefore be called an epiphanic place, an intersection of time and eternity. The shrines of the saints who founded Sufi schools, especially, are experienced as centers of spiritual power: Moinuddin Chishti (d. 1236) in Ajmer, India; Bâbâ Farîd (d. 1266) in Pâkpattan, Pakistan; and Nizammudin Aulia (d. 1325) and his disciple Amir

Khusrau (d. 1325) in Delhi. The veneration of Sufi saints is part of a widespread popular hetero-dox Islam in Pakistan and India.

The most vital moment of celebration is the commemoration of the *'urs* ("marriage") of the saint, that is, when he was "annihilated" into union with his Beloved at his passing away. *Dargahs* have become places of spiritual guidance and mystical teaching, with single and some-times plural succession to the leadership of the saint and his tomb.[33]

The shrines of the great Sufis of the past were and still are the centers of *samâ'* in Pakistan and India. The main performers are the *qawwals*, with a repertoire in which the verses of Amir Khusrau occupy a central position. He is cherished as the founding father of *qawwali* and, through his ardent poetical address to his *murshid* Nizamuddin Aulia, as providing the model of the master-disciple relationship.[34]

Musical Power

As the core of the power transmission of the saints and their successors, poetry has priority in *samâ'*. However, Chishtiyya tradition holds that musical rendering is indispensable in trans-forming poetical words into an emotional and spiritual experience for the listener. The emo-tional effect of music on the receptive listener is considered to be immediate, with music transcending comprehension.

In her analyses of *qawwali*, Qureshi specifies how music performed in *samâ'* is conceived as having its own power. However, Sufis do not simply equate musical power with spiritual power. Music is considered problematic, since the love emotion that it may arouse is aspecific. Texts and contexts determine whether it will acquire spiritual or profane qualities. Therefore, special care by spiritual supervisors is called for.

Chishtiyya Sufism embraces music, but this tradition is embedded in Islam, in which music is viewed as a delicate subject, to say the least. Although the Qu'ran does not directly prohibit music, Islamic theological tradition has often ostracized music as dangerous and illicit. The tradition does accept cantillation (ritual chanting) of religious texts, above all the Qu'ran (*qir-â'ah*), and even cultivates it, emphasizing the beauty of the vocal rendering, but cantillation is considered "nonmusic." Another case of nonmusic is *adhân*, the call to prayer.[35] Problems arise in the a "musicalization" of religious practice, such as the development of musical elements for their own sake or the use of musical instruments. Both are found to a greater or lesser degree in the *qawwali* at *samâ'*, which makes it theologically suspect. Therefore, music in *samâ'* is kept under strict supervision. The primacy of poetry over music is stressed, and the musicians are submitted to a position of clientship to the spiritual *dargah* leaders, who act as patrons.[36]

Movements and Ecstasy

Listeners express their response in movements conceived as related to emotional and spiritual arousal. Qureshi discerns three stages within a continuum of increasing intensity, each with its relevant terms and movements, counting a relatively neutral but receptive state as zero. They range from "activated devotional attitude," through becoming "deeply moved, overcome with spiritual emotion," to being "transported, self obliterated." In the former two stages, the listener is held to have self-control, but not in the latter: it is here that trance (*behoshî*) or ecstasy (*wajd, hâl*) may set in.[37] Qureshi adds a list of expressive manifestations and their specific terms, ranging from mild to strong arousal. The former finds its expression in, for example, the swaying of the head and the raising of an arm, and the latter in sudden uncontrolled movements, standing up, and dancing. The spiritual leader constantly monitors both the devotees and the group of *qawwals*. The latter should incite and guide the arousal to ecstasy, as well as its ebbing away.[38]

In order to generate and guide spiritual arousal during *samâ'*, the *qawwals* supply a strong metric and rhythmic framework with a regular and short-term stress pattern, which is acoustically intensified by handclaps and drumming. The emphatic stress of the beat (*zarb*) is directly linked with *zikr*. It is also compared to the heartbeat and is considered essential to move the soul, together with pattern repetition and the melodic aspect. When the spiritual leader and/or *qawwal* recognize a sympathetic response in one or more devotees, the musicians apply a technique of intensification in order to further arouse and strengthen the spiritual emotion: gradual increase in the speed of delivery. Given the priority of poetry, the *qawwal* seeks to convey the text message as clearly as possible, using a strong voice, high volume, and clear enunciation. High volume is further achieved by the group of *qawwals* engaging in responsorial singing, which reinforces the words. Alternation between solo and group makes possible a continuous presentation of text. The text content is semantically clarified by visual presentation: certain words are accompanied by gestures.[39]

All these textual and musical aspects create a relentless performance, one that leaves no room for distraction or for rest and that is intended to focus the listener's attention on a single point. The musical procedures have a potentially overpowering effect on the listener, which, in a basic way, is in line with the poetry's appeal to submission.

Listening as Prior to Performing: The Low Status of Musicians

Qureshi points to the ideological distinction between listening and performing in *qawwali*: listening is intended for spiritual advancement, while performing is seen by Sufis as totally subservient to that. She emphasizes the paradox in the *qawwals'* work: they occupy a totally insignificant social position and yet they play an essential role in the Sufi ritual of *samâ'*. *Qawwals* are considered to be service professionals and are wholly dependent on the spiritual leader(s) of the shrine, with whom they are not expected to interact socially. Nevertheless, the lead singer can originate a strategy to generate and stimulate emotional and spiritual arousal, even though his behavior is closely monitored by the presiding sheikh.[40]

Many aspects of the *samâ'* performance reflect the subordinate position of the musicians in *dargah qawwali* and, more fundamentally, the differentiation between musical power and spiritual power. Music is considered a medium rather than a focus during the listeners' inner concentration on the mystical quest. Similar observations have been made by J. M. Pacholczyk about Sufi practice in Kashmir.[41] In the seating arrangement, the audience does not face the performers, except for the spiritual leader, who controls the *qawwals*. *Qawwals* should not attract undue attention to their person or behavior. They are expected to restrain themselves in making expressive gestures to underline words, to dress simply, and to limit their musical sophistication. Performance should not be so artful or theatrical that it becomes conspicuous as the focus of the ritual; if it does, the spiritual nature of the ritual will be distorted.[42]

The misgivings about musicians may be motivated by the problem that there is no generally accepted answer to the question of whether and, if so, how musical power relates to spiritual power. The art of the *qawwals'* musical seduction remains open to suspicion: Is it divine—or demonic?

A further reason for Sufis to hold *qawwals* in low esteem is that these "technicians of ecstasy" are professionals, who have an economic interest in *samâ'*. Because of this basic hybridity of their participation, *qawwals* are not expected to follow a spiritual path as disciples, except in rare cases; they are not seen as devotees, not even as Sufis. A performer cannot claim spiritual authority.[43] If a *qawwali* group is believed to have a spiritual effect, that is only because its members are empowered in their endeavor by performing at a center of spiritual power—the *dargah*—and because they are supervised by a *pir* or a sheikh. Thus, the music may performatively bring the content of the poetry into presence.

Musicians' Strategy

Since the general orientation of the ritual is climactic, music is applied to generate, reinforce, increase, and bring to rest states of arousal. Each individual emotional or spiritual state, as observed through its manifestation, is liable to intensification. The *qawwals* are constantly assessing the audience in order to form a strategy. The relevant issues for them are the state—

253

observed or desired—and the status of the listeners. Because *qawwali* is intended to serve various listeners' diverse and changing spiritual needs, the performers have developed a flexible music practice, both in repertoire and in form. When they see fit, or are admonished to by supervising sheikhs, they can repeat phrases or parts thereof and insert verses. They may enhance their music with techniques borrowed from classical Indian music or introduce tunes from popular and folk music traditions, especially when such tunes are enjoying current success. A high-status public may even accept a purely musical insertion. An example is the use of solmization syllables (*tarana*), a technique derived from classical music practice. In order to intensify a state, the musicians apply various techniques, the main ones being multiple repetition (*takrâr*) and acceleration.

Status is relevant to the choice of the poetical and musical genre. Listeners with a high status, in the spiritual or worldly sense, are likely to prefer poems in Farsi or Hindi, a sophisticated style, classical music, a complex rhythm, and a restrained style of performance. Listeners with a low status tend to be attracted to Urdu texts, a simple style, popular music, a simple rhythm, and exuberant, explicit delivery.[44]

The Musicalization of *Qawwali*

Public interest in *qawwali* has been booming since the 1980s, first in Pakistan and India, then later also abroad. It has taken *qawwali* far outside the Sufi shrines. The key artist in this, Nusrat, stems from a family of classical music vocalists (*khayal, dhrupad*) and instrumentalists. His first teacher was his father, Ustad Fateh Ali Khan, a singer of classical Indian-Pakistani music and *qawwali*, an instrumentalist, and a scholar. He taught Nusrat *tabla* and classical vocal music. After his father's death in 1964, Nusrat was instructed by two of his uncles. It was then that he started to concentrate on *qawwali*. He further developed the hybrid genre of concert *qawwali*—a fusion of classical and light-classical Indo-Pakistani music and *qawwali* as practiced at the Sufi *dargahs*. Nusrat formed a group with his brother Ustad Farukh Fateh Ali Khan, the latter's son Rahat, and various others.

One of the most striking features of concert *qawwali* when compared to *dargah* practice is the absence of spiritual supervision at concerts, as well as a strong tendency toward musicalization by vocal virtuosity. The singers-musicians are not subordinated to a sheikh or *pir*, in a patron-client relationship, nor is assessment of the spiritual nature of the audience response considered essential. Concert *qawwali* is not tied to a sacred place like a *dargah*, as an epiphanic place of spiritual power. Especially in a concert context, *qawwali* "spirituality" has acquired an economic dimension and become a commercial selling point. Obviously, spiritual assessment—

like that carried out at *dargahs*—would be counterproductive here, serving as a source of possible exclusion.

Nusrat heralded the emancipation of *qawwali* from its spiritually and economically dependent position at *dargahs*. Apart from developing himself into a magnificent performer, he became an independent musical entrepreneur after the Western model. In a reversal of relationships, religion now served music.

The fact that Nusrat was honored in Pakistan as an independent musical performer—that is, independent of *dargah* supervision—culminated in his receiving the Pride of Performance Award from the Pakistani government in 1986.[45] He had to face a situation like that encountered by European composers at the end of the eighteenth and the beginning of the nineteenth centuries, as they freed themselves from court and church.[46] Like them, he presented himself on the market and exploited divergent routes, geared to different venues, between popularization and creating exclusivity.

As performers, Nusrat and his group did not subject themselves to an inconspicuous position, placed on a secondary plane, shielded from eye contact with the public. On the contrary, Nusrat was the center of attention on the concert stage, elevated spatially above his audience. After each concert item he got applause, which theatrically underlined the change of *qawwali* from *dargah* to stage performance. He was usually treated as a diva, both on and off stage. Unlike *dargah qawwals*, he attracted much visual attention through gestures and facial expressions, and through their intensification. His emphatic movements of head and arms to the beat, and his raising of hands and arms, incited enthusiasm and mild arousal.[47] Analyzed in terms of Qureshi's "Application of Status Referent,"[48] his exuberant, explicit presentation, with its extensive demonstrative gestures, his "acting out" the song, has the "lower status" orientation. This is underlined by his preference for singing Urdu texts in his Pakistani concerts.

Nusrat's Pakistani public, and to an extent his public in the West, responded in much stronger ways than is usual in *dargah qawwali*. Their movements were quite hyperbolic. In Lahore, the audience made gestures and movements that manifested mild to strong arousal even before Nusrat had started to sing. Already at the very beginning of his performance, many people cried out (*âwâz nikâlnâ*), some swayed their heads or torsos as though in a trance, while others raised both arms (*hâth batânâ*), stood up (*kharâ honâ*), or danced (*raqs*). A similar reaction can be seen in Chicago. From the perspective of Qureshi's *dargah* analysis, this behavior resembles that of what she calls the "common" audience, as opposed to the "sophisticated" one.[49] Whereas these expressions are relatively rare and individual at the *dargah qawwali* that has been observed, at concert *qawwali* they involve most of the audience. This could be called the "democratization of ecstatic behavior": anybody can involve him- or herself in it and no spiritual authority is monitoring it for authenticity.

Qureshi notes about *dargah qawwali*: "Once a state of intense arousal has been reached, the manifestations of the state are entirely expressive, not referential."[50] In concert *qawwali* this is much less evident, especially since many people seem to manifest ecstatic behavior even when they have hardly been exposed to the music. It is quite likely that, to a much greater extent than in *dargah qawwali*, the expressive behavior of the audience at concert *qawwali* has become part of the performance. In comparison to *dargah qawwali*, the practice of Nusrat and his Pakistani public tended toward a representation of Sufi traditions rather than participation in them.

On the global scale, Nusrat's role was shaped by a process of decontextualization and recontextualization as "world music." A twofold persona—the diva and the pop star—was projected upon him, and to an extent he accepted it. The diva figure in Western classical music has a musical foundation of virtuosity; the pop star depends largely on seductive physical behavior, with an overpowering, multimedia backing. Both are expected to arouse large audiences to ecstasy, for which they have developed relevant techniques. This double projection on Nusrat involved despiritualization, though spiritual arguments were employed to achieve it.

The Spiritualization of *Qawwali*

Nusrat musicalized *qawwali*, but he also spiritualized his concert practice. He always stressed that the Sufi mystic tradition was the root of his art. He emphasized the hierarchy between spiritual power and musical power, subjecting the latter to the former.[51] Using the characteristic figure of the disempowerment of the self, he placed his art in the perspective of the canonical Sufi tradition of Chishtiyya medieval mystics, both in the context of Pakistani and Western concert presentations and in information in the booklets accompanying his CDs.

As an authorization of his art, Nusrat stressed time and again his spiritual calling. He reported that in 1964, a few days after his father's death, he had a dream vision of himself performing at an unknown place. His father had taken him there and told him to sing. When Nusrat expressed his inability to do so, his father said that he would sing along with him. Nusrat began to sing, and he was still singing when he awoke. He told his uncles about the dream, and they asked him to describe the place where it all happened. According to them, it was the *dargah* of Moinuddin Chishti, in Ajmer, India. This *dargah* is nothing less than the Mecca of Indian-Pakistani *qawwali*, as the saint is the founder of the music-loving Chishtiyya order. Forty days (for Muslims, an auspicious period) after the death of Nusrat's father, the family received a letter from the Ajmer *dargah*. After a period of prayer, its spiritual leaders had received a dream that Nusrat would be the successor to his father.[52] So, although his concert *qawwali* lacked a spatial connection to a *dargah*, it acquired a powerful dream-vision one.

The poetry of the Sufi founder saints, in particular texts by Amir Khusrau, occupied a central place in Nusrat's singing. In his interviews he stressed their work as great missionaries of Islam and the role of music in it: "Through music, the Sufis were able to make those whom they wished to convert admire the splendours of the Koran."[53] By placing his father in this lineage of saints, Nusrat implicitly made himself part of it, combining the transmission of musical and of spiritual power. Nusrat said several times that, thanks to his ancestors (who apparently included missionary saints), he was imparting the Sufi message to the world. He universalized its content, saying: "I'd like to give the world a message of love, knowledge and humanity. Our Sufi music is a bridge to other nations. It invites people to get closer in love and brotherhood."[54] Nusrat's conviction is double-faceted, combining the Western concept of universal brotherhood with the aspiration of Islam to create a universal community of believers (*uma*).

Indeed, interpreting the message of the Ajmer *dargah* spiritual leaders as a confirmation of his mission, Nusrat seems to have assumed the roles of both musician and sheikh. In concert *qawwali*, there is a change in the division of spiritual and musical power. As the main singer, he was responsible for the event. A shift of authority seemed to have taken place, which also involved imbalance in the relation between God and man as conceived in Islam. It was the musician who became the object of veneration in concert *qawwali*. The use of certain artificial means—such as extreme electronic amplification and huge venues—emphasized this shift to the deification of the artist.

Virtuosity is an interesting aspect of concert *qawwali*. In a Western context it is a celebration of human vitality, dexterity, and control; the kind of ecstasy that is to be evoked in the public is related to individual human excellence. At the same time, vocal virtuosity, especially, is not only an affair of musical technique: in opera, coloratura virtuosity is usually connected with the extreme emotional state of the protagonist; the fact that the words sung in such a passage usually cannot be understood because of the speed and high register at which they are uttered only underlines this. Nusrat's virtuosity—particularly the most "musical" one, which uses meaningless sounds and syllables—needed justification in a Pakistani Muslim context. But how can one justify virtuosity as "spiritual"? It is striking that Nusrat's musical brilliance in the solmization episodes manifests the same passion as in the poetry-bound ones—like Western opera coloraturas, these episodes are not simply cases of technical bravado. In fact, the audience is given the impression that Nusrat's nonsense-syllable passages are an exemplification of the ecstasy about which the text speaks, a kind of glossolalia.

Again: The Power of Music

In accordance with *qawwali* practice, Nusrat stressed the power of music. He was convinced that it was music that empowered the medieval Islamic mission in India and Pakistan. According to him, Sufi poetry "can only really reach people if it is sung"; otherwise "it remains in the book. . . . the music backing will give the text all its majesty."[55] Nusrat even went so far as to state that for those who do not understand the words of *qawwali*—for example, his Western public—"the exact effect sought by the master's words will be created by the *music alone*."[56] This points clearly to the Janus-faced process of concert *qawwali*, that is, the musicalization of a spiritual practice and the spiritualization/respiritualization of musical performance. Given this stance, one may understand Nusrat's objection to some of Michael Brook's cuts and editing, which Brook considered purely musical, for the *Mustt mustt* CD. In an interview with Helen Jerome, Brook states: "We made some edits that were not acceptable to Nusrat, because we'd cut a phrase in half—sometimes there were actual lyrics that we made nonsense of. . . . Sometimes even though they were just singing Sa Re Ga [solmization] we had interfered with the meaning of the phrase."[57] The latter observation is an interesting one. Of course, Nusrat's objection might stem from formal musical criteria, but it may also have been motivated by his belief that musical episodes with nonsense syllables, no less than texted ones, harbor spiritual power if performed in the spirit of a saint's lineage. Unlike the Western practice of treating musical sound as an object to edit at will, Nusrat may have approached the recording as a transmission of power in which certain formal entities should be kept intact.

Yet compared to *dargah qawwali*, a reversal has taken place in Nusrat's practice. Instead of being curtailed as a spiritually suspect medium, the musical component has become the principal one, its power being recognized in a new way as indispensable for a present-day spreading of Islam, in the form of a generalized Sufi message.

The Figure of Submission; Revelation

While Nusrat's performance became an act that used the power of the stage, he was still employing the traditional *qawwali* poetical figure of complete disempowerment, as in the *Mustt mustt* CD. The figure of submission is present in several ways in his practice, again in a double fashion. Interestingly, he used the figure of annihilation not only in relation to the saints, the Prophet, and Allah, but also to music: "But what counts for me is my total immersion in my art."[58] Similarly, for him not only is the Qu'ran a result of revelation, but so too is music: "It's revealed to the soul. It's mental work that stems from the atmosphere. It connects to the soul."[59] An altered notion of submission from the Sufi context seems to mingle with the nineteenth-century European topos of the disempowerment of the genius-artist: the more he is disempowered of his own volition, the more he becomes an instrument of inspiration. This was held by some influential thinkers (e.g., Schopenhauer) to be especially true for music, seen as privileged among the arts because it was the most direct expression of the "World Soul."

Differentiation in Concert *Qawwali*

Catering to the needs of different performance situations, Nusrat maintained and greatly enlarged the flexibility of *dargah qawwals* in repertoire and formal musical aspects. He generally preserved traditional *qawwali* characteristics—such as rhythmic energy, ecstatic performance, tempo acceleration, and intensification of text delivery—in his concert performances. But in Pakistan he emphasized the language of Sufi poetry much more than he did in Western venues.[60] In the Pakistani context, he preferred to do popular *ghazals* in Urdu and to remain relatively close to the *dargah* musical format, while in his concert series at the prestigious Théâtre de la Ville de Paris, he tended to sing in the high-status language Farsi, with long episodes in Indian-Pakistani classical music style, in order to meet the expectation of "authenticity" and musical exclusivity. He was greatly transgressing the narrow limits of his *dargah* colleagues here, expanding enormously the responsorial *qawwali* form between lead singer and chorus with long virtuoso solo passages.

In the latter performances, the vocal sound is very often "musicalized"; what is sung is not poetry but vocalizations as well as Sa-Re-Ga solmization syllables (*taranas*). This could be called the instrumentalization of vocality. At the same time, as if to balance this musicalization, the Paris concerts emphatically show the traditional *dargah samâ'* poetical structure of *hamd*, *na't*, and *manqabat*, making explicit the spiritual chain of power.[61]

A further step toward musicalization is found on his most famous CD for the global market, *Mustt mustt*. Only two of the ten items (the eleventh being a remix of the first) have lyrics; the others employ vocalization and solmization. This is a far cry from *dargah qawwali*, with its strong emphasis on the primary position of poetry. Nusrat was well aware of this differentiation within the practice of concert *qawwali* and consciously developed it. Considering music an international language that makes words superfluous, he stressed improvisation and faster tempi much more in the West than he did in India and Pakistan.[62]

259

Concert *Qawwali* as an Empowerment of Pakistani Nationalism

In the Lahore concert, Nusrat was welcomed as a Pakistani hero. In Missolz's documentary, Pakistani employees of Oriental Stars Production in London mix a concept of religious purity with nationalist issues when they discuss his music. One of them says: "People have forgotten the sacred aim of Islam. India is stealing his [Nusrat's] music. They use his songs and tunes for their films. . . . that's dishonest." These remarks should be understood in the context of Pakistan's ambition to be a "pure" state in the religious sense. This would ideally mean that the secular domain would be spiritualized, obliterating the distinction between "worldly" and "religious." Nusrat's family, particularly his father, had been in contact with Muhammad Iqbal, the great designer of Pakistan as, literally, a "pure state." Nusrat himself sang *ghazals* written by this poet. No doubt Nusrat knew about Iqbal's ideas about creating a new state as a Muslim polity, in which all aspects of life would be rethought and reshaped. Concert *qawwali* may be conceived as a musical proposal in that direction.

In a sense, Nusrat's practice may be considered an attempt to "convert" Indian-Pakistani classical music, which is rooted in courtesan culture, into an Islamic art by means of popular Sufi *qawwali*. Its ideal was to recompose the secular through the spiritual, by which the Sufi musico-poetic legacy was made to play a nationalist role. Ironically, concert *qawwali*, being a very hybrid music, combining courtesan and shrine traditions, is musically empowering the concept of a pure Islamic nation; conversely, a notion of Islam as an all-encompassing social, cultural, and political revolutionary force is empowering a stage concert practice that originated in the West. The enthusiastic and ecstatic (or quasi-ecstatic) response of the Lahore concert audience may have been spiritually motivated, but it was probably at the same time, and with the same gestures, an expression of nationalism. This combination was also audible in President Parvez Musharraf's address at the inauguration of the National Academy of Performing Arts in Karachi in 2005, when he praised Nusrat for being instrumental in creating both a gentle image of Pakistan and an enlightened one of Islam.[63]

One is tempted to read the Lahore public's ecstatic behavior as not the outcome of *fanâ'* (a spiritualized state) but rather an utterance of *Rausch* (German for "intoxication"), as expounded in Nietzsche's *Götzendämmerung* (*Twilight of the Gods*), that is, the feeling of an increase of power and fullness, idealizing the world (hence a politicized act).[64]

Western Musicalization and the Spiritualization of *Qawwali*

Nusrat's Western concerts and CDs were generally accompanied by printed information about his Sufi background, often in a language similar to that used in commercials. For example, the

Opus CD, which was released in France, speaks of a "voice from heaven." The Ocora Paris series provides translations of the texts sung. Nusrat himself was eloquent about his credo. Consequently, the attention of the Western publics of CD and concert *qawwali* has been bent toward connecting music and spirituality.

The Western reception of Nusrat's art may well have been helped by the fact that audiences in Europe and the Americas had been prepared for the figure of the charismatic Oriental artist-missionary. Earlier examples include Inayat Khan and Rabindranath Tagore (both before the Second World War) and Ravi Shankar (since the late 1950s), who was well versed in presenting his sitar recitals as events with spiritual overtones—or rather fundamentals.[65] The reception of Nusrat may be taken as part of a romantic necessity to recover or replace religion. As in these earlier examples, in concert *qawwali* we encounter the strong attribution of a spiritual agency to an "other" that is a composite of both music and Orient.

One symptom of this aspect of the Western reception of Nusrat's music is the Messianic title of Missolz's documentary film about him. To call this film *The Last Prophet* implies, in a Muslim context, the transference of the status of Muhammad to a rather suspect subject (a musician, of all people), which, if the Prophet were not a human being, would count as blasphemy. Yet to bestow such an epithet on an artist is not uncommon in a Western context, with its tradition of individualism and cult of genius. The implication of this daring title is that the Sufi chain of spiritual power has collapsed, to make room for an unmediated connection between a present-day musician and the divine.

The ready reception of Nusrat as an artist-missionary may have been strengthened by another factor in recent Western culture: the concept of music *as* religion. This concept has been developed by German poets and philosophers since the late eighteenth and the early nineteenth centuries in relation to classical instrumental music. It can also be found in popular music, as the hit "God is a DJ," by Faithless, from their album *Sunday 8 pm* (1999), can testify. In this hit, religious experiences and expectations are projected onto musical structures and processes. Both the processes of musicalization (including the instrumentalization of vocality) and the spiritualization of *qawwali* by Nusrat fit well into the concept of music as religion.[66]

A third factor may be the recent European interest in intoxication (*Rausch*).[67] N. Lebovic, in *Dionysian Politics and the Discourse of "Rausch,"* identifies three historical moments of *Rausch* conceptualization. The first, in the late eighteenth century, was an early romantic reaction to rational Enlightenment; the second, in late romantic Europe, manifested a strong emphasis on love;[68] and the third, in the 1920s, was a conceptualization and politicization of both earlier moments.

Unlike the Western CDs for classical music listeners, the Realworld CDs *Mustt mustt* (1990) and especially *Night Song* (1995), which were destined for the popular music market, offer little information about Nusrat's Sufi background. The booklet accompanying the former CD contains barely more than three lines about Nusrat and *qawwali*, while it amply discusses purely musical experiments and innovations. The cover text of *Night Song* is limited to linking the CD with its predecessor. Only one of the English titles—"Intoxicated"—may betray the background to the music, and only in a covert way. What remains is the association between music and a very general notion of emotionality or spirituality. This attitude is also conspicuous in Peter Gabriel's comments about Nusrat quoted earlier. In all this, Nusrat's art is largely stripped of its rich Sufi mystical background. Western publics tend to consider experiences of *musst*, or "intoxication," as religious in themselves, without any reference to God or saints. Virtually nothing in *Mustt mustt* or its successor discloses the original motivation of the overpowering quality of *qawwali* music, that is, the desire to disempower the listener in order to make him or her available to the Beloved's power of love.

However, popular music *qawwali* does offer some parallels to the figure of disempowerment and submission. When we listen to *Mustt mustt*—the "intoxication" song of the Lahore concert—in the Massive Attack remix on the Realworld CD, we find the same strong emphasis on the beat structure as in *qawwali*. While the remix omits the usual intensifier of *qawwali* (the increase in tempo), it has done something else: it has mechanized the beat structure to absolute regularity, in conformity with recent Western popular music practices. Although the remixers could not have been aware of the *zikr* background to the strong beat in *qawwali*, they have, with their percussive machine, provided a kind of simulacrum of it. The mechanicity of beat production suggests the presence of something absolute, a regularity that is inhuman, although produced by humans. This suggestion is greatly enhanced by the extreme loudness with which this music is usually played. (The *Mustt mustt* remix was a dance club hit in 1990.) The experience of the inhuman—in this case, the loud "absolute" regularity—can easily shift into an interpretation of it as something supra-individual and ultimately something "divine." In the case of the *Mustt mustt* remix, such an interpretation is helped by the editing technique. The vocal sounds are subjected to different degrees of reverberation and to a layering of overlapping phrase repetitions with decreasing loudness. These echo effects—a nonhuman phenomenon (though, again, produced by humans)—have been used for centuries as a musico-theatrical device to suggest the supernatural, sometimes more specifically a divine presence, from Monteverdi through Bach and contemporaries into the nineteenth and the twentieth centuries.[69]

The inhumanity of "absolute" regularity, clad in the nonhumanity of echo, is presented so loudly that the listener is forced to choose between submission and resistance. The music presses the listener toward the former, since the vocal sounds of Nusrat fade out several times as though they were drowning in the "absolute" beat structure. The testimonies of participants in dance events also point to the desired experience of ecstasy or intoxication, transgressing the boundaries of the individual self; this seems psychologically (which is not the same as spiritually) similar to the *dargah* situation. In this context, the mystical or quasi-mystical aura of *qawwali* may well have promoted its acceptance.[70]

If the listener chooses submission, what kind of *musst*, or "intoxication," will be effected in him or her? Is there any qualification in the music, text, or context that suggests that a "power of love" is at work? The listener is certainly overwhelmed by power—and, while submitting, is largely disempowered. It is a power of human origin that appears as both inhuman and nonhuman—"absolute" regularity, artificial echo, excessive electrical amplification—and that thereby suggests something greater than man (although actually lesser, since it is manmade), in other words, something that used to be called God.[71] Although music in Western popular *qawwali* has now been freed from spiritual *dargah* supervision, its listeners are ready to submit to a new authoritative presence: a musical one. To be overpowered by sonic inhumanity and nonhumanity constructed by man, may in the end lead to an "intoxication" by deep alienation, which only man can produce and experience.

Appendix: An Email Conversation with Dr. Regula Qureshi on "Ecstasy," May 9, 2007

1.

RDG: In your book you describe different stages of ecstasy through which members of the audience may go during a *mahfil* [*samâ'*]. Do or don't the musicians also experience ecstasy in its various stages while playing? Are they or are they not expected to?

RQ: They are not expected to, because that would interfere with their mandate to transmit the sonic message to those who have come to listen with the purpose of gaining spiritual advancement. This is why the Sufi assembly is called a gathering for spiritual listening (*mahfil-e-samâ'*, or just *samâ'*), not a performance. A number of serious *qawwals*, however, are Sufis and disciples of a sheikh, and as such spiritually affected by what they are singing. My *qawwali* teacher, Meraj Ahmad, told me of another *qawwal* who was overcome by emotion during his singing and started to weep. The sheikh told him to leave the singing and sit down. Meraj explained, and that was confirmed by the sheikh when I talked to him later, that his responsibility was to convey the spiritual message to the members of the Sufi community.

2.

RDG: Do participants—sheikhs/*pirs*, and audience—differentiate between trance and ecstasy?

RQ: Words are difficult here, first of all because of the language. There are several terms in Urdu/Persian and they are used in different, nuanced ways—not according to any scheme.

RDG: Do you make such a differentiation?

RQ: In a general way I see ecstasy as denoting a state of transport, not necessarily a loss of consciousness—which is generally denoted by the term *trance*. In the end, I am very uncomfortable about pinning down other people's interior experiences, and when I used both these terms on page 121 in my book it was to try to approximate the range of meanings embedded in the Urdu terms. I try to listen to what Sufis have to say themselves, but they are more likely to use metaphors denoting an altered state, or "vanishing" within the sheikh, the saint, and ultimately God (or all of them becoming one and the same). Of course, there is no reason why *ecstasy* and *trance* should not become the words for this experience for English speakers.

I want to add that the sheikhs and even the *qawwals* I worked with were very literate, spiritually so as well, as were their audiences. The big concert stage *qawwali* event is more recent and has turned the whole thing into much more of a spectacle. Public spectacles at large shrine assemblies are very common in Pakistan, and performers like Nusrat were used to singing to "crowds" rather than to a few individual Sufis who were all known to them and to each other. Amazingly, Nusrat always retained the integrity of his spiritual song texts, even before uncomprehending audiences.

John Cage and the Mystification of Musical Silence

Jael Kraut

Artistic silence has always been entangled with various forms of power. Silence has often been imposed on artists in all major religious traditions in both the Orient and the Occident. Mystical traditions seem especially disaffected with speech (e.g., the writings of Dionysius the Areopagite, Jakob Boehme, and Meister Eckhardt, and parallels in Zen, Taoist, and Sufi texts), and the radical wings of monotheist religions have tended to suppress or at least curb all forms of human expression by calling for iconoclasm, rejecting the imitation of nature, and prohibiting (certain) music. In the twentieth century, however, appeals for silence have come from leading artists themselves rather than from the legatees of religious traditions. Cultural philosophers such as Susan Sontag and George Steiner have stipulated that within the historical context of nihilism, political inhumanity, the totalitarian reign of technology and mass culture, together with the devastating consequences of the last for humans and nature, the artist is imprisoned in the consciousness of his time and place in history. It is in this context that many artists choose the rhetorical act of silence, expressing their reluctance to communicate or to produce, firmly put into words by James Purdy in *Cabot Wright Begins*: "I won't be a writer in a place and time like this."[1] Overwhelmed by a feeling of disempowerment in the all-embracing "noise" of the twentieth century, the artist found that he "has nothing to say," and says this by using the powerful and "most fatal weapon of silence."[2]

Whereas the appeals to silence of many twentieth-century artists seem vehement criticisms of the actual historical situation, another group of artists emphasizes the revaluation of the ancient mystical values of silence.

Within the domain of music, composers such as John Cage and Toru Takemitsu suggest that they use the power of silence in order to reestablish a spiritual relationship with the nonhuman (God, nature). They emphasize silence as a "means" to religious empowerment, supposed to unify self-isolated humankind with the cosmos and nature. For them, musical silence seeks to renounce human power in an overpopulated and overmanipulated world. Other contemporary composers for whom silence plays such a role are Arvo Pärt, John Tavener, and Henryk Górecki. They actually seek to revive medieval Christian mysticism, particularly from the Orthodox tradition. Because of their meditative, hypnotic, and repetitive music, they are often called "holy minimalists."

In this essay, I will focus on a composer who made brilliant use of silence with reference mysticism: John Cage, the "composer" who composed no music—or silence. I will engage the theme of power on two levels. First, I will demonstrate, by examining the genesis of Cage's most famous and radical silent piece, *4′33″*, that Cage's musical silence would already have made perfect sense if he had called it a natural reaction to the art practices in the context of the twentieth century. His composed silence could have answered the critical avant-garde call for the *dépassement de l'art*, which, according to the Cobra painter Constant Nieuwenhuys, "transforms art into a power for spiritual health," since it signifies "the power of the individual to free himself from the ruling aesthetic and place himself above it."[3] Silence would then be the artist's ultimate weapon. But—and this constitutes the second level on which I address the theme of power—Cage denied that he was working toward the demise of art, and one does not find this assertion in the majority of postwar interpretations of his works and writings. This stance facilitated the composer's cultural survival, allowing him to evade what is "frightening, confusing, or difficult in the social realm," while his anticritical stance contributed to his empowerment as a musically incompetent composer—a characterization Cage himself cheerfully accepted.

Silencing Social Music

Cage's initial impetus, together with the conclusions of his early critics, would indicate that he should fit perfectly into the avant-garde strategy of the destruction of art in response to the social and technological conditions of the twentieth century. In an in-depth analysis of Cage's writings and compositions, Douglas Kahn suggests that throughout his entire life and career Cage seems to have been guided by the "fantasy" of "silencing the social."[4] For an oratorical contest during his high school days, Cage already presented a text in which he said:

> One of the greatest blessings that the United States could receive in the near future would be to have her industries halted, her business discontinued, her people speechless, a great

pause in the world of affairs created, and finally to have everything stopped that runs, until everyone should hear the last wheel go around and the last echo fade away . . . then, in that moment of complete intermission, of undisturbed calm, would be the hour most conducive to the birth of a Pan-American Conscience.[5]

After he had established himself as a composer, music became the appropriate means by which to achieve his goal of silencing the social. Paradoxically, in order for music to accomplish the ambitious program of this "grand silencing," music must first itself be silenced. Music is a social phenomenon; it is produced in and around social institutions, according to rules passed down in musical traditions.

Silencing the established practices of music in his time was particularly difficult for Cage, who, in carrying out this program, needed to surpass his teacher Arnold Schoenberg, the composer who had put an end to tonality, hence, to the basic principle of Western music. In fact, Schoenberg's field of musical innovation involved harmony, dynamics, and timbre; the musical instruments he used were traditional. It might not be surprising, then, that Cage focused on silencing instruments as a means to extend the reach of his "music." From now on, any noise produced by any object that had previously been considered unmusical would constitute the sound of music, and, inversely, what traditionally had been considered a musical instrument would from now on have the same status as any other object in the world.

In 1938 Cage began to have some success with the prepared piano. By adding screws, bolts, and pieces of felt inserted between the strings, he completely transformed the piano, producing timbres reminiscent of various percussive instruments. The following year, he composed *The Wonderful Widow of Eighteen Springs*, a piece for voice and closed piano. He muted the vocal line by deleting the original punctuation of the text he was adapting, using capital letters, and only allowing three pitches—moreover, he instructed the singer to negate the rhythm, structure, and sense of Joyce's literary "voice." The accompaniment consisted in tapping and knocking on the wooden cover over the inaccessible piano keys. The piano, that preeminent instrument of romantic expression, had to remain closed. Reduced to the primordial, it became merely a sonorous surface, just a "something," an object closed, heavy, massive, and dense. Indeed, composing music for a closed piano not only means losing the accepted possibilities of the instrument as a means for human expression but also implies putting an end to a certain culture, that is, to Western culture and its specific cultural objects.

Although European composers were the first to begin the process of reorganizing and disintegrating the traditional musical system, according to many critics, they were still composing music. Cage, by contrast, effectively crossed the border between the musical and the formerly unmusical. He began a process through which what general consensus considers to be music is lost. Paul Henry Lang confirms this by stressing that Schoenberg's twelve-tone system remains on the side of music because it still "has a 'tonality' represented in certain concretely defined melodic steps":

> New tonality does not mean a lack of tonal unity, for without such unity there can be no music. Music rests on melody, and every melody has a certain construction regulating the relationship of the various pitches. Only that music could be called atonal whose melody would show no system of relationship between its various pitches; but such music no longer belongs to the domain of aesthetics, that is, it is no longer art, it is not music, it is merely a conglomeration of unrelated sounds.[6]

Of course, one may question the melodic features of Schoenberg's music, especially his dodeca-phonic works. But Adorno supports Lang's argument, too. In spite of the criticism addressed to Schoenberg and his students in Adorno's *Philosophy of New Music,* for him too the Second Viennese School (together with composers such as Bartok, Stravinsky, and Hindemith) was still on the side of music, whereas the composers who followed—such as Boulez, Stockhausen, and Cage—were not. According to Adorno, although the latter pretended to be spiritual, in reality they had lost the ability to compose music. As he puts it:

> His [Schoenberg's] most recent followers blithely short-circuit the antinomy that he rightly tried to deal with. They are intentionally indifferent to whether the music makes sense and is articulated—a consideration that caused Schoenberg's hesitations—and believe that the preparation of tones is already composition as soon as one has dismissed from composition everything by which it actually becomes a composition. They never get farther than abstract negation, and take off on an empty, high-spirited trip, through thinkably complex scores, in which nothing actually occurs; this seems to authorize them to write one score after another, without any constraints at all.[7]

Douglas Kahn writes: "Cage played a unique role in that he took the avant-garde strategy to its logical conclusion."[8] He rightly suggests that Cage concluded the avant-garde strategy, but he is wrong in calling him unique. We must remember that Cage was very much influenced by the aesthetic views held by artists in Europe, where he spent almost two years and which he contin-ued to visit throughout his entire life. In Europe many artistic movements, such as Dada, surre-alism, de Stijl, constructivism, Cobra, and the Lettrist International, searched for techniques that would go beyond art in order to reinvent it. A salient example is Guy Debord, who made the film *Hurlements en faveur de Sade* (*Howls for Sade*) in 1952. In this film, the silence of the last twenty-four minutes stands for the "necessary silence of all artistic expression" in a world where "we are locked into relations of production that contradict the necessary development of productive forces, in the sphere of culture *as well*."[9] Debord explicitly suggests that in Cage he felt he had found a brother in arms. As he wrote to a friend: "I heard that last year an American musician called John Cage brought together an audience and invited them to listen to ten minutes of perfect silence. *The course of history, mister*."[10]

For Cage, however, silencing what is socially and traditionally understood as music meant, inversely, that "nothing was lost when everything was given away. In fact, everything is gained."[11] According to him, the future of music does not reside in turning to atonality, dodecaphony, and serialism, which is, as Cage argues, "simply the maintenance of an ambiguous tonal state of affaires."[12] Indeed, he urged "a way out" of the process of music disintegration, but, instead of considering his music to be antimusic, he purported to bring a "new music," which implies a "new listening." Although his work thus appears to fit perfectly into the avant-garde strategy, the composer himself radically refutes such claims.

Cage's Turn to Religion

Cage's idea of new music and new listening could only be achieved by taking on aspects of Eastern traditions, initially from India. While working with the dancer Merce Cunningham, Cage wrote the suite *Amores*, which consisted of two pieces for prepared piano and two pieces for percussion trio. It was "an attempt to express in combination the erotic and the tranquil, two of the permanent emotions of Indian tradition."[13] Increasingly fascinated by the possibilities that Indian philosophy offered to his music, he read *The Dance of Shiva* by art historian Ananda K. Coomaraswamy.[14] Ideas deriving from Indian aesthetics are first evident in the ballet *The Seasons*, particularly in the hour-long series of short pieces for prepared piano, the *Sonatas and Preludes*, in which Cage aims to portray the eight "permanent emotions" or *rasas* of Indian aesthetics—the erotic, the heroic, the odious, anger, mirth, fear, sorrow, and the wondrous—and their common tendency toward tranquility, *shanti-rasa*. According to Cage, however, the decisive step in his genesis as an artist and composer—as a revolutionary—was made when he attended courses at Columbia University given by Daisetz Teitaro Suzuki, who revealed Zen to him. The Buddhist ideal of the negation of the will (the negation of desire and control)—of disempowerment—prompted him to develop an aesthetic and spiritual silence in both his life and his work.

In 1948, he presented the lecture "In Defense of Satie"—which created a scandal at Black Mountain College—in which he pronounced that European music had stopped being musical in the Renaissance, because from that time on harmonic structure determined how music had to be composed. He expands this claim in the article "Forerunners of Modern Music," published a year later, in which he writes that "the material of music is sound and silence," that composing consists in integrating these two, and that, most importantly, music must rediscover its relation to nature.

The more Cage immersed himself in religion, the more his initial critical attitude toward the historical situation faded into the background. In consequence, his arguments take an ambiguous turn, particularly when it comes to defining nature. With the aim of determining not "the nature of music as essence, but the essence of music as nature,"[15] Cage suggests that he opposes classical and romantic ideas of music, particularly those of self-expression. In the conventional conception of music, in addition to form and structure, a composition involves expression; one hears not only sounds or silence but also subjectivity. "Are sounds just sounds or are they Beethoven? People aren't sounds, are they?"[16] Within the framework of Zen Buddhism, the role of the composer, as Cage saw it, ceases to be one of manipulating sonorous material and imposing human expression upon it. The principle of his method of composition became one of "letting the sounds be themselves," which means that humans should quit turning sounds into what he calls a " Frankenstein monster," that is, abortive, manipulated attempts to re-create what they take to be themselves.[17]

Although Cage explicitly refers to the Renaissance as the period in which music lost its essence as nature, one would assume that he might oppose the denatured concept of nature in a capitalist age, in which it has come to be conceived as "raw reality, and the given that one has to receive and master."[18] In the Renaissance, nature was defined from the perspective of a philosophy of representation, in which the subject is opposed to the object. The ideal of this perspective was the "mastery of nature" in order to alleviate the human condition, a position associated with Descartes. From this standpoint, art is a practice that uses knowledge to produce artificiality with the view of establishing a human order. Cage seems to consider the dominance of harmonic structure from the Renaissance onward exemplary for such an establishment of a human order in the field of music. But one may very well argue, as Mikel Dufrenne suggests, that human intervention in nature does not necessarily imply the "denaturalization of nature" and that, on the contrary, it may very well be a "new affirmation of nature." This would be entirely consistent with Aristotle's definition of art (*technē*) as the means by which nature comes into its own by exceeding its natural state or form. In this definition, only by becoming something other, by becoming art, does nature fulfill the naturalness to which it is destined, and consequently only in the hands of humanity, in its *technē* or technique, can nature be exposed. It also links up to the Japanese composer Toru Takemitsu's ideas about nature: "I strive to create an unnatural environment in my own world. That is really a *natural* thing to do."[19]

If one follows Dufrenne's argument, only in the twentieth century was nature (including humanity) increasingly reduced to a mere object. Moreover, Cage himself repeatedly refers to the transformations of sounds by means of technology and mass media—phenomena that obviously do not belong to the Renaissance. As Douglas Kahn emphasizes:

Sounds proliferated by incorporating a greater diversity of cultural codes and worldly sources and generated still greater variety through internal means; the sheer number of sounds increased as they became freighted with multiple, shifting allusions and meanings. Sounds themselves took on multiple personalities, and the nature of sound became less natural. . . . Under the guise of a new aurality, an opening up to the sounds of the world, Cage built a musical bulwark against auditive culture, one founded on a musical identification with nature itself.[20]

One might presume, then, that Cage contrasts the Buddhist ideal of interpenetration and nonobstruction—as propagated by Suzuki—to the twentieth-century conception of nature as something entirely other or nonhuman. In relation to music, interpenetration and nonobstruction mean that intentional sound should not get in the way of another sound or silence, and silence should not get in the way of another silence or sound. Inversely, it means that sounds and silences may finally interpenetrate; all sounds and silences are equal and thus have the same value. Cage, however, formulates his assertions as if there were no reference to conditions in the twentieth century, as when he stresses that we should give up "everything that belongs to humanity—for a musician, the giving up of music," which will lead to "the world of nature, where, gradually or suddenly, one sees that humanity and nature, not separate, are in this world together."[21]

One presumes that his ideal of the dehumanization of sounds implies equally that humanity loses its power over "natural" sounds, which today for the most part have become subject to human manipulation. As time went on, Cage adopted an ambiguous attitude toward manipulated sounds. As Kahn writes: "Just as he incorporated noise as extra-musical sound into music, so too did he accommodate urban noise through acts of composition and musical listening."[22] Kahn does not hesitate to add that "Cage seeks a musical identification with nature, but . . . the nature he has in mind is exceedingly manipulated." Moreover, a similar ambiguity can be found in Cage's attitude toward musical instruments. Because of their determinate effects, he rejects any traditional musical instrument—"we must dispense with instruments altogether and get used to working with tools"[23]—while he ardently pleads for the use of technology (tape-recorders, loudspeakers, photoelectric cells) in music. Since electronic media can exist only on the basis of quantitative mathematics, and hence are a purely human construction and absolutely absent in nature, it is clear that the sound-transforming techniques of technology do more damage to sound's proximity of nature than any traditional instrument, so his rejection of former musical instruments is not altogether convincing.

Aesthetic of Absence

Apart from ambiguities regarding the historical implications of his work, one finds a mystification of Cagean silence at another level. As Cage increasingly engaged in musical silence, his initial criticism of society seemed to fade into the background. After visiting an anechoic chamber, a space in which all sounds are absorbed by the walls, Cage felt he had proven empirically that silence does not exist—in the sense of a situation in which there is no sound at all. In the anechoic chamber Cage expected to hear silence, but, as he wrote later, he heard two sounds, one high and one low. The engineer in charge informed him that the high one was his own nervous system, the low one the circulation of his blood. Cage had gone to a place where he expected complete silence, and yet sound was discernible. The conclusion he drew from this experience was that, in musical terms, conventionally intended silence indicated by pauses in scores turns out to be an illusion. In fact, as Cage suggests, those pauses are filled with sounds, "the sounds that happen to be in the environment."[24]

In asserting the identity of silence and sound, Cage was claiming that silence, as intended by composers in the past, turns out to be a relative concept; pauses in a composition create silence only in relation to the intended, that is, to the written sounds. But a pause in a composition does not create a pause in the totality of sounds in the world. That is why silence is an illusion, and that is why a pause in a composition is, as Cage emphasizes, a "so-called silence."[25] Calling silence in a musical work an illusion because it cannot completely silence sounds in the world outside the composition presupposes that the separation between the artwork and life is abandoned. When the performing musicians keep silent, the people in the concert hall produce the sounds. When traditional composers wrote pauses in their compositions, they did not think about the noises of the world. Their intentional object was limited to the composition. When the composition constitutes the intentional object and not "the world as a kind of total-object,"[26] a pause means silence. Cage's claim that a pause is only a so-called silence holds only insofar as the phenomenological concept of differentiality in intentionality has been abandoned and the world is considered as a raw sonorous unity. This is precisely what Cage wants. He writes: "Yes! I do not discriminate between intention and non-intention, the splits, subject-object, art-life, etc. disappear, and identification has been made with the material."[27]

In erasing the boundaries between art and life, Cage finds the ultimate disempowerment of the composer as well as of the performer, on the one hand, and the ultimate personal empowerment, on the other. He realizes this in the piece that turned the entire history of music composition upside down: the silence piece of 1952 entitled *4'33"*. The idea for the piece had occurred to him much earlier. In 1948, Cage wrote that he had the desire to "compose a piece of uninterrupted silence and sell it to the Muzak Co. It will be 3 or 4½ minutes long—these being the standards lengths of 'canned' music—and its title will be 'silent prayer.'" Although many people might embrace the idea of silent Muzak, it has probably never been bought by the Muzak Company. As Cage's favorite piece, *4'33"* would ultimately become the manifestation of his concept of silence as something that does not exist, never existed, and will not exist. The indeterminacy of the work becomes a means of manifesting the nonexistence of silence, that is, the work is reduced to sounds the composer cannot control, simply because he cannot know in advance what sounds may present themselves during a performance of the work.

Conclusion

Many twentieth-century spiritual composers share a rejection of the Enlightenment values associated with classical music. They seem convinced that since the seventeenth century, at least, humanity has lost something vital, and they believe that humanism and reason have blinded us to the sacred. In response, they seek to rediscover a sacred nature in music, beyond intellectual understanding. This turn to ancient religiosity, together with the rejection of rationalism, is not altogether surprising. Music has not been exempt from naïve scientific objectivism and the transformations of the world through technology. Excessive intellectualism contributed to a musical culture characterized by a lack of spiritual ideals, submission to materialism, and technicalism. This prompted composers to bring forth alternative attitudes. Yet the danger is that mysticism "can betray itself and deteriorate into self-deception, folly, and escapism. For mysticism can be and has been used simply to evade that which is frightening, confusing, or difficult *in* the social realm."[28]

The question remains whether Cage's (non)music, or silence, is—in addition to being an attempt to offer modern humankind a sort of formula for spiritual enlightenment—the most radical modernist response to the conditions of the twentieth century. Toru Takamitsu writes:

Significant in this century are the troubles brought on by modernization and the pessimism that developed along with technology. These things have ruled us beyond imagination.

Now we are in the midst of a potential war crisis symbolized by nuclear weapons. More-over, a distrust of things religious breeds a great pessimism, and feelings of powerlessness grip us. In such circumstances the great and immediate problem is survival.[29]

In calling his composed silence "new music" and "new listening," while substantiating this with quotes from Zen Buddhism and Meister Eckhart, Cage seemed reluctant to acknowledge the negativity at the heart of his work and, overlooking the critique immanent to it, dispossessed it of its historical meaning. What took place, then, was a twofold mystification of his ideas on silence: with reference to religiosity, Cagean silence literally has a mystical signification, with the result that the historical and critical implications of artistic silence are mystified as well. This twofold mystification of silence led to contradictions between his statements, on the one hand, and his work, on the other.

Is it not possible, then, that Cage's radical silence—"I have nothing to say, and I say it," he said—is in reality the most drastic means of survival or empowerment for a "disempowered" composer? Based on the motto "let the sounds be themselves," Cage made history as the first music composer who did not compose any music. His aim was, he suggested, to produce noth-ing (nothing more than nothing), or something, which for him is the same. The reason he gives for this is that "composing no music is easier than effectively composing music," "simpler, that is for me, because it happens that I write music."[30] He calls his disempowerment spiritual enlightenment. But from a historical perspective, his intentional silence can hardly be consid-ered other than the last convulsion of a composer who is silenced by his time and, consequently, as a desperate scream motivated by the eternal "Will to Power"—obstinately repressed by him but nevertheless discernable in his unintentional silence, that is to say, his project of the mysti-fication of silence. Cage devoted all of his intellectual capacity to convincing his audience of the importance of the revaluation of ancient mystical values of silence. In this, he unquestionably was driven by the ideal of "a better world," as he would often say. But, as I have attempted to demonstrate, precisely his dominant interest in relief through mysticism turned his eyes and ears away from a necessary critical approach to typical twentieth-century phenomena, such as technology, capitalism, pollution, and global oppression.

Cage's silent music, which is nothing but the absence of music, does express a certain refusal of contemporary culture. But at the same time it perfectly fits Debord's description of the modern artist who finds it "necessary to mask the real dialectic of modern art by reducing everything to a satisfying positivity of nothingness that justifies its own existence tautologically by the mere fact that it exists, which is to say that it is granted recognition within the specta-cle."[31] And Debord does not hesitate to add: "The emptiness of life must now be furnished with the emptiness of culture."[32]

Maternal Martyrdom

Alien3 and the Power of the Female Martyr

Laura Copier

One of the key Hollywood action heroines of the 1980s and 1990s is Lieutenant Ellen Ripley (played by Sigourney Weaver) of the science fiction film series *Alien*. More than any other genre, the science fiction film has served to reinforce stereotypical notions of masculinity and femininity; it is a subspecies even more thoroughly dominated by males than the Western is.[1] The character of Ripley has had a profound influence on the genre of the action film, to such an extent that she may serve as the prototype for a new female lead that differs from the typical science fiction and fantasy film heroine. The *Alien* series presents a strong woman who possesses several classic heroic traits: Ripley is smart, competent, moral, and courageous.

However, apart from these typical masculine qualities, Ripley also embodies a very feminine quality: a mothering instinct. This instinct was predominantly latent in *Alien*, although it almost got her killed as she searched for her lost cat.[2] In the sequel, *Aliens*, where Ripley discovers a little girl named Newt, she begins to transform from the accidental heroine of the first film into the Good Mother of the second.[3] The character Newt functions as a surrogate for that daughter. Ripley actively sets up a new nuclear family, consisting of herself, Newt, and Corporal Dwayne Hicks. At the end of the film, Ripley goes to great lengths to rescue her new "family" from the impending nuclear detonation of the planet. Unfortunately, Ripley's newly forged family is wiped out at the beginning of *Alien3*.[4] After the narrow escape at the end of *Aliens*, Ripley ends up all alone on a planet populated by monkish men only. Here, her femininity, read as the transgression of being a woman among men, becomes a pronounced aspect of her character.

More importantly, Ripley's perennial battle with the alien(s) reaches its climax. In the final scene of *Alien3*, which is the catalyst for this essay, Ripley dies a martyr's death. She willingly plunges to death in a cauldron of molten lead. The reason for her self-chosen death, particularly when viewed in terms of the entire trilogy of *Alien* films, is plain: Ripley carries an alien inside her; to make matters worse, it is on the verge of being born—that is to say, the alien will violently and lethally break out of Ripley's body, killing her in the process. This interiority of the alien is the final frontier for Ripley. Her battles against the aliens in the previous episodes of the saga were violent but clear-cut: the breed had to be annihilated by all means and at all costs. Here, Ripley's own life is directly implicated with the survival of the alien. In the end, Ripley is both the source of and the solution to the problem of the film. Her reproductive function provided the womb for the queen alien, while at the same time she is the only one capable of killing it.

The traumatic event of an alien birth is by no means novel within the *Alien* series; in the two preceding films several characters fell victim to this gruesome death. Ripley's destiny is cleverly foreshadowed in *Aliens*, when she—just awake after fifty-seven years of sleep—is troubled by the nightmare of herself giving birth to an alien.[5] *Alien3* finally displays this unthinkable act and, more importantly, the representation of Ripley's final act is influenced by intertextual and iconographical elements from classical martyrdom discourse. The question, then, when Ripley's martyrdom is read against classical martyrdom, is to what extent does this contemporary and popular representation reconfigure its historical predecessors?

Preposterous Constellations of Female Martyrs

In this essay, I will focus on the recycling of biblical and early Christian images and narrative structures regarding the end of time and martyrdom or self-sacrifice in contemporary Hollywood cinema. I intend to analyze to what extent representations of martyrs and self-sacrifice are informed by traditional religious notions of martyrs and self-sacrifice, and how these notions are reproduced but also transformed and redirected in the process of transmission. Hollywood cinema can be regarded as a site of reuse and reinterpretation of Christian and non-Christian visual and textual traditions. However, these adaptations and interpretations are performed within a secular, at least not (explicitly) religious system.

My methodological framework for integrating visual and linguistic traditions of interpretation will build on Mieke Bal's approach in *Quoting Caravaggio: Contemporary Art, Preposterous History*. Bal addresses a key question about representation in art. She states that art is inevitably engaged with what came before it and that that engagement is an active reworking. The question is: "Who illuminates—helps us understand—whom?"[6] One may adopt the traditional view, which regards ancient art as the source, a foundational influence on everything that follows in its wake. However, as Bal contends, "the problem with this view is that we can only see what we already know, or think we know."[7] This conception of the relationship between source and adaptation is based on recognition. To escape this deadlock between past and present, specifically the dominating influence of the past (what came first) over the present (what came later, or after), Bal proposes the term *preposterous history*. Preposterous history is "the reversal of what came chronologically first (pre-) as an aftereffect behind (post-) its later recycling."[8] The past should not be understood as a bound, coherent point of departure or origin, against which all later forms are to be evaluated. Rather, past and present engage in a dialogue, which brings about transformations between them. To set up such a dialogue between contemporary culture, in this case Hollywood cinema, and the art of the past, biblical images and stories, quotation can function as a mediator. Quotation, which consists of both iconography and intertextuality, can be defined as the recasting of past images, which not only is important to contemporary art but also affects the original source of the images, for which it, in turn, becomes a source. In the practice of quotation, we see preposterous history at work.

If one applies Bal's theory of quotation to *Alien*, certain elements of ancient religious texts exert their power in and on the new text. Therefore I will examine the influence of the precedent text. Once the historical source is traced, I will analyze in what ways the new text is an active intervention in the earlier material. And finally, I will attempt to define the transfers of meaning from past to present and from present to past. This implies a radical rethinking of Hollywood as a mere duplicator or recycler of "original" images and narrative structures. Here, one could perceive the original to be functioning as an aftereffect caused by the images of Hollywood cinema.

This article explores the representation of female martyrdom, exemplified by the case of Perpetua. The contemporary example of Ripley functions as my starting point in this exploration. My aim is not to contrast these female representations with representations of male martyrdom or to point out the difference between male and female martyrdom. Rather, female martyrdom, in my view, should be regarded as a separate entity. Its significance lies in the fact that women who chose the role of the martyr, determined by masculine values as this concept may be, in their act of martyrdom, at least temporarily, transgressed the prevailing binary.

Although some discursive elements of male martyrdom are relevant for female martyrdom as well, such as the defiance of authority and the manifestation of visions, a simple comparison between the two would reduce the significance of the female martyr. Specifically, I develop my position in contradistinction to Elizabeth Castelli's *Martyrdom and Memory: Early Christian Culture Making*, whose final assessment of female martyrdom deems it no more than a "Pyrrhic victory," meaning that women could endure the most gruesome acts of physical torture but in the end they still remained, and were valued by society as, women.[9] Instead, I would argue that these martyrs lay bare a gendered continuum between masculinity and femininity. The crucial marker of the female, the ability to have children, is a recurring element in classical martyr stories. The repetition of the maternal in contemporary martyr discourse is of particular interest to me.

Subsequently, the passion of Perpetua will be read against a secular and contemporary manifestation of female martyrdom: the final scene of *Alien3*. I address two readings of the *Alien* film series. The films of the *Alien* series have been subject to extensive analysis in film studies, particularly with regard to the representation of their female hero. Analogous to the classical martyrs, the character of Ripley, the self-sacrificial heroine of *Alien3*, is endowed with feminine as well as masculine traits. The two readings on which I focus appear to be different: while the first proposes a "positive" evaluation of the female heroine, the second uncovers a "fundamental problem" within the general representation of women in film, and hence cannot but be negative in conclusion. Yet the two readings share a common denominator: both highlight the conflation of the female with the maternal. The concept of the maternal functions here to address the representation of the female martyr, since notions of maternity shape both classical as well as contemporary instances of female martyrdom.

I contend that it is through the maternal, the figure of the mother, or put bluntly, the determinism of woman as mother, that the preposterous turn between past, the classical martyrs, and present, the character of Ripley, and vice versa can be made. In order to make that turn, I want to point out the a priori preposterous nature of the two components in my constellation of cultural texts. As Castelli argues, martyr stories exemplify the "culture making" dimensions of martyrdom that "depend upon repetition and dynamics of recognition."[10] The continual retelling and rereading of this story in literature as well as the visual arts raises the question of historical accuracy and the relevance of the past today. Castelli inquires into the status of the historical predecessor as well as into its "function as a meaningful resource for the present."[11] Castelli's argument has influenced my argument. Factual historicity recedes. The question of whether Perpetua, or any of the other classical martyrs, is an actual historical figure cannot be unequivocally answered. However, that question is irrelevant, Castelli argues, since the "commemorative narratives and representations take on lives of their own in rereadings, retellings, reinscriptions."[12] Crucial in this quote is the "lives of their own" these martyrs take on. These "lives" should be understood as ahistorical, that is to say, they exceed their historical context.

278

The crux of her argument regarding martyrdom and history resonates with my approach of history as preposterous in Bal's sense. If there is a history, Castelli claims, it "oscillates and adapts itself over time, sacrificing none of its authority in its changing focus, its amplification of details, and its *transformation* of its object."[13]

This formulation exemplifies the analytical usage of Bal's concept of preposterous history. Although my prime object, the contemporary manifestation of female martyrdom in Hollywood cinema, may be centuries away from Castelli's object, her method of reading the object—through quotation, citation, allusion, and iconography—is as relevant for my project as for hers. The discourse of martyrdom is so powerful and authoritative precisely because of its adaptability and, critically, the transformation of the object that it allows. The object is not just appropriated and translated, but changed inherently.

The second element in my preposterous constellation, the film *Alien3*, displays a similar form of historical transformation. The adaptability of the film rests on a particular technological quality, namely, the DVD player. I want to emphasize an important but often overlooked connection between the substance, the material of film—celluloid—and the analysis of film. In her book entitled *Death 24x a Second: Stillness and the Moving Image*, Laura Mulvey addresses the impact of the digital revolution on cinema.[14] New technologies such as video, but more importantly DVD, have transformed the way we experience film. The experience of watching a film on DVD is "far removed from that of the traditional cinema audience bound to watch a film in its given order at 24 frames a second," Mulvey claims.[15] A new kind of interactive spectatorship is introduced, as the viewer is capable of skipping, repeating, slowing down, speeding up, and reversing the traditional flow of cinema.

This type of spectatorship has implications, Mulvey argues, "for the cohesion of narrative, which comes under pressure from external discourses, that is, production context, anecdote, history."[16] This argument has far-reaching consequences for traditional methods of film theory and film analysis. The release of old films in a special edition format, which often includes restored and previously unseen material, Mulvey argues, "transforms the ways in which old films are consumed."[17] Moreover, a restored and extended version of a film can, and perhaps should, be a motivation for the analysis of a new—because transformed—object. Here one can observe the link between Castelli and Mulvey. In their work, they emphasize the transformative powers of, respectively, history and technology. I call the DVD an instance of preposterous technology. In the case of *Alien3*, one should reconsider earlier interpretations, since, thanks to the DVD, a crucial augmentation has been incorporated into the film text: an alternative ending that has not been seen before in the film version. Before discussing the preposterousness of the film, which is located in both its main character and its several endings, I will set out the preposterous history of the female martyr Perpetua.

Classical Female Martyrs and Martyrdom

In the Christian discourse of martyrdom, gender and power often work in conflicting ways. Although one can claim martyrdom to be what one commentator called an "equal opportunity employer" for women and men, martyrdom largely draws on and generates ideals of "masculinity."[18] In the historical context, martyr images frequently entail masculine notions of identity, such as gaining power over one's opponents, self-mastery, and endurance.[19] As Castelli remarks, "the martyr's death is a masculine death, even when (or perhaps especially when) it is suffered by a woman."[20]

However, Castelli continues, notions of masculine and feminine within the discourse of martyrdom are at the same time "ambivalent" and "unstable." Gender is "malleable" to a certain extent, because women can take on male characteristics. One explanation for this ambivalence resides in the status of gender as "a dimension of worldliness that can be left behind with enthusiasm and without regret," Castelli states. The spiritual act of martyrdom transcends the earthly sufferings of the flesh and renders that flesh, whether male or female, obsolete. However, Castelli adds, this dynamic at the same time preserves the intrinsic dichotomy between male and female: "the gender binary need not always be binding though its intrinsic value system . . . [yet] remains relentlessly intact."[21] Women can be martyrs on the condition that they abandon their femininity and adopt the masculine values of strength, endurance, and steadfastness. Hence, gender difference is at once transgressed and reaffirmed by the female martyr who dies like a man. Castelli's evaluation of martyrdom as a domain where gender rules may be transgressed, even though ultimately they are reaffirmed, opens up a range of possible readings of female martyrs. Here, the Christian martyr Perpetua serves as the basis for my discussion of female martyrdom.

The third-century Christian and partly autobiographical text *Passion of Perpetua and Felicitas* recounts the imprisonment, dreams, visions, and ultimate death in the arena of the young Roman Perpetua and the slave woman Felicitas. It is no exaggeration to claim that Perpetua is the most famous female martyr in Western culture, perhaps exceeded only by the illustrious Joan of Arc. The key point that I want to highlight is the gender transformation that Perpetua experiences in her vision the night before she is to be martyred. It is important to note that she undergoes a transformation in her way of thinking about herself as a woman and, crucially, as a mother. In Perpetua's account the reader can trace her decision to become a martyr and to break away from traditional female and family patterns. The case of Perpetua is thus useful in two ways: it serves as a classic instance of female martyrdom as well as an example of the complex association and connection between the feminine maternal and the masculine martyr.

The martyrdom of Perpetua has been the subject of much scholarly attention because it consists of an autobiographical section, the prison diary of Perpetua, and a prologue and epilogue written by an anonymous editor. Its authenticity generally undisputed, the diary presents the earliest extant writing by a Christian woman. Perpetua belonged to a group of Christians who were arrested and subsequently executed. In her diary Perpetua recounts the sufferings of prison life, her strained relationship with her father, who desperately tried to convince Perpetua to abandon her Christian faith, and, above all, the visions she receives. Especially her fourth vision has earned the attention of feminist scholars.

In this fourth and final vision, Perpetua finds herself in the arena facing an Egyptian opponent.[22] She is stripped of her clothes and at that moment discovers that she has become a man: "And I was stripped naked, and I became a man." So, in this dream, the physical markers of the male sex have replaced the markers of Perpetua's female sex. The implication of this change is that Perpetua's womanly weakness, a weakness that is taken to be physical as well as mental, is replaced by masculine strength, in the physical and mental way. Her mental strength and fervor, already immense, as the story time and again points out, is matched by an equally powerful physical strength. Perpetua's masculine mind, ready to face martyrdom, fits her male body, which will serve as the vehicle of that martyrdom. In the remainder of her vision, Perpetua defeats her Egyptian adversary by stepping on his head and leaves the arena victoriously through the Gate of Life. This divine vision provides Perpetua with the mental strength and conviction that she will be victorious in the case of the real execution, which will take place the next day.

According to the editor who introduces the account of Perpetua's death, she acted exceptionally bravely. The gladiator who was supposed to kill Perpetua was unable to do so.[23] Perpetua guided and steadied his sword to her neck, which the editor views as a truly courageous act: "Perchance so great a woman could not else have been slain . . . had she not herself so willed it."[24] Perpetua's shift from femininity to masculinity is different from Thecla's shift, in another early Christian martyr text, in that Perpetua undergoes a symbolic physical change. Her body takes on male characteristics in her vision, in contrast to Thecla, who hides the female characteristics of her body. Perpetua's masculine transformation also entails her repudiation of maternity, ultimately of her own child. Perpetua's body, from the onset of the story marked as a maternal body capable of having children and feeding them, is adjusted to her mind. As a result, after her vision, Perpetua's mind and body are aligned—they both have, in a symbolical manner, become masculine.

Margaret Miles provides an explanation for Perpetua's miraculous gender transformation. The metaphor of "becoming male" was frequently used for and used by women "who undertook to live an uncompromising Christian faith" and by women who "sought union with Christ in martyrdom."[25] Perpetua's vision seems directly related to this metaphor. More importantly, its physically powerful image provided her with the strength to prevail in the arena. In concordance with Miles's interpretation, Castelli argues that Perpetua's martyrdom problematizes conventional thought on the constrictions of gender: "Perpetua's spiritual progress is marked by the social moving away from conventional female roles."[26]

The text recounts how Perpetua, the daughter, moves away from her father, who begs her to give up her faith to survive persecution by the Roman authorities. In the final move, which completes Perpetua's detachment from femininity, she gives up her baby, refusing the maternal function.[27] Gradually stripping off what Castelli describes as "the cultural attributions of the female body,"[28] a process by which even the physical marks of femaleness have been removed, Perpetua is ready to enact her martyr's death. Here, the potential conflict between the roles of mother and martyr becomes apparent. Perpetua's story points to the incompatibility between these roles: mothers cannot be martyrs and vice versa. The two roles are mutually exclusive.

Perpetua may have been in doubt as to whether she should, or could, combine the roles of Roman mother and Christian martyr.[29] Initially, she had allowed her family to take care of her infant son, but after her sentencing she wanted to have her son with her in prison. Her father refused. From that moment, Perpetua is no longer a mother. She is strengthened in this decision by the appearance of a sign of divine approval: her baby has no more need of her breast. Unlike the mother of 4 Maccabees, she gives up her son and dies alone. So, Perpetua's story adds another characteristic to the female martyr: next to the renunciation of femininity, these women deal with the impossibility of being a mother and a martyr at the same time. Perpetua's vision of becoming male is a literal representation of this impossibility, whereas simultaneously the vision provides her a momentary way out of this impossibility, or suspends the impossibility temporarily. However, once Perpetua fulfills her actual martyrdom, both her femininity and her maternity are again important characteristics of the female martyr.

The Muscular Mother

The question I wish to address next is: How are these elements from the early discourse of female martyrdom reconfigured in contemporary and popular representations of female martyrdom? In the second part of this essay, I will contrast the contemporary representation of a female martyr, Ripley, to the classical portrayals of female martyrdom. Apart from Mulvey's work mentioned above, my reading of Ripley will be informed by two key books on cinema and femininity. The first is Yvonne Tasker, *Spectacular Bodies*, and the second is Barbara Creed, *The Monstrous-Feminine*.[30] Both are firmly positioned within the feminist project of analyzing representations of the feminine in cinema, and both address the connection between gender and genre. Tasker looks at the action cinema of the 1980s, whereas Creed studies both horror and, to a lesser degree, science fiction film.

It should come as no surprise that both authors address either the *Alien* series—a film series that not only perfectly displays the hybridization of the action, horror, and science fiction genre but also features a strong woman as its lead character—or *Alien3* in detail. Tasker and Creed are of particular interest to me, since they both investigate the concept of gender. Tasker's undertaking seems to be more positive in that she looks for representations that exceed the traditional representations of women in film. The advent of the female action hero, not unlike the female martyr, opens up and broadens traditional imagery. Creed strikes a more somber tone in her analysis of the female as monstrous; nevertheless, her interpretation of the maternal is indispensable to my reading of Ripley. In what follows, I will contrast the analyses of Tasker and Creed to my own reading of Ripley, which is influenced by these two readings but, crucially, also expands on them. After that, I will return to Mulvey's work to address the preposterous nature of cinema, *Alien3*, and particularly Ripley as a female martyr, in itself.

The muscular Hollywood cinema of the 1980s and 1990s, characterized by male stars such as Bruce Willis, Sylvester Stallone, and Arnold Schwarzenegger, is the focus of Yvonne Tasker's 1993 study *Spectacular Bodies*. Aware of the emergence of the female action hero as the center of the action narrative, Tasker decides to focus on the representation of masculinity and femininity in the genre. An important parallel between the values of the classical martyr and the contemporary action film hero must immediately be asserted. Both discourses emphasize the courage, steadfastness, determination, and physical strength of its respective "heroes." Yvonne Tasker's reading of *Alien* and *Aliens* focuses on the masculine or what she terms "musculine" nature of the heroine Ripley. The term "musculinity" to her suggests "the extent to which a physical definition of masculinity in terms of a developed musculature is not limited to the male body within representation."[31] Hence, Tasker argues, in certain cases female action heroes can be just as physically and mentally strong as their male counterparts. Her conclusion, "musculinity indicates the way in which the signifiers of strength are not limited to male characters," opens up the possible comparison between female martyrs and female action heroes.[32]

Tasker's concept of musculinity is indispensable for my discussion of female martyrs. It signifies the sliding scale between male and female aspects as well as the attendant notions of femininity and masculinity. As I have argued above, the classical female martyr stories transgress and modify gender categories. In this sense, the musculine character of Ripley can be seen as a contemporary representation of the earlier paradigm set by Perpetua. Ripley, as we shall see, resembles Perpetua in her exceptional courage and her problematic function as a mother. Yet, despite the representation of a strong, gun-wielding woman in the film, Tasker, rightfully yet with a tinge of disappointment, remarks that these types of heroines always at a certain point are connected to configurations of motherhood, or as she puts it, "the ways in which image-makers have dealt with the 'problem' of the action heroine, mobilizing configurations of motherhood."[33] The maternal is again a crucial element in the restriction of a femininity that attempts to go beyond its set limits. As a musculine heroine Ripley transgresses the limitations of her gender, Tasker argues, but only to a certain point. Eventually, the "maternal bond" is invoked and Ripley is as much maternal as she is musculine.[34]

Hence, maternity forms the outer boundary of the "musculinity" of female heroines like Ripley. Consequently, the three concepts that I will bring into play are musculinity, maternity, and martyrdom. If martyrdom in the classical estimation was open to women, it could only be achieved by letting go of typical feminine traits, most importantly motherhood. In Ripley, the reverse picture seems to emerge: motherhood and martyrdom are knotted together. She embraces her motherhood at the moment of her sacrificial death. This analysis points to a significant revision in the martyrological discourse discussed so far, which construes maternity and martyrdom as mutually exclusive.

Despite her musculine qualities, the character of Ripley is eventually put back into her feminine position. Ripley, as a pop culture symbol, or even an icon, offers a manifold and yet ambiguous image of femininity. Despite Ripley's transgressive qualities, what Tasker calls symbolic and iconographic transgression[35]—a strong woman at the narrative center of the action-adventure film—Ripley's character balances a strong maternal side with a musculine side. Hence, following Tasker's line of argumentation, one could read both films as representations of a brave woman who exhibits heroic qualities without sacrificing her nurturing ones. However, in what follows I would argue that the positive portrayal of a brave and heroic femininity in the first two *Alien* films is undercut by the final installment of the series.

In *Alien3* the rejection and derision of femininity is strongly motivated by the film's plot. Ripley finds herself stranded on the distant planet Fiorina 161, inhabited only by males, and dangerous ones to boot. The planet is a prison colony for rapists and murderers. With shaved heads, dressed in sackcloth, the men have taken a vow to have no contact with women. In this way, the film turns the prisoners into a group of monks. In addition, the prisoners have adopted an apocalyptic philosophy advocated by the spiritual leader of the prisoners, Dillon. The arrival of the woman Ripley—as well as the queen alien she is carrying inside her, unbeknownst to herself and the others—poses a threat to the closed community. The female outsider is viewed with a mixture of disgust and lust: she is repellent yet dangerously attractive to this group of rapists. Ripley's most visible sign of her femininity, her hair, is shaved off after her arrival—the prison complex is infested with lice—and the underwear she wore during her hypersleep is replaced with the standard sackcloth couture.[36] Ripley is rid of the external markers of her femininity in order to endure in an exclusively male environment. Despite these efforts to de-feminize Ripley, as Thomas Doherty argues in his essay on the *Alien* trilogy, her presence in this all-male environment "discombobulates the monastic social order."[37] Furthermore, in *Alien3*, the "de-sexing" of Ripley is a forced act of submission to the status quo.

The gender ambiguity as a result of such practices is, Castelli argues, generally taken as a sign of "special holiness."[38] The film certainly telegraphs, that is to say, makes visually palpable in practically every scene of the film, the singularity of Ripley. Yet her nascent holiness is not enacted until the very end. Instead, Ripley's curbed femininity is alluring: a group of prisoners attempt to rape her.[39] An enraged Dillon manages to save her in the nick of time. Later, the lethality of femininity is further articulated in a love scene between Ripley and Clemens, the prison doctor, who is also a prisoner (a slightly more privileged transgressor among transgres-sors): after they have made love, Clemens is "punished" for his offense and killed by an alien. Ripley's sexual ambiguity is coupled with the literal "killing off" of the romantic subplot.

Perhaps the word *romantic* is an ill-fitting adjective. As Doherty argues, "in the only inter-human sex act of the series, she [Ripley] coolly propositions and mates with Clemens."[40] Never-theless, these two instances of male sexual intrusion into the female body, with its lethal consequences, indicate the increasingly "untouchable" nature of the Ripley character.[41] Ripley's physical transformation, with its markers of untouchable holiness, is finally completed with the accompanying act that will conclude her conversion. Her death in the flames of the furnace is represented as a holy sacrifice, finishing the process of her becoming a holy woman or even a saint. The de-sexualized, masculine, musculine, holy body, which still holds the physical allure of the female body, as proposed by Tasker, stands in sharp contrast to the monstrous nature of female corporeality Creed suggests. The second reading of the *Alien* series that I will elaborate on, exemplified by Creed's work, stresses the hyper-feminine, monstrously maternal side of Ripley.

The Monstrous Mother

In her book entitled *The Monstrous-Feminine*, Barbara Creed discusses various representations of women as abject in horror film.[42] Vampires, witches, and the possessed woman, among others, constitute the appearance of the female monster or, as Creed calls it, the monstrous-feminine. The monstrous-feminine is not just a persistent character in horror films; it has a long history, ranging from classic mythology and the Bible to Freud. The recurring trait of the manifestations of the female monster, as of stereotypes of the feminine in general, Creed argues, is that woman is defined in terms of her sexuality. Creed's main point is that "when woman is represented as monstrous it is almost always in relation to her mothering and reproductive functions."[43] The abject in *Alien3* is connected with the monstrous act of childbearing. Ripley's act of voluntary death and the monstrous act of giving birth to the alien collide in the final scene of *Alien3*. The scene is a prime example of the tension between the female as strong and masculine and the female reduced to a particular bodily function and typified as abject. Tasker's reading of Ripley stresses maternity as the outer border of female "musculinity," the boundary that a heroic femininity may not cross. Motherhood "saves" Ripley from becoming too masculine. In Creed's reading, however, it is not so much gender transgression or ambivalence that is threatening, but the maternal itself that is disgusting or abject. As Creed asserts, "woman's birth-giving function has provided the horror film with an important source of its most horrific images."[44]

Creed refers to Julia Kristeva's theory of the abject and the maternal. In her book *Powers of Horror*, Kristeva formulates the concept of the abject as that which does not "respect borders, positions, rules"; that which "disturbs identity, system, order."[45] The abject body, as opposed to the clean and proper body, is a body that has lost form and integrity. In Kristeva's view, the image of woman's body, because of its maternal functions, acknowledges its "debt to nature" and consequently is more likely to signify the abject.[46] "The maternal womb," she argues, "represents the utmost in abjection for it contains a new life form which will pass from inside to outside bringing with it traces of its contamination—blood, afterbirth, faeces."[47] This capacity to transgress the border between the body's inside and outside is what makes the maternal womb the site of the abject.

The quadrilogy of *Alien* films, starting with *Alien*, followed by the sequel *Aliens* and *Alien3*—which was originally supposed to finish the series—and finally *Alien: Resurrection* effectively uses the associations of giving birth with the uncanny, the iconography of the intrauterine, and the alien.[48] The first two films explore the parallels between Ripley and the alien, yet *Alien3* takes the similarities between woman and monster to its logical conclusion. As I have mentioned, Ripley turns out to be impregnated by the alien.[49] She is carrying an alien queen, capable of giving birth to thousands of aliens, in her womb. The birth of the queen would mean the certain end of humanity. Here, the contours of Ripley's sacrifice and imminent martyrdom become apparent. Ripley has no other option than to abort the alien fetus, the contamination, the "foreign tissue" that has invaded her body, which means she will have to kill herself as well.[50]

As Creed remarks with regard to the final scene of *Alien3*:

In possibly the most stunning sequence in the *Alien* trilogy, Ripley throws herself backwards into the fiery furnace. A close-up shot reveals an expression of ecstasy on her face as she plummets backwards into the void. At the same time, the alien bursts forth. Ripley brings her arms forward, enclosing the *infant* queen in an embrace both *maternal* and murderous—an embrace that ensures the alien will die alongside its surrogate *mother*.[51]

Notice Creed's choice of words: "infant," "maternal," and "mother." In the context of Creed's analysis of this scene, with its emphasis on Ripley's maternal relationship to the alien, an important feature is finally integrated in the martyrdom discourse. The mutually exclusive concepts of martyrdom and maternity are forged together in Ripley's final act. The close, physical bond between Ripley and her monstrous offspring necessarily leads to the sacrificial ending of *Alien3*. The alien, emerging from Ripley's inmost parts, violently given birth to, is an irrevocable part of, Ripley herself. The demarcation between human and monster is transgressed to the extent that the mere killing of the monstrous infant would not suffice. Ripley's martyrdom resides precisely in the perverse negation of the border between human and not-human/monster, reinforcing Kristeva's reading of the maternal as abject. Ripley has served as a fertile womb for a monstrous other.[52] The possibility that she may give birth to the alien, and thus become the "godmother" of a new breed of aliens, leaves her no other option than to kill the thing that is most intimate to her while also most radically different.

It seems to me that, on the basis of Tasker and Creed's analysis of the *Alien* series, Ripley's transgressive potential resides in the permutation of two opposing elements, masculinity and femininity, here consistently figured as the monstrous maternal. On the one hand, Ripley moves away from maternity in favor of masculinity. Yet, as Tasker argues, maternity comes back to claim her as female. On the other hand, Ripley is too maternal. Or, as Creed would say, she is dangerous because of her maternal, reproductive potential. In a sense, both positions come down to the problematic, but somehow inevitable, relation between femininity and maternity. In her battle against the excessive manifestation of the maternal, the queen alien located inside her womb, Ripley seems to counter it by her own variety of equally lethal maternity. Her deadly embrace of the newborn alien queen simultaneously activates maternal as well as martyrlike images. Put differently, the maternal is a condition for her act of martyrdom. Unlike her previous encounters with the alien(s), where she was simply trying to annihilate them and make sure she herself got away safely, the fact that she has given birth to one of them makes her involvement in its total destruction a matter of life and death. Crucially, her maternal and reproductive connection with this breed of alien leaves her no other option than the self-chosen death of herself and her monstrous child. Thus, the significance of *Alien3* is located in the coupling of the mother and the martyr.

If the analysis of Ripley as a contemporary martyr would end here, one could contend that the preposterous turn has been rewarding: the earlier discourse of the classical martyr stories serves as the template for the later cinematic discourse of the *Alien* series, altering both discourses: Ripley is imbued with intertextual and iconographical characteristics of Perpetua, placing her in a line of female martyrs. The constellation of concepts that govern the construction of the female martyr—femininity, masculinity, and maternity—are reconfigured in the Ripley character and her final act. In turn, the classical martyr Perpetua can be preposterously read as a representation of gender crossing and, more specifically, as displaying signs of musculinity. The maternal aspect, explicitly present in the case of Perpetua, is similar to Ripley's maternity and equally ambiguous. The classical conception of the coupling of martyrdom and maternity deemed the two mutually exclusive. The contemporary conception of the strong, masculine yet maternal woman as hero and martyr, exemplified in the work of Tasker and Creed, turns out to be just as problematic. Either the masculine/musculine is eventually kept at bay through the maternal, as Tasker argues, or the maternal turned monstrous simply overshadows all other characteristics a woman may have, as Creed maintains.

My analysis of Ripley would be positioned between the classical and the contemporary conceptions. Arguing against Tasker, I would say that the maternal does not merely function as a device to curb too much musculinity, or put the transgressive woman back in her "natural," nurturing position. Rather, the maternal enforces the musculine traits of Ripley; specifically, in the very musculine aspect of the severe physical pain that she has to endure. Similarly, Creed's accentuation of the monstrous maternal as all encompassing takes away the courageous nature of Ripley's humanitarian act—an act performed to counter directly the potential lethal fertility principle of the alien. The character of Ripley and the act of martyrdom she performs seem to me to supersede previous readings. She is positioned neither on the side of the masculine nor on the reductive side of the maternal. However, my analysis does not stop at this particular ending of *Alien3*. One more analytical turn must be made.

Preposterous Technology and Alternative Endings

In the opening to this essay, I mentioned Laura Mulvey's argument that the digital technology of the DVD has a major impact on the viewing and analysis of film. Films in a digital format, in contrast to celluloid, are capable of reversing the flow of spectatorship and academic analysis. This reversal of a flow is in itself preposterous; it challenges the common perception that films and analyses have a clear-cut beginning, middle, and end—the idea that films have stable endings and academic articles have logical conclusions. Endings, both in film as well as in academia, signal a definite stop to the processes of viewing and analyzing. However, the advent of digital film opens up the possibility of slowing down, speeding up, repeating, skipping, and looking again at the separate images that constitute the medium. Hence, a clear ending is never fully reached and can be postponed perpetually. Moreover, the digital format not only allows for the interruption and the reversal of the flow of images, it also frequently adds new textual streams to the already-existing film text. With regard to *Alien3*, both these possibilities of the digital format, the reversal of the flow and the addition of new text, can lead to a new analysis of the film. As I hope to show, the addition of an alternative ending to the existing film text fundamentally challenges previous analyses of the film, including my own.

At the time of the film's release in 1992, it was widely reported that the studio Twentieth Century Fox had taken *Alien3* out of director David Fincher's hands before its theatrical release and reedited the film without his consent. In 2003, the *Alien Quadrilogy* DVD box set and special edition was released. This special edition contains the theatrical release as well as an alternative "work print" cut of *Alien3*. This work print, previously unavailable, is the closest approximation of Fincher's original vision of the film.

The ending of the film was much discussed during production. The most important difference between the 1992 theatrical version (111 minutes long) and the 2003 special edition / work print (139 minutes) is the sacrificial ending. In the special edition version, the scene where Ripley falls into the molten lead—and this is the crucial difference—contains no shot of the alien (in *Alien* terminology called a "chestburster") emerging from her body. The focus of the discussion was precisely whether the alien in Ripley's body should emerge at the end of the film. In all, according to James Swallow, whose book on David Fincher charts the troubled production process of *Alien3*, there were no fewer than four different versions of the ending.[53] In the first version, the alien emerges first, and then Ripley dives into the molten metal. In the second version, the alien does not emerge. Instead, blood blooms out of Ripley's chest as she is falling. This ending was discarded as being "too religious . . . and vulgar."[54] This second version appears to have been shot by Fincher, but so far these outtakes are not available.

In the third ending, chosen for the theatrical version (TV), the alien emerges during Ripley's fall. In contrast, the fourth ending, the work print ending that is available on the special edition release of the film (SE), refrains from showing the alien altogether. Moreover, the scene in which Ripley makes her final decision to drop into the lead is longer: she needs more time to build up her courage. The subsequent death scene consists of an alternate take: the alien does not burst forth from her body, Ripley seems more lifelike (in contrast to the obvious puppet used in the original shot), the fall is much shorter and takes place in slow motion, and Ripley's body can be seen to burn up just before it hits the lead.

Thus, the crucial difference between these two versions (the TV and SE versions) is tied to the decisive choice between showing and not showing the alien. Before I turn to that discussion, though, an iconographic consequence of this presence and absence needs to be noted. The fact that the alien bursts out in the theatrical version forces Ripley to struggle with it. She clutches the creature to her breast to prevent it from jumping away from her. However, if we remember Creed's analysis of this particular part of the climax of *Alien3*, a different reading can be posited. Creed perceives what I label a struggle not as a struggle but in terms of maternal love, lethal love, but maternal love nonetheless.

In the SE version Ripley neither wrestles with nor cradles the alien, because it is absent. This absence, however, produces a postural, physical difference in Ripley's death dive. She plummets into the fire with her arms outstretched. This signifies and underscores two connotations. First, stretching the arms is associated with the joy of deliberately jumping from great heights, as in bungee jumping. The person jumping stretches out in order to fully experience the sensation of flight. As such, this gesture emphasizes the voluntary and conscious dimension of Ripley's act. Second, extending both arms instantaneously triggers an iconographical association with Christ's crucifixion. Thus, in the SE version, the voluntary and martyrlike nature of Ripley's choice is accentuated by the nonappearance of the alien. This absence causes the entire mother/maternal association to remain absent. In this version, Ripley is more a martyr than a mother. More important, though, is that the SE ending reaffirms and reiterates the classical discourse on female martyrdom, precisely because the maternal aspect in Ripley's martyrdom is absent. Instead, she is depicted as the strong, conscious, determined, and, above all, active creator of her own destiny.

Finally, I want to look in more detail at the consequences the presence or absence of the alien has for the reading of the martyrdom of Ripley. The first choice is whether the alien should burst out of Ripley's chest at all, thus giving the audience the paradigmatic thrill and satisfaction of the horror film's gory finale. The second decision is whether Ripley should dive *before* the manifestation of the beast or *after* it has revealed itself.

The chain of events is open to several variations, and when we compare these three versions, Ripley's act of martyrdom takes on different implications. Fincher was strongly in favor of not showing the alien, simply because he thought it was not necessary. In addition, Fincher supported Ripley's willfully, proactively, taking her life *before* the creature bursts out: "if she gets ripped apart before she falls into the fire, that's not sacrifice, that's janitorial service. To knowingly step into the void carrying this thing inside her seemed to me to be more regal."[55] The essential word Fincher uses in his description of the meaning and purpose of the final scene is *sacrifice*. Ripley's death should be self-chosen and actively pursued. Her act of deliberately falling, arms outstretched, into the fire bestows upon her the noble status of the martyr; she is not the passive victim of a monster that is stronger than she is. Thus, Ripley should demonstrate the agency and self-mastery to destroy her body. Eventually, the theatrical ending adheres to this scenario, yet at the same time it grants the audience the spectacle of the chestburster: the creature emerges from Ripley's chest during her fall. This ending seems a perfect Hollywood compromise. However, as a result—and this can be observed in Creed's analysis of this scene—the theatrical ending activates the seemingly inevitable return to the archetype of the mother and child. By comparing Ripley with the unfortunate mother of the monstrous child, the alien, Creed and the film effectively restore Ripley to the maternal function. In Creed's analysis, Ripley's monstrous maternity eclipses the sacrificial nature of her act.

I would, however, posit a more ambivalent reading of the theatrical ending of the film, particularly when compared to the SE version. In contrast to the SE ending, which reaffirms a classical martyr discourse, the maternity evoked in the TV version signals a preposterous vacillation between past and present representations of martyrdom. On the one hand, this ending reconnects Ripley as a female heroine to motherliness, which, according to both Tasker and Creed, is ideologically cumbersome. But on the other hand, and this is the point I wish to stress, Ripley's maternal aspect reconceives classical martyrdom discourse, which presupposes that mothers cannot become martyrs, only women made male can become martyrs. In this sense, a motherly martyr critically reconceives that older discourse: the mother and the martyr become newly related in distinction to the classical examples. Critically, Ripley's maternity does not take away from her martyr's act of self-sacrifice for humanity. In consequence, the potential reduction of Ripley to her assigned gender position of the archetypal mother is effectively dislocated: in her final sacrificial act, mother and martyr are not parted but imparted.

Notes

Introduction, by Meerten B. ter Borg and Jan Willem van Henten

1. Directed by Tom Shadyac, screenplay by Steve Koren, Mark O'Keefe, and Steve Oedekerk, Spyglass Entertainment/Universal, 2003.

2. Further discussion can be found in Jan Willem van Henten, "Playing God in the Movies: *Bruce Almighty* and the Preposterous History of Genesis 1:26–27," in *Creation and Creativity: From Genesis to Genetics and Back*, ed. A. Hunter and C. Vander Stichele (Sheffield: Phoenix Press, 2006), 125–41.

3. See, e.g., Frank J. Manuel, *The Prophets of Paris* (Cambridge: Harvard University Press, 1962).

4. See Talal Asad, ed., *Anthropology and the Colonial Encounter* (London: Ithaca Press, 1973), and Peter Pels and Oscar Salemink, eds., *Colonial Subjects: Essays on the Practical History of Anthropology* (Ann Arbor: University of Michigan Press, 1999).

5. See Peter L. Berger, *The Desecularization of the World: Resurgent Religion and World Politics* (Grand Rapids, Mich.: Eerdmans, 1999).

6. See Hent de Vries, ed., *Religion: Beyond a Concept* (New York: Fordham University Press, 2008). De Vries's "Introduction: Why Still Religion?" to this first volume in The Future of the Religious Past series discusses some of the various approaches to "religion" and arguments concerning its presence in the contemporary world.

7. On the ambiguity of religion, see esp. R. Scott Appleby, *The Ambivalence of the Sacred: Religion, Violence, and Reconciliation* (Lanham, Md.: Rowman & Littlefield Publishers, 2000).

8. For assessments of the different conceptions of religion and of power, see, e.g., Jan G. Platvoet and Arie L. Molendijk, eds., *The Pragmatics of Defining Religion: Contexts, Concepts and Contests* (Leiden: Brill, 1999). For definitions of power, see: Stewart R. Clegg, David Courpasson, and Nelson Phillips, *Power and Organizations* (London: Sage, 2006), and Stewart R. Clegg, *Frameworks of Power* (London: Sage, 1989).

9. See Thomas Hobbes, *Leviathan*, ed. C. B. McPherson (Harmondsworth, Middlesex: Penguin, 1968).

10. Karl Marx and Friedrich Engels, *The Communist Manifesto* (New York: Penguin, 1998).

11. Juergensmeyer's article can be considered a synthesis of his previous work about religion and violence, as elaborated in his *Terror in the Mind of God: The Global Rise of Religious Violence* (Berkeley: University of California Press, 2003).

12. Jan Willem van Henten, "Internet Martyrs and Violence: Victims and/or Perpetrators?" in *Sanctified Aggression: Legacies of Biblical and Post-Biblical Vocabularies of Violence*, ed. Jonneke Bekkenkamp and Yvonne Sherwood (London: Continuum, 2004), 193–212. See also the paper by Anna-Karina Hermkens in this volume.

13. Max Weber, *Wirtschaft und Gesellschaft* (Tübingen: J. C. B. Mohr–Paul Siebeck, 1922), 310.

14. See Mieke Bal and Miguel Á. Hernández-Navarro, *2MOVE: Video, Art, Migration* (Murica, Spain: Cendeac 2008).

15. Appleby, *Ambivalence of the Sacred*, 28. Appleby also makes a (normative) distinction between "strong religion" and "weak religion," depending upon the position of religious actors, especially leaders. "Strong religion" presupposes that religious institutions are well developed and secure, that adherents are "literate" in doctrinal and moral teachings, that there is a plurality of interpretations as well as respect for nonbelievers, that its informed interpreters counter religion's capacity for violence, and that they establish a tradition of education in the theology of peace, moral formation in peace building, and training in conflict resolution (ibid., 75–79).

16. Manuel Castells, *The Information Age: Economy, Society and Culture*, 3 vols. (Oxford: Blackwell, 1996–98).

The Recovery of Perverted Religion: Internal Power Processes and the Vicissitudes of Religious Experience, by André Droogers

1. Gabriel García Márquez, *Collected Stories* (New York: Harper Perennial Classics, 1999), 247–54. The full text can also be found at http://iws.ccccd.edu/jmiller/handsome.htm (accessed October 10, 2006). Rubem Alves (*The Poet, the Warrior, the Prophet* [London: SCM, 2002], 23–24) uses the same story but with a different analysis. For the sake of the argument, I have adopted some of the changes Alves introduces in Márquez's story and have also added some elements myself.

2. See André Droogers, "The Power Dimensions of the Christian Community: An Anthropological Model," *Religion: A Journal of Religion and Religions* 33, no. 3 (2003): 263–80.

3. André Droogers, "Symbols of Marginality in the Biographies of Religious and Secular Innovators: A Comparative Study of the Lives of Jesus, Waldes, Booth, Kimbangu, Buddha, Mohammed and Marx," *Numen* 27, no. 1 (1980):105–21.

4. Roland Barthes, *Livres, Textes, Entretiens, 1977–1980*, vol. 5 of *Oeuvres complètes* (Paris: Seuil, 2002), 431–32.

5. Linda Sexton, *Ordinarily Sacred* (Charlottesville: The University Press of Virginia, 1982), 34.

6. Mario Quintana, *Caderno H* (Porto Alegre: Globo, 1983), 54. My translation.

7. Sally McFague, *Metaphoric Theology* (London: SCM, 1983), 13.

8. Karla Poewe, "On the Metonymic Structure of Religious Experiences: The Example of Charismatic Christianity," *Cultural Dynamics* 2, no. 4 (1989): 361–80.

9. For a useful overview, see: Barbara Boudewijnse, "The Conceptualization of Ritual: A History of Its Problematic Aspects," *Jaarboek voor Liturgie-onderzoek* 11 (1992): 31–56.

10. William James, *The Varieties of Religious Experience: A Study in Human Nature* (1902; New York: Mentor Books, 1958). See also Birgit Meyer, "Religious Sensations: Why Media, Aesthetics, and Power Matter in the Study of Contemporary Religion," in *Religion: Beyond a Concept*, ed. Hent de Vries (New York: Fordham University Press, 2008), 706–7.

11. André Droogers, "Methodological Ludism: Beyond Religionism and Reductionism," in *Conflicts in Social Science*, ed. Anton van Harskamp (London: Routledge, 1996), 53.

12. Victor Turner, *The Anthropology of Performance* (New York: PAJ Publications, 1989), 25, 169.

13. André Droogers, "Syncretism," in *International Encyclopedia of the Social and Behavioral Sciences* (London: Elsevier, 2001), 15386–88.

14. André Droogers, "Syncretism and Fundamentalism: A Comparison," *Social Compass* 52, no. 4 (2005): 463–71.

15. André Droogers, "Defining Religion: A Social Science Approach," in *The Oxford Handbook of the Sociology of Religion*, ed. Peter Clarke (Oxford: Oxford University Press, 2009), 263–79.

16. Stanley Johannesen, "Third-Generation Pentecostal Language: Continuity and Change in Collective Perceptions," in *Charismatic Christianity as a Global Culture*, ed. Karla Poewe (Columbia: University of South Carolina Press, 1994), 175–99.

17. Allan Anderson, *An Introduction to Pentecostalism: Global Charismatic Christianity* (Cambridge: Cambridge University Press, 2004), 1.

18. Els Jacobs, "The Feminine Way 'O Jeito Feminino': Religion, Power and Identity in South Brazilian Base Communities," Ph.D. thesis (Amsterdam: Vrije Universiteit, 2002), 151.

Symbolic Violence: Religion and Empowerment, by Mark Juergensmeyer

1. Interview with Abdul Aziz Rantisi, co-founder and political leader of Hamas, Khan Yunis, Gaza, March 1, 1998. By "religion," in this essay I mean the traditions of religious symbols.

2. Cynthia Keppley Mahmood, *Fighting for Faith and Nation: Dialogues with Sikh Militants* (Philadelphia: University of Pennsylvania Press, 1996), 188.

3. Interview with Takeshi Nakamura, Tokyo, January 12, 1996. See the full interview with Nakamura (a pseudonym) in my book *Terror in the Mind of God: The Global Rise of Religious Violence* (Berkeley: University of California Press, 2003), 106–13.

4. See ibid., 124–28.

5. Interview with Mahmud Abouhalima, convicted co-conspirator in the 1993 World Trade Center bombing, at the federal penitentiary, Lompoc, California, September 30, 1997.

6. For recent scholarship on religion and sacrifice, see, e.g.: Maurice Bloch, *Prey into Hunter* (Cambridge: Cambridge University Press, 1992); René Girard, *Violence and the Sacred*, trans. Patrick Gregory (Baltimore: Johns Hopkins University Press, 1977), and idem, *The Scapegoat*, trans. Yvonne Freccero (Baltimore: Johns Hopkins University Press, 1986); Walter Burkert, *Homo Necans: The Anthropology of Ancient Greek Sacrificial Ritual and Myth*, trans. Peter Bing (Berkeley: University of California Press, 1972); Walter Burkert, René Girard, and Jonathan Z. Smith, *Violent Origins: Ritual Killing and Cultural Formation*, ed. Robert G. Hamerton-Kelly (Stanford: Stanford University Press, 1987); Eli Sagan, *The Lust to Annihilate: A Psychoanalytic Study of Violence in Ancient Greek Culture* (New York: The Psychohistory Press, 1972), and idem, *Cannibalism: Human Aggression and Cultural Form* (New York: Psychohistory Press, 1974). For a review of some of the scholarship, see Richard D. Hecht, "Studies on Sacrifice, 1970–1980," *Religious Studies Review* 8, no. 3 (1982): 13–19.

7. Sigmund Freud, *Totem and Taboo: Some Points of Agreement Between the Mental Lives of Savages and Neurotics*, trans. James Strachey (1913; New York: W. W. Norton and Co., 1962).

8. See, e.g., Henri Hubert and Marcel Mauss, *Sacrifice: Its Nature and Function* (1898; Chicago: University of Chicago Press, 1964).

9. Tim LaHaye and Jerry Jenkins, *Left Behind: A Novel of the Earth's Last Days* (Carol Stream, Ill.: Tyndale House Publishers, 1996). This is the first in the series; the twelfth, and presumably last, was

published in 2004. Since then a new series has begun, a kind of prequel to the original series, published under the heading *Before They Were Left Behind*.

10. Juergensmeyer, *Terror in the Mind of God*, 148–66.

11. Shoko Asahara, *Disaster Approaches the Land of the Rising Sun: Shoko Asahara's Apocalyptic Predictions* (Shizuoka, Japan: Aum Publishing Company, 1995).

12. See Ian Reader, *Religious Violence in Contemporary Japan: The Case of Aum Shinrikyo* (Honolulu: University of Hawai'i Press, 2000), and my case study of Aum in *Terror in the Mind of God*, 103–18.

13. St. Augustine, *City of God* (New York: Modern Library, 1994). Originally written in Latin sometime after the fall of Rome to the invading Goths in the fifth century.

14. The literature on just-war theory is considerable. See, e.g., Michael Walzer, *Just and Unjust Wars* (New York: Basic Books, 1977), and John Kelsay and James Turner Johnson, eds., *Just War and Jihad* (Boulder, Colo.: Greenwood Press, 1991).

15. Reinhold Niebuhr, "Why the Christian Church Is Not Pacifist," in *The Essential Reinhold Niebuhr*, ed. Robert McAfee Brown (New Haven: Yale University Press, 1987). Originally published in *Christian Century* in 1940.

16. Girard, *Violence and the Sacred*.

17. Gandhi, writing in *Young India*, September 23, 1926. I explore Gandhi's ideas further in my book *Gandhi's Way: A Handbook of Conflict Resolution* (Berkeley: University of California Press, 2005, rev. ed.).

Political Theology: The Authority of God, by Avishai Margalit

1. Carl Schmitt, *Political Theology: Four Chapters on the Concept of Sovereignty*, trans. George Schwab (Cambridge: MIT Press, 1985), 36.

Explaining the Global Religious Revival, by Talal Asad

NOTE: This essay first appeared in *Religion and Society*, ed. Gerrie ter Haar and Yoshio Tsuruoka (Leiden: Brill, 2007), 83–103. It appears here by permission of Koninklijke Brill NV.

1. Barbara Crossette, "Study Warns of Stagnation in Arab Societies," *The New York Times*, July 2, 2002; Thomas Freedman, "Editorial Desk" section, *The New York Times*, July 3, 2002.

2. And yet some years previously Friedman had noted with great satisfaction that "in the globalization system, the United States is now the sole and dominant superpower and all other nations are subordinate to it to one degree or another" (Thomas L. Friedman, *The Lexus and the Olive Tree* [New York: Farrar, Strauss and Giroux, 1999]). If this relationship has any meaning, it signifies a continuous intervention in the conditions of life of subordinate nations—by economic, cultural, and military means. Clearly the hostilities expressed in those nations toward America are not unrelated to its status as "the sole and dominant superpower." But then clarity of thought has never been one of Friedman's great virtues.

3. For the Egyptian situation in the seventies and eighties, see Heba Handoussa, "Crisis and Challenge: Prospects for the 1990s," in *Employment and Structural Adjustment: Egypt in the 1990s*, ed. H. Handoussa and G. Potter (Cairo: AUC Press, 1991). See also the empirically useful—but theoretically often questionable—comparative study by Clement Henry and Robert Springborg, *Globalization and the Politics of Development in the Middle East* (Cambridge: Cambridge University Press, 2001).

4. It has been claimed, incidentally, that such economic improvements as there have been recently in Egypt can be attributed to the large amount of aid received from the United States. But in reply it has been pointed out that, although U.S. aid was useful in improving Egyptian infrastructure, most of the aid money has gone back to the States because it was tied to American goods (including military hardware) and American consultants. Perhaps the most significant consequence of the aid for Egypt's political economy has been the emergence of local businessmen loyal to U.S. interests. Thus the way this aid has been given and used has reinforced class privileges in Egypt and the spread of American consumer culture.

5. The Egyptian political economist Galal Amin has written an incisive critique of the report's methodology, entitled "al-Taghrib wa-l-ightirab fi taqrir al-tanmiya al-insaniyya al-'arabiyya," in *Wajhat Nazar* 4, no.46 (November 2002). Among other things, he argues that the indices chosen by the report reflect not merely "deficits" in Arab society—as explicitly intended by its authors—but political economic pressures from a co-opting world power: the United States.

6. Gilles Kepel was one of the first to describe this repression in his *The Prophet and the Pharaoh* (London: Saqi Books, 1985).

7. A classic study of the movement is Richard Mitchell, *The Society of the Muslim Brothers* (Oxford: Oxford University Press, 1969); a useful study of the militants who broke away from the mainstream Muslim Brothers in an extremist direction is Kepel, *The Prophet and Pharaoh.*

8. See Olivier Roy, *Globalized Islam: The Search for a New Ummah* (New York: Columbia University Press, 2004).

9. The European Council for Fatwa and Research attempts to deal with this dual belonging at the level of "the jurisprudence of Muslim minorities" (*fiqh al-aqalliyāt*). See its Web site: www.ecfr.org.

10. This is the view of specialists on contemporary Islam such as Gilles Keppel.

11. The destruction of human lives and property carried out by U.S. occupying forces in Iraq is as striking, in its own way, as the murder and mayhem perpetrated by the insurgents.

12. See, e.g., the work of Gema Martin-Munoz, who makes a strong case for explaining the Islamic revival in terms of cultural identity.

13. The classical Arabic word for "to give" is the same as the word for "to guide"—*hada*—and it occurs with great frequency throughout the Qur'an. It is central to the opening chapter of the Qur'an, the *fatiha*, recited in every prayer, and is the object of subsequent writing, both pietistic and theological. Gratitude is continually expressed for God's gifts (*ni'māt*) in everyday formulas (e.g., *al-hamdu lillah*). Another verb used in the Qur'an for giving is *a'tā*, having the general sense of giving a thing—and sometimes of endowing it with an attribute. God gives life to things and gives them their nature. If God's guidance is a gift to the faithful Muslim, it addresses him or her uniquely, describing the way to follow the nature of things. Gifts are, however, ambiguous: although they are given gratuitously and received freely, they must not be rejected, and—as the anthropologist Marcel Mauss first pointed out—they have the power to draw a return. Because gifts have this power, they may (like all powerful things) be dangerous. But the gifts that God bestows on mankind cannot be reciprocated in kind: humans cannot give God any*thing* because he lacks no*thing*. Humans can, nevertheless, give thanks (*shukr*) for his bounty and an acknowledgment of obligation—which in relation to God means willing obedience.

14. I borrow this idea of enchantment from Jane Bennett's *The Enchantment of Modern Life* (Princeton: Princeton University Press, 2001). Bennett points out that enchantment as a mode of being in the world is present in a positive way in secular modernity.

15. The Qur'an refers many times to God's "signs" (*ayāt*) in the world, and commentators usually regard this as its attempt to persuade by reference to evidence. Since all the "signs" referred to in the

Qur'an were familiar to early listeners, and since most later Muslim listeners needed no convincing of its divine status, I think more is involved here than an exercise in forensics. Many Muslim readers of the Qur'an regard the reference to these signs as an invitation to listeners to participate in "wondrous encounters" through an alert use of their senses.

16. See, e.g., the religious scholar Amy Hollywood, who in "Gender, Agency, and the Divine in Religious Historiography," *Journal of Religion* 84, no. 4 (2004), wrestles with the old question "How seriously should one take the beliefs of religious subjects?" through the social science binary between describing (including mistaken beliefs) and explaining (scientifically valid accounts). She turns to the distinction between History 1 (the history of capital and of progressive liberation, based on homogeneous time) and History 2 (the history of precapitalism, based on beliefs about the supernatural and on nonhomogeneous time) made by the postcolonial historian Dipesh Chakrabarty. This allows her to make a plea for listening to discourses that are disruptive of rational history but that at the same time don't close off the possibility of criticizing obstacles to liberation. (Chakrabarty speaks of a dialectic between History 1 and History 2.) Hollywood is right to worry about these things, but her solution doesn't seem to me satisfactory because it doesn't go beyond an assertive moralism. She needs to consider why she *wants* to write something that is disruptive of "rational" history and why "liberation" matters. What are the stakes here?

17. See, e.g., Sayyid Yasin et al., eds., *al-Turāth wa tahadiyyāt al-'asr fi al-watan al-'arabi aw al-asāla wa al-mu'āsira* (Beirut, 1985). The secularist Yasin engaged in a well-known debate with the moderate Islamist Kamal Abu Magd (founder of the Centre Party, *hizb al-wasat*, which the government has refused to register) in the columns of the daily paper *al-Ahram*—May 30, June 8, June 20, 1994.

18. For a well-known discussion of this assumption in modern Western culture, see Lionel Trilling, *Sincerity and Authenticity* (Cambridge: Harvard University Press, 1972).

19. Various professional syndicates (lawyers, doctors, engineers) are important centers of Islamist opposition.

20. Herbert Butterfield's well-known comment is especially apposite here: "The issue between Protestants and Catholics in the sixteenth century was an issue of their world and not of our world, and we are definitely being unhistorical, we are forgetting that Protestantism and Catholicism have both had a long history since 1517, if we argue from a rash analogy that the one was fighting for something like our modern world while the other was trying to prevent its coming" (*The Whig Interpretation of History* [New York: W. W. Norton, 1965], 36–37).

21. The most famous argument along these lines is, of course, Thomas S. Kuhn, *The Structure of Scientific Revolutions* (Chicago: University of Chicago Press, 1962).

22. Peter L. Berger, "The Desecularization of the World: A Global Overview," in *The Desecularization of the World: Resurgent Religion and World Politics*, ed. Peter L. Berger et al. (Grand Rapids, Mich.: W. B. Eerdmans, 1999), 11.

23. Karen Armstrong, "Spiritual Prozac," *New Statesman and Society*, July 21, 1995.

24. David Harvey, *The Condition of Postmodernity: An Enquiry into the Origins of Cultural Change* (Oxford: Blackwell, 1991), 41. Harvey's particular reference here is to the Catholic theologian Rocco Buttiglione, whom he regards as an influential spokesman for one stream of "postmodernism." Although Harvey is critical of "postmodernist" thought, he sees it as a *symptom* of something real—a shift in the political economy of late capitalism. He proposes that a great range of disparate developments, styles, and attitudes should be brought together under a single name ("postmodernity") and that *that* singularity is a symptom of "a loss of faith" on the part of members of the New Left who have been seduced by it (see,

e.g., 353–55). In other words, he suggests that there *is* a crisis of Enlightenment thought—a general loss of faith in universal reason and emancipation—but maintains that "postmodernists" fail to identify its singular (material) cause.

25. Colin Campbell, *The Romantic Ethic and the Spirit of Modern Consumerism* (Writersprintshop, 2005).

26. In an intriguing article entitled "Enlightenment Fears, Fears of Enlightenment," Lorraine Daston writes: "In keeping with the opposition of natural facts to human artifacts, the errors that most terrified Enlightenment savants in theory and practice were errors of construction, the fear of fashioning a world not reflected in sensation but made up by the imagination. Sensory infirmities worried Enlightenment epistemologists relatively little, prejudices and misconceptions instilled by bad education rather more so, the distortions wrought by strong passions still more, and the unruly creations of the imagination most of all" (in *What's Left of Enlightenment?* ed. Keith M. Baker and P. H. Reill [Stanford: Stanford University Press, 2001], 118–19). For Enlightenment epistemologists, then, "religion" (an unruly creation of the imagination) constituted an obstacle to the sound accumulation of "facts."

27. Lorraine Daston, "Scientific Error and the Ethos of Belief," *Social Research* 72, no. 1 (2005).

28. See Gerhard Oestreich, *Neostoicism and the Early Modern State* (Cambridge: Cambridge University Press, 1982), esp. chap. 3, "The Main Political Work of Lipsius." For the Neostoics, the state's neutrality toward the religious beliefs of its subjects is a second-best solution for securing stable power: the best is an enforced religious uniformity.

29. But even classical Qur'anic exegetes have recognized that the Qur'an consists of clear passages (*nusūs*) and obscure ones (*mutashābihāt*), which are subject to various interpretations.

30. See Baber Johansen for an elaboration of this point in *Contingency in a Sacred Law* (Leiden: Brill, 1999).

31. Talal Asad, "Anthropological Conceptions of Religion: Reflections on Geertz," *Man* 18 (1983); *Genealogies of Religion: Discipline and Reasons of Power in Christianity and Islam* (Baltimore: Johns Hopkins University Press, 1993); "On Re-reading a Modern Classic: W. C. Smith's *The Meaning and End of Religion*," *History of Religions* 40, no. 3 (2001), reprinted as "Reading a Modern Classic: W. C. Smith's *The Meaning and End of Religion*," in *Religion and Media*, ed. Hent de Vries and Samuel Weber (Stanford: Stanford University Press, 2001), 131–47.

Seeing Nationhood: Images of American Identity, by David Morgan

1. The first phrase is from John Winthrop's sermon of 1630 on the *Arbella*, the ship bringing colonizers to Massachusetts Bay; the second is from President Woodrow Wilson's request to Congress on April 2, 1917, to declare war on Germany—Woodrow Wilson, *War Messages*, 65th Cong., 1st Sess. Senate Doc. No. 5, Serial No. 7264, Washington, D.C., 1917, p. 5.

2. Letter to John Canfield, January 6, 1783, quoted in Harlow Giles Unger, *Noah Webster: The Life and Times of an American Patriot* (New York: John Wiley & Sons, 1998), 59.

3. Washington Irving, "Rip Van Winkle," in *The Complete Tales of Washington Irving*, ed. and introd. Charles Nieder (New York: Da Capo Press, 1998), 10.

4. Christopher Looby, *Voicing America: Language, Literary Form, and the Origin of the United States* (Chicago: University of Chicago Press, 1996), 95.

5. On illustrated religious texts and antebellum American understandings of the nation and its purpose, see David Morgan, *Protestants and Pictures: Religion, Visual Culture, and the Age of American Mass-Production* (New York: Oxford University Press, 1999), 13–39; on illustrated schoolbooks and related iconography, see David Morgan, "For Christ and the Republic: Protestant Illustration and the History of Literacy in Nineteenth-Century America," in *The Visual Culture of American Religions*, ed. David Morgan and Sally M. Promey (Berkeley: University of California Press, 2001), 49–67.

6. For a detailed discussion of the importance of the image of Washington in American public culture, see Karal Ann Marling, *George Washington Slept Here: Colonial Revivals and American Culture, 1876–1986* (Cambridge: Harvard University Press, 1988).

7. Instructive studies of state iconography and the ceremonial use of art and architecture in Washington are: Vivien Green Fryd, *Art and Empire: The Politics of Ethnicity in the U.S. Capitol, 1815–1860* (New Haven: Yale University Press, 1992), and Jeffrey F. Meyer, *Myths in Stone: Religious Dimensions of Washington, D.C.* (Berkeley: University of California Press, 2001).

8. See the illustration heading chapter 38 of the edition published by John P. Jewett in 1853.

9. On the visual portrayal of African Americans in the nineteenth century, see Albert Boime, *The Art of Exclusion: Representing Blacks in the Nineteenth Century* (Washington, D.C.: Smithsonian Institution Press, 1990). For a discussion of Thomas Ball's Freedman's Monument, see Kirk Savage, *Standing Soldiers, Kneeling Slaves: Race, War, and Monument in Nineteenth-Century America* (Princeton: Princeton University Press, 1997), 89–92, and 89–128 for placement of this monument within the larger national campaigns to memorialize emancipation.

10. Admiral [David] Porter, *Incidents and Anecdotes of the Civil War* (New York: D. Appleton and Company, 1885), 295.

11. Ibid.

12. Ibid., 296.

13. Frederick Douglass, "Oration on the Occasion of the Unveiling of the Freedmen's Monument," in *Masterpieces of Negro Eloquence 1818–1913*, ed. Alice Moore Dunbar (Mineola, N.Y.: Dover Publications, 2000), 91.

14. Ibid., 92.

15. Eugene Lawrence, "The European Congress," *Harper's Weekly* 22, no. 1122 (June 29, 1878): 511.

16. See W. N. Medlicott, *The Congress of Berlin and After: A Diplomatic History of the Near Eastern Settlement, 1878–1880* (London: F. Cass, 1963), 6–7, 206.

17. For extensive discussion of this trope, see Brian W. Dippie, *The Vanishing Indian: White Attitudes and U.S. Indian Policy* (Lawrence: University Press of Kansas, 1982).

18. "Address of the Rev. Samuel Eastman," *American Tract Magazine* 2, no. 7 (June 1827): 166. For an instructive discussion of photographs of Native Americans as the "vanishing race," see Martha A. Sandweiss, *Print the Legend: Photography and the American West* (New Haven: Yale University Press, 2002), 217–19, 249–54, 260–66.

19. Ibid., 167.

20. Katherine Bowden was the lecturer; see a publicity memo of September 12, 1951, in the Bowden Papers, Valparaiso University.

21. In his famous "I have a dream" speech, delivered from the steps of the Lincoln Memorial in Washington, D.C., on August 28, 1963, King urged his audience to "continue to work with the faith that unearned suffering is redemptive."

22. Adam Badeau, *The Vagabond* (New York: Rudd & Carleton, 1859), 123.

23. Ibid., 124. An insightful study of American landscape painting and the national mythos is Angela Miller, *The Empire of the Eye: Landscape Representation and American Cultural Politics, 1825–1875* (Ithaca: Cornell University Press, 1993).

24. Badeau, *Vagabond*, 125.

25. Quoted in Andrew Wilton and Tim Barringer, *American Sublime: Landscape Painting in the United States 1820–1880* (London: Tate Publishing, 2002), 138.

26. Rev. W. W. Everts, "The Social Position and Influence of Cities," in *Words in Earnest* (New York: Edward H. Fletcher, 1851), 11.

27. John Steinbeck, *The Grapes of Wrath* (New York: Viking, 1989), 301.

28. Ibid., 341.

29. Ibid., 527. Cf. the words of Jesus: "Father, forgive them; for they know not what they do," Luke 23:34.

30. Steinbeck, *Grapes of Wrath*, 175.

31. Philip K. Dick, *Blade Runner (Do Androids Dream of Electric Sheep)* (New York: Ballantine Books, 1968), 119.

32. Ibid., 124.

33. On Iturbide and her photographs, see *Images of the Spirit: Photographs by Graciela Iturbide* (New York: Aperature, 1996).

The Visible and the Invisible in South Asia, by Peter van der Veer

NOTE: This paper was first given as a key-note address at a conference entitled Secularism, Religious Nationalism, and the State: Visual Practices and Public Subjects, organized at the American University of Beirut in April 2005. I want to thank Dr Maha Yahya for her invitation.

1. Marc Shell, *Children of the Earth: Literature, Politics, and Nationhood* (New York: Oxford University Press, 1993.)

2. See my discussion of Habermas and Koselleck in "Secrecy and Publicity in the South Asian Public Arena," in *Public Islam and the Common Good*, ed. Armando Salvatore and Dale Eickelman (Leiden: Brill, 2004), 29–53.

3. Benedict Anderson, *Imagined Communities* (London: Verso, 1991).

4. See my discussion in *Religious Nationalism* (Berkeley: University of California Press, 1994).

5. Talal Asad, *Genealogies of Religion: Discipline and Reasons of Power in Christianity and Islam* (Baltimore; Johns Hopkins University Press, 1993).

The Power of Mary in Secessionist Warfare: Catholicism and Political Crisis in Bougainville, Papua New Guinea, by Anna-Karina Hermkens

NOTE: The research on which this article is based was made possible by the Netherlands Organisation for Scientific Research (NWO) and the Institute for Gender Studies and the Department of Cultural Anthropology at the Radboud University Nijmegen. Parts of this article have been published in Anna-Karina

Hermkens, "Religion in War and Peace: Unraveling Mary's Intervention in the Bougainville Crisis," *Culture and Religion* 8, no. 3 (2007): 263–76.

1. Volker Böge and Lorraine Garasu, "Papua New Guinea: A Success Story of Post-conflict Peacebuilding in Bougainville," in *Searching for Peace in Asia Pacific: An Overview of Conflict Prevention and Peacebuilding Activities*, ed. Annelies Heijmans, Nicola Simmons, and Hans van de Veen (London: Lynne Rienner Publishers, 2004), 565.

2. Marilyn Taleo Havini, "The Role of Bougainville Women in the War and Peace Process," in *Building Peace in Bougainville*, ed. Geoff Harris, Naihuwo Ahai, and Rebecca Spence (The Centre for Peace Studies, University of New England, Australia, and the National Research Institute, 1999), 39.

3. Böge and Garasu, "Peacebuilding in Bougainville," 570.

4. The Koromira district has been renowned for its support for the secessionist movement, and it harbors many ex–BRA combatants.

5. Robert Orsi, "Everyday Miracles: The Study of Lived Religion," in *Lived Religion in America: Toward a History of Practice*, ed. David Hall (Princeton: Princeton University Press, 1997), 3–21.

6. Donald Denoon, *Getting under the Skin: The Bougainville Copper Agreement and the Creation of the Panguna Mine* (Melbourne: Melbourne University Press, 2000).

7. Anthony J. Regan, *The Bougainville Conflict: Origins and Development, Main "Actors," and Strategies for Its Resolution* (Faculty of Law, University of Papua New Guinea, 1996), 71. In 2005, ten billion kina equaled approximately 2.4 billion euros.

8. Andy Carl and Lorraine Garasu, "Chronology," in *Weaving Consensus: The Papua New Guinea–Bougainville Peace Process*, ed. Andy Carl and Lorraine Garasu, special issue, *Accord: Informing and Strengthening Peace Processes* 12 (London: Conciliation Resources, 2002): 96.

9. Ibid.

10. Anthony J. Regan, "Why a Neutral Peace Monitoring Force? The Bougainville Conflict and the Peace Process," in *Without a Gun: Australians' Experiences Monitoring Peace in Bougainville, 1997–2001*, ed. Monica Wehner and Donald Denoon (Canberra: Pandanus Books, 2001), 2. Douglas Oliver, *Black Islanders: A Personal Perspective of Bougainville 1937–1991* (Melbourne: Hyland House, 1991), 21–56, argues that the colonial and recent oppression by white missionaries, plantation owners, and colonial administration added to the growing antiwhite and anticolonial sentiments among Bougainvilleans.

11. In 1962, a UN visiting mission to Bougainville heard its inhabitants' grievances, and speakers asked that the UN mandate be transferred from Australia to the United States.

12. James Griffin, "Napdakoe Navitu," in *Micronationalist Movements in Papua New Guinea*, ed. R. J. May, Political and Social Change Monograph 1 (Canberra: Research School of Pacific Studies, Australian National University, 1982), 113–38.

13. In this process, the name *North Solomons* was adopted.

14. Regan, "Why a Neutral Peace Monitoring Force?" 3.

15. Patrick F. Gesch, "'We have our own ways too'—The Dilemma of Reconstruction on Bougainville," *Contemporary PNG Studies: DWU Research Journal* 2 (2005): 95.

16. Patrick Howley, *Breaking Spears and Mending Hearts: Peacemakers and Restorative Justice in Bougainville* (London: Federation Press, 2002), 33.

17. Ibid., 34–35.

18. Ibid., 27.

19. Regan, "The Bougainville Conflict," 71–72.

20. Ibid., 10, and Howley, "Breaking Spears," 41, 43–53.

21. Regan, "Why a Neutral Peace Monitoring Force?" 10–14. Peter Sohia, "Early Interventions," in *Weaving Consensus: The Papua New Guinea–Bougainville Peace Process*, ed. Andy Carl and Lorraine Garasu, special issue, *Accord: Informing and Strengthening Peace Processes* 12 (London: Conciliation Resources, 2002): 16–23, analyzes the various negotiations between Bougainville and the Papua New Guinea government from the 1980s to the mid-1990s. He argues that, despite the collapse of all of these efforts and repeated returns to violence, they form part of an important cumulative process toward peace.

22. Although it was agreed that the Panguna mine will not reopen and the Papua New Guinea national government, which maintains control of mining operations in the autonomous province, has placed a moratorium on all further mining at Panguna, recent leaders of the AGB have suggested that the mine should be reopened to finance the costly rebuilding of Bougainville.

23. Anthony Regan, "Bougainville: Beyond Survival," *Cultural Survival Quarterly* 26, no. 3 (2002). Today, Dameng's ideas are upheld mainly in the no-go zones (the Panguna mine in central Bougainville and the Buin area in the south), which are sealed off from the rest of Bougainville by the Me'ekamui government. However, especially in the districts of Kieta and Koromira, many people adhere to (parts of) Dameng's and Ona's ideology.

24. James Tanis, "Reconciliation: My Side of the Island," in *Weaving Consensus: The Papua New Guinea–Bougainville Peace Process*, ed. Andy Carl and Lorraine Garasu, special issue, *Accord: Informing and Strengthening Peace Processes* 12 (London: Conciliation Resources, 2002): 60.

25. Ibid.

26. Bronwen Dougles, "Power, Discourse and the Appropriation of God: Christianity and Subversion in a Melanesian Context," *History and Anthropology* 9, no. 1 (1995): 57.

27. Tanis "Reconciliation," 60.

28. Elizabeth Ibua Momis, "The Bougainville Catholic Church and 'Indigenisation,' " in *Bougainville Before the Conflict*, ed. Anthony J. Regan and Helga M. Griffin (Canberra: Pandanus Books, The Australian National University, 2005), 326.

29. Slightly less than one percent reported themselves as non-Christians, and another two percent did not indicate a religion (National Statistical Office, *2000 National Census: North Solomons Provincial Report* [Port Moresby: National Statistical Office, 2002], 19).

30. H. Laracy, *Marists and Melanesians: A History of Catholic Missions in the Solomon Islands* (Canberra: Australian National University, 1976), 54–55.

31. M. O'Callaghan, *Enemies Within: Papua New Guinea, Australia and the Sandline Crisis, The Inside Story* (Sydney: Doubleday, 1999), 17.

32. In June 2006, Father Unabali became auxiliary bishop of Bougainville.

33. One year later, on April 30, 1998, a ceasefire agreement was signed by all parties, officially ending the crisis. Obviously, the crisis did not end this simply. Although a treaty was signed, Ona was not present, as he stayed out of the peace process. The BRA was represented by BRA leaders Sam Kauona and the current president of the ABG, Joseph Kabui. Moreover, hostilities between various Bougainville groups continued. Nevertheless, among Catholics there is a general conviction that the pilgrimage of the statue of Fatima marked a turning point in the crisis.

34. Shane McLeod, "Bougainville—The Man Who Would Be King," foreign correspondent ABC broadcast, May 17, 2005, http://www.abc.net.au/foreign/content/2005/s1372909.htm (last visited October 13, 2006).

35. "Ona's Legacy Still Lives," *Post Courier* 4, August 2006, http://www.postcourier.com.pg/20060804/frhome.htm (last visited October 13, 2006).

36. Thomas J. Csordas, *Language, Charisma, and Creativity: The Ritual Life of a Religious Movement* (Berkeley: University of California Press, 1997), 205.

37. Ruddy Doom and Koen Vlassenroot, *Kony's Message: A New Koine? The Lord's Resistance Army in Northern Uganda* (Oxford: Oxford Journals / Royal African Society, 1999), 98.

38. Ibid.

39. Mircea Eliade, *The Sacred and the Profane: The Nature of Religion* (New York: Harper & Row, 1961).

40. Wayne Coles-Janess, "Interview with Francis Ona," *World in Focus*, broadcast, March 4, 1997.

41. Jill Nash, "The Red and the Black: Bougainvillean Perceptions of Other Papua New Guineans," *Pacific Studies* 13, no. 2 (1990): 1–17.

42. Rosemary Radford Ruether, "Christians Must Challenge American Messianic Nationalism: A Call to the Churches," 2004, http://www.psr.edu/page.cfm?l = 62&id = 1802 (last visited June 12, 2006).

43. Max Watts, "The Napoleon of Mekamui: Francis Ona's Role and Plekhanov," *Counterpunch*, July 30/31, 2005, http://www.counterpunch.org/watts07302005.html (last visited October 15, 2006).

44. Nigel Cooper, *The Bougainville Land Crisis of 1969*, Macmillan Brown Occasional Paper Series 31 (Christchurch, New Zealand: Macmillan Brown Centre for Pacific Studies, University of Canterbury, 1992).

45. Over time, the aims of the organization became directed toward greater self-determination for Bougainville, including independence from Papua New Guinea. The Napidakoe Navitu group thus appears to have become integrated into the wider autonomy movement of Bougainville. See Oliver, "Black Islanders," 184–85, and Griffin, "Napdakoe Navitu," 113–38.

46. Thomas Hylland Eriksen, *Ethnicity and Nationalism: Anthropological Perspectives*, 2d ed. (London: Pluto Press, 2002), 107.

47. See also Marjo de Theije, "Local Protest and Transnational Catholicism in Brazil," *Focaal* 47 (2006): 77–89, and Dougles, "Power, Discourse and the Appropriation of God," 57.

48. Anna-Karina Hermkens, "Religion in War and Peace: Unravelling Mary's Intervention in the Bougainville Crisis," *Culture and Religion* 8, no. 3 (2007): 263–76.

49. Andrew Lattas, *Cultures of Secrecy: Reinventing Race in Bush Kaliai Cargo Cults* (Madison: University of Wisconsin Press, 1998), 267.

50. Michael W. Young, "Commemorating Missionary Heroes: Local Christianity and Narratives of Nationalism," in *Narratives of Nation in the South Pacific*, ed. Ton Otto and Nicholas Thomas (Newark, N.J.: Harwood Academic Publishers, 1997), 91.

51. Anthony D. Smith, *Chosen Peoples: Sacred Sources of National Identity* (Oxford: Oxford University Press, 2003), 15.

52. Bruce Kapferer, *Legends of People, Myths of State: Violence, Intolerance and Political Culture in Sri Lanka and Australia* (Washington, D.C.: Smithsonian Institute Press, 1988). Kapferer's emphasis on the religious aspects of nationalism is described by Eriksen, "Ethnicity and Nationalism," 106, 111.

53. Margaret Jolly, "Woman-Nation-State in Vanuatu: Women as Signs and Subjects in the Discourses of *Kastom*, Modernity and Christianity," in *Narratives of Nation in the South Pacific*, ed. Ton Otto and Nicholas Thomas (Newark, N.J.: Harwood Academic Publishers, 1997), 133–34.

54. F. B. Bird, "Charisma and Leadership in New Religious Movements," in *Handbook of Cults and Sects in America*, vol. B, ed. D. G. Bromley and J. K. Hadden (Greenwich, Conn.: JAI, 1993), 76.

55. D. Madsen and P. Snow, *The Charismatic Bond* (Cambridge: Harvard University Press, 1991).

The Mourid Brotherhood at the Center of Senegalese Political Life: A Dialectic of State and Religious Power, by Cheikh Guèye and Olivia Gervasoni

1. A movement named "and japalé Abdoulaye Wade nguir Serigne Touba [together support Abdoulaye Wade for Serigne Touba]" was formed in 2001 to uphold Wade's electoral ambitions.

2. Fernand Dumont, *La pensée de Cheikh Amadou Bamba, fondateur du mouridisme sénégalais* (Dakar: Les Nouvelles Éditions Africaines, 1975), 47.

3. The name *dahira* refers to a sort of religious council that also deals with social affairs, a Mourid association attempting to establish in towns a spirit of solidarity and the collective practice of shared beliefs.

4. Christian Coulon, *Le marabout et le prince (Islam et pouvoir au Sénégal)* (Paris: Pédone, 1981); D. B. Cruise O'Brien, *The Mourids of Senegal: The Political and Economic Organization of an Islamic Brotherhood* (Oxford: Oxford University Press, 1971).

5. Interview with Ousseynou Fall, General Secretary for the Citizens' Movement, Dakar, May 17, 2001.

6. Ibid.

7. Ibid.

8. Interview with Ibrahima Sall, General Secretary for RAMOU (Mourid gathering), an organization renamed Tawfikhoul Hady, grouping together personalities from the brotherhood (marabouts, businessmen, political leaders, men in different legal domains, international consultants) whose stated objective is to carry out lobbying and bring about action for the development of the town of Touba, Dakar, April 19, 2001.

9. Interview with Madické Wade, campaigner for the Citizens' Movement, Saint-Louis, May 9, 2001.

10. Interview with Atou Diagne, President of the Hizbut Tarqiyya, Dakar, April 2, 2001.

11. These subjects were interviewed in Dakar on the following dates: Madické Niang, March 25, 2001; Souleymane Ndéné Ndiaye, March 23, 2001; Moustapha Sourang, June 8, 2001; Modou Diagne Fada, May 2, 2001; Kansoumbaly Ndiaye, April 25, 2001; Oumar Sarr, May 16, 2001; Ablaye Faye, June 6, 2001.

12. These subjects were interviewed in Dakar on the following dates: Serigne Abdou Fatah, May 23, 2001; Madior Bouna Niang, May 16, 2001; Cheikh Bamba Sall, May 5, 2001; Modou Amar, May 4, 2001.

13. These subjects were interviewed in Dakar on the following dates: Boubakar Thioube, May 14, 2001; Talla Sylla, May 31, 2001.

14. Moriba Magassouba, *L'Islam au Sénégal, demain les mollahs? La question musulmane et les partis politiques au Sénégal de 1946 à nos jours* (Paris: "Les Afriques," 1985), 212.

15. Ibid., 212n6.

16. Amadou Diaw, Pape Diop, Pape Souleymane Kandji, Samba Thiam, "L'état Mouride se resserre autour de Me Wade," *L'Info 7*, Dakar, no. 619 (October 27, 2000): 3–4.

Sharia and State in the Sudan: From Late Colonialism to Late Islamism, by Shamil Jeppie

1. A more correct transliteration of *sharia* would be *sharī'ah*, but I have adopted a simplified form in this essay. The word is conventionally translated "Islamic law," although it literally means "the path," as in "the path to the water."

2. See Sayyid Abu Rannat, "The Relationship Between Islamic and Customary Law in the Sudan," *Journal of African Law* 4, no. 1 (1960): 9–16, and Zaki Mustafa, *The Common Law in the Sudan: an Account of the "Justice, Equity and Good Conscience Provision"* (Oxford: Oxford University Press, 1971).

3. See, e.g., the discussion in the penultimate and final chapters of Wael Hallaq, *A History of Islamic Legal Theories* (Cambridge: Cambridge University Press, 1997).

4. Cited in Ali Suleman Fadlalla, "The Development of the Legal System in the Sudan since Independence," in *Law, Society, and National Identity*, ed. J. M. Abun-Nasr et al. (Hamburg: Helmut Buske Verlag, 1990), 199–209.

5. For an introduction to these schools, see N. J. Coulson, *An Introduction to Islamic Law* (Edinburgh: Edinburgh University Press, 1964).

6. On the application of these legal techniques, called *talfiq* and *takhayyur*, see ibid., 185–201 and 208.

7. Carol Fluehr-Lobban, *Islamic Law and Society in the Sudan* (London: Frank Cass, 1987).

8. Heather Sharkey-Balasubramanian, "The Egyptian Colonial Presence in the Anglo-Egyptian Sudan 1898–1932," in *White Nile, Black Blood*, ed. Stephanie Beswick and Jay Spaulding (Lawrenceville, N.J.: Red Sea Press, 1999).

9. The Egyptian Grand Qadis in the Sudan were: Shaykh Muhammad Shakir (1900–4), Sh. Muhammad Harun (1904), Sh. Mustafa al-Maraghi (1904–19)), Sh. Muhammad Amin Quraa (1919–32), Sh. Nuaman al-Jarim (1932–41), Sh. Hasan Mamun (1941–47), Sh. Hasan Muddathir (1956).

10. See Mustafa, *The Common Law in the Sudan*.

11. Sections 5 & 9 of the Civil Justice Ordinance of 1929 (previously sections 3 & 4 of CJO of 1900) read: "Where in any suit or other proceedings in a civil court any question arises regarding succession, inheritance, wills, legacies, gifts, marriage, family relations, or the constitution of wakfs the rule of decision shall be: (a) any custom applicable to the parties concerned, which is not contrary to justice, equity and good conscience, and has not been by this or any other enactment altered or abolished and has not been declared void by decision of a competent court; (b) the Mohammedan Law, in cases where the parties are Mohammedans, except in so far as that law has been modified by such custom as above mentioned."

12. See *The Laws of Sudan*, vol. 2, title 28: *sharia*.

13. Between 1902 and 1979, sixty-two circulars were issued. They have all been translated and published in Carolyn Fluehr-Lobban and Hatim Babiker, "Circulars of the Shari'a Courts in the Sudan (Manshurat el-mahakim el-shari'a fi Sudan), 1902–979," *Journal of African Law* 27, no. 2 (1983): 79–140.

14. Salman M. A. Salman, "Lay Tribunals in the Sudan: An Historical and Socio-legal Analysis," *Journal of Legal Pluralism* 21 (1983): 61–128.

15. Sharkey-Balasubramanian, "The Egyptian Colonial Presence."

16. Mudadthir 'Abd al-Rahim, *Imperialism and Nationalism in the Sudan: A Study in Constitutional and Political Development 1899–1956* (Oxford: Oxford University Press, 1969), 51.

17. See A. H. M. Kirk-Greene, *The Sudan Political Service: A Preliminary Profile* (Oxford: Oxford University Press,1982).

18. Mahmood Mamdani, *Citizen and Subject: Contemporary Africa and the Legacy of Late Colonialism* (Oxford: James Currey, 1996).

19. 'Abd al-Rahim, *Imperialism and Nationalism*, 70.

20. Salman, "Lay Tribunals in the Sudan."

21. Cited in 'Abd al-Rahim, *Imperialism and Nationalism*, 103.

22. Yoshiko Kurita, *Ali Abd al-Latif wa thawra 1924* (Cairo: 1997).

23. A. H. M. Kirk-Greene, *Nationalism and Arcadianism in the Sudan: The Janus Factor in the Political Service Memoirs* (Oxford: Oxford University Press, 1993).

24. 'Abd al-Rahim, *Imperialism and Nationalism*, 127.

25. Salman, "Lay Tribunals in the Sudan."

26. Abdel Salam Sidahmed, *Politics and Islam in Contemporary Sudan* (Richmond: 1997), 45.

27. Salman, "Lay Tribunals in the Sudan," and 'Abd al-Rahim, *Imperialism and Nationalism*.

28. Mustafa, *The Common Law in the Sudan*, chap. 8.

29. For a survey of how recent scholars have dealt with the question of *ijtihad* ("exercise of independent judicial judgment"), see Hallaq, *Introduction to Islamic Legal Theories*.

30. Martin Daly, "The Transfer of Power in the Sudan," in *Decolonization and African Independence: The Transfer of Power 1960–1980* (New Haven: Yale University Press, 1988), 185–97.

31. 'Abd al-Rahim, *Imperialism and Nationalism*, 226.

32. Nikolas Rose, *Powers of Freedom: Reframing Political Thought* (Cambridge: Cambridge University Press, 1999), 27.

33. For a report on the faculty of law, see W. L. Twining, "Legal Studies at the University of Khartoum," *Journal of African Law* 6, no. 2 (1962): 145–49. The author reports that more than 50 percent of the students took five years for the four-year LLB; then the course was extended to five years. The first doctorate was awarded in 1961, for a thesis on Islamic law.

34. Salman M. A. Salman, "Legal Profession in the Sudan: A Study of Legal and Professional Pluralism," in *Lawyers in the Third World: Comparative and Developmental Perspectives*, ed. C. J. Dias et al. (Uppsala: Scandinavian Institute for African Studies, 1981), 226–47.

35. Ibid.

36. Ibid.

37. Salman, "Lay Tribunals in the Sudan."

38. Abdullahi Ahmed An-Na'im, "Constitutionalism and Islamization in the Sudan," *Africa Today* 36, nos. 3 and 4 (1989): 11–28.

39. On this incident, see Gabriel Warburg, *Islam, Nationalism, and Communism in a Traditional Society: The Case of Sudan* (London: Frank Cass, 1978), 116–17.

40. See Sidahmed, *Politics and Islam*, 89–94.

41. See Hasan al-Turabi, "The Islamic State," in John Esposito, *The Voices of Resurgent Islam*, ed. John Esposito (New York: Oxford University Press, 1983), 241–51.

42. See Abdelwahab El-Affendi, *Turabi's Revolution: Islam and Power in Sudan* (London: Grey Seal, 1991), and Hasan al-Turabi's interview in Mohamed E. Hamdi, *The Making of an Islamic Political Leader: Conversations with Hasan al-Turabi* (Boulder, Colo.: Westview Press, 1998), 25.

43. See chap. 4 of Sidahmed, *Politics and Islam*.

44. On this period, see N. A. Akolawin, "Sudan," in *Annual Survey of African Law*, vol. 5 (1971), and Akolawin on Sudan in ibid., vol. 6 (1972): 36–49.

45. Akolawin, "Sudan."

46. Salman, "Legal Profession in the Sudan."

47. *Authentic English Translation of the Permanent Constitution of the Sudan*, Khartoum, issued on May 8, 1973.

48. Carey N. Gordon, "The Islamic Legal Revolution: The Case of Sudan," *The International Lawyer* 19, no. 3 (1985): 793–816.

49. On aspects of the relationship between women and the law, see Sondra Hale, *Gender Politics in Sudan: Islamism, Socialism, and the State* (Boulder, Colo.: Westview Press, 1997), 137–39.

50. See Sidahmed, *Politics and Islam*, and El-Affendi, *Turabi's Revolution*.

51. On certain technical and legal aspects, see Abdullahi Ahmed An-Na'im, *Toward an Islamic Reformation: Civil Liberties, Human Rights, and International Law* (Syracuse, N.Y.: Syracuse University Press, 1990), 127–31.

52. Turabi, in Hamdi, *The Making of an Islamic Political Leader*, 25.

53. El-Affendi, *Turabi's Revolution*, 124.

54. Gordon, "The Islamic Legal Revolution."

55. The State v. Laleet Ratinlal Shah. See ibid.

56. John Makec, "Sudan," in *Yearbook of Islamic and Middle Eastern Law* 3 (1996): 251–73.

57. Cited in Sidahmed, *Politics and Islam*, 63.

58. Ibid., 64.

59. Ibid., 65.

60. Carolyn Fluehr-Lobban, "*Sharia* in the Sudan: History and Trends since Independence," in *Africa Today* 28, no. 2 (1981): 69–77.

61. Sidahmed, *Politics and Islam*, 172.

62. This point is based on discussions with Sudanese political figures in London in May 2000.

63. Abdel Salam Sidahmed, "Sudan: Ideology and Pragmatism," in *Islamic Fundamentalism*, ed. A. S. Sidahmed and A. Ehteshami (Boulder, Colo: Westview Press, 1996), 179–98.

64. See El-Affendi, *Turabi's Revolution*, 81–82.

65. Fluehr-Lobban, *Islamic Law and Society in the Sudan*.

66. Ibid., 50.

67. Dina Sheikh el Din Osman, "The Legal Status of Muslim Women in the Sudan," in *Women and Development in Africa*, ed. Gideon S. Were (Nairobi, 1985), 124–42.

68. Fluehr-Lobban, *Islamic Law and Society*, 46–48.

69. Ibid., 50.

70. Osman, "The Legal Status of Muslim Women."

71. M. W. Daly and Ahmad Alawad Sikainga, eds., *Civil War in the Sudan* (London, British Academic Press, 1993).

72. An-Na'im, "Constitutionalism and Islamization."

73. "Sudan," in Dieter Nohlen et al., eds., *Elections in Africa: A Data Handbook* (Oxford: Oxford University Press, 1990).

74. See the appendixes in Ann Mosely Lesch, *The Sudan: Contested National Identities* (Bloomington: Indiana University Press, 1998).

75. El-Affendi, *Turabi's Revolution*, 183. Sidahmed puts it in the following terms: "the Islamic state-model has become as ambiguous as the strategy of transition to it. The emphasis shifted from the Muslim society at large to the Islamist movement. . . . questions of models, ideologies, and strategies are to be left to the discretion of the movement. . . . An Islamic state is one governed by Islamists!" (Sidahmed, "Sudan," 96).

76. Leon Trotsky, *Our Political Tasks*, pamphlet, 1904.

77. See Article 43(d) and Part 8 (Articles 131–35) of "Constitution of the Republic of Sudan," issued March 1999, in *Constitutions of the Countries of the World*, ed. Gisbert H. Flanz (Dobbs Ferry, N.Y.: Oceana Publications, 1971–).

78. Dr. Khalafalla el-Rasheed, "Internal Discussions in the National Commission for the Constitution," in the third session of *Constitutional Perspectives on the Sudan (Proceedings of the IDF Seminar)*, ed. Michael Hoebink, Durham Middle East Paper no. 62, (Durham, 1999), 61–95.

79. Dr. Amin Mekki Medani's statement in ibid.

"Bolivarian" Anti-Semitism, by Claudio Lomnitz and Rafael Sánchez

NOTE: This essay first appeared as "United by Hate: The Uses of Anti-Semitism in Chávez's Venezuela," in the *Boston Review*, July/August 2009.

1. http://www.gobiernoenlinea.gob.ve/docMgr/sharedfiles/Chavez_visita_Centro_Manantial_de_los_suenos24122005.pdf;Sábado, 24 de diciembre de 2005.

2. "Judeofobia endógena," *El Universal*, March 8, 2009.

3. Ibid.

4. "Antisemitic Religious Prosecution from Hugo Chavez's Regime," http://www.youtube.com/watch?v=eKWGA510zbE.

5. "Asi opina Chávez de los judios," http://www.youtube.com/watch?v=0Rnr-b1g4ic.

6. In Telesur (telesur.net). A cartoon by the cartoonist Varela in Telesur on January 13, 2009, emphasizes this point by showing a Judaized Uncle Sam sharing Gaza with an Israeli Jew.

7. For a partial list of these expressions, see the website of the Anti-Defamation League, http://www.adl.org/main_Anti_Semitism_International/Chavez_VenezuelaeUnder_Threat.htm.

8. Martín Sánchez, editor of *Aporrea*, removed Silva's note from the website on February 6, that is, a week after the attack on the synagogue, http://www.aporrea.org/actualidad/a71876.html.

9. For Ceresole's Holocaust denial, see his *Caudillo, ejército, pueblo: La Venezuela del Comandante Chávez* (Madrid: Estudios hispanos-árabes, 2000), 14–27. See also: *Terrorismo fundamentalista judío* (Buenos Aires: CEAM, 1996); *El nacionaljudaísmo* (Madrid: Libertarias, 1997); *La falsificación de la realidad* (Madrid: Libertarias, 1998); and *La conquista del imperio americano* (Madrid: AlÁndalus, 1998).

10. *Aló Presidente*, program no. 255, May 21, 2006, http://alopresidente.gob.ve/component/option,com_docman/Itemid,0/task,doc_view/gid,184/.

11. Ceresole, *Caudillo, ejército, y pueblo*, 29.

12. Ibid, 9.

13. http://www.hrw.org/reports/2008/venezuela0908/pp.1–2.

14. Ceresole, *Caudillo, ejército, y pueblo*, 20.

15. "Chávez condena ataque a sinagoga en Caracas," February 1, 2009, http://www2.esmas.com/noticierostelevisa/internacional/0523/chavez-conden a-ataque-sinagoga-caracas.

16. Associated Press, September 12, 2006.

17. Ceresole, *Caudillo, ejército, y pueblo*, 30.

18. Human Rights Watch, 3–4.

19. Hugo Chavez, "Rojo y piragua," September 12, 2006, www.youtube.com/watch?v=kKATJTWb_h8.

20. "Fiscal se pronuncia ante declaraciones del CEV Y CICPC en caso del padre Piñango," http:„ww.mci.gob.veoticiàs625fiiscal_se_pronuncia.htm l, 28 April 2006.

21. "Isaías Rodríguez, Venezuelan Attorney General," April 26, 2006, http://www.youtube.com/results?search_type = &search_query = "Isaías;plRodríguez%2C + Venezuelan + Attorney + General%2C" + +&a q = f.

22. "La descarga de Mario Silva al 'pato' Roland Carreño," July 6, 2008, file:///Volumes/Crucial%20/» %20La%20descarga%20de%20Mario%20Silva%20al%20"pato"%20Roland%20Carren~o%20en%20 Noticias24.com.webarchive.

23. Hugo Chávez, "Fue una victoria de mierda, " December 5, 2007, http://www.youtube.com/watch?v = ed7gB2MmSmM.

24. Lina Ron, "Los chavistas somos como el Guaire . . .," October 12, 2008, http://www.noticias24.com/actualidad/noticia/18666/lina-ron-los-chavistas-somos-como-el-guaire/.

25. Jorge Castañeda, "The Plot Against the Castros," *Newsweek*, March 14, 2009.

26. Teodoro Petkoff, "Chávez y la Sinagoga," *TalCual*, February 12. 2009.

The Power of the Less Powerful: Making Memory on a Pilgrimage to Lourdes by Catrien Notermans

NOTE: I thank NORFACE (New Opportunities for Research Funding Co-operation in Europe) and NWO (the Netherlands Organisation for Scientific Research) for funding part of this research. I also thank Trudy van Helmond, pilgrimage coordinator of the Dutch health care insurance company VGZ. She kindly accepted me as a volunteer in the June pilgrimage in 2004 and critically read my work before publication. I also thank the pilgrims for sharing with me their moving stories. Part of the data in this article has been published in Catrien Notermans, "Loss and Healing: A Marian Pilgrimage in Secular Dutch Society," *Ethnology* 46, no. 3 (2007): 217–33.

1. Pierre Nora, "Between Memory and History: Les Lieux de Memoire," *Representations* 26 (1989): 7–24.

2. Anna-Karina Hermkens, Willy Jansen, and Catrien Notermans, eds., *Moved by Mary: The Power of Pilgrimage in the Modern World* (Aldershot: Ashgate, 2009). In this volume, different case studies show how dominant and subdominant people use Marian devotion to cope with the problems they must face in the modern world.

3. Michael Jackson, *The Politics of Storytelling: Violence, Transgression, and Intersubjectivity* (Copenhagen: Museum Tusculanum Press, 2002), 17.

4. Arthur Kleinman, Veena Das, and Margaret Lock, eds., *Social Suffering* (Berkeley: University of California Press, 1997).

5. Mieke Bal, Jonathan Crewe, and Leo Spitzer, eds., *Acts of Memory: Cultural Recall in the Present* (Hanover: University Press of New England, 1999).

6. Simon Coleman and John Eade, eds., *Reframing Pilgrimage: Cultures in Motion* (London: Routledge, 2004).

7. Jill Dubisch, " 'Heartland of America': Memory, Motion, and the (Re)Construction of History on a Motorcycle Pilgrimage," and Katharina Schramm, "Coming Home to the Motherland: Pilgrimage Tourism in Ghana," both in *Reframing Pilgrimage: Cultures in Motion*, ed. Simon Coleman and John Eade (London: Routledge, 2004).

8. For more information about people's identification with Mary, see Catrien Notermans, "Local and Global Images of Mary: An Ethnographic Study of a Powerful Symbol," *Anthropos* 103, no. 2 (2008): 471–81.

9. James Dow, "Universal Aspects of Symbolic Healing: A Theoretical Synthesis," *American Anthropologist* 88, no. 1 (1986): 56–69; Marina Roseman, "Head, Heart, Odor, and Shadow: The Structure of the Self, the Emotional World, and Ritual Performance among Senoi Temiar," *Ethos* 18, no. 3 (1990): 227–50.

10. For more information on the background and organization of this particular pilgrimage, see Catrien Notermans, "Loss and Healing: A Marian Pilgrimage in Secular Dutch Society," *Ethnology* 46, no. 3 (2008).

11. Jackson, *The Politics of Storytelling*, 15.

12. Dubisch, "'Heartland of America,'" 128.

13. Some studies confirming the healing aspects of religious storytelling are: Karen McCarthy Brown, *Mama Lola: A Vodou Priestess in Brooklyn* (Berkeley: University of California Press, 2001); Clifford Geertz, *The Interpretation of Cultures* (New York: Basic Books, 1973); and Robert Orsi, *Thank You, St. Jude: Women's Devotion to the Patron Saint of Hopeless Causes* (New Haven: Yale University Press, 1998).

14. Dubisch, "'Heartland of America,'" 106.

"Without my headscarf I feel naked": "Veiling," *Laïcité,* Politics, and Islamist Discourse in North Cameroon, by José C. M. van Santen

NOTE: The research for this essay is related to the Netherlands Organisation for Scientific Research (NWO) program the Future of the Religious Past and is part of the subprogram Islam in Africa: Globalization and Moving Frontiers.

1. Markha G. Valenta, "How to Recognize a Muslim When You See One: Western Secularism and the Politics of Conversion," in *Political Theologies: Public Religions in a Post-Secular World*, ed. Hent de Vries and Lawrence E. Sullivan (New York: Fordham University Press, 2006): 444–74.

2. Ibid., 753n3.

3. Ibid. In European countries with a Muslim majority, such as Turkey, it is also part of the political debate, related to tensions between the norms of secular democracy and the principles of religious tolerance.

4. The term *fundamental* is much debated. Karin Willemse and I have chosen to use it for reasons of comparison. In an article in preparation (José C. M. van Santen and Karin Willemse, "The Issue of Islamic Fundamentalism: Masculinities and Femininities"), we state: "Though first used in the United States at the beginning of the twentieth century, the term *fundamentalism* is often automatically read as Islamic fundamentalism." See also José C. M. van Santen and Karin Willemse, "Fundamentalismen: Discourses over mannelijkheid en vrouwelijkheid, Discussiestuk Lova Studiedag 28–5-1999," *Lova Tijdschrift* 20, no. 1 (1999), 4–13. Fundamentalism has become a prominent focus of the imagery through which Islam is presented to the Western public. Bobby Sayyid (*A Fundamental Fear: Eurocentrism and the Emergence of Islamism* [London: Zed Books, 1997]) even refers to this labeling as "demonology." For this reason, many scholars denounce the term *fundamentalism*, preferring other terms such as *Islamic resurgence, revivalism, activism,* or even *extremism* and *militantism* (M. Choueiri Youssef, *Islamic Fundamentalism* [London: Twayne Publishers, 1990]; John. H Hawley and Wayne L. Proudfoot, "Introduction," in *Fundamentalism*

and Gender, ed. John Stratton Hawley [New York: Oxford University Press, 1994], 1–44; Laurence J. Silberstein, "Religion, Ideology, Modernity: Theoretical Issues in the Study of Jewish Fundamentalism," in *Jewish Fundamentalism in Comparative Perspective: Religion, Ideology, and the Crisis of Modernity*, ed. Laurence Silberstein [New York: New York University Press, 1993], 1–13). Others prefer local terms, which for anthropologists seem the best solution, given that they usually work in specific cultural settings. When discussing a more particular form of political Islam, most scholars use the term *Islamism* to refer to movements "usually aiming at an Islamic state that would enforce at least some Islamic laws and customs, including those related to sex segregation, and some economic measures and Qur'anic punishments" (Nikki Keddie, quoted in Azza M. Karam, *Women, Islamisms and the State: Contemporary Feminisms in Egypt* [New York: Macmillan, 1998], 16). Willemse and I hold that "Islamism" should be distinguished from processes of "Islamization." The last term refers to processes of conversion to Islam in general, whether by force or by consent, whether today or in the past. We speak of "Islamic reform movements" when we discuss nameable groups that reformulate Islamic practices or redefine certain Islamic values in reference to specific contexts. We use the term *Islamist* to indicate individuals or groups with access to sources of power, whether economic, political, moral, or military, which they use to enforce their redefinitions of Islam within the Muslim (and possibly even non-Muslim) community at large. We would suggest that the problems surrounding a concept such as fundamentalism should not blind us to the possibilities that it offers for comparison and analysis of similar global processes. Furthermore, despite the problematic nature of the term, researchers must come to terms with it, however politically incorrect it may be. Despite criticisms and protests, whether in academic or popular sites, fundamentalism as a concept seems here to stay. Therefore, the most relevant question is: How can we compare supposedly "fundamentalist" movements in various regions? In this we share the opinion of Gita Sahgal and Nira Yuval-Davis ('The Uses of Fundamentalism: Response to Nederveen Pieterse," *Women Against Fundamentalism* 5 [1994]: 7–9), who suggest that "Islamism" can be applied to specific cases of political Islam, while "fundamentalism" may be used when we want to "create links across religious and cultural specifics" while not denying "difference in context and circumstances" (ibid., 9). Willemse and I have chosen to use *fundamentalisms* in the plural, thus suggesting the pluriform nature of the phenomenon denoted by the term; see also Karin Willemse, *One Foot in Heaven: Narratives on Gender and Islam in Darfur, West-Sudan* (Leiden: Brill, 2006).

5. Talal Asad, "Trying to Understand French Secularism," in *Political Theologies: Public Religions in a Post-Secular World*, ed. Hent de Vries and Lawrence E. Sullivan (New York: Fordham University Press, 2006), 494–526.

6. Private Islamic institutions are usually founded by a single person—often a religious leader who is financially backed by an Islamic NGO. The 2006 annual report of the secretary for "Islamic education" mentions for the province Extrême Nord alone eight "Franco- Arab" schools; these were founded by the "Association Culturelle Islamique du Cameroun." They have existed since the colonial period, but subsidies from the Ministry of Education stopped in 2000. Sixteen private primary Islamic schools have been founded since 1993 and are functioning with the authorization of the Ministry of Education; four are functioning without this authorization; and seven are in an advanced stage of construction. As for secondary schools, three are functioning with the authorization of the ministry (with a total of 1,218 pupils, of whom 718 are girls and 500 boys), and three without this authorization (with a total of 180 pupils, of whom 143 are girls). Throughout Cameroon sixteen secondary private Islamic schools are functioning.

7. Michel-Rolph Trouillot, "The Anthropology of the State in the Age of Globalisation," *Current Anthropology* 42, no. 1 (February 2001): 125–38.

8. Talal Asad holds that a single case can very well be taken as an example. In matters of religion, we should not just come up with deconstructions or simple definitions but should look at concrete historical processes, staying close to the ways religion is articulated and talking about religion in the singular (as cited by Birgit Meyer during the Future of the Religious Past conference in June 2005 in Amsterdam).

9. Journalists hardly ever demonstrate historical consciousness. In our own societies we have a history of veiling, too. In every biblical painting, women wear head garments, as was common in European societies. One can see this in Tracy Chevalier, *Girl with a Pearl Earring* (London: HarperCollins, 1999), inspired by the famous painting of Johannes Vermeer. The protagonist of the book feels "naked" when she is seen without her headgear. Until recently a headscarf was either obligatory while performing Catholic prayers or part of a new fashion, as in the 1960s, when Brigitte Bardot often wore a headscarf.

10. Valenta, "How to Recognize a Muslim When You See One," 465.

11. Asad, "Trying to Understand French Secularism," 502.

12. Asad, reflecting on the restatement in France of *laïcité* from an anthropological perspective and discussing the Stasi commission report, states that the commission's concern with the desires of pupils is expressed in a distinction between those who didn't really want to wear the headscarf and those who did. Solicitude for the "real" desires of the pupils applied only to girls who wore the headscarf. No thought appears to have been given to determining the "real" desires of girls who did not wear the headscarf. Was it possible, he asks, that some of them secretly wanted to wear a headscarf but were ashamed to do so because of what their French peers and people in the street might think and say (Asad, "Trying to Understand French Secularism," 503)?

13. As argued also by Paul Mepschen in 2004, http://www.grenzeloos.org/artikel/viewartikel.php/id/593.html.

14. Lila Abu-Lughod, *Veiled Sentiments* (Berkeley: University of California Press, 1986); Fatima Mernissi, *Beyond the Veil: Male-Female Dynamics in a Modern Muslim Society* (New York: Halsted Press [John Wiley Sons, Inc.], 1975); Fariba Adelkhah, *La revolution sous le voile* (Paris: Karthala, 1991); Nawal El Saadawi, *The Hidden Face of Eve: Women in the Arab World* (London: Zed Press, 1980).

15. Djibril Samb, *Comprendre la laïcité* (Dakar: Les nouvelles Editions Africaines du Sénégal, 2005). Grace Davie, a well-known British sociologist of religion, describes *laïcité* as "a neutral space privileging no religion in particular and effecting this policy by excluding the discussion of religion from all state institutions, including the school system" (*Religion in Modern Europe: A Memory Mutates* [Oxford: Oxford University Press, 2000], 19, cited in Talal Asad, "Trying to Understand French Secularism," 497). Asad considers this description to be too simple, but a thorough account of the matter is outside the scope of the present essay.

16. For an account of some of this history, see Yolande Jansen, "*Laïcité*, or the Politics of Republican Secularism," in *Political Theologies: Public Religions in a Post-Secular World*, ed. Hent de Vries and Lawrence E. Sullivan (New York: Fordham University Press, 2006), 475–93.

17. From the Preamble to the Constitution of the Republic of Cameroon, Law No 96–06 of January 18, 1996, to amend the Constitution of June 2, 1972. Part 12, Special Provisions, art. 65. The Preamble shall be part and parcel of this Constitution.

18. In Holland—not a fully laical state—opposition to the headscarf in schools eventually led to more pragmatic solutions: wearing a *badmuts* ("bath cap") during natural science lessons to prevent the headscarf from catching fire. However, headscarves are usually allowed at universities and for people working in public administration, though the *nikab* (the veil covering the face as well) is controversial and not

allowed in many public spaces. In Holland a law (23) permits the foundation of religious schools, so Islamic schools have been introduced into the Dutch educational landscape. In Britain the headscarf is not forbidden, and the country has an "à la carte policy": each school has a special working group that decides on individual cases; children may be absent from certain lessons or attend segregated ones (for sex education, swimming, physical exercise, etc.). In October 2006, some girls wearing the *nikab* had to leave secondary school. The topic is also an issue in Middle Eastern societies: in Egypt a new order was introduced in October 2006 that forbids *nikabs* on university campuses, to prevent (terrorist) men from disguising themselves in women's dress.

19. The word *hijab* is mentioned eight times in the Qur'an:

Chapter 7, verse 46: The *hijab* is mentioned as the wall that separates people in paradise from those in hell.

Chapter 38, verse 32: The *hijab* is used in the sense of a "covered sun" when Salomon was absent-minded during morning prayers due to the return of his horses.

Chapter 41, verse 5: This verse informs the *koraichite* unbelievers (inhabitants of Mecca) that the "voice" of the message does not get through to them due to a *hijab* ("curtain") that separates them from the Prophet.

Chapter 17, verse 45: Mention of the *hijab* here is the same as in Chapter 83, verse 15.

Chapter 42, verse 51: God informs us that, being invisible, he addresses the human being only from behind a *hijab*.

Chapter 19, verse 17: The voluntary isolation of Mary, at the moment she becomes pregnant, is considered to be a *hijab*, which protects her from the gaze of other humans.

Chapter 33, verse 53: Those who believe do not enter the rooms of the Prophet, except in the event that they have been invited to dinner. . . . When they ask something (addressing his wives), they should do so behind a curtain (*hijab*). That is better for your own heart as well as those of the Prophet's wives. In that way they do not insult God's messenger, nor marry his wives after he did so (Abderrahmane Fraikech, lawyer, in *Sisyphe*, November 15, 2004, un regard féministe sur le monde, site d'information, d'analyse et d'opinion indépendant, http://sisyphe.org).

20. Why and how the *hijab* is worn within this group, whose members were Islamized only in the twentieth century, is an intriguing phenomenon worthy of an essay in itself. In Cameroon, they settled in certain economic niches, so they do a little fishing, raise a little rice, and keep some cattle. See Diny M. E. van Est, *Vissen in Andermans Vijver: Beheer en strijdige belangen onder Mousgoum en Kotoko in de Logone overstromingsvlakte van Noord-kameroen* (Leiden: CML, 1999).

21. Actually the Germans came first, in 1900. The French and English divided the northern areas after the First World War. See José C. M. van Santen, *They Leave Their Jars Behind: The Conversion of Mafa Women to Islam (North Cameroon)* (Leiden: Vena Publications, 1993).

22. Roy Olivier, *L'Islam mondialisé* (Paris: Editions du Seuil, 2002).

23. Salma Nageeb, "Negotiating Development: Translocal Gendered Spaces in Muslim Societies, A Methodology Paper" (Universität Bielefeld: working paper, 2005), has examined a similar development in the Sudan.

24. Personal observation.

25. Personal observation during the *fête nationale de la jeunesse* on February 11, 2005.

26. These "Pakistani" men—whether they really come from Pakistan or from other regions in the Middle East is not clear—refused to speak to me, because my face was not covered "properly." I have never had such an experience in my years of talking openly with *marabouts* and *imams* in the region.

27. Here is a typical comment: "They just walk around in the streets of town, these adolescent girls. They search for boys, they often get pregnant out of wedlock . . . prostitution is a serious problem of modern times." Fear of such a situation often leads fathers to arrange forced marriages for their daughters. They are terrified that their daughters "will miss the wedding boat." Many of these girls walk away after one or two years of marriage, to "wander around" afterward. But it is also true that many girls do not get married at all. The economic situation is largely responsible, as marriage demands an enormous investment from both the groom's family and the bride's. During women's day, on March 8, 2004, women's groups marched in the street to demonstrate against forced marriages for young girls (*contre les mariages précoces*). These marches were organized by a southern Cameroonian Christian sociologist working in the north.

28. Annie Lebeuf, "L'origine et la constitution des principaux kotoko (Cameroun septentrional)," in *Contributions de la recherche ethnologique à l'histoire des civilisations du Cameroun*, ed. C. Tardits (Paris: CNRS, 1981), 1209–18; Vivana Paques, *Le roi pecheur et le roi chasseur* (Strasbourg: Travaux de l'Institut de l'Anthropologie de Strasbourg, 1977).

29. Eldridge Mohammadou, *Les royaumes foulbe du plateau de l'Adamaoua au XIX siècle* (Tokyo: ILCAA, 1978); idem, *Le royaume du Wandala ou Mandara au XIXe siècle* (Tokyo: ILCAA, 1982); idem, *Les lamidats du Diamare et du Mayo Louti au XIXe siècle* (Tokyo: ILCAA, 1988).

30. Van Santen, *They Leave Their Jars Behind*; Kees Schilder, *Quest for Self-Esteem: State Islam and Mundang Ethnicity in Northern Cameroon* (London: Avebury, 1994). Fulbe of Diamaré and Kalfou did not succeed in penetrating the regions adjacent to the Logone River, where the Massa and Toupouri lived.

31. Henry Tourneux and Olivier Iyébi-Mandjek, *L'école dans une petite ville africaine Maroua, Cameroun* (Paris: Karthala, 1994).

32. Van Santen, *They Leave Their Jars Behind*; Philip Burnham, *The Politics of Cultural Difference in Northern Cameroon* (Edinburgh: Edinburgh University Press, 1996).

33. Mahmood Mamdani, "The Politics of Peasant Ethnic Communities and Urban Civil Society: Reflections on an African Dilemma," in *Disappearing Peasantries? Rural Labour in Africa, Asia and Latin America*, ed. Deborah Brysceson, Cristóbal Kay, and Jos Mooij (London: Intermediate Technology Publications, 2000), 99–112.

34. Van Santen, *They Leave Their Jars Behind*; José C. M. van Santen, "Islamisation in North Cameroon: Political Processes and Individual Choices," *Anthropos* 7 (2002): 67–97.

35. Van Santen, *They Leave Their Jars Behind*, 28.

36. Mamdani, 'The Politics of Peasant Ethnic Communities and Urban Civil Society," 103–4.

37. José C. M. van Santen, "Islam, Gender and Urbanisation among the Mafa of North Cameroon: The Differing Commitment to 'Home' among Muslims and non-Muslims," *Africa* 68, no. 3 (1998): 403–24.

38. José C. M. van Santen, "Règles d'accès au foncier et occupation du sol dans un contexte de migration: Le cas de Mafa Kilda," in *Savanes africaines: Des espaces en mutation, des acteurs face à de nouveaux défis*, ed. J. Y. Jamin, L. Seiny Boukar, and C. Floret (Montpellier/N'Djamena: Cirad/Prasac, 2003).

39. Tourneux and Iyébi-Mandjek, *L'école dans une petite ville africaine Maroua, Cameroun*.

40. Renaud Santerre, "L'école coranique de la savanne camerounaise" (Ph.D. thesis, Université de Paris, 1968), 146.

41. Tourneux and Iyébi-Mandjek, *L'école dans une petite ville africaine Maroua, Cameroun*.

42. Ibid., 100.

43. Van Santen, *They Leave Their Jars Behind*, 28; Mamdani, 'The Politics of Peasant Ethnic Communities and Urban Civil Society."

44. Tourneux and Iyébi-Mandjek, *L'école dans une petite ville africaine Maroua, Cameroun*, 108, and oral information.

45. Hamadou Adama, Dean of the Faculty of History at Ngaoundèrè University, Cameroon, mentions that between 1980 and 1990 not a single founder or teacher sent his own child to Islamic schools in North Cameroon.

46. I attended this workshop, given that at the time I was joint director of the Centre of Environment and Development Studies (CEDC—Antenne de l'Úniversité de Dschang) in North Cameroon—the area in which I have been carrying out fieldwork since 1986.

47. This intriguing workshop has been analyzed elsewhere: José C. M. Van Santen, "'Will I send my boy or my girl to school?' NGO concepts of 'gender,' Islam, and Public Space in North Cameroon," given at the panel Islam and the Modern State in Africa (and Elsewhere), Issues of Citizenship and the Place of Religion in the Public Sphere, NWO Future of the Religious Past conference, June 26–27, 2006, Amsterdam.

48. Recently Islamized people are usually unable to read or write themselves, but they do send their children to Qur'anic schools. In traditional Qur'anic schools, there are as many girls as boys, and many *marabouts* were of the opinion that girls learn faster and in general have more knowledge.

49. Uthman dan Fodio, "Nur al-albab" and "Irshad al-Ikhwan ila ahkam," cited in I. A. Ogunbiyi, "The Position of Muslim Women as Stated by Uthman dan Fodio," *ODU* 2 (1969): 43–60.

50. Uthman dan Fodio, "Irshad al-Ikhwan cala jawaz," cited in Ogunbiyi, "The Position of Muslim Women as Stated by Uthman dan Fodio."

51. Uthman dan Fodio, "Ihya al-sunna," cited in Ogunbiyi, "The Position of Muslim Women as Stated by Uthman dan Fodio."

52. Jean Boyd and Alhadju Shaku Shagari, "The Fulani Women Poets," in *Pastoralists of the West African Savanna*, ed. Mahdi Adamu and A. H. M. Kirk-Greene (Manchester: Manchester University Press, 1986).

Religion and Powerlessness: Elena in *Nothing is Missing,* by Mieke Bal

1. Mieke Bal and Miguel Á. Hernández-Navarro, *2MOVE: Video, Art, Migration* (Murcia, Spain: Cendeac, 2008).

Music, Religion, and Power: *Qawwali* as Empowering Disempowerment, by Rokus de Groot

1. Regula B. Qureshi, *Sufi Music of India and Pakistan: Sound, Context, and Meaning in Qawwali* (Cambridge: Cambridge University Press, 1986), xv.

2. See, for the discussion of a similar issue in the context of Christianity, the analysis of Augustine's thoughts on music by Sander van Maas, *Doorbraak en Idolatrie: Olivier Messiaen en het geloof in de muziek* (Delft: Eburon, 2003), 91–112, and in idem, *The Reinvention of Religious Music: Olivier Messiaen's Breakthrough to the Beyond* (New York: Fordham University Press, 2009), 78–80. Augustine considered music essential but dangerous in the context of liturgy.

3. Gerry Farrell, *Indian Music and the West* (Oxford: Oxford University Press, 1997), 205.

4. *Dam mast mast, dam mast dekho phirte hain dam mast Ali, Ali dam mast Qalandar, mast, mast sakhi Lal Qalandar mast mast.* I thank Dr. Dick Plukker of the India Instituut (Amsterdam) for the translation.

5. Jérôme de Missolz, *Nusrat Fateh Ali Khan, Le dernier Prophète.* DVD Arte Video 1996, 18'.50"–22'.12".

6. Nusrat Fateh Ali Khan contributed to the sound tracks of *The Last Temptation of Christ* (Martin Scorsese, 1988), *The Bandit Queen* (Shekhar Kapoor, 1994), *Natural Born Killers* (Oliver Stone, 1994), and *Dead Man Walking* (Tim Robbins, 1995).

7. The *qalandar* ("wandering dervish") mentioned in the poem was Muhammad Uthman Marandi (1177–1274). Nicknamed Lal Shahbaz Qalandar, he is still a popular patron saint of Sindh. He was a mystic and a missionary for Islam and is reported to have preached tolerance between Islam and Hinduism. His magnificent tomb at Sehwan remains the focus of mass pilgrimage, by both Muslims and Hindus.

8. "Solmization" is singing not text but the names of the musical notes one is rendering, like *do-re-mi-fa-sol-la-ti* in the European music tradition, and *Sa-Re-Ga-Ma-Pa-Dha-Ni* in the Indian one. These names denote relative pitches. If one takes *Sa* or *do* as C, then Indian *Re, Ga,* etc., and European *re, mi,* etc., refer to D, E, etc.

9. A cadenza is a standard formula that ends a prosodic section in music.

10. Missolz, *Nusrat Fateh Ali Khan,* 47'.02"–50'.59".

11. Repeated alternation between solo and group singing.

12. Missolz, *Nusrat Fateh Ali Khan,* 50'.59"–52'.19".

13. *Musst musst,* Realworld 0777 7862212 3, 1990. Peter Gabriel played a key role in introducing Nusrat to the global market.

14. The beat is eighty to the minute.

15. From the website www.WOMAD.org: "the central aim of the WOMAD festival—to bring together and to celebrate many forms of music, arts and dance drawn from countries and cultures all over the world.//WOMAD was originally inspired by Peter Gabriel: 'Pure enthusiasm for music from around the world led us to the idea of WOMAD in 1980 and thus to the first WOMAD festival in 1982. . . ., the festivals have also allowed many different audiences to gain an insight into cultures other than their own through the enjoyment of music. Music is a universal language, it draws people together and proves, as well as anything, the stupidity of racism.' As an organization, WOMAD now works in many different ways, but our aims are always the same—at festivals, performance events, through recorded releases and through educational projects, we aim to excite, to inform, and to create awareness of the worth and potential of a multicultural society."

16. Missolz, *Nusrat Fateh Ali Khan,* 22'.41"–23'.53".

17. Qureshi, *Sufi Music,* discusses a number of cases in which several people enter into trance; at *'urs* festivals (commemoration of the demise of Sufi saints), trance behavior may be seen among large numbers of people.

18. A. Schimmel, *Mystical Dimensions of Islam* (Chapel Hill: University of North Carolina Press, 1978), 178.

19. Schimmel, ibid., refers to Nwyia's proposal to translate *wajd* as "instasy," since the mystic may experience—or express himself as—being carried inside rather than outside himself.

20. Qureshi, *Sufi Music,* 80–81.

21. Ibid., 81.

22. *Mathnawî* 1.30, translation by R. A. Nicholson, *The Mathnawî of Jalalu'ddîn Rûmî* (London: Gibb Memorial Trust, 1926, rpt. 1990), 2:6.

23. Qureshi, *Sufi Music*, 23–24.

24. Ibid., 82.

25. Schimmel, *Mystical Dimensions*, 180.

26. Qureshi, *Sufi Music*, 82.

27. Ibid., 107.

28. Ibid., 122–23.

29. V. S. Naipaul, *Among the Believers: An Islamic Journey* (1981; London: Picador, 2001), 142.

30. Qureshi, *Sufi Music*, 117.

31. Ibid., 123.

32. Ibid., 81.

33. Ibid., 93, 115.

34. Ibid., 1, 103.

35. Ibid., 81; S. H. Nasr, "Islam and Music: The Legal and Spiritual Dimensions," in *Enchanting Powers: Music in the World's Religions*, ed. Lawrence E. Sullivan (Cambridge: Harvard University Press, 1997), 219–35.

36. Qureshi, *Sufi Music*, 81.

37. Qureshi, *Sufi Music*, does not differentiate between trance and ecstasy. Further research is necessary here as far as *qawwali* is concerned. In the Missolz *dargah* episode, it seems that the subject undergoes a narrowing down of consciousness, which would usually be associated with the notion of trance (ecstasy being connected with a widening of consciousness). One might ask: Is trance more readily linked to audition (especially in the case of repetitive sounds and music), and ecstasy to vision, especially in relation to the singularity of the sublime or divine? How do trance and ecstasy relate to submission?

38. Qureshi, *Sufi Music*, 119, table 24; 121, table 25; 126.

39. Ibid., 59, table 6 and discussion.

40. Ibid., 92, 97, 111–12, 136.

41. Jósef M. Pacholczyk, *Sûfyâna Mûsîqî: The Classical Music of Kashmir* (Berlin: Verlag für Wissenschaft und Bildung, 1996).

42. Qureshi, *Sufi Music*, 114, 118, 218.

43. Ibid., 111–12, 128, 130, 137–38. The musicians cannot even follow their economic purpose directly. They are dependent on donations given during the *samâ'*; however, these are handed over not to them but to the spiritual leaders, who divide them up, thereby confirming that *samâ'* is not a material transaction. It is therefore in the musicians' interest to comply with the spiritual needs of the listeners and the directions given by the spiritual leaders (ibid., 138).

44. Ibid., 3; 19–20; 47; 187–90; 201–5; table 34, 214–17; 223–26.

45. Although his art was in fact put to another service, the first word of the award should be read as "*National* Pride"; see also later in this essay the section "Concert *Qawwali* as an Empowerment of Pakistani Nationalism."

46. H. Sabbe, *"All that music": Een antropologie van de westerse cultuur* (Leuven: Acco, 1996), Introduction.

47. Qureshi, *Sufi Music*, table 25, *hâth uthânâ, hâth batânâ*.

48. Ibid., table 34.

49. Ibid., 189.

50. Ibid., 221.

51. See notes to the Audio CD *Nusrat Fateh Ali Khan en concert à Paris*, Ocora C 559073, 1997, recorded 1988, 4:13.

52. Missolz, *Nusrat Fateh Ali Khan*.

53. Audio CD *Nusrat Fateh Ali Khan en concert à Paris*, Ocora, 4:12.

54. Missolz, *Nusrat Fateh Ali Khan*.

55. Audio CD *Nusrat Fateh Ali Khan en concert à Paris*, Ocora, 4:13.

56. Ibid., my italics.

57. Notes to the Audio CD *Musst musst*, Realworld 0777 7862212 3, 1990.

58. Audio CD *Nusrat Fateh Ali Khan en concert à Paris*, Ocora, 4: 12.

59. Missolz, *Nusrat Fateh Ali Khan*.

60. Compare the Lahore performance with the Chicago one in Missolz, *Nusrat Fateh Ali Khan*, and compare his *Opus* CD (Vanstory 12001, 2000), a 1995 recording of a Lahore concert, with the *Nusrat Fateh Ali Khan en concert à Paris* CD series, Ocora.

61. Audio CD *Nusrat Fateh Ali Khan en concert à Paris*, Ocora, vols. 1, 2, and 4.

62. Missolz, *Nusrat Fateh Ali Khan*, 51':46'.

63. P.-A. Baud, *Nusrat Fateh Ali Khan, le messager du qawwali* (Paris: Demi-Lune, 2008), 108.

64. Friedrich Nietzsche, *Götzendämmerung*, vol. 6 of *Sämtliche Werke: Kritische Studienausgabe*, ed. Giorgio Colli and Massino Montinari (Berlin:: De Gruyter, 1980).

65. See: Farrell, *Indian Music and the West*, chap. 5; Rokus de Groot, "The Reception in the Netherlands of an Indian Singing Saint: Meerabai in Film, in Translation and in Concert," *Tijdschrift van de Koninklijke Vereniging voor Nederlandse Muziekgeschiedenis* 56, no. 1 (2006): 25–65; idem, "Oriental Identities in Western Music," in *Redefining Musical Identities in the Twenty-first Century* (Zwolle: ARTEZ, 2007), 87–99; idem, "Rabindranath Tagore and Frederik van Eeden: Reception of a 'Poet-King' in the Netherlands," in *Essays on the History of North Indian Music*, ed. J. Bor et al. (New Delhi: Manohar, 2009), 521–76.

66. The popularity of *qawwali* in the West since the mid-1980s is surprising. While discussing a newspaper review, Farrell, *Indian Music and the West*, 206, notes, on the one hand: "All the prerequisites for entry into the aural universe of Western popular culture are there: it sounds like something else which is recognizable—in this case soul music . . .—and yet it retains some oriental distance, making it ultimately unknowable and hence attractive (ancient tradition, mystical overtones); even so, the Western audience can impose its own cultural values on it—it is good to move to (percussion, 'shuffling, driving beat')." On the other hand, he observes that in these very years: "On the global stage, fundamentalist Islam was rapidly replacing communism as the main perceived ideological threat to Western capitalism" (208).

67. N. Lebovic, *Dionysian Politics and The Discourse of 'Rausch'* (Los Angeles: UCLA Center for European and Eurasian Studies, 2004), paper 4, discerns the following three historical moments of thought on intoxication: early Romanticism (Goethe, the Grimm brothers, Hölderlin), late Romanticism (different stances of Nietzsche), and the 1920s conceptualization and politicization of both earlier moments (Lages, Benjamin). Note that the Grimm brothers point to the novelty of the subject: "a new poetic talk, Rausch means also dizziness, the soul's drunkenness, the delight of the inner faculties that lead to self forgetfulness" (2). While Nietzsche stresses a polarity between Dionysian *Rausch* and Apollonian order in *Der Geburt der Tragödie* (*The Birth of Tragedy*; 1872), he takes intoxication to be both Dionysian and Apollonian in *Twilight of the Gods* (1889).

68. See some reviews discussed in Farrell, *Indian Music and the West*. A review of the 1988 Queen Elisabeth Hall concert "compared the ecstatic delivery and rhythmic energy of the music [by Nusrat and group] to that of James Brown" etc. (207).

69. Rokus de Groot, "De eigenzinnige echo: Betekenisanalyse van echo-personificaties in muziekdramatische werken," *Tijdschrift voor Muziektheorie* 4, no. 1 (1999): 40–52.

70. Cf. Nietzsche's "the belief in ecstasy" ("der Glaube an den Rausch"), as discussed in *Morgenröte: Gedanken über die moralischen Vorurtiele* (*Daybreak: Thoughts on the Prejudices of Morality*), vol. 3 of *Sämtliche Werke: Kritische Studienausgabe*, ed. Giorgio Colli and Massino Montinari (1881; Berlin, Munich: DTV / De Gruyter, 1980), no. 50. Nietzsche notes: "Intoxication counts as the real life, as the proper I."

71. In this case, a "God" who counts as external in a situation of duality.

John Cage and the Mystification of Musical Silence, by Jael Kraut

1. Quoted by George Steiner in *Language and Silence* (New York: Atheneum, 1967), 69.

2. Kafka writes in "Das Schweigen der Sirenen": "Now, the Sirens have an even more terrible weapon than their singing, namely, their silence" (*Nachgelassene Schriften und Fragmente* [Frankfurt am Main: Fischer, 1989], 40).

3. Constant Nieuwenhuys, "Manifesto," in *Reflex* (Amsterdam) 1 (September-October, 1948), trans. Leonard Bright, rpt. in Kristine Stiles and Peter Howard Selz, *Theories and Documents of Contemporary Art: A Sourcebook of Artists' Writings* (Berkeley: University of California Press, 1996), 204–8.

4. Douglas Kahn, "John Cage: Silence and Silencing," in Kahn, *Noise, Water, Meat: A History of Sound in the Arts* (Cambridge: MIT Press, 1999), 176.

5. John Cage, "Other People Think" (1927), in *John Cage*; ed. Richard Kostelanetz (New York: Praeger, 1970), 21–24.

6. Paul Henry Lang, *Music in Western Civilization* (New York: Norton, 1941), 991.

7. Theodor W. Adorno, "The Aging of New Music" (1956), in *Essays on Music / Theodor W. Adorno*, ed. Richard Leppert (Berkeley: University of California Press, 2000), 187.

8. Kahn, *Noise, Water, Meat*, 164.

9. Guy-Ernest Debord, "One More Try If You Want to be Situationists," in *Potlatch*, no. 29 (Paris: November 5, 1957), trans. John Sepley, published on Situationist International Online: www.cddc.vt.edu/sionline.

10. Debord, in an undated letter to Gil J. Wolman (probably from 1953), quoted in Wolman, *Défense de mourir* (Paris: Allia, 2001), 182. The translation of this quotation is my own.

11. Cage, "Experimental Music" (1958), in Cage, *Silence: Lectures and Writings* (Cambridge: MIT Press, 1971), 8.

12. Cage, "A Composer's Confessions" (1948), in *John Cage: Writer*, ed. Richard Kostelanetz (New York: Limelight, 1993), 40.

13. Ibid.

14. For an extensive study of Asian influences on Cage, see David W. Patterson, "Cage and Asia: History and Sources," in *The Cambridge Companion to John Cage*, ed. David Nicholls (Cambridge: Cambridge University Press, 2002), 44–48.

15. Daniel Charles, *Gloses sur John Cage* (Paris: Union Générale d'Editions, 1978), 17.

16. Cage, *Silence*, 41.

17. Ibid., 36.

18. Mikel Dufrenne, *Vocabulaire d'esthétique*, ed. Étienne Souriau, 2004, s.v. "Nature" (Paris: Presses Universitaires de France, 2004) 1056.

19. Toru Takemitsu, "Nature and Music," "Sound of East, Sound of West," in Takemitsu, *Confronting Silence: Selected Writings* (Berkeley: Fallen Leaf Press, 1995), 16.

20. Kahn, *Noise, Water, Meat*, 162.

21. Cage, *Silence*, 41.

22. Kahn, *Noise, Water, Meat*, 193.

23. John Cage, "Rhythm etc.," in Cage, *Module, Proportion, Symmetry, Rhythm* (New York: György Kepes, 1966), 197.

24. Cage, *Silence*, 12.

25. Ibid., 14.

26. Edmund Husserl, *Ding und Raum* (Hamburg: Meiner, 1991), 81.

27. Cage, *Silence*, 14.

28. Roger S. Gottlieb, "The Transcendence of Justice and the Justice of Transcendence: Mysticism, Deep Ecology, and Political Life," *Journal of the American Academy of Religion* 67 (March 1999): 152.

29. Takemitsu, "Sound of East, Sound of West," in *Confronting Silence*, 59.

30. Cage, *Silence*, 111.

31. In *Internationale Situationniste*, no. 9 (August 1964), rpt. in Guy Debord, *Oeuvres*, ed. Jean-Louis Rançon and Alice Debord (Paris: Gallimard, 2006), 1054; trans. Thomas Y. Levin, published on Situationist International Online: www.cddc.vt.edu/sionline

32. Ibid.

Maternal Martyrdom: *Alien3* and the Power of the Female Martyr, by Laura Copier

1. Rebecca Bell-Metereau, *Hollywood Androgyny* (New York: Columbia University Press, 1985), 209. An exception to the rule is the science fiction television series *Star Trek*, which features many female characters.

2. *Alien* (USA: Ridley Scott, 1979). In one of the first articles on *Alien*, Judith Newton reads Ripley's search for Jonesey the cat as "as impulsive, humanitarian, and therefore traditionally feminine action" (Judith Newton, "Feminism and Anxiety in Alien," in *Alien Zone: Cultural Theory and Contemporary Science Fiction Cinema*, ed. Annette Kuhn [London: Verso, 1990], 82–87; originally published in *Science Fiction Studies* 7, no. 3 [1980]). This, Newton suggests, robs Ripley of her feminist qualities and "subtly reinvests [her] with traditionally feminine qualities" (86).

3. *Aliens* (USA: James Cameron, 1986). The sequel also reveals an important aspect of Ripley's character background: the fact that she has a daughter. Due to Ripley's "hypersleep," which lasted over fifty-seven years, her daughter has died of old age by the time Ripley is rescued and awake again in *Aliens*.

4. *Alien3* (USA: David Fincher, 1992).

5. As Lynda K. Bundtzen remarks concerning this scene, the spectator's confusion about the actual status of a scene (is it a dream or is it real?) is a common "cinematic trick, we believe the dream to be reality, and the film thereby enacts an unthinkable horror, the potential birth of Alien otherness in Ripley's body" (L. K. Bundtzen, "Monstrous Mothers: Medusa, Grendel, and Now Alien," in *The Gendered Cyborg:*

A Reader, ed. Gill Kirkup, Linda Janes, Kathryn Woodward, and Fiona Hovenden [London: Routledge, 2000], 106). Ripley's dream can also be read as a sign of premonition.

6. Mieke Bal, *Quoting Caravaggio: Contemporary Art, Preposterous History* (Chicago: University of Chicago Press, 1996), 3.

7. Ibid.

8. Ibid., 7.

9. Elizabeth Castelli, *Martyrdom and Memory: Early Christian Culture Making* (New York: Columbia University Press, 2004), 67.

10. Ibid., 136.

11. Ibid.

12. Ibid.

13. Ibid., 137, my emphasis.

14. Laura Mulvey, *Death 24x a Second: Stillness and the Moving Image* (London: Reaktion, 2006).

15. Ibid., 27.

16. Ibid.

17. Ibid., 21.

18. Gail Corrington Streete, "Women as Sources of Redemption and Knowledge in Early Christian Traditions," in *Women and Christian Origins*, ed. Ross Shepard Kramer and Mary Rose D'Angelo (New York: Oxford University Press, 1999), 349.

19. Todd Penner and Caroline Vander Stichele, "The Tyranny of the Martyr: Violence and Victimization in Martyrdom Discourse and the Movies of Lars von Trier," in *Sanctified Aggression: Legacies of Biblical and Post Biblical Vocabularies of Violence*, ed. Jonneke Bekkenkamp and Yvonne Sherwood (London: Continuum, 2003), 177.

20. Castelli, *Martyrdom and Memory*, 62.

21. Ibid., 63.

22. Perpetua interprets her own vision, and particularly her Egyptian adversary, as a metaphor of the battle she, as a Christian, will have to wage against the devil (personified by the Egyptian). She writes in her diary: "And I awoke; and I understood that I should fight, not with beasts but against the devil; but I knew that mine was the victory" ("The Martyrdom of Saints Perpetua and Felicitas," in *The Acts of the Christian Martyrs*, trans. Herbert Musurillo [Oxford: Oxford University Press, 1972]). All following references to the source text are taken from Musurillo.

23. Ibid., 21.9.

24. Ibid., 21.10.

25. Margaret R. Miles, *Carnal Knowing: Female Nakedness and Religious Meaning in the Christian West* (New York: Vintage Books, 1989), 55.

26. Elizabeth Castelli, " 'I Will Make Mary Male': Pieties of the Body and Gender Transformation of Christian Women in Late Antiquity," in *Body Guards: The Cultural Politics of Gender Ambiguity*, ed. Julia Epstein and Kristina Straub (New York: Routledge, 1991), 35.

27. "The Martyrdom of Saints Perpetua and Felicitas," 6.8. Mary R. Lefkowitz states that many of the stories of Christian women martyrs display a "surprising eagerness to abandon young infants." Felicitas gives away her newborn daughter. Similarly, Lefkowitz mentions the case of Eutychia and the Greek myth of the women of Thebes, who abandoned and in some cases murdered their sons (Mary R. Lefkowitz, "The Motivations for St. Perpetua's Martyrdom," *Journal of the American Academy of Religion* 44, no. 3 [1976]: 419).

28. Castelli, "'I Will Make Mary Male,'" 35.

29. Yvonne Tasker, *Spectacular Bodies: Gender, Genre and the Action Cinema* (London: Routledge, 1993), mentions the publicity shot for *Aliens* of Weaver "clutching a child in one arm, weapon in another" (151). This image perfectly encapsulates the ambiguity of the musculine action heroine. Unfortunately, Tasker does not expand on this. Instead, she emphasizes the vulnerability of the heroine and focuses on the threat of rape.

30. Tasker, *Spectacular Bodies*, n. 26; Barbara Creed, *The Monstrous-Feminine: Film, Feminism, Psychoanalysis* (London: Routledge, 1993).

31. Ibid., 3.

32. Ibid., 149.

33. Ibid., 15.

34. Ibid., 152. The spectacle of a woman with a shaved head should not be underestimated: the publicity material of *Alien3* strongly capitalizes on the actress's bald head. Many of the publicity shots show Sigourney Weaver lit from behind, thus putting extra emphasis on her baldness. The act of shaving off her hair is, surprisingly enough, not shown in the film. In contrast, in a recent film, *V for Vendetta* (USA: James McTeigue, 2005), the actual act of shaving is prominently featured. The actress Nathalie Portman, as the character of Evey Hammond, is shaved in real time, in a long take that lasts several minutes.

35. Tasker, *Spectacular Bodies*, 15 and 143.

36. This scene provides an interesting parallel with the Joan of Arc story: like Ripley, Joan was harassed and supposedly raped by her male guards while awaiting her final sentence. Again, Tasker's argument that the musculine woman is in greater risk of being raped, as a punishment for her (tress-)passing, reverberates in this scene of the film.

37. Thomas Doherty, "Genre, Gender, and the *Aliens* Trilogy," in *The Dread of Difference: Gender and the Horror Film*, ed. Barry Keith Grant (Austin: University of Texas Press: 1996), 181–99.

38. Castelli, "'I Will Make Mary Male,'" 43.

39. Judith Halberstam offers an interesting reading of Ripley's masculinity in *Female Masculinity* (Durham, N.C.: Duke University Press, 1998). She argues that the transgressive potential of the Ripley character is undercut by her "resolute heterosexuality" (28). Even though Halberstam discusses *Aliens*, her analysis is also applicable to *Alien3*. It is only when female masculinity is coupled with lesbian desire, which can be observed in *Alien: Resurrection*, that female masculinity is perceived as "threatening and indeed 'alien'" (28).

40. Doherty, "Genre, Gender, and the *Aliens* Trilogy," 193.

41. For a critique of the concept of abjection, and particularly its misogynistic connotations, see Rosalind E. Krauss, "The Destiny of the *Informe*," in *Formless: A User's Guide*, ed. Yve-Alain Bois and Rosalind E. Krauss (New York: Zone Books, 1997), 235–52. The genealogy of the concept is traced back to the work of Georges Bataille, whose understanding of abjection is devoid of its later misogyny. As Krauss argues, it is through Kristeva's indebtness to Jean-Paul Sartre's conceptualization of the *visqueux* ("slimy") that her conception of the abject has become infused with the stereotype of "female as degenerate."

42. Creed, *The Monstrous-Feminine*, n. 27.

43. Ibid., 7.

44. Ibid., 50.

45. Julia Kristeva, *Powers of Horror: An Essay on Abjection* (New York: Columbia University Press, 1982), 4; Creed, *The Monstrous-Feminine*, 8.

46. Ibid., 11.

47. Ibid., 49. The act of impregnation is not shown, only suggested. In the opening sequence of *Alien3*, short shots of the escape pod, which besides Ripley, Newt, Hicks, and Bishop also contains an alien, are interspersed with the credit roll. In the first scene of the film, it becomes clear that Ripley is the only survivor and that her fellow travelers all have fallen victim to the alien. The body of Hicks looks as if it was ripped open by a chestburster. Ripley's body is apparently unscarred. Yet, on the basis of the opening sequence, which contains x-ray shots depicting the strangulation mechanism of the so-called face hugger of one (or several) unidentified members of the crew, we can assume that Ripley was indeed attacked by an alien.

48. *Alien: Resurrection* (USA: Jean-Pierre Jeunet, 1997).

49. The sacrificial aspect of Ripley's death is abundantly clear. Creed, *The Monstrous-Feminine*, 52, even ventures to compare the scene with the death scene in Carl Dreyer's *The Passion of Joan of Arc* (USA: Carl Theodore Dreyer, 1928). Indeed, *Alien3* offers several instances of intertextuality, both on the level of the narrative as well as on the level of iconography.

50. The horrendous scene of Ripley giving birth is certainly not unique in the *Alien* trilogy. The primal scene in this respect occurs in *Alien*, according to Barbara Creed, "Alien and the Monstrous-Feminine," in *The Gendered Cyborg: A Reader*, ed. Gill Kirkup, Linda Janes, Kathryn Woodward, and Fiona Hovenden (London: Routledge: 2000), 124–35, first published in *Alien Zone* (1990), excerpted from Creed's "Horror and the Monstrous-Feminine: An Imaginary Abjection," *Screen* 28, no. 2 (1987). One of the male members of the crew, Kane, is orally raped. The tail of the alien penetrates his mouth in order to implant itself inside his stomach. After this rape, during which Kane is in a comalike state and the alien grows inside him, the birth scene occurs quite unexpectedly when an apparently normal Kane and the rest of the crew are having dinner. In *Aliens*, the android Bishop becomes the host to the alien. In one of the final scenes of the film, he is literally ripped apart by the violent emergence of the monster. It comes as no surprise that Ripley has to experience the same horror. This death, a recurring trademark of the entire trilogy, seems a fitting way of dying for its heroine. The crucial difference between Kane and Bishop, on the one hand, and Ripley, on the other, is that Ripley is able to destroy the alien. Perhaps the fact that she is a woman, and as such better equipped by nature to give birth, comes into play.

51. Creed, *The Monstrous-Feminine*, 52, my emphasis.

52. James Swallow, *Dark Eye: The Films of David Fincher* (London: Reynolds and Hearn, 2003), 34–61. On the alternate endings of the film, see pp. 54–55.

53. Ibid., n. 48.

54. Ibid., 55. The fact that these outtakes are not included on this particular special edition does not exclude the possibility of their surfacing in a later and "improved" special edition of the film. As a result, the flow of analysis is extended and a definitive, conclusive reading of the film is deferred once more.

55. Swallow, *Dark Eye*, 55.

Contributors

Talal Asad was born in Saudi Arabia and educated in Britain. He now teaches anthropology at the Graduate Center of the City University of New York. His most recent book is entitled *Formations of the Secular: Christianity, Islam, Modernity* (2003).

Mieke Bal, a cultural theorist and critic, is Royal Netherlands Academy of Arts and Sciences Professor (KNAW). She is based at the Amsterdam School for Cultural Analysis (ASCA), University of Amsterdam. Her areas of interest range from biblical and classical antiquity to seventeenth-century and contemporary art and modern literature, feminism, and migratory culture. Her many books include *A Mieke Bal Reader* (2006), *Travelling Concepts in the Humanities* (2002), and *Narratology* (3d ed., 2009). Bal is also a video artist; her experimental documentaries on migration include *A Thousand and One Days*, *Colony*, and the installation *Nothing Is Missing*. Her work is exhibited internationally. Occasionally she acts as an independent curator.

Meerten B. ter Borg is a sociologist and philosopher. He is Professor in the Sociology of Religion, specializing in noninstitutional and implicit forms of religion, at the University of Leiden. Among his publications in English is the contribution "Religious Power" in the *Oxford Handbook on the Sociology of Religion* (2008).

Laura Copier has studied film and television at the University of Amsterdam and completed her Ph.D. at ASCA. Her dissertation is titled "Preposterous Revelations: Visions of Apocalypse and Martyrdom in Hollywood Cinema, 1980–2000." Currently, she is a lecturer in the Media and Culture Department and the Department of Religious Studies at the University of Amsterdam.

André Droogers is Emeritus Professor of Cultural Anthropology, especially anthropology of religion and symbolic anthropology, at the VU University Amsterdam. His numerous publications address such themes as Pentecostalism, syncretism, religion and play, changing worldviews in the Netherlands, and religion and power. He is the coordinator of research programs on changing worldviews in the Netherlands and on conversion careers and cultural politics in global Pentecostalism. He is co-founder of the Hollenweger Center for the Interdisciplinary Study of Pentecostal and Charismatic Movements.

Olivia Gervasoni has worked since 2007 at the Delegation of the European Commission in Maputo (Mozambique), after having worked for OFPRA (Fontenay Sous Bois) from 2004 until 2007. She co-edited an article with Cheigh Guèye after having carried out research in Senegal in the context of her studies at the Institut d'Études Politiques of Aix en Provence and at the Université Panthéon Sorbonne in Paris. She has also worked as a stageaire at the first private radio station in Senegal.

Rokus de Groot, a musicologist and composer, conducts research on music of the twentieth and twenty-first centuries, especially on the systematics and aesthetics of composition, the interaction between different cultural traditions, and (re)conceptualizations of past and present religious and spiritual ideas. He holds the chair of musicology at the University of Amsterdam, after occupying the chair Music in the Netherlands since 1600 at the University of Utrecht from 1994 to 2000. Recently he co-edited, with Albert van der Schoot, *Redefining Musical Identities: Reorientations at the Waning of Modernism* (2007), and he has published "Perspectives of Polyphony in Edward Said's Writings," in *Edward Said and Critical Decolonization*, ed. F. Ghazoul (2007). He has composed music in which singers, musicians, and dancers from different traditions cooperate, such as *Song of Songs: The Love of Mirabai* (New Delhi, 2005) and *Layla and Majnun: A Composition about the Night* (Amsterdam, 2006).

Cheikh Guèye is the Head of Methods and Approaches at the Executive Secretariat of ENDA Third World. He has a Ph.D. from Université Louis Pasteur de Strasbourg and is co-founder of the recently established Center for Research on Social Policies in Senegal. His work for the NWO-ASSR project Islam in Africa deals with gender, identity, and Mourid transnational networks in Senegal, and his publications concern urban issues in countries of the global South.

Jan Willem van Henten is Professor of New Testament and Vice-Dean of Humanities and Director of the Graduate School for Humanities at the University of Amsterdam. His research interests concern Second Temple Judaism and Early Christianity, as well as the topics of martyrdom and the nexus of religion and violence in various contexts. He is the co-author, with Friedrich Avemarie, of *Martyrdom and Noble Death: Selected Texts from Graeco-Roman, Jewish, and Christian Antiquity* (2002).

Anna-Karina Hermkens is an anthropologist who works as a postdoctoral researcher at the Faculty of Religious Studies, Radboud University Nijmegen. Her fields of interest are material culture studies, gender, and religion and conflict. She is co-editor of *Moved by Mary: The Power of Pilgrimage in the Modern World* (2009) and has published on religion and conflict in several journals. Her most recent research concentrates on conflict and postconflict areas in Papua New Guinea and Indonesia, with an emphasis on the relation between religion, violence, and the (female) body.

Shamil Jeppie teaches in the Department of Historical Studies at the University of Cape Town, South Africa. He has written on various aspects of African history, and the subject of his essay in this volume is part of a project looking at the ways in which colonialism and Islamic law interacted.

Mark Juergensmeyer is Professor of Sociology and Global Studies and Director of the Orfalea Center for Global and International Studies at the University of California, Santa Barbara. He is author or editor of twenty books, including *The Oxford Handbook of Global Religions* (2006) and *Terror in the Mind of God: The Global Rise of Religious Violence* (2000).

Jael Kraut is a Ph.D. Fellow at ASCA. At present, she is preparing her dissertation, in the Department of Musicology at the University of Amsterdam, on silence in relation to twentieth-century musical compositions.

Claudio Lomnitz is Professor of Anthropology and Director of the Center for the Study of Race and Ethnicity at Columbia University. Among his publications are *Death and the Idea of Mexico* (2005), *Deep Mexico, Silent Mexico: An Anthropology of Nationalism* (2001), and *Exits from the Labyrinth: Culture and Ideology in the Mexican National Space* (1992).

Avishai Margalit is the George F. Kennan Professor at the Institute for Advanced Study in Princeton and Professor Emeritus in Philosophy at Hebrew University. Among his publications are *Occidentalism: The West in the Eyes of Its Enemies* (with Ian Buruma, 2004), *The Ethics of Memory* (2002), *Views in Review: Politics and Culture in the State of the Jews* (1998), *The Decent Society* (1996), and *Idolatry* (with Moshe Halbertal, 1992).

David Morgan is Professor of Religion at Duke University. He is the author of several books, most recently *The Lure of Images: A History of Religion and Visual Images in America* (2007).

327

Morgan is co-editor of the journal *Material Religion* and of a book series, Religion, Media, and Culture, at Routledge.

Catrien Notermans is Senior Researcher in the Department of Cultural Anthropology at Radboud University Nijmegen. Her fields of interest include religion, pilgrimage, kinship, and gender. She is the author of "Local and Global Icons of Mary: An Ethnographic Study of a Powerful Symbol," *Anthropos* (2008), and the co-editor of *Moved by Mary: The Power of Pilgrimage in the Modern World* (2009).

Rafael Sánchez is Assistant Professor of Latin American and Caribbean Studies at New York University. His publications focus on media, politics, populism, and spirit mediumship. He is the author of *Dancing Jacobins: A Genealogy of Latin American Populism* (forthcoming), and his current project, *The Fate of Sovereignty in the Landscape of the City*, focuses on urban imaginaries and territorializing practices in Caracas under the current Chávez regime.

José C. M. van Santen is Assistant Professor in the Department of Cultural Anthropology at Leiden University, where she has served as Joint Director of the Ph.D. Research School CNWS (School of Asian, African, and Amerindian Studies). Her Ph.D. dissertation is entitled "Processes of Islamisation and Its Effects on Gender Relations in North Cameroon." Since 2001, she has also worked as Director of Scientific Research at the Centre de l'Étude de l'Environnement et de Développement in Maroua, North Cameroon. Her work for the NWO-ASSR project Islam in Africa deals with gender, the influence of transnational networks, and the (re)construction of youth identity.

Peter van der Veer is University Professor at Utrecht University. He works on religion, nationalism, and imperialism in India, China, and Europe. Among his many publications are *Gods on Earth: The Management of Religious Experience and Identity in a North Indian Pilgrimage* (1988), *Religious Nationalism: Hindus and Muslims in India* (1994), and *Imperial Encounters: Religion and Modernity in India and Britain* (2001). He is now preparing a book on the comparison of religion and nationalism in India and China.

Index